Cisco ThousandEyes

Digital Experience Monitoring and Troubleshooting

Aaron Trompeter

Robert Webb

T0292823

Cisco Press

Cisco ThousandEyes: Digital Experience Monitoring and Troubleshooting

Aaron Trompeter, Robert Webb

Published by:
Cisco Press
Hoboken, New Jersey

1 2024

Library of Congress Control Number: 2024942159

ISBN-13: 978-0-13-830918-3
ISBN-10: 0-13-830918-3

Warning and Disclaimer

This book is designed to provide information about using Cisco's ThousandEyes platform to monitor networks, applications, and dependency services that impact user experience. Every effort has been made to make this book as complete and as accurate as possible, but no warranty or fitness is implied.

The information is provided on an "as is" basis. The authors, Cisco Press, and Cisco Systems, Inc. shall have neither liability nor responsibility to any person or entity with respect to any loss or damages arising from the information contained in this book or from the use of the discs or programs that may accompany it.

The opinions expressed in this book belong to the author and are not necessarily those of Cisco Systems, Inc.

Trademark Acknowledgments

All terms mentioned in this book that are known to be trademarks or service marks have been appropriately capitalized. Cisco Press or Cisco Systems, Inc., cannot attest to the accuracy of this information. Use of a term in this book should not be regarded as affecting the validity of any trademark or service mark.

Special Sales

For information about buying this title in bulk quantities, or for special sales opportunities (which may include electronic versions; custom cover designs; and content particular to your business, training goals, marketing focus, or branding interests), please contact our corporate sales department at corpsales@pearsoned.com or (800) 382-3419.

For government sales inquiries, please contact governmentsales@pearsoned.com.

For questions about sales outside the U.S., please contact intlcs@pearson.com.

Feedback Information

At Cisco Press, our goal is to create in-depth technical books of the highest quality and value. Each book is crafted with care and precision, undergoing rigorous development that involves the unique expertise of members from the professional technical community.

Readers' feedback is a natural continuation of this process. If you have any comments regarding how we could improve the quality of this book, or otherwise alter it to better suit your needs, you can contact us through email at feedback@ciscopress.com. Please make sure to include the book title and ISBN in your message.

We greatly appreciate your assistance.

Please contact us with concerns about any potential bias at https://www.pearson.com/report-bias.html.

GM K12, Early Career and Professional Learning: Soo Kang

Alliances Manager, Cisco Press: Caroline Antonio

Director, ITP Product Management: Brett Bartow

Executive Editor: Nancy Davis

Managing Editor: Sandra Schroeder

Development Editor: Ellie C. Bru

Senior Project Editor: Tonya Simpson

Copy Editor: Bill McManus

Technical Editors: Jeffrey Drury, Collin Sullivan

Editorial Assistant: Cindy Teeters

Cover Designer: Chuti Prasertsith

Composition: codeMantra

Indexer: Timothy Wright

Proofreader: Barbara Mack

Americas Headquarters	Asia Pacific Headquarters	Europe Headquarters
Cisco Systems, Inc.	Cisco Systems (USA) Pte. Ltd.	Cisco Systems International BV Amsterdam,
San Jose, CA	Singapore	The Netherlands

Cisco has more than 200 offices worldwide. Addresses, phone numbers, and fax numbers are listed on the Cisco Website at **www.cisco.com/go/offices**.

Cisco and the Cisco logo are trademarks or registered trademarks of Cisco and/or its affiliates in the U.S. and other countries. To view a list of Cisco trademarks, go to this URL: www.cisco.com/go/trademarks. Third party trademarks mentioned are the property of their respective owners. The use of the word partner does not imply a partnership relationship between Cisco and any other company. (1110R)

About the Authors

Aaron Trompeter is a technical solutions architect within the ThousandEyes global enterprise segment at Cisco, focusing on visibility and operational awareness for on-prem, SaaS, and cloud native. In this role, he aligns his passion for education and learning with his motivation for helping the infrastructure community grow and learn to harness tools to provide use cases that fit each organization. Prior to this role, Aaron spent 6 years as a data center TSA within Cisco and had a few other roles within Cisco as a service provider specialist and software engineer in the Cloud Engineering unit. Aaron has more than 20 years of experience in the IT and engineering areas and has continued to focus on networking and software.

Rob Webb began his technical career when, at 17 years old, he enlisted in the military as a teletype technician. His military service spanned more than 28 years, during which time he trained and worked in telecommunications systems, F-4 and F-16 avionics systems, and, eventually, Cyber Warfare Operations. Most of this time was spent working part-time in the Air National Guard. This allowed Rob to not only get the benefits of military training and experience but also to pursue a full-time career outside the military. He went from pulling cable to IT professional services to protocol analysis to pre-sales engineering/solutions architecture. Rob even ran his own consulting service, WEBNET Communication, where he achieved industry-recognized certifications in protocol analysis, which include Certified Network Expert (CNX), Sniffer Certified (SCM), and Certified NetAnalyst.

Rob has spent his career solving complex problems for customers and helping them design and implement monitoring solutions so they can better solve those problems themselves. He has spent many hours collecting and analyzing packets to understand not only what is happening in each situation, but also what should be happening and what can be done to improve it. He often refers to these as opportunities for optimization. Rob joined ThousandEyes as a sales engineer in March, 2020.

When Rob is not working, he keeps busy by enjoying outdoor activities such as fishing and photography. Now he combines the two in his sportfishing photography. You can follow Rob on LinkedIn (www.linkedin.com/in/robertwebbcyberguy) or Instagram (@photographyinspiredbylife).

About the Technical Reviewers

Jeff Drury is a passionate technologist and self-proclaimed nerd. While at Cisco, Jeff has worked with large enterprise customers to build and enhance their data center and observability architectures. Jeff has also been an advocate of automation and programmability by developing and leading several internal and external training sessions. Prior to joining Cisco, Jeff was Director of Engineering at a regional VAR, where he built several teams and mentored early-in-career engineers. Jeff is an avid cyclist who loves to go on adventures with his wife and two teenage sons.

Collin Sullivan works as a solutions engineer at ThousandEyes and has specialized in helping enterprise customers design and implement infrastructure and hybrid-cloud monitoring strategies. Collin has worked with customers across verticals such as financial, manufacturing, healthcare, and technology. Before ThousandEyes, Collin worked as a consultant for Cisco, focused on the industrial wireless space, but started his journey at Cisco working in Advanced Lab Operations as part of a team that rapidly rebuilt customers' networks in Cisco's mock data centers when outages or issues occurred to determine root cause. In that sense, Collin's whole career has been focused on network issues and helping customers avoid and identify bottlenecks. When you can't find Collin reading or writing about networks, he is typically enjoying a cold beverage on the beach.

Dedications

Aaron Trompeter

I would like to dedicate this book to my family: my wife, Sarah, encouraged me to keep pushing and never procrastinate; my son, Aiden, cheered me on when writing the book through the weekends and at night; and my mother and sister said, "just do it," and, "if you want it, go get it." I could not have even started this book without the support of my family.

Rob Webb

I would like to dedicate this book to my sister, Sue, who has always been my inspiration to do more, learn more, and pay better attention to the details. To my wonderful daughter, Lauren, who is sick of hearing me talk about this book but puts up with me all the same. And to my customers over the years for trusting me to help solve some really challenging issues we have run into. Without you, I would never have had the stories to share or the experience to sound like I know what I am talking about. The best advice I have for all of you is this: when you get stuck on a problem, call your mom. Not to get technical advice, but to take a break from the technical for a few minutes. Also, she'll appreciate it.

Acknowledgments

Aaron's Acknowledgments

Rob Webb, thank you for saying, "this sounds like a great idea, it will be fun." Barry Wayne, thanks for recommending Rob. Collin Sullivan and Jeff Drury, we could not have done this without you guys. Jason Warfield and Bill Donoghue, you guys allowed me onto the ThousandEyes team and have always encouraged the team to push and promote the platform.

Rob's Acknowledgments

I'd like to thank Bill Donoghue, who trusted me when I wanted to do things a little different from what is "normal" in our field. Bill helped me to start telling my stories over a decade ago. Also, I thank Bernie Clairmont for continually setting aside time for us to brainstorm ideas and work through issues that I may be struggling with. It was Bernie who provided the framework for the Output/Input/Processes methodology (see Chapter 7). Thanks to Jim Marcel, Greg Mathews, and Joe Clark, who helped me learn many lessons as they trusted me to restore or improve services to their organization more times that I can count...thank you for helping me build stories worth sharing. Finally, thank you, Aaron, for inviting me to join in the writing of this book and giving me a place to share my stories and experience.

Contents at a Glance

Reader Services

Register your copy at www.ciscopress.com/title/9780138309183 for convenient access to downloads, updates, and corrections as they become available. To start the registration process, go to www.ciscopress.com/register and log in or create an account*. Enter the product ISBN 9780138309183 and click Submit. When the process is complete, you will find any available bonus content under Registered Products.

*Be sure to check the box that you would like to hear from us to receive exclusive discounts on future editions of this product.

Contents

Command Syntax Conventions

The conventions used to present command syntax in this book are the same conventions used in the IOS Command Reference. The Command Reference describes these conventions as follows:

- **Boldface** indicates commands and keywords that are entered literally as shown. In actual configuration examples and output (not general command syntax), boldface indicates commands that are manually input by the user (such as a **show** command).

- *Italic* indicates arguments for which you supply actual values.

- Vertical bars (|) separate alternative, mutually exclusive elements.

- Square brackets ([ ]) indicate an optional element.

- Braces ({ }) indicate a required choice.

- Braces within brackets ([{ }]) indicate a required choice within an optional element.

Introduction

You might have heard Cisco ThousandEyes referred to as the "Google Maps for the Internet," the Internet visibility platform that the world's biggest brands and fastest growing startups rely on to ensure they're delivering the best possible digital experiences. This comparison isn't far from the truth. In this book we review some basic network concepts before jumping into the installation of agents. We explore where to deploy the agents and why. We look at test creation, when to use certain tests, and the objective of those tests. As we build on each chapter, you will learn how to look at alerts and what to do with them. Next, we look at operationalizing ThousandEyes through integration with other Cisco platforms and third-party apps. The goal of the book is to get you up to speed with the ThousandEyes platform quickly so that you can start creating value for your business.

Goals, Objectives, and Approach of the Book

This book was written with the intent to help IT professionals better understand how to use Cisco ThousandEyes. We cover many how-to topics, some of which are not always obvious in the product documentation available online. Additionally, by describing real-world experiences where ThousandEyes helped to solve complex problems, we hope to help you consider additional use cases and ways to leverage the information provided by the ThousandEyes platform.

Before you begin reading the hands-on chapters, we highly recommend that you create your own free 15-day trial account, which will allow you to follow along with recommended configurations, tips, and best practices throughout the book. The link www.thousandeyes.com/booktrial provides an easy way to start your new trial account. This account will provide you with access to ThousandEyes resources such as Internet Insight and many of the Cloud Agents and enable you to install your own Enterprise and Endpoint Agents.

This book is our attempt to truly teach you how to think about ThousandEyes holistically as opposed to simply telling you what to do.

You should understand that due to the dynamic nature of Software as a Service (SaaS) hosting combined with the fast-paced innovation in which Cisco ThousandEyes operates, many changes are occurring weekly to this product. You can view and keep track of these changes, along with the dates they were implemented, in the ThousandEyes Changelog (https://docs.thousandeyes.com/whats-new/changelog). Over the course of writing this book, several features and product names have changed in Cisco ThousandEyes. For example, with Endpoint Agents, Automated Session Tests (ASTs) are now referred to as Dynamic Tests. Depending on when a particular chapter was written, you might see either of these names used. Additionally, the version of Views has recently changed from Views 1.0 to Views 2.0 for most Cloud Agent and Enterprise Agent tests. Endpoint Agent views will likely have changed by the time this book is published.

While some of the stories in this book are taken directly from our experience in using ThousandEyes to troubleshoot and solve a given problem, other stories describe how a problem was analyzed and resolved using traditional methods, followed by analysis of how the same problem could be solved much faster by using ThousandEyes. What used to take hours, sometimes days, to collect and analyze can now often be done in seconds, minimizing the requirement for extensive packet collections.

Who Should Read This Book?

While the obvious audience would be anyone who works with ThousandEyes in their jobs, this book has been written with a far broader audience in mind: network administrators, DevOps engineers, and IT professionals who are responsible for managing and optimizing the performance of an organization's network infrastructure and applications.

Anyone who intends to apply for an IT position with a company that uses ThousandEyes should absolutely read this book. For that matter, anyone who is looking to learn about new tools and troubleshooting methodologies for network and application performance would benefit from reading this material. Because this book includes the ability to create your very own ThousandEyes demo account, it opens the field to anyone who is interested in modern IT operations and digital experience monitoring.

How This Book Is Organized

The book is organized into 13 chapters:

- **Chapter 1, "Introduction to ThousandEyes and Its Capabilities":** This chapter describes the origins of ThousandEyes and introduces some of its key use cases. It also addresses fundamental networking concepts that you need to maximize your understanding of the technologies, tests, and metrics discussed throughout the book.

- **Chapter 2, "Agent Setup":** This chapter explains agents in ThousandEyes, including Cloud (Public) Agents, Enterprise (Private) Agents, and Endpoint (User) Agents, which are all used to initiate tests.

- **Chapter 3, "Configuring Tests":** This chapter addresses the different ThousandEyes tests that can be deployed as well as the parameters that are generally used for each test type.

- **Chapter 4, "Configuring Alerts":** Once you understand the tests and test types, it's time to learn about how ThousandEyes alerts when thresholds are exceeded or certain conditions are or are not met.

- **Chapter 5, "Dashboards":** This chapter discusses how ThousandEyes dashboards allow metrics to be viewed across tests, agents, locations, and more.

- **Chapter 6, "Monitoring and Troubleshooting Network Performance Issues":** This chapter covers the different tests used to provide both end-to-end metrics and hop-by-hop metrics. Understanding how these tests are executed in detail will help you to troubleshoot issues when they arise.

- **Chapter 7, "Scripted Synthetic User Testing with Transaction Tests":** This chapter explains how ThousandEyes enables customers to record multistep, transaction test scripts and then deploy them as a synthetic test. These Transaction tests exercise the target application by accessing multiple pages and even authenticating (where applicable).

- **Chapter 8, "Integrations":** ThousandEyes has the capability to integrate not only with other Cisco products, such as Application Dynamics (AppD), but also any applications using webhooks. Recently, ThousandEyes has added the capability to export OTel data from the API in addition to the traditional query method. This chapter discusses these various integrations and how they are beneficial.

- **Chapter 9, "Best Practices: Test Optimization, Collaboration, and Stories from the Field":** Because all networks are different, sometimes tests need to be "tweaked" to achieve the best results. This chapter covers many of these scenarios and discusses how and when to tweak.

- **Chapter 10, "Device Monitoring":** This chapter explains how ThousandEyes monitors devices via SNMP. This enhances the traditional Path Visualization described throughout the book with device-level metrics such as CPU, Memory, Error, and Discards.

- **Chapter 11, "Account Administration":** This chapter gets into the weeds of account administration, including adding users and defining their roles within ThousandEyes, which is critical to operating a comprehensive and secure SaaS platform.

- **Chapter 12, "Automation—Use Cases and Case Studies":** This chapter relates some of the field experiences of the authors, providing insight into the application of ThousandEyes. The ability to automate the deployment of agents and tests is critical to some of our largest customers, and this chapter provides some examples of this.

- **Chapter 13, "Business Strategy for Engineers":** This chapter discusses how ThousandEyes plays a part in your company's business strategy and what that means to a network engineer.

Figure Credits

Figures 8-7 through 8-23 © 2024 ServiceNow

Figure 9-43 inset courtesy of Defense Logistics Agency

Chapter 1

Introduction to ThousandEyes and Its Capabilities

Note that our intent for this book is to guide your learning, not to be a step-by-step instruction manual. You should use the information contained here to understand the ThousandEyes product and how to leverage the information it provides to aid in your monitoring and troubleshooting of networks, applications, and overall user experience. The Cisco ThousandEyes product team is constantly innovating and improving product workflow and navigation. This results in product changes that might not have made it into this publication. However, the basic concepts of how to use Cisco ThousandEyes to troubleshoot your environment remain the same. We, the authors, hope you not only enjoy reading this book, but also that the lessons described within remain with you throughout your career, regardless of which tools you happen to be using to accomplish your job.

How ThousandEyes Was Conceived

Back in the late 2000s at the UCLA Internet Research Lab, then PhD students Mohit Lad and Ricardo Oliveira made a bet on the future of business. More specifically, they believed that the Internet was on its way to becoming the new enterprise backbone, and that it would become the medium by which every company would conduct its business— how money would exchange hands, how applications and services would get delivered to customers, how employees would communicate with each other, and so forth.

Lad and Oliveira knew that if they were right, businesses would be opening themselves up to an incredible amount of risk because they'd be relying on the Internet, which they recognized as an unregulated, highly distributed collection of independent networks that operate on a chain of trust and are rife with bad actors. Worse, they knew these businesses would have no visibility into—and no control over—the Internet, the vast majority of the service delivery chain that their most mission-critical applications, services, and websites would take to get to their customers and employees.

Lad and Oliveira also knew that if their prediction proved true, businesses would need an entirely new kind of network and infrastructure monitoring software: one that could see beyond a company's internal network and into the very complex and massive system that is the Internet. Businesses would need to see every handoff from one provider to the next—to know, with certainty, that their services were getting delivered to their customers or employees, and that they were delivering the highest quality digital experiences possible. And even before something would go wrong, they would need to be able to instantly see exactly where the delivery chain was breaking so they could fix it, fast, before it started impacting their revenue, damaging their brand reputation, or halting their employee productivity.

In 2010, after spending years researching the way the Internet works and how to measure it, Lad and Oliveira won a modest grant from the National Science Foundation that gave them just enough funds to bootstrap their business, buy a few used servers, and, in true Silicon Valley fashion, set up shop in a garage in Mountain View. So began ThousandEyes on its journey to becoming the "Google Maps for the Internet," the Internet visibility platform that the world's biggest brands and fastest growing startups rely on to ensure they're delivering the best possible digital experiences.

In 2020, ThousandEyes was acquired by Cisco, where ThousandEyes continues to grow and be a part of many integrations within the Cisco product line, specifically its core Enterprise Networking, Cloud, and AppDynamics portfolios to enhance visibility across the enterprise, Internet, and the cloud.

Understanding ThousandEyes Use Cases

ThousandEyes has a diverse range of use cases spanning network, application, and cloud monitoring, SaaS, and even more than you might expect.

- **Network performance monitoring:** ThousandEyes goes beyond traditional monitoring solutions by offering in-depth insights into network performance. The platform utilizes everyday network protocols such as ICMP and TCP, but also dives into areas like TCP Selective Acknowledgments (SACK) to provide comprehensive metrics such as throughput, latency, loss, and jitter. Additionally, ThousandEyes can monitor the WAN, MPLS, and various connections that connect different locations. It also provides insights into SD-WAN, covering both underlay and overlay perspectives.

- **Application Performance Monitoring (APM):** ThousandEyes offers a wealth of monitoring options from the application perspective. It goes beyond simple HTTP tests to measure page load times, DNS resolution times, and SSL/TLS negotiation times. It can even simulate scripted transactions to emulate user experiences and troubleshoot performance issues.

- **Cloud and Hybrid Monitoring:** ThousandEyes addresses the unique challenges of cloud and hybrid environments. With path visibility, it shows end-to-end metrics while identifying issues and providing detailed information beyond your network. For cloud monitoring, ThousandEyes enables visibility from inside the network to the cloud providers such as Amazon Web Services (AWS), Google Cloud Platform (GCP), and Microsoft Azure.

- **Internet and DNS Monitoring:** ThousandEyes offers powerful capabilities for Internet and DNS monitoring. With Cloud Agents or cloud vantage points in many ISPs and broadband networks, ThousandEyes can monitor from the origin network to specific ISPs. For DNS, ThousandEyes monitors external and on-prem DNS, including authoritative and caching servers, enabling troubleshooting of availability, performance, and security issues.

- **Collaboration Monitoring:** ThousandEyes can monitor voice and video traffic using SIP and RTP, with specific codecs and DSCP values to simulate calls. It also monitors automatic sessions for Cisco Webex and other vendors, logging data on user experiences and identifying issues outside your network. Additionally, it monitors group chat applications like Webex Teams and Slack.

Fundamental Network Metrics

Several chapters in this book present use cases of actual ThousandEyes customers to give you an idea of how ThousandEyes is used in practice. Many of the use cases involve network fundamentals such as packet loss and throughput, so this section provides a quick refresher on those fundamentals.

It's the Network

Why would we title this section "It's the Network"? Well, for one, we've heard that exact statement thousands of times working in IT. But also because sometimes it really is the network causing the issue. We have seen things overlooked and misread too many times to ever take for granted it isn't the network causing an operational performance problem. Although experience should tell us that most of the time when we hear either "it's the network" or "it's not the network," we should be thinking, "How do you know? What metrics are you monitoring?"

ThousandEyes easily addresses these hasty conclusions by providing a method to triage the fault domain and show what is responsible for the impact to operational performance.

Operational Impact

Most engineers are surprised (and some even doubtful) when they hear us say that there are only two network metrics that impact operational performance of a TCP application: packet loss and latency. If neither of these metrics has changed but performance has degraded, then it *is not the network* causing the poor performance. In the context of UDP applications for voice and video, jitter is an important metric, but jitter has no performance impact on TCP-based applications.

If you are wondering why bandwidth isn't included as a third metric that impacts operational performance, more than likely you have run into issues caused by a lack of bandwidth triggering poor application performance. The truth is that the only time bandwidth impacts network operations is when it affects packet loss, latency, or both. A lack of bandwidth can cause an increase in packet loss or an increase in latency, but if neither of those two primary metrics is impacted, bandwidth (regardless of the percent in use) is not causing operational issues for your TCP application(s).

Packet Loss

Packet loss often creates a much larger performance degradation than most people think. One factor that weighs heavily on how much packet loss is acceptable is the type of application being impacted. As an example, email would be more tolerant of packet loss than, say, a virtual desktop session.

Figure 1-1 is from a ThousandEyes test that shows packet loss occurring between Dallas, TX, and a server hosting www.google.com.

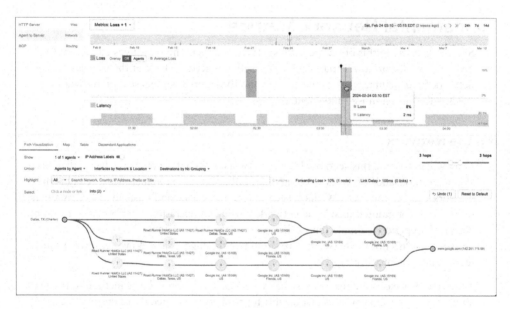

Figure 1-1 *Packet Loss*

When a host sending TCP segments to another host realizes that it has not heard its data acknowledged in too long of a period, it must resend that data. The host does not know (or really care) why the segments were not acknowledged. When the sending host's TCP retransmit timer expires, it retransmits the segments. However, this also causes the sending host to go into a TCP congestion avoidance algorithm. In this scenario, the host is likely to revert to TCP slow start. This is like driving on a highway at 80 miles per hour and then having to stop to pay a toll. The amount of time it takes to pay the toll is likely minimal. However, slowing down and speeding back up takes time…and TCP does not accelerate very well. TCP goes into slow start, assuming the network is congested. Then it tests the network to see if it is safe to send more data. A TCP host sending data to another host begins each TCP session in slow start. Also, if the TCP retransmit timer expires on a host, it may return to slow start in the middle of a TCP session. Without going too in depth into TCP slow start and congestion avoidance, just remember that the process costs in terms of performance and user experience.

Table 1-1 shows a representation of two hosts in slow start where host one is sending data to host two. Host two is acknowledging the data received. Host one must wait on Acknowledgements to be returned to it before it can continue transmitting data.

Table 1-1 *TCP Slow Start and Delay ACK*

Host Sending Data	Host Receiving Data
Send 2 segments	
	Send 1 ACK (both segments)
Send 3 segments	
	Send 1 ACK (first 2 segments) (3rd segment = TCP Delay ACK)
Send 4 segments	
	Send 2 ACKs (last segment above and first segment + next 2 segments) (4th segment = TCP Delay ACK)
Send 6 segments	
	Send 3 ACKs (last segment above and first segment + next 2 segments + next 2 segments) (6th segment = TCP Delay ACK)
Send 9 segments	
	Send 5 ACKs
Send 14 segments	

What causes packet loss? There are two primary types of packet loss: errors and discards. Both result in the same cost in terms of performance; however, knowing the differences can greatly aid in identifying fault domains.

Errors

Errors are caused by some type of hardware issue. An error is reported when packets are corrupted and can no longer be recognized or trusted by whatever device is next receiving them (and performing a CRC/FCS check). That device could be the destination host, but often these errors are reported by routers and switches. When an error is reported, it is not reported back to the host sending the original packet, or even to the last hop forwarding the packet. Well, not since X.25 anyway. And yes, we have troubleshot X.25 circuits. But that's another story for another time. Today, error correction occurs on the sending host and generally because of a timer expiring. Errors are caused by a physical corruption to the data such as bad cabling, corrosion, loose connectors, malfunctioning hardware, or electromagnetic noise interfering with the signal. The good thing is there is a very small fault domain when dealing with errors. If it is an outbound error, the problem is likely on the device reporting the error. If it is an inbound error, the problem is between the last device that preformed a CRC check and the device reporting the error.

Discards

Both errors and discards result in the same amount of performance degradation. Discards are an indication of a capacity issue. When an interface card or a system cannot keep up with the amount of data it needs to process or transfer, it will first buffer (or queue) some data. When the queue is full, it will start dropping data. This is a very simplistic version of what is occurring, but it makes the point.

Inbound discards are simply a system reporting that it is unable to keep up with the number of packets it is receiving. Outbound discards appear when the system is unable to offload the data onto the network as fast as it is coming in. Think of inbound discards as a system notifying the administrator that it is overloaded, and think of outbound discards as a system notifying the administrator that the circuit (or queue if QoS/DSCP is in use) is overloaded. One thing to keep in mind when troubleshooting discards is that inbound discards are more likely impacted by the number of packets processed than by the number of bytes, whereas outbound discards are most likely due to the number of bytes being forwarded to a given queue on the outbound interface.

Because of the speed of hardware available today, inbound discards should be rare unless that system has not been properly sized for the way it is being utilized. Inbound discards might also occur when process switching is being used. Process switching is when the router is inspecting all packets in software at Layer 3 instead of in its hardware. This creates slower forwarding decisions, higher CPU utilization, and sometimes inbound discards. Whenever you see inbound discards, your first two questions should be the following:

1. Did the packets per second (pps) metric increase?

2. Is this router process switching?

Why is the packets per second metric such a big deal? Why not just look at bytes?

First, packets are processed by header, not by payload. In making forwarding (or processing) decisions, a system needs to inspect the packet header of each packet (hopefully in hardware and not software). Additionally, depending upon the size of the packet, the number of packets it takes to equal a given amount of bandwidth can vary greatly. For example, something as small as 10 Mbps of data on a network can vary anywhere from less than 1,000 pps to about 20,000 pps depending on the size of the packet:

800 pps × 1,500 bytes = 9.6 Mbps

19,000 pps × 64 bytes = 9.7 Mbps

In Figure 1-2, ThousandEyes is using its Devices View (SNMP from an Enterprise Agent) to show outbound discards on an interface. While the metric shows only 4.33 pps discarded, keep in mind this is over a 5-minute period (11:45–11:50). This indicates that the interface dropped about 1,300 packets during this timeframe.

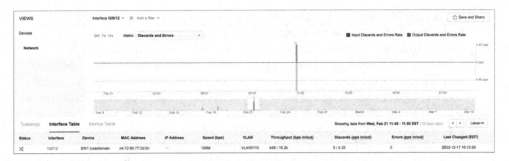

Figure 1-2 *Outbound Discards*

Network Latency

Bidirectional network latency is often measured by sending a packet from a host to the destination, making note of the time the packet left the interface until the time a response is received. This is often accomplished by using Ping, which is an application native to most IP-based hosts that leverages the ICMP protocol to communicate. With Ping, the first host issues an ICMP Echo (type 8, code 0) and the second host (the destination) responds with an ICMP Echo Reply (type 0, code 0). However, latency is best measured using the same protocol/port as the application being monitored. There are several methods available to do just this; however, there are advantages and disadvantages in how they are used and interpreted.

One method we'll examine in this book is the TCP 3-way handshake. This is where the first host (generally the client) sends a TCP packet with the SYN bit set to 1 to the second host (generally a server). This method forces (should force) an immediate response from the second host to either send a SYN/ACK (when the port requested is available) or an RST (when the port is not active or is unavailable). With either response, a very good measurement can be taken, as the second host is not waiting to collect data but simply responding to a request for a connection.

The second method is simply to use TCP sequence numbers (SEQ) and Acknowledgements (ACKs). Round-trip times for data can be measured this way. It is a very accurate way of measuring latency, but it will include TCP protocol delays. TCP protocol delays, such as TCP Delay ACK, will impact this measurement, making latency appear to be higher than what is occurring on the network. With TCP Delay ACK, when a host receives TCP data segments (containing payload), instead of ACKing every segment received, it will only ACK every other segment (a typical TCP Delay ACK value is two segments). This is common TCP default behavior and reduces the number of packets placed on the network. While this is a form of latency and can play an important role in overall performance (such as its role in TCP slow start), it should not be calculated when determining latency due to the network. Therefore, this type of measurement is not recommended in calculating metrics such as Maximum Theoretical Throughput (discussed later in this chapter).

The third method leverages TCP Selective Acknowledgements (SACK). ThousandEyes uses this method to test end-to-end agent-to-server network metrics such as packet loss and latency. The first host (client or agent) establishes a TCP connection with the target host. Then the first host sends a data segment (payload) to the target; however, it skips the first byte that the target is expecting to receive. This forces the target to immediately respond with a request for the first byte of data. The target will issue this response every time it receives a segment that does not include that first byte it is expecting. Now, if SACK is used (it must be agreed to by both hosts during the 3-way handshake), the target will indicate which segments it has received each time it notifies the first host that it is looking for that first byte of data. This allows a one-to-one correlation between the packet/segment sent to the target and the response/ACK/SACK returned. Because these responses are sent immediately, there is only network latency involved and no TCP protocol delay.

Figure 1-3 shows end-to-end bidirectional network latency (4 ms) between a ThousandEyes Cloud Agent in Chicago, IL, and a server hosting www.google.com.

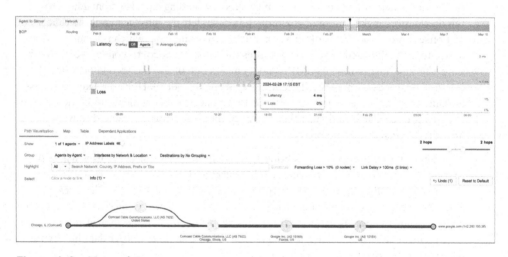

Figure 1-3   *Network Latency*

Five sources of latency combine to make up network latency:

- **Serialization delay:** Directly related to interface speed or bandwidth

- **Queuing delay:** Only impacts operations during times of congestion

- **Distance delay:** A little faster than one-half the speed of light (for fiber optics)

- **Routing/switching delay:** Also known as forwarding delay

- **Protocol delay:** Wi-Fi RTS/CTS, TCP Delay ACK, etc.

Serialization Delay

Serialization is the process of taking a packet from a parallel bus inside a computing system and placing it, one bit at a time, onto the network. The faster the interface, the shorter the delay. A T1 interface (1.544 Mbps) can serialize a full-size packet (1,500 bytes) in about 8 ms:

$$1,500 \text{ B} \times 8 = 12,000 \text{ b}$$

$$12,000 / 1,544,000 = 0.007772020725389 \text{ second}$$

The same interface can serialize a 64-byte packet in under 0.4 ms. Generally, most networks today should have very little serialization delay.

Queuing Delay

Think of traveling through an airport. When you stand in line for security screening, you are in a queue. If you get to the airport at 4:00 a.m. and there in no one in front of you, you can go right into the screening process (analogous to serialization). However, if you get there at 8:00 a.m. on a Monday morning, there may be a significant line ahead of you. This wait time is *queuing delay*. You are waiting for those ahead of you to be screened (serialized). Same with networking. Queuing delay happens only when multiple packets need to be processed (inbound or outbound) and have to wait on other packets that arrived ahead of them. If multiple queues are employed, such as with DSCP, then you are only impacted by the depth of the queue you are in. In no way does QoS/DSCP or any type of priority queuing make a network run any faster. What a well-architected and properly implemented queuing strategy should do is make a network more consistent. High-priority queues should perform much like the network does when there is no congestion, regardless of the amount of traffic.

Figure 1-4 shows a ThousandEyes test running between Orlando, FL, and Dallas, TX, where the Path Visualization identifies one link in the path that changes the DSCP markings from 46 (Express Forwarding/EF) to 0 (Best Effort).

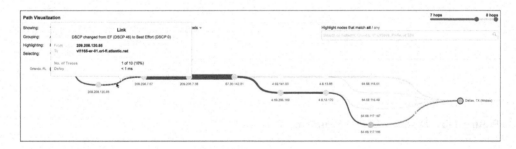

Figure 1-4   *DSCP Changes in Path*

Distance Delay

Distance delay is often the most significant source of latency over a wide-area network or over the Internet.

■ The speed of light traveling on fiber is about 5.50 microseconds per kilometer.

- The speed of electricity traveling on copper is about 5.56 microseconds per kilometer.

- The speed of microwave communication is about 3.30 microseconds per kilometer.

This means that over fiber, packets travel about 125 miles per millisecond. Actual latency is considerably slower than this. If two hosts are 3,000 miles apart, you will never see only 50-ms latency (3,000 × 2 / 125 = 48 ms) because this is not a straight fiber run between two points. There will be relays and routers (hops) that the packets must cross. At best, you might see 60 ms. But even that is being hopeful. That said, if you see 100 ms or higher, then it's time to figure out why. Is it distance, or something else, consuming most of the time?

In Figure 1-5, a test running from Seattle, WA, to login.live.com (Microsoft) is encountering over 250-ms latency on a regular basis. When we use ThousandEyes to provide path visualization, we see that this agent is being sent to Singapore to log into Microsoft. Sometimes simply pinging is not enough.

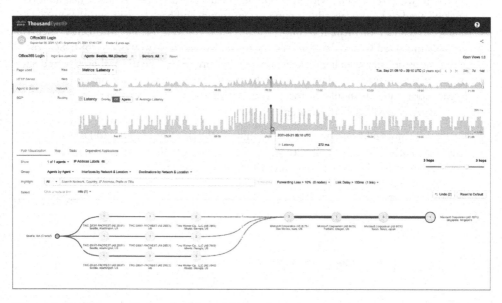

Figure 1-5   *Distance Delay: Seattle to Microsoft*

Routing/Switching Delay

Routing/switching delay, also referred to as forwarding delay, is the amount of time it takes for a given router or switch to process an incoming packet and forward it to the proper outbound interface. This should be a sub-millisecond decision made in hardware. However, if a router is process switching, it may take considerably longer. Although even then it is generally a small amount of delay because inbound queues are generally much smaller than outbound queues and will likely result in discarded packets if the load is significant.

Protocol Delay

Protocol delay is mostly seen only when dealing with Wi-Fi in today's networking environments. Back in the day, half-duplex Ethernet used carrier-sense multiple access with collision detection (CSMA/CD), which introduced a type of protocol delay. However, that has been overcome by technology with today's full-duplex operations. Wireless/Wi-Fi access points use a similar technology that allows them to communicate with multiple clients. They now use carrier-sense multiple access with collision avoidance (CSMA/CA). Additionally, Wi-Fi uses Clear-to-Send/Request-to-Send (CTS/RTS) to avoid host data colliding and becoming corrupted. All of these technologies operate at very fast speeds, but they do amount to some level of protocol delay.

TCP Delay ACK and TCP slow start are also forms of protocol delay. By avoiding using measurement methods that include these delays (as previously discussed) you can understand the latency associated with the network without including additional latency injected by the protocol.

To summarize this section, here is a list of key metrics to remember:

- **Packet loss**

  - **Outbound errors:** Check the device reporting the errors

  - **Inbound errors:** Fault domain between the device reporting errors and the previous CRC check

  - **Outbound discards:** Bandwidth/queue capacity

  - **Inbound discards:** System capacity (note pps)—beware of process switching

- **Network latency:** When looking at latency over a consistent WAN or Internet path, the minimum amount of network latency generally provides a good reference for distance. Latency spikes above minimum provide a good reference as to queuing delay. Using ThousandEyes, test different QoS/DSCP queues and compare for consistency. If higher priority queues are not providing more consistent latency (fewer spikes), then reexamine your queuing architecture and implementation.

  - **Serialization delay:** Speed of interface/bandwidth

  - **Queuing delay:** Latency above minimum indicates congestion

  - **Distance delay:** Likely the main source of latency for WAN and Internet paths

  - **Forwarding delay:** Should be minimal unless process switching (look for inbound discards)

  - **Protocol delay:** Primarily wireless and TCP/IP

Maximum Theoretical Throughput

A ThousandEyes customer was recently attempting to transfer files using Common Internet File System (CIFS) over Server Message Block (SMB). The files were being copied between two servers, one onsite in Vancouver and the other in the AWS East 1 region.

The customer had an Internet tunnel connecting the locations. The customer had provisioned a 1-Gbps circuit between these locations. Their issue was that it would take 7 hours to transfer a 40-GB file, putting the effective throughput at the following:

40 GB = 42,949,672,960 B = 343,597,383,680 b

7 hours = 25,200 seconds

Roughly 13 Mbps average

Note that this is calculating application throughput (payload) and does not take into consideration the overhead of Ethernet, IP, and TCP headers.

A primary metric to look at whenever we are asked to troubleshoot a throughput issue is Maximum Theoretical Throughput (MTT). This is a calculated value of the maximum throughput that can be achieved for a given TCP session based on the amount of the network latency encountered. This metric uses a Data Block Size (DBS) and divides that value by the actual measured network latency (DBS / latency = MTT). This calculation assumes unlimited bandwidth and no packet loss. Now, the DBS can never be larger than the TCP Receive Window (RWIN) of the receiving host. It could be smaller if the application imposes greater limits or if the sending host is going through a congestion avoidance algorithm. But the *maximum* value that is possible is when the DBS = RWIN. So, we will use RWIN initially to see if better throughput is even possible.

Unfortunately, the customer had not yet installed an Enterprise Agent in either Vancouver or in AWS East. We did have an Enterprise Agent available in their Plano, TX, data center with a direct tunnel to Vancouver. So, we decided to begin testing from there. We set up a network-to-server test using TCP port 445, the same port SMB uses. We pointed this test directly at the server in Vancouver. This not only provided a quick graphical representation of the network latency (see Figure 1-6) but also allowed us to collect packets associated with the Vancouver server and be able to see its TCP window size (RWIN).

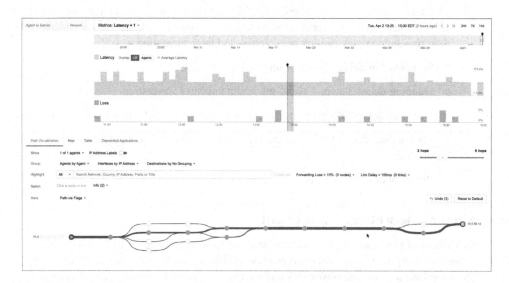

Figure 1-6   *Latency from Plano to Vancouver*

Figure 1-6 shows the network latency to be as low as 51 ms, with occasional spikes. So, for MTT, we will start with the smallest value.

Although a packet capture is not an exposed feature of ThousandEyes agents, the ThousandEyes support team can assist when packet captures are needed. Note that only packets associated with the agent as the source or destination IP address will be collected. Here is a link to a ThousandEyes document with additional information on generating packet captures:

https://docs.thousandeyes.com/product-documentation/global-vantage-points/enterprise-agents/troubleshooting/how-to-generate-packet-captures

This was used to collect packets while the network test was being executed (see Figure 1-7). Most modern TCP implementations on hosts today allow for TCP window scaling. Since the traditional TCP window was limited to a 2-byte field in the TCP header, the maximum value it could be was 65535 (FFFF). Window scaling provides a multiplier that allows for window sizes up to 1 GB. The Vancouver server showed a window size of 512 bytes with a scale factor of 256:

$$512 \times 256 = 131{,}072 \text{ bytes}$$

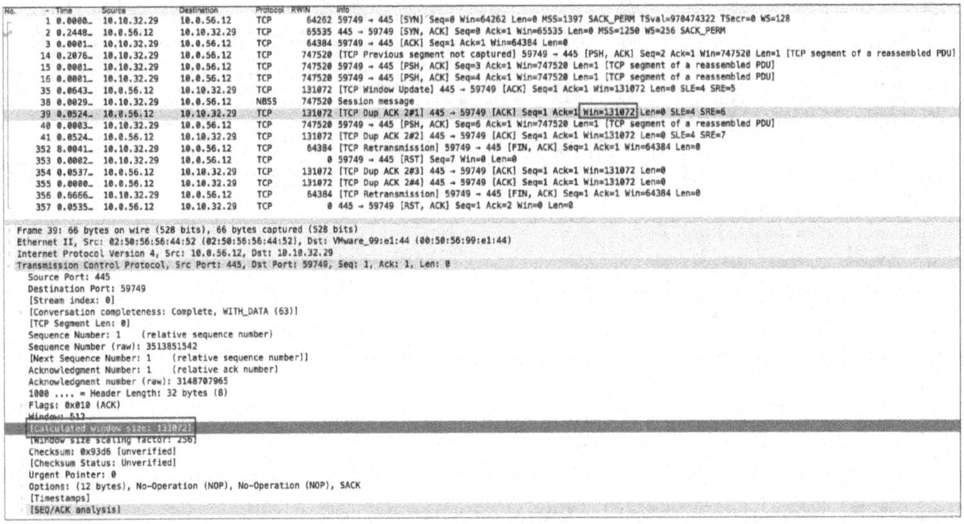

Figure 1-7 *Vancouver TCP Header RWIN = 131,072 Bytes*

This represents the most data this server is willing to risk in flight at any given time. The term *in flight* represents the amount of data that has been transmitted from the sending host but has yet to be acknowledged. Because no more than 131,072 bytes can be risked, that also means that no more than 131,072 bytes can be sent per network round trip, which is measured as latency. This provides us with a method to mathematically calculate the MTT. Keep in mind that the actual throughput may be less, but it cannot be more for a given TCP session.

$131{,}072 \times 8 = 1{,}048{,}576$ bits

RWIN/Latency = MTT

$1{,}048{,}576 / .051 = 20{,}560{,}314$ bps ~ 20 Mbps

This shows a maximum throughput from Plano to the Vancouver server to be around 20 Mbps.

Figures 1-7 and 1-8 show packet captures taken of the test running between the Enterprise Agent and the Vancouver server. Each figure reveals a different window size coming from the Vancouver server. The math related to each window size is calculated following the figures.

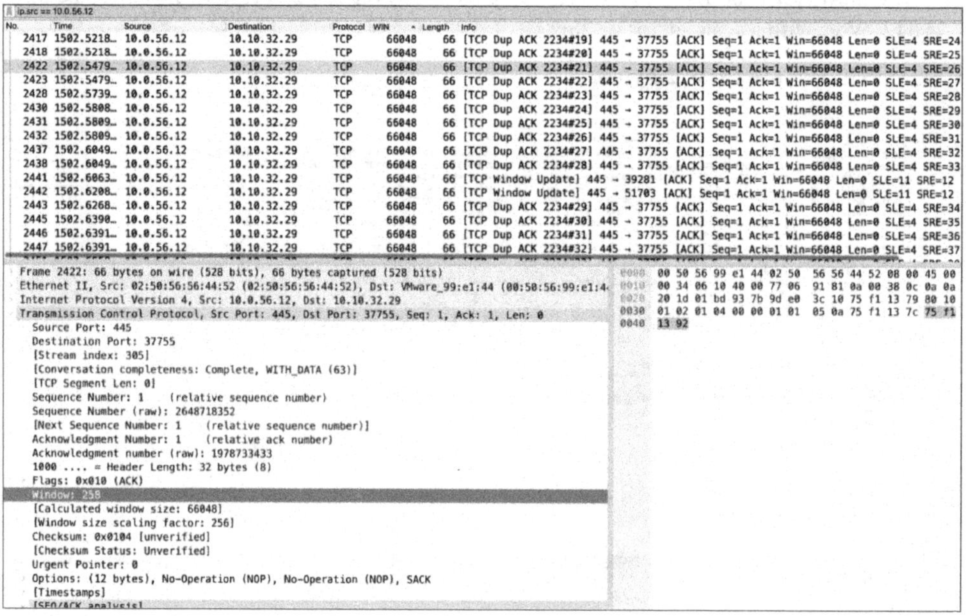

Figure 1-8 *Vancouver TCP Header RWIN = 66,048 Bytes*

However, taking additional (longer duration) packet captures revealed that at times the TCP window drops to as low as 66,048 bytes (528,384 bits):

$66{,}048 \times 8 = 528{,}384$ bits

RWIN/Latency = MTT

$528{,}384 / .051 = 10{,}360{,}470$ bps ~ 10 Mbps

Now, to be a bit more accurate, Plano to Vancouver (PLN to VAN) latency averages around 79 ms (see Figure 1-9) over a 24-hour period. This would affect throughput as follows:

$131,072 \times 8 = 1,048,576 / .079 = 13,273,113$ bps ~ 13 Mbps

$66,048 \times 8 = 528,384 / .079 = 6,688,405$ bps ~ 6.6 Mbps

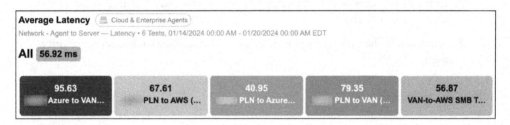

Figure 1-9 *Latency 24-Hour Averages*

Note we now have a measurement for Azure to Vancouver as well at 95 ms:

$131,072 \times 8 = 1,048,576 / .095 = 11,037,642$ bps ~ 11 Mbps

$66,048 \times 8 = 528,384 / .095 = 5,561,936$ bps ~ 5.5 Mbps

What remains missing from the equation is testing between AWS and Vancouver. Although basic latency tests (ping) show similar results with both Azure and AWS testing, they provide only a spot check of latency and lack the 24-hour average shown in Figure 1-9.

Results

All testing and conclusions are based on data transfers "to" Vancouver. Additional testing would be required to calculate MTT for Vancouver to AWS.

The results of this basic analysis demonstrate that the throughput may very well be "as expected" given the server's limited Receive Window capacity and the network latency. While faster throughputs may be achieved by increasing the Receive Window on the Vancouver server, the window size setting is likely considerably larger than the operation tested window size. Improvement in throughput will require one of three things:

- Increased operational window size

- Decreased latency (distance is generally the biggest factor in latency and not one easily overcome)

- Increase the number of simultaneous TCP sessions (aka threads) used in the file transfers (may require third-party software)

Review Questions

Answer the following questions. Check your answers against those provided in Appendix A, "Answers to Review Questions."

1. Where is the most likely fault domain when a device is showing inbound discards on an interface?

2. Of the five sources of network latency, which is most likely the largest contributor to latency over a WAN?

3. What should the expected result be of placing an application in a higher priority queue (DSCP)?

Chapter 2

Agent Setup

ThousandEyes Agents are compact pieces of code designed to run on a Linux platform. These agents serve as vantage points, enabling users to execute a range of tests across various locations. By serving as vantage points, they offer valuable insights into network and application performance. Agents come in several variations, including Enterprise Agents, Cloud Agents, and Endpoint Agents. In this chapter, we delve into each type of agent and explore its capabilities.

Enterprise Agents

Enterprise Agents hold a pivotal role in monitoring your organization's network from within its infrastructure. These agents offer comprehensive visibility into internal networks and critical infrastructure components, facilitating accurate performance assessment. In this section, we delve into the specifics of Enterprise Agents, covering their installation process, types, and strategic placement to ensure optimal vantage points.

Before diving into the discussion of how Enterprise Agents function, it's essential to ensure that the network is primed for the setup. Enterprise Agents have specific dependencies and require communication with ThousandEyes servers and other endpoints. Figure 2-1 shows the protocols, ports, and destination addresses that are necessary for this communication. Be certain that your firewall or proxy settings allow for this seamless interaction; each domain will need to be resolvable from the agent location.

Protocol	Port	Destination Address and/or Name	Notes
TCP, UDP	53	DNS Server IP Address(es)	Domain Name Service
UDP	123	NTP Server Domain Names or IP Addresses	Time Synchronization
TCP	443	c1.thousandeyes.com, c1.agt.thousandeyes.com, sc1.thousandeyes.com, crashreports.thousandeyes.com, crashreports.agt.thousandeyes.com, bbot-sentry-proxy.thousandeyes.com, data1.agt.thousandeyes.com, api.thousandeyes.com, registry.agt.thousandeyes.com	ThousandEyes Agent Infrastructure
TCP	80	archive.ubuntu.com, archive.canonical.com, security.ubuntu.com	Ubuntu Linux Package Repository
TCP	443	changelogs.ubuntu.com	Ubuntu Linux Package Repository
TCP	80 or 443	apt.thousandeyes.com	ThousandEyes APT Package Repository
TCP	443	Agent IP Address	Inbound to the Agent
TCP	22	Agent IP Address	Inbound to the Agent

Protocol	ICMP Types
IPv4	3, 11

Figure 2-1 *Firewall Rules*

Enterprise Agent Installation

The installation of ThousandEyes Enterprise Agents can be achieved through various methods, ranging from virtual machines to installations on Cisco devices. In this first section, we explore how to install Enterprise Agents on Cisco devices utilizing the Cisco Application Framework. This approach leverages the integration capabilities of Cisco devices to enhance network visibility and performance monitoring.

Cisco Application Framework Installation

Cisco has introduced a groundbreaking framework for efficient application and hardware resource management on network devices. This framework, known as the Cisco Application Framework or Cisco IOx (IOS + Linux), marks a significant advancement. Cisco IOx has been designed specifically for hosting applications on Internet of Things (IoT) network devices, which execute compact applications.

The IOx framework enables a pivotal leap in network device capabilities, optimizing the deployment of small applications across IoT networks. It's important to note that the IOx framework may not be available on all Cisco devices. As a best practice, consulting the release notes to confirm compatibility is highly recommended when considering the integration of ThousandEyes.

The introduction of the Cisco Application Framework (CAF) presents an efficient solution for deploying the ThousandEyes Enterprise Agent within a Docker container on the device. This framework addresses the challenges posed by the previous installation methods, making the process significantly smoother. Previously, the installation process often involved the use of Guest shell and other methods that were cumbersome.

Before proceeding into the CAF-based installation of the ThousandEyes (TE) agent, a few prerequisites need to be met:

- **Proper licenses:** It's essential to ensure that you possess the appropriate licenses. By default, the Cisco DNA Advantage license permits users to start utilizing both the Cisco Application Framework (CAF) and Cisco IOx.

- **Compatible code version:** To ensure seamless integration, it's crucial to enable the appropriate code version. For instance, for Cisco IOS-XE environments, version 17.6.1 is recommended. Similarly, for Nexus environments, version 10.3.3 is advised.

The following steps demonstrate how to utilize a Cisco Catalyst 9300 switch as an example. This process is supported on various devices, including Catalyst 9300/8000 and various ISR, ASR, and Nexus 9000 platforms, but the focus here is to demonstrate the Docker installation procedure using the Cisco Application Framework. This framework, supported on a range of devices, introduces a new command, **app-hosting**, that plays a pivotal role in initializing the device to host containerized applications. If you are using Catalyst-Center, Meraki, or Cisco SDWAN, we cover those topics in Chapter 8, "Integrations."

Step 1.   Enable the IOx to enable the application hosting on the Catalyst 9000:

```
C9K# conf t
C9K(config)1# iox
C9K(config)1# exit
```

Step 2.   There are two ways to install the application to the device. The first is the traditional way, using flash or SSD. The second way is to use the new **app-hosting** command to also download the application.

For the traditional method, use SCP, FTP, TFTP, or USB storage to copy the Docker image to the switch's flash: directory:

```
C9K# copy scp://thousandeyes@10.100.21.239/thousandeyes-
enterprise-agent-4.4.2.cisco.tar flash:
```

Verify the contents:

```
C9K# dir flash: | i .tar
      253960   -rw-          178872320   Mar 27 2021 00:03:32
+00:00   thousandeyes-enterprise-agent-3.0.cat9k.tar
```

Using the **app-hosting** command enables you to effortlessly pull down the desired application, similar to executing a **docker pull** command. On your Cisco switch, input the following command, replacing **DESIRED_APP_ID** with the name you have chosen for your Enterprise Agent:

```
C9K# app-hosting install appid DESIRED_APP_ID package
https://downloads.thousandeyes.com/enterprise-agent/
thousandeyes-enterprise-agent-4.4.2.cisco.tar
```

After successfully retrieving the application using either of the preceding two methods, you're now ready to advance to the installation phase.

Step 3.   Configure the AppGigabitEthernet port (see Figure 2-2).

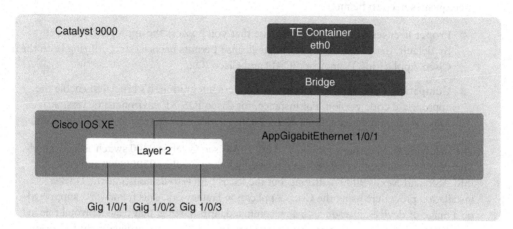

Figure 2-2   *Virtual Switch Connection*

AppGigabitEthernet is an internal virtual data port that is hardware-switched to the front-panel data ports. The AppGigabitEthernet port can be configured as a trunk port and allow a specific VLAN for application traffic.

a. Enter privileged EXEC mode. Ensure your device allows the user to enter privileged EXEC mode when making changes or configuring:

```
C9K# enable
C9K# config t
```

b. Access the interface. Enter the following command to access the specific AppGigabitEthernet port (replace **1/0/1** with the appropriate port number):

```
C9K# interface AppGigabitEthernet1/0/1
```

c. Define the allowed VLAN. Specify the allowed VLAN for application traffic using the following command (replace **<vlan-id>** with the desired VLAN ID):

```
C9k# switchport trunk allowed vlan <vlan-id>
```

d. Configure the port to operate in trunk mode:

```
C9K# switchport mode trunk
```

Step 4. Assign an IP address to the application, either statically or dynamically.

For static configurations:

```
C9K(config)# app-hosting appid <app-name>
C9K(config-app-hosting)# app-vnic AppGigabitEthernet trunk
C9K(config-config-app-hosting-trunk)# vlan <vlan-id>
guest-interface 0
C9K(config-config-app-hosting-vlan-access-ip)# guest-
ipaddress x.x.x.x netmask x.x.x.x
C9K(config-config-app-hosting-vlan-access-ip)# app-default-
gateway x.x.x.x guest-interface 0
```

For dynamic (DHCP) configurations:

```
C9K# conf t
```

Enter configuration commands, one per line. End with Ctrl-Z.

```
C9K(config)# app-hosting appid <app-name>
C9K(config-app-hosting)# app-vnic AppGigabitEthernet trunk
C9K(config-config-app-hosting-trunk)#  vlan <vlan-id>
guest-interface 0
C9K(config-app-hosting)# app-resource docker
```

Note The container will assume that DHCP is being used because the IP address was not specified. Ensure that the VLAN used is a Layer 2 VLAN.

Step 5. To obtain the ThousandEyes account token, log in to the platform and follow the next steps:

   a. Navigate to **Cloud & Enterprise Agents**.

   b. Click **Agent Settings**.

   c. Click the **Add New Enterprise Agent** button.

   d. Click the **Cisco Application Hosting** tab.

   e. Copy the **Account Group Token** from this section (see Figure 2-3).

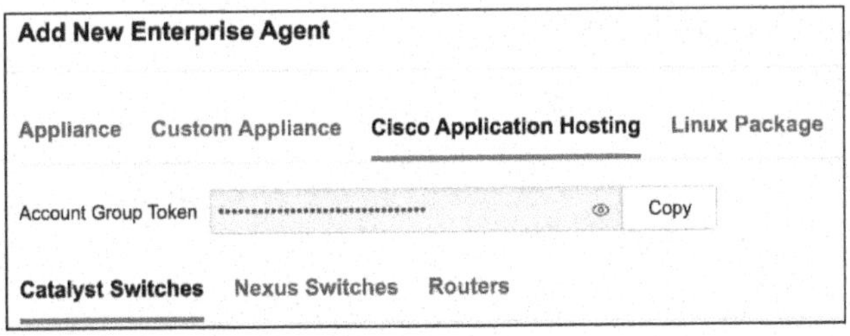

Figure 2-3 *Account Group Token*

The account token will allow the Enterprise Agent to register to the ThousandEyes collector and then be placed into the correct account group.

At this point we should have established a connection to the AppGigabitEthernet port, with a proper IP scheme and ThousandEyes token. We show the entire snippet using a static IP address using the **app-hosting** command in Example 2-1.

```
C9K# conf t
```

Enter configuration commands, one per line. End with Ctrl-Z.

Example 2-1 *Static IP Configuration*

```
C9K(config)# app-hosting appid <app-name>
C9K(config-app-hosting)# app-vnic AppGigabitEthernet trunk
C9K(config-config-app-hosting-trunk)# vlan <vlan-id> guest-interface 0
C9K(config-config-app-hosting-vlan-access-ip)# guest-ipaddress x.x.x.x netmask
  x.x.x.x
C9K(config-config-app-hosting-vlan-access-ip)# app-default-gateway x.x.x.x
  guest-interface 0
C9K(config-app-hosting)# app-resource docker
C9K(config-app-hosting-docker)# prepend-pkg-opts
C9K(config-app-hosting-docker)# run-opts 1 "-e TEAGENT_ACCOUNT_TOKEN=xxxxxxxxxx"
C9K(config-app-hosting-docker)# name-server0 x.x.x
C9K(config-app-hosting)# start
C9K(config-app-hosting)# end
```

Note   In Example 2-1, the **name-server** is for DNS. If you do not add **name-server**, you will not be able to resolve domain names. The **run-opts** command enables the user to also add more Docker runtime options; for example: **run-opts 2 "--hostname Cisco-Docker"**.

Step 6.   Verify that the container and application are running:

```
C9K# sh app-hosting list
App id State
-----------------------------------------------------------
thousandeyes_enterprise_agent RUNNING
```

To verify in detail, see Example 2-2.

Example 2-2   *The* show app-hosting detail *Command*

```
C9Kt# show app-hosting detail appid thousandeyes_enterprise_agent
App id              : thousandeyes_enterprise_agent
Owner               : iox
State               : RUNNING
Application
  Type              : docker
  Name              : ThousandEyes Enterprise Agent
  Version           : 4.4.2
  Description       :
  Author            : ThousandEyes <support@thousandeyes.com>
  Path              : flash:thousandeyes-enterprise-agent-4.4.2.cisco.tar
  URL Path          :
Activated profile name : custom


Resource reservation
  Memory            : 500 MB
  Disk              : 1 MB
  CPU               : 1850 units
  VCPU              : 1
Attached devices
  Type              Name              Alias
-----------------------------------------------
  serial/shell    iox_console_shell   serial0
  serial/aux      iox_console_aux     serial1
  serial/syslog   iox_syslog          serial2
  serial/trace    iox_trace           serial3


Network interfaces
  -------------------------------------
eth0:
  MAC address       : 52:54:dd:d:38:3d
  Network name      : mgmt-bridge-v21
Docker
------
Run-time information
  Command           :
  Entry-point       : /sbin/my_init
  Run options in use : -e TEAGENT_ACCOUNT_TOKEN=TOKEN_NOT_SET
--hostname=$(SYSTEM_NAME) --cap-add=NET_ADMIN --mount
type=tmpfs,destination=/var/log/agent,tmpfs-size=140m --mount
type=tmpfs,destination=/var/lib/te-agent/data,tmpfs-size=200m -v
$(APP_DATA)/data:/var/lib/te-agent -e TEAGENT_PROXY_TYPE=DIRECT -e
```

```
TEAGENT_PROXY_LOCATION= -e TEAGENT_PROXY_USER= -e
TEAGENT_PROXY_AUTH_TYPE= -e TEAGENT_PROXY_PASS= -e
TEAGENT_PROXY_BYPASS_LIST= -e TEAGENT_KDC_USER= -e TEAGENT_KDC_PASS=
-e TEAGENT_KDC_REALM= -e TEAGENT_KDC_HOST= -e TEAGENT_KDC_PORT=88 -e
TEAGENT_KERBEROS_WHITELIST= -e TEAGENT_KERBEROS_RDNS=1 -e PROXY_APT=
-e APT_PROXY_USER= -e APT_PROXY_PASS= -e APT_PROXY_LOCATION= -e
TEAGENT_AUTO_UPDATES=1 -e
TEAGENT_ACCOUNT_TOKEN=nfhjzm8e8ikg07d4n31wcsws9bakcloh --hostname
Cisco-Docker

  Package run options  : -e TEAGENT_ACCOUNT_TOKEN=TOKEN_NOT_SET
--hostname=$(SYSTEM_NAME) --cap-add=NET_ADMIN --mount
type=tmpfs,destination=/var/log/agent,tmpfs-size=140m --mount
type=tmpfs,destination=/var/lib/te-agent/data,tmpfs-size=200m -v
$(APP_DATA)/data:/var/lib/te-agent -e TEAGENT_PROXY_TYPE=DIRECT -e
TEAGENT_PROXY_LOCATION= -e TEAGENT_PROXY_USER= -e
TEAGENT_PROXY_AUTH_TYPE= -e TEAGENT_PROXY_PASS= -e
TEAGENT_PROXY_BYPASS_LIST= -e TEAGENT_KDC_USER= -e TEAGENT_KDC_PASS=
-e TEAGENT_KDC_REALM= -e TEAGENT_KDC_HOST= -e TEAGENT_KDC_PORT=88 -e
TEAGENT_KERBEROS_WHITELIST= -e TEAGENT_KERBEROS_RDNS=1 -e PROXY_APT=
-e APT_PROXY_USER= -e APT_PROXY_PASS= -e APT_PROXY_LOCATION= -e
TEAGENT_AUTO_UPDATES=1

Application health information
  Status            : 0
  Last probe error  :
  Last probe output :
```

Step 7.   Finally, verify in the ThousandEyes UI that the agent is up and running and that an IP address is assigned. From the Agent Settings in the UI, we can see that the agent is online, its IP addresses (private and public), and what platform it is sitting on (see Figure 2-4).

Please refer to the following for additional information about **app-hosting** supported commands:

- Troubleshooting: Appendix B
- Supported **app-hosting** commands: Appendix B
- Cisco Catalyst Center (formerly DNA Center): See Chapter 8, "Integrations"

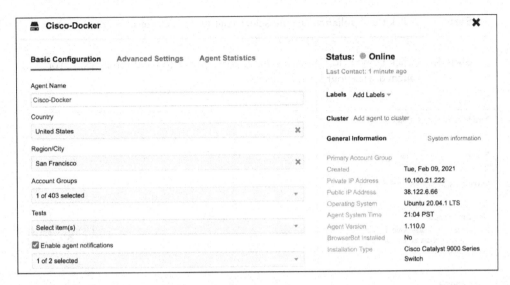

Figure 2-4 *Agent Verification*

Open Virtual Appliance Installation

Another option for installing the ThousandEyes agent is to utilize an Open Virtualization Appliance (OVA) or virtual machine (VM). This approach grants users the flexibility to install the TE agent within a range of virtual infrastructure platforms, including VMware, Microsoft Hyper-V, and even VirtualBox. The OVA presents a prebuilt TE agent, which streamlines the process because it can be swiftly imported into the virtual network.

Before proceeding with the installation of the TE agent using the OVA, there are some prerequisites to address:

- **Firewall configuration or proxy settings:** Ensure that the necessary adjustments have been made to your firewall configuration or proxy settings. This will ensure smooth communication between the virtual appliance and external servers.

- **Memory allocation:** Allocate a minimum of 2 GB of memory to the virtual machine in which the TE agent will reside. This allocation is essential for optimal performance as well to ensure the OVA is able to run a browser bot in order to run web layer testing.

This discussion assumes that you possess a basic understanding of virtualization, as this forms the foundation for deploying the TE agent using this method.

To add a new Enterprise Agent from the ThousandEyes user interface, follow these steps (see Figure 2-5):

Step 1.   Navigate to **Cloud & Enterprise Agents > Agent Settings**.

Step 2.   Click the **Add New Enterprise Agent** button.

Step 3.   Click the **Appliance** tab and select your preference for deploying a virtual appliance as an Enterprise Agent.

Step 4.   Click **Download-OVA.** This image corresponds to the desired VM flavor aligned with your intended use.

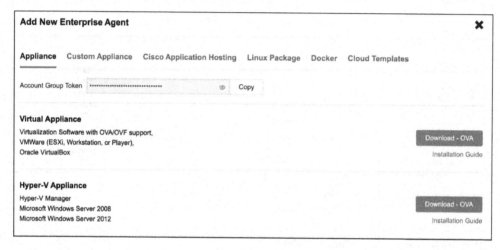

Figure 2-5   *Agent OVA Download*

For this demonstration, we'll illustrate the process using Oracle VM VirtualBox (see Figure 2-6).

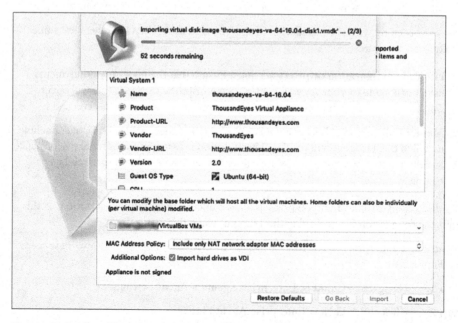

Figure 2-6   *Installing a New VM Enterprise Agent*

Regardless of the chosen platform, a crucial step in the installation process is to configure the network connection for your virtual machine. This step ensures that the guest VM enjoys unhindered access to both the network and the Internet. To achieve this, you need to opt for a bridged network connection (see Figure 2-7), which will facilitate seamless communication.

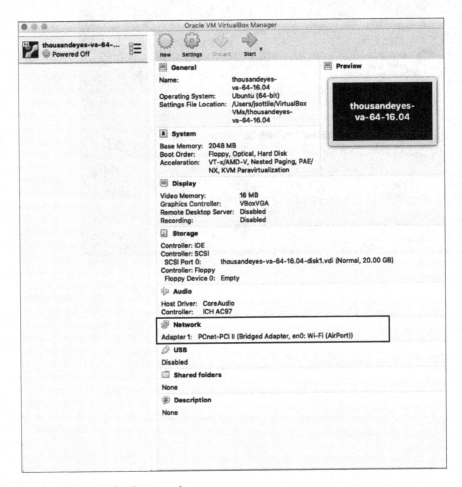

Figure 2-7 *Bridged Network*

Now, let's configure the appliance.

Upon starting the VM, you will encounter a screen displaying the necessary credentials along with the IP address for accessing the management console (see Figure 2-8). To proceed with the configuration, access the console by navigating to the provided IP address using a web browser. Enter the designated user credentials (username and password) to gain access to the management console.

Once you're logged into the platform, you'll be directed through a process to update your web interface password, as shown in Figure 2-9.

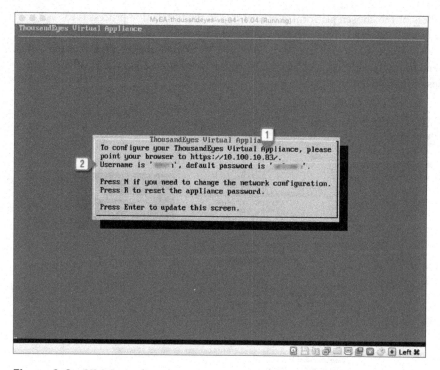

Figure 2-8   *VM Console*

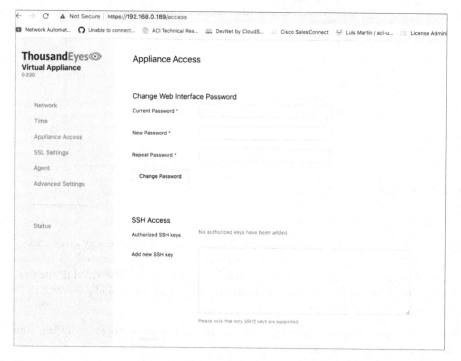

Figure 2-9   *Updating Web Interface Password*

With the password successfully changed, the next step is to associate the virtual appliance with your designated ThousandEyes account group. To accomplish this, you'll need to provide the token group associated with your account. The following steps outline the process in the ThousandEyes user interface:

Step 1.   Navigate to **Cloud & Enterprise Agents > Agent Settings.**

Step 2.   Click the **Add New Enterprise Agent** button.

Step 3.   Click the **Appliance** tab (see Figure 2-10).

Add New Enterprise Agent   ✖

Appliance   Custom Appliance   Cisco Application Hosting   Linux Package   Docker   Cloud Templates

Account Group Token   ·····························   👁   Copy

Virtual Appliance
Virtualization Software with OVA/OVF support,
VMWare (ESXi, Workstation, or Player),
Oracle VirtualBox

Download - OVA
Installation Guide

Figure 2-10   *Associating the Virtual Appliance with Your ThousandEyes Account Group*

Step 4.   Copy the **Account Group Token.**

Step 5.   After copying the Account Group Token, navigate back to the virtual appliance interface and click **Agent.** Complete the token application process by pasting the token into the Account Group Token field, as shown in Figure 2-11.

ThousandEyes
Virtual Appliance
0.230

Agent

Network

Time

Appliance Access

SSL Settings

Agent

Advanced Settings

Status

Account Group Token   52ks837phekg9c8stxuxc2dctp9w4mlf

Agent has been set up with this token.
To change the account group token for this agent, first reset agent state in the Advanced Settings .

Browserbot   Yes   No

Enable Crash Reports   Yes   No

Save Changes

Figure 2-11   *Inserting the Token into the Virtual Appliance*

After successfully linking the account token, the next step involves a thorough review of the virtual appliance settings. This verification process is crucial to ensure that all configurations are accurate and aligned with your requirements.

The most extensive segment we will delve into is the Network section. Within this section, you'll verify and configure several critical components (see Figure 2-12 to follow all the required entries):

- **Static or DHCP:** In the Configure IPv4 Address field, confirm whether the network connection will utilize a static IP address configuration or DHCP for dynamic allocation.

- **IP address:** Verify the correctness of the assigned IP address to ensure seamless communication.

- **Subnet mask:** Double-check the subnet mask setting in the Netmask field to guarantee proper network segmentation.

- **Gateway:** Review and configure the gateway address to enable efficient network routing.

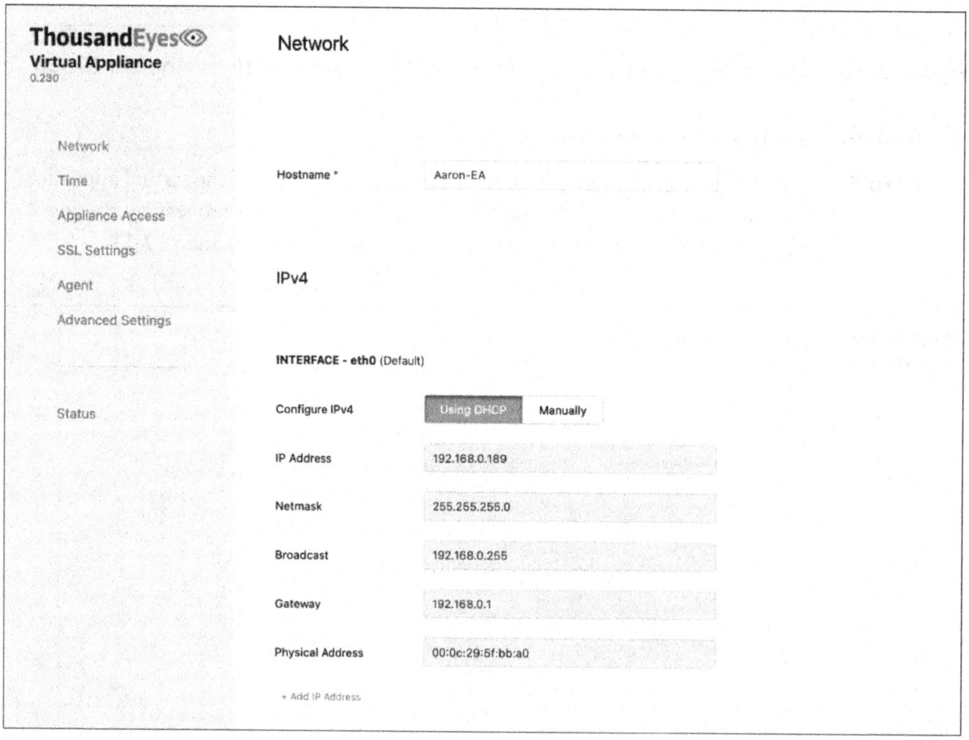

Figure 2-12   *Network Settings*

The Network section also encompasses the integration of IPv6 and DNS configurations (see Figure 2-13). These components play a crucial role in establishing comprehensive network functionality:

- **IPv6 configuration:** If IPv6 is a requirement, ensure that the appropriate settings are configured to support this protocol effectively.

- **DNS settings:** Verify and adjust Domain Name System settings as needed, ensuring accurate name resolution for smooth network communication.

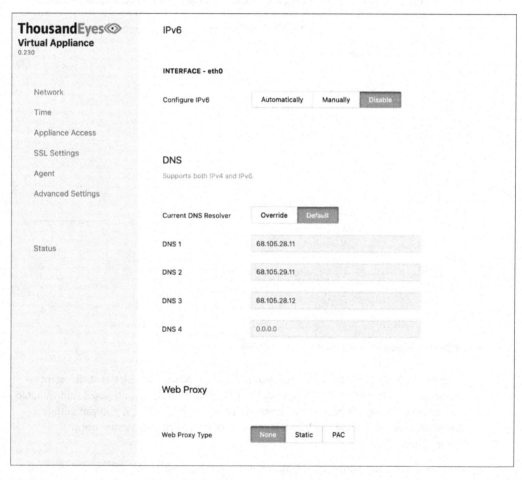

Figure 2-13 *Network Settings for IPv6 and DNS*

Finally, the Network section also provides an option to add certificate authority (CA) certificates and to use Apt Proxy if required (see Figure 2-14). These settings add another layer of configurational depth to ensure a secure and efficient network environment.

- **CA certificates:** If CA certificates are essential for secure communication, you can specify and configure these certificates in the Add CA Certificate field of the Network section.

- **Apt Proxy:** For streamlined package management, you have the option to define an Apt Proxy if needed, enhancing the efficiency of software updates and installations.

Figure 2-14   *Certificate Authority and Apt Proxy Options*

After successfully applying your configurations, it's essential to verify that the agent is operational and functioning as intended. Click the **Status** section, and you'll find valuable indicators of the agent's health and connectivity status. If necessary, you can initiate a diagnostic test by clicking the **Run Diagnostics** option to further ensure optimal performance.

For troubleshooting purposes, the Status section also provides the option to download logs (see Figure 2-15). These logs serve as valuable resources for in-depth analysis, aiding in the identification and resolution of any potential issues. For further information on troubleshooting, see Appendix B.

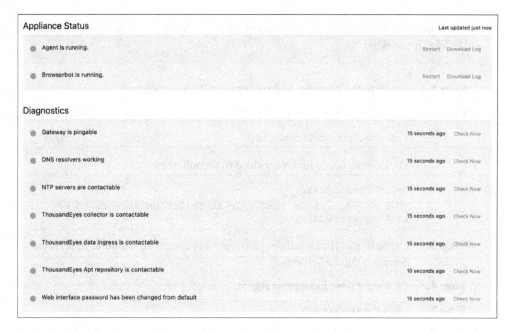

Figure 2-15   *Virtual Appliance Status Settings*

Enterprise Agent Using Docker

This Enterprise Agent provides flexibility and scalability, making it ideal for containerized environments. This section shows you how to set up the agent and integrate it with your existing Docker infrastructure.

The Docker container Enterprise Agent is currently supported on 64-bit Linux distributions running Kernel version 3.10 or newer, such as

- Ubuntu 14.04 LTR or newer

- Debian 7.7 or newer

- Red Hat Enterprise Linux 7

- CentOS 7

- Fedora 24 or newer

- Oracle Linux 7 or newer

- openSUSE 13.2 or newer

See the official Docker documentation for other options.

The following steps outline how to install Enterprise Agent on Docker.

> **Note** This discussion assumes that you understand basic concepts of **docker** commands and Docker networking.

Step 1. Log in to the host that will support the Docker container.

Step 2. Ensure Docker is running properly; to verify you can run a **docker** command:

```
$ docker run hello-world
```

The output should look very close to the following:

```
Hello from Docker.
This message shows that your installation appears to be
working correctly.
```

Step 3. Log in to the ThousandEyes platform and navigate to **Cloud & Enterprise Agents > Agent Settings**.

Step 4. Click **Add New Enterprise Agent**.

Step 5. Click the **Docker** tab.

Step 6. Using the ThousandEyes template (see Figure 2-16), specify the name of the agent for the Docker infrastructure and specify the directory in which to store persistent agent files.

After you have completed the template, copy the CLI and paste it into the Docker host. Example 2-3 shows the Docker Installation process and run options (note that the name **ThousandEyes** is the docker name and can be anything).

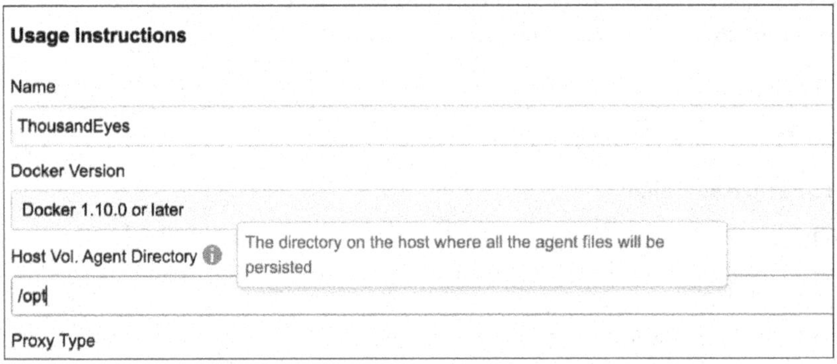

Usage Instructions
Name
ThousandEyes
Docker Version
Docker 1.10.0 or later
Host Vol. Agent Directory ⓘ   The directory on the host where all the agent files will be persisted
/opt
Proxy Type

Figure 2-16 *Docker Template*

Example 2-3 *Docker Install Example*

```
docker pull thousandeyes/enterprise-agent > /dev/null 2>&1
docker stop 'ThousandEyes' > /dev/null 2>&1
docker rm 'ThousandEyes' > /dev/null 2>&1
docker run \
  --hostname='ThousandEyes' \
  --memory=2g \
  --memory-swap=2g \
  --detach=true \
  --tty=true \
  --shm-size=512M \
  -e TEAGENT_ACCOUNT_TOKEN=52ks837phekg9c8stxuxc2dctp9w4mlf \
  -e TEAGENT_INET=4 \
  -v '/opt/thousandeyes/ThousandEyes/te-agent':/var/lib/te-agent \
  -v '/opt/thousandeyes/ThousandEyes/te-browserbot':/var/lib/te-browserbot \
  -v '/opt/thousandeyes/ThousandEyes/log/':/var/log/agent \
  --cap-add=NET_ADMIN \
  --cap-add=SYS_ADMIN \
  --name 'ThousandEyes' \
  --restart=unless-stopped \
  --security-opt apparmor=docker_sandbox \
  --security-opt seccomp=/var/docker/configs/te-seccomp.json \
  thousandeyes/enterprise-agent /sbin/my_init
```

Docker will install the agent and restart the container. To verify the container is up and running, use the CLI command **docker ps**. The output should look like the following:

```
CONTAINER ID IMAGE                              COMMAND        CREATED
STATUS        PORTS NAMES
400b4ad7bb34 thousandeyes/enterprise-agent "/sbin/my_init" 2 minutes
ago  Up 2 minutes      <agent-name>
```

By default, Docker will use the bridged network, like a virtual appliance. This bridge will use Docker0. This network will use an assigned IP space within that Docker network. With that said, NAT will be used to communicate outside the Docker network—this is the default behavior of a Docker bridged network. Decide which Docker network you want to use and plan accordingly.

There will be a vETH for each, and Docker will use DHCP for the IPs. Finally, Docker will copy /etc/resolve.conf for DNS. If there is a reason to use another DNS server, use the following runtime option:

```
--dns=<dns-server>
```

From the host, you can use **ip address show**, **ifconfig**, or **ipconfig**, depending on what OS you are on. Figure 2-17 shows the Docker0 and vETH.

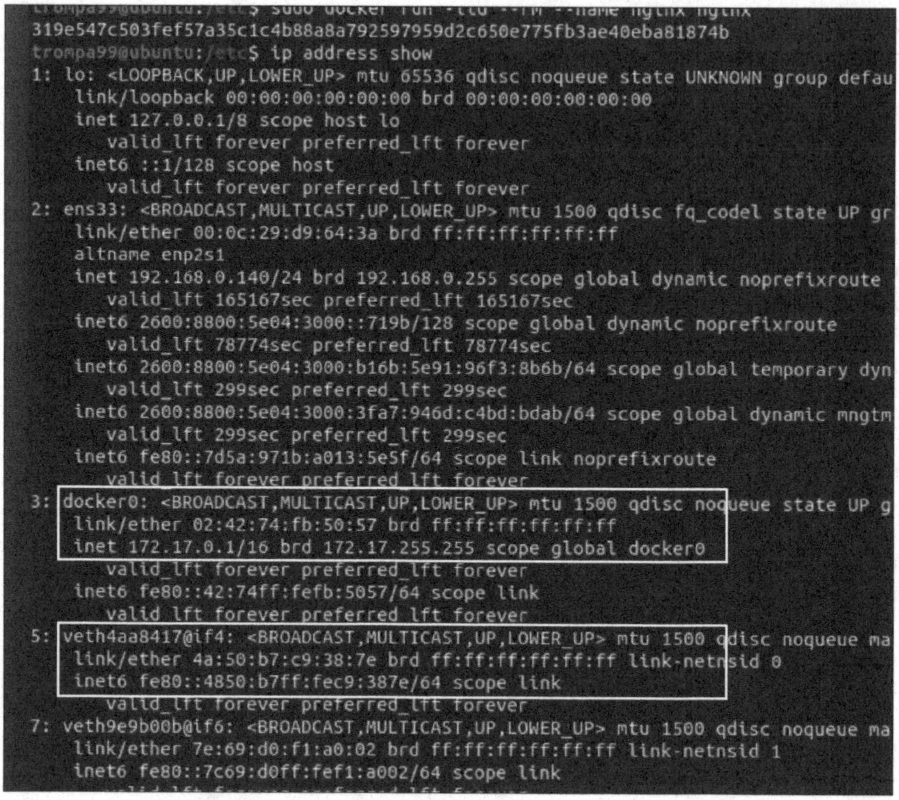

Figure 2-17 *Verifying Docker IP and Network*

If you have a use case in which you need to run agent-to-agent tests, you must ensure that you have the proper ports opened, because the default bridge does not do this. By default, ThousandEyes will use port 49153, which you can alter if needed.

Using one of the following methods in the **docker run** command will suffice:

```
--expose 49153/udp\
--publish 49153:49153/udp\
```

Or another method, depending on use cases:

```
-p 80:80 -Webserver nginx
```

Using **-p** will expose the Docker port to the host port; Figure 2-18 shows port 80.

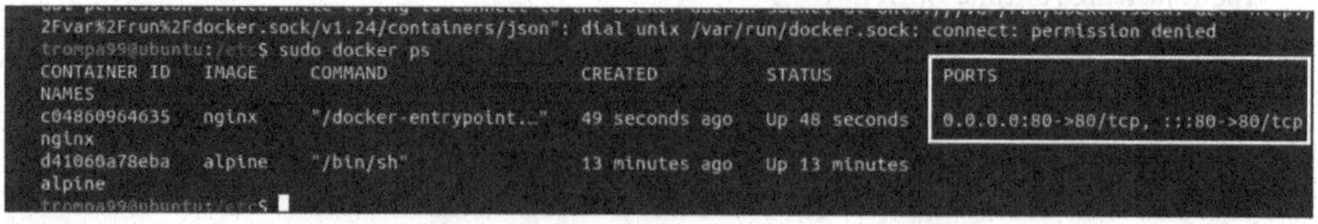

Figure 2-18 *Verifying Docker Ports*

To verify what ports are being used, try **docker ps** as shown in Figure 2-18.

Once you have the Docker agent configured properly, go back to the ThousandEyes UI and verify the agent is up and running. Navigate to **Agent Settings**, click the Agent, and verify the Status and IP info (see Figure 2-19).

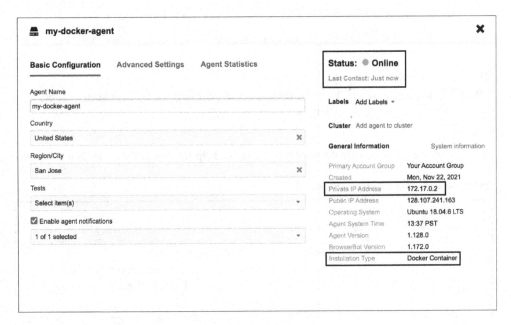

Figure 2-19 *Docker Enterprise Agent Status*

For more details on troubleshooting, see Appendix B.

Enterprise Agent Using Linux

The last Enterprise Agent option we will discuss is applying the agent on a Linux distribution such as Red Hat, CentOS, or Ubuntu. We will discuss other Linux flavors later in this section; for now, we will use some of the more popular platforms.

From the Agent Settings in the ThousandEyes UI:

Step 1.   Click **Add New Enterprise Agent.**

Step 2.   Click the **Linux Package** tab. You should see three Linux commands.

Step 3.   Copy all three commands and run them from the Linux distribution. The first command uses **curl** to download the enterprise agent to the Linux distribution:

```
curl -Os https://downloads.thousandeyes.com/agent/install_
thousandeyes.sh
```

The second command, **chmod**, is used in Linux to modify the permissions and access mode of files and directories. These are the permissions that control who can read, write, and execute the file.

```
chmod +x install_thousandeyes.sh
```

The last command ties the token account group to the agent you are installing:

```
sudo ./install_thousandeyes.sh -b <Account Group Installation
Token>
```

> **Note**   You can remove the -b option if you do not want BrowserBot, but keep in mind this will limit the testing to only network testing.

To view other options for the shell script, use the **help** option, as shown in Example 2-4.

Example 2-4   *Linux* **help** *Command*

```
$ ./install_thousandeyes.sh --help
Usage: ./install_thousandeyes.sh [-b [-L] [-W]] [-f] [-h] [-I INSTALL_LOG]
  [-l LOG_PATH] [-t PROXY_TYPE -P PROXY_LOCATION [-U PROXY_USER -u PROXY_PASS]]
  [-r REPO] [-s] [-v AGENT_VERSION] [-O] ACCOUNT_TOKEN
  -b                  Also install BrowserBot, an agent component that collects
                      Page Load and Transaction test data using an instance
                      of the Chromium browser
  -L                  Also install international language packages for BrowserBot
  (requires -b)
  -W                  Install BrowserBot without its recommended packages
  (e.g. te-xvfb) (requires -b)
  -f                  Force batch mode
  -h                  Print this message
  -I <INSTALL_LOG>    Set the install log location to INSTALL_LOG
  -l <LOG_PATH>       Set the log path to LOG_PATH
  -t <PROXY_TYPE>     Set the proxy type: DIRECT (default, no proxy), STATIC,
  or PAC
  -P <PROXY_LOCATION> Set the proxy location, format depends on PROXY_TYPE
                          DIRECT
                              PROXY_LOCATION is an invalid option for DIRECT
                          STATIC
                              host:port for hostname or IPv4 address
                              [IPv6 IP]:port for IPv6 address
                          PAC
                              URL where PAC file can be found
  -U <PROXY_USER>     Set the proxy user to PROXY_USER
  -u <PROXY_PASS>     Set the proxy password to PROXY_PASS
```

```
-a <PROXY_AUTH_TYPE>    Set the proxy authentication type: BASIC (default), NTLM
-r <REPO>               Force the installer to install from REPO (overriding
original ones)
-s                      Skip the repository creation
-v <AGENT_VERSION>      Specify agent version
-O                      Install the agent, but do not start the agent services
```

Once the installation completes, the Enterprise Agent will start automatically. Normally, within a minute the Enterprise Agent will appear under Cloud and Enterprise Agent > Agent Settings.

To avoid synchronization issues with the ThousandEyes collector, it is strongly recommended that you install a Network Time Protocol (NTP) package. Please refer to the specific Linux distribution documentation for instructions.

At the time of writing this book, the following Linux distributions are supported:

- Amazon Linux 2

- Oracle Linux 7 and 8

- Red Hat Enterprise Linux and CentOS 7

- Red Hat Enterprise Linux 8 and 9

- Ubuntu 20.04

Ensure your life cycle is up to date and not out of support.

Enterprise Agent Utilization

Now that we have explored a few Enterprise Agent options, we need to be strategic and understand that Enterprise Agents can reach a certain utilization point where only a certain number of tests can be run. With that said, Enterprise Agents have inherent limitations—each one possesses a finite capacity to execute a specific number of tests concurrently, contingent upon the type of test. Should the number of tests exceed the Enterprise Agent's capacity, certain test rounds might remain unexecuted, causing gaps in the timeline of test results. To circumvent this scenario without modifying test configurations, ThousandEyes offers a solution called *Clusters*. This entails the aggregation of multiple agents into a unified entity, or *Cluster*, which serves as the source for a particular test.

In the process of clustering, the individual agents maintain their unique *agent_id* while simultaneously sharing a common *v_agent_id*. Test assignments are designated to this virtual agent identifier, with tasks being evenly distributed among agents within the cluster based on their current utilization. It's close to the concept of HSRP, where a virtual IP is utilized.

The optimal strategy for resolving utilization issues revolves around augmenting the cluster by adding more agents. Given that the execution time of a test is predominantly contingent upon network or server response times, bolstering hardware resources such as RAM, CPU speed, or I/O hardware on the system hosting the Enterprise Agent typically proves ineffective in mitigating utilization concerns.

Before we get into clustering agents, let's take a few moments and look at agent utilization.

Elevated utilization can arise from a single prolonged test or a collection of extended tests. It could also stem from numerous tests making incremental contributions, or even a combination of these factors. *Long-running tests* are tests that surpass their designated Timeout value for completion or those with completion times that constitute a substantial portion of the test's Timeout setting. This is particularly pertinent if the Timeout value has been augmented from its default.

Instances where test targets fail to respond often lead to tests exceeding their Timeout period. The extent of time consumed by a test directly corresponds to its contribution to the queue's utilization. Consequently, a protracted test is more likely to elevate the utilization level.

Alternatively, high utilization might result from a multitude of tests, none of which are necessarily long-running. It's important to note that there isn't a definitive number of tests in a queue that invariably leads to high utilization. The threshold varies based on the unique characteristics of the queue and the tests it encompasses. In Figure 2-20 you can see which test is associated to that certain queue.

Queue Name	Test Types Assigned to Queue
Browser	• Page Load tests • Transaction tests
General	• All Network Layer tests • All DNS Layer tests • HTTP Server tests
Bandwidth	• All tests with Bandwidth metrics • All tests with Throughput metrics
Voice	• All Voice Layer tests

Figure 2-20   *Enterprise Agent Queue*

Understanding the specific queue helps users identify which tests could potentially burden the agent. It's important to note, however, that the utilization percentage within one queue remains independent of the utilization in other queues. For instance, elevated utilization in the Browser queue will not impact the utilization levels in the remaining three queues.

To delve deeper into tests that might be contributing to high utilization, consider these pointers. After identifying the queue responsible for the issue, it's wise to perform a quick sanity check.

- **Reduce test frequency:** Scale back the frequency of tests within the problematic queue.

- **Adjust Timeout settings:** Lower the Timeout values for these tests.

- **Ensure test responsiveness:** Verify that all tests are yielding responsive results.

- **Examine page load tests:** Scrutinize page load tests for any missing objects that could trigger extended timeouts.

If, after the completion of the sanity check and the identification of the specific queue causing the issues, you find that the utilization challenges persist, it might be time to explore more advanced solutions. This brings us to the next section, where we will delve into a powerful strategy known as *Agent Clustering*. This technique holds the potential to address utilization concerns effectively and optimize the performance of your ThousandEyes agents.

Agent Cluster and Agent Clustering

An Agent *Cluster* is a strategic approach within ThousandEyes that involves grouping multiple individual agents together into a unified entity, or cluster. This cluster functions as a single source for executing tests, enabling efficient resource utilization, and having improved test execution and enhanced scalability. By consolidating agents into clusters, organizations can better manage their testing activities, optimize performance, and address utilization challenges in a more streamlined manner.

Tests assigned to a cluster are intelligently distributed among its member agents based on their respective utilization levels. When a new agent is added to the cluster, the tests previously assigned to that agent are seamlessly divided among the cluster members to maintain equilibrium. If a cluster member is removed, the tests originally assigned to that agent are automatically redistributed among the remaining cluster members to ensure ongoing efficiency.

Individual agent utilization is displayed within the agent statistics in the ThousandEyes UI under the Agent Settings page, while the aggregate cluster utilization reflects the average across all cluster members. When incorporating a new agent into an established cluster, the following actions occur:

- All tests assigned to the new agent are inherited by the cluster.

- Any group assignments linked to the new agent are disregarded.

- The cluster's settings, such as the Verify SSL Certificates configuration, continue to apply.

The following are the steps to create a cluster:

Step 1.   From the ThousandEyes UI, navigate to Agent Settings. From the Enterprise Agent views, click the agent you want to add to a cluster. Then click **Add Agent to Cluster** (see Figure 2-21).

Basic Configuration	Advanced Settings	Agent Statistics		Status: ● **Online**
				Last Contact: Just now
Agent Name				
LinuxBox				Labels Add Labels ▾
Country				Cluster Add agent to cluster
United States			×	
				General Information System information

Figure 2-21   *Adding an Agent to a Cluster*

Step 2.   Add the agent to a new cluster by entering the cluster name in the field below the Add to New Cluster radio button and clicking **Add**, as shown in Figure 2-22. (The Add to Existing Cluster radio button is described in Step 4.)

Add Agent to Cluster   ✖

◉ **Add to new cluster**
You'll be able to add additional agents to the new cluster after creation. Test assignments will be transferred to the new cluster.

Cluster-1

○ **Add to existing cluster**
Add extra capacity to an existing cluster. Test and account assignments will be transferred to the selected cluster.

Figure 2-22   *Creating a New Cluster*

Step 3.   From the ThousandEyes UI in Agent Settings, navigate to **Enterprise Agent > Agents**, and notice there is a new icon showing it's in a cluster (see Figure 2-23).

Figure 2-23   *Agent Views with Cluster Icon*

Step 4.   To add additional agents to the new cluster, click the agent you want to add to the cluster and click the **Add to Existing Cluster** radio button to display the list of available clusters (see Figure 2-24). Select the appropriate cluster name and click **Add**.

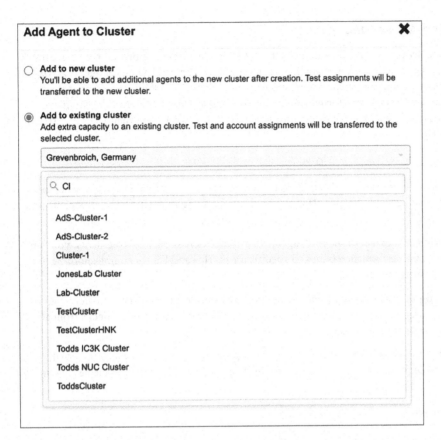

Figure 2-24   *Adding Agents to an Existing Cluster*

The following is a list of Agent Clustering best practices:

- Agents should be running the same version of both operating system and agent software.

- Agents should have similar hardware configuration.

- Agents should be in the same physical location.

- Agents should be running the same components (i.e., all agents run both agent and BrowserBot, or just agent).

- All agents must be owned by the same account group (i.e., use the same account token).

- All agents must be using the same address family (no mixing of IPv4 agents with IPv6 agents).

- Using a cluster as a target for agent-to-agent tests will work fine, unless all agents are behind the same NAT. In this scenario, you'll need to create a firewall rule for the target.

Enterprise Agent Placement

Strategically placing agents within your network architecture is a pivotal factor in establishing effective network and application monitoring. The positioning of agents across key points in your infrastructure allows for comprehensive visibility, enabling you to monitor and optimize performance seamlessly. This section delves into the significance of agent placement and explores various agent types, emphasizing their roles in different scenarios.

The following list explains why agent placement matters:

- **End-to-end visibility:** Placing agents at strategic junctures provides a holistic view of your network's health. This encompasses both internal network components and external services involved in application delivery.

- **Precise issue isolation:** With agents distributed across network segments, you can pinpoint performance issues to specific areas. This accelerates troubleshooting and minimizes downtime.

- **Realistic monitoring:** Agents positioned where users access services offer insights into user experience, helping identify potential performance bottlenecks from an end-user perspective.

- **SLA validation:** Strategic placement of agents enables you to monitor external service providers, validating service level agreements (SLAs) and ensuring they meet defined expectations.

The following are the various types of agent:

- **Virtual Machine (VM) Agents:** Deploying agents within virtual environments like VMware or VirtualBox provides flexibility and cost-efficiency and is ideal for internal network monitoring and possibly spinning up faster. The question is, will the vantage point be effective?

- **Cisco Device Agents:** Placing agents on Cisco devices with Cisco Application Framework (IOx) support offers insights into network traffic flow and performance at critical junctions. Placing an agent on a Cisco device allows the vantage point to be closest to a user if placed in the access layer.

- **Docker Container Agents:** Dockerized agents run alongside applications in containers, delivering performance insights at an application-specific level. Using Docker to host the Enterprise Agent is similar to the virtual appliance. Do you need metrics from the virtual switch or maybe a Kubernetes cluster, or maybe just from Docker? Where do you need the vantage point?

- **Linux Platform Agent:** The Enterprise Agent is based on Linux, so some administrators might prefer not to use Docker or a virtual appliance. Using a Linux-based agent might provide better metrics from the server to the destination. The question remains, does this give the vantage point you need?

Strategically placing agents optimizes your network and application monitoring strategy, offering diverse insights into performance metrics. Whether through VMs, Cisco switches, Docker containers, or Linux servers, agent placement plays a pivotal role in ensuring smooth operations and delivering exceptional user experiences.

With a comprehensive understanding of Enterprise Agents in place, let's delve into Cisco's internal perspective on these agents. Cisco's utilization of Enterprise Agents is multifaceted, and they prove invaluable in scenarios where monitoring Software as a Service (SaaS) or hybrid applications is essential. This capability enables agents to provide insights from within the network and extend outward, optimizing visibility and troubleshooting capabilities.

Remember, a meticulous monitoring strategy hinges on the precise positioning of these agents. Whether you seek to monitor internal traffic, external interactions, specific application performance, or even user experience, the right agent, positioned strategically, holds the key.

So, as you embark on the journey of crafting a robust monitoring framework, harness the wisdom of agent placement. Align it with your organization's goals, strive to eliminate blind spots, and empower your team to spot issues before they escalate. Ultimately, it's this strategic orchestration of agents that will elevate your network and application monitoring to unprecedented heights.

In the next section, we will pivot our focus to Cloud Agents. These agents offer a unique perspective, functioning as a vantage point positioned outside the network, allowing for a meticulous examination from an external standpoint.

Cloud Agents

Cloud Agents present a distinctive perspective, capitalizing on vantage points dispersed across various Internet service providers (ISPs) and cloud service providers (CSPs). Unlike their counterparts, Cloud Agents are entirely managed by ThousandEyes, freeing customers from administrative tasks and offering immediate configuration of tests.

Distributed across numerous cities and countries, Cloud Agents extend an "outside-in" view, allowing for meticulous examination of web-based applications and API endpoints. While Enterprise Agents afford users an insight from within the network outward, Cloud Agents flip the paradigm, granting insights from the external environment.

This vantage point is invaluable in comprehending behaviors within ISPs and enabling the aggregation of agents in specific regions, for specific tests. This aggregation yields precise metrics that administrators can utilize proactively to fine-tune their network strategies.

At the time of writing, ThousandEyes boasts a network of approximately 230+ agents strategically positioned across the globe. These agents are connected to a spectrum of ISPs, ranging from Tier 1, 2, and 3 providers to broadband service providers and regional data centers belonging to major cloud providers. Figure 2-25 shows approximately where agents are located across the world.

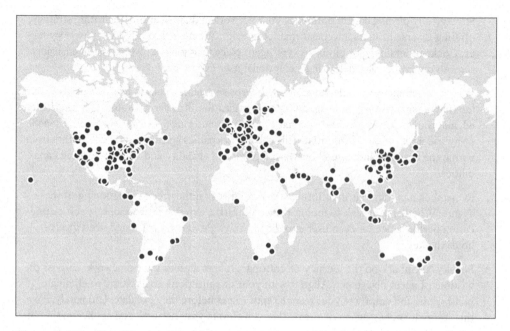

Figure 2-25   *Cloud Agents Worldview*

Cloud Agents offer a majority of the configuration options available with Enterprise Agents, but it's important to note that, due to their shared usage across multiple customers, certain features of Cloud Agents have inherent restrictions. For instance, configuring Cloud Agents to perform Web Layer tests through a proxy server is not feasible. Such configuration would necessitate all tests run by the agent to funnel through the proxy, rendering it incompatible. In cases that require testing of a cloud-based proxy server, opting for an Enterprise Agent or Endpoint Agent is recommended. Another limit that can cause an issue with strategy is that throughout testing, Enterprise Agents will need to be used from end to end to also support this type of test. We will dive into types of tests and best practices with each agent type in Chapter 3, "Configure Tests."

Endpoint Agents

Endpoint Agents are instrumental in capturing insights into user experience and application performance from the end user's perspective. This section shows you how to install and configure endpoint agents on users' devices to gain a comprehensive understanding of their digital experience.

Endpoint Agents are supported on both Microsoft Windows and Apple macOS machines. The installation process is painless, but there are a few basic things to point out.

To install an Endpoint Agent on Windows or macOS, navigate to **Endpoint Agents > Agent Settings** and click the **Add New Endpoint Agent** button, which will open the screen shown in Figure 2-26.

Figure 2-26 *Endpoint Agent Installation*

Windows users need to determine whether they are using x86 or x64. Once that is done, click **Download** and follow the wizard to install the agent. Once the agent has been installed:

- **macOS users:** After installing the .pkg file, make sure to open the installation-config.te-endpoint file to register the agent. Without this step, the application will run but the agent will not appear in the agent settings. To verify the application is running, check under Spotlight Search or in the Applications folder.

- **Windows users:** Once the file has been installed, the agent will not create an entry in the application menu, but you should see the application in the path c:/program files/thousandeyes.

Once you have deemed the application is up and running, go back to the ThousandEyes UI, choose **Endpoint Agents > Agent Settings**, and you should see an entry like that shown in Figure 2-27.

Figure 2-27 *Endpoint Agent Status*

To scale the installation with scripts in Windows, use the following steps:

Step 1.   Download the Endpoint Agent MSI installer.

Step 2.   Open Command Prompt as an administrator.

Step 3. Use the **msiexec.exe** command to silently install the agent on multiple machines (replace **<path_to_msi>** with the actual path to the MSI installer and **<path_to_log>** with the desired log file path):

```
msiexec.exe /i <path_to_msi> /quiet /norestart /qn /l*vx
<path_to_log>
```

To scale the installation with scripts in macOS, use the following steps:

Step 1. Download the Endpoint Agent .pkg installer.

Step 2. Open Terminal.

Step 3. Use the **installer** command to deploy the agent on multiple Macs (replace /path/to/application.pkg with the actual path to the .pkg file):

```
sudo installer -pkg /path/to/application.pkg -target
/Applications
```

Review Questions

Answer the following questions. Check your answers against those provided in Appendix A, "Answers to Review Questions."

1. What are the three main types of agents in ThousandEyes, and what are their primary use cases?

2. How do you install an Enterprise Agent on a Cisco device using the Cisco Application Framework?

3. What are some prerequisites for installing an Enterprise Agent?

4. What are the key differences between Cloud Agents and Enterprise Agents?

5. When might you choose to use an Endpoint Agent instead of an Enterprise Agent?

Chapter 3

Configuring Tests

The ThousandEyes platform empowers you to oversee assets essential to your organization's operations. While network monitoring might be the first thing that comes to mind, ThousandEyes provides a much broader perspective, enabling you to monitor any device your network reaches. Reflecting on the previous chapter, consider: Where should I position vantage points? What specific metrics should I track? Which applications and networks are indispensable to the business? By pondering these inquiries, you can explore additional use cases and effectively implement these assessments within the platform. This chapter delves into tests that will be configured on the agents we built in Chapter 2, "Agent Setup": Enterprise Agents, Endpoint Agents, and Cloud Agents.

Tests for Enterprise and Cloud Agents

When we look at testing, Figure 3-1 shows the granularity that you can perform with the ThousandEyes platform at each layer of your organization's operations. This section describes each of the five layers and the test types that you can conduct.

Routing Layer

When creating tests, you have the option to specify either a URL or an IP address as the destination. If you choose a URL, ThousandEyes' layered BGP tests will automatically monitor reachability and path changes for the associated prefix. Conversely, when you select an IP address, the focus shifts to a more network-centric test. In this case, the ThousandEyes platform monitors the Internet-routed prefix corresponding to that IP.

In addition to providing support for monitoring BGP reachability and path changes for prefixes through layered BGP tests, the ThousandEyes team has introduced a powerful feature that offers inside-out BGP visibility. With the ThousandEyes platform's private eBGP peer capability, your network administrators can configure their BGP speakers to peer with the ThousandEyes route collector. This unique capability enables you to observe the reachability of each BGP target from the vantage point of your own networks, enhancing your network monitoring and management capabilities.

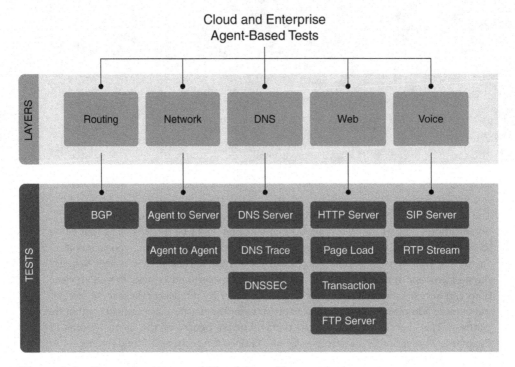

Figure 3-1 *Enterprise Agent and Cloud Agent Tests*

Routing changes, errors, and leaks can disrupt traffic paths, potentially causing sudden outages or interruptions that affect network performance. ThousandEyes monitors BGP routes from both corporate and service provider networks, providing visibility into inbound routes to your prefixes and outbound routes to key services and endpoints.

ThousandEyes monitoring enables quick responses to issues such as local misconfigurations, peering changes, and route hijackings. ThousandEyes collects BGP data through a combination of public and private monitors. With 45 public monitors located worldwide, you can observe inbound routes from each of these locations to your prefixes. Additionally, private monitors offer insights into outbound routing from your address space to crucial services and endpoints. This is especially valuable for understanding routing between offices, data centers, or critical external cloud providers.

ThousandEyes also tracks essential routing metrics, including path changes, reachability, and updates. These metrics can be comprehended within the context of BGP route visualization, illustrating the historical and current autonomous system (AS) paths taken by traffic from all monitors to the destination. You can also gain insights into routing outages. The intelligent algorithms of the ThousandEyes platform identify and provide data on reachability outages, including their global and local impact, as well as the networks most likely to contain the root cause of routing issues.

Setting up tests and collecting data is straightforward. BGP data is available for any test that includes network measurements and as a standalone test for a specific prefix, which is the focus of this chapter. Alerts and notifications can be configured with customizable threshold metrics from path changes, reachability, or other situations where the next hop AS changes or when a more specific prefix is detected. These alerts are especially useful for detecting routing errors and malicious activity, which we delve into in Chapter 4, "Alerts."

Now, let's explore the concepts of BGP route leaks and BGP route hijacking.

A *BGP route leak* is akin to making a mistake when giving directions on the Internet. It occurs when one AS unintentionally informs another AS about a route it shouldn't have. This mistake violates established rules and policies for sharing directions and often is the result of an administrator inadvertently changing a configuration.

In contrast, *BGP route hijacking*, also known as *prefix hijacking* and *IP hijacking*, involves the unauthorized takeover of groups of IP addresses. This is accomplished by manipulating Internet routing tables reliant on BGP.

When announcing a prefix using BGP, an IPv4 or IPv6 address block is specified along with a path of AS numbers, indicating the autonomous systems that traffic must traverse to reach the announced address block. Through malicious manipulation of BGP IP prefixes, an attacker can divert traffic, potentially intercepting or altering it. This is a common tactic employed by hackers looking to manipulate corporate traffic. They exploit vulnerabilities in BGP to reset neighbor relationships, remove routes, inject fake routes into the routing table, and create traffic blackholes.

While BGP route hijacking may seem daunting, it's important to note that there are numerous mechanisms to secure BGP. The key is not only to implement these security measures but also to monitor and ensure that the policies in place are enforced. ThousandEyes provides alerts for these policies and associated metrics, allowing you to maintain a secure and well-monitored BGP environment.

In the next section, we look deeper into BGP monitoring for specific prefixes, addressing concerns such as hijacks and leaks.

Configure Inside-Out BGP Visibility

To configure inside-out BGP visibility in the ThousandEyes UI, navigate to **Cloud & Enterprise Agents > BGP Monitors** and click **Add Private BGP Monitor** (see Figure 3-2).

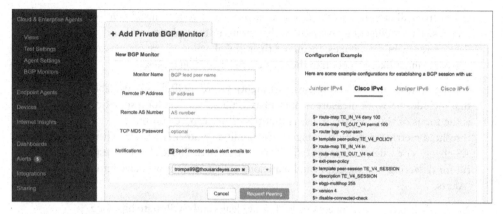

Figure 3-2   *Adding a Private BGP Monitor*

Complete the following fields in the New BGP Monitor section:

- **Monitor Name:** Enter the name you wish to show in the list of BGP monitors.

- **Remote IP Address:** Enter the external (non RFC 1918) address allocated to your router.

- **Remote AS Number:** Enter your autonomous system number. You must maintain your own AS number in order to configure peering with the ThousandEyes route collector.

- **TCP MD5 Password:** Optionally, enter the authentication key used to establish the peering session on your router.

Note in the Configuration Example section on the right in Figure 3-2 that ThousandEyes has configuration templates for Cisco and Juniper for both IPv4 and IPv6. The configuration consists of setting up BGP for external multihop and remote AS 65315.

After you have populated the fields, click **Request Peering**. You'll then see the dialog box shown in Figure 3-3 that describes the peering request process. Click **OK**.

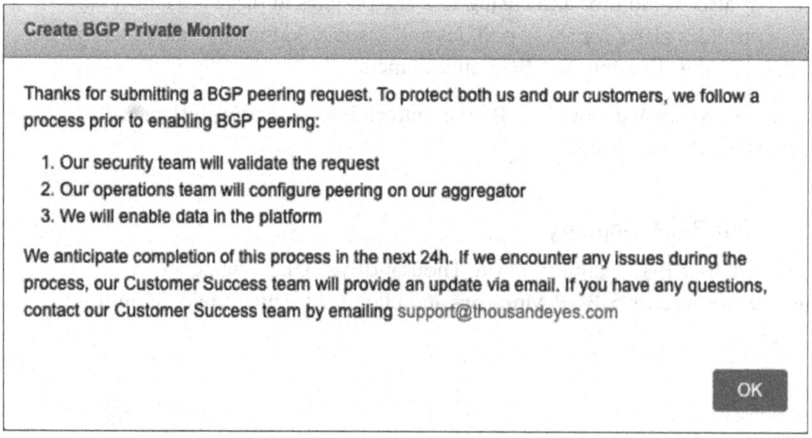

Create BGP Private Monitor

Thanks for submitting a BGP peering request. To protect both us and our customers, we follow a process prior to enabling BGP peering:

1. Our security team will validate the request
2. Our operations team will configure peering on our aggregator
3. We will enable data in the platform

We anticipate completion of this process in the next 24h. If we encounter any issues during the process, our Customer Success team will provide an update via email. If you have any questions, contact our Customer Success team by emailing support@thousandeyes.com

OK

Figure 3-3   *BGP Peering Request*

Once this request is complete, the configuration will need to be configured on the router.

The highlights of the configuration are the following:

```
ebgp-multihop ttl-value
```

The TTL value for eBGP multihop must be in the range 2 to 255 (it is set to 255 in the ThousandEyes template). You must manually reset the BGP sessions after using this command:

```
neighbor <peer-ip> remote-as 65315
```

The ThousandEyes Autonomous System number (ASN) (65315) and peer IP will be supplied via email once the request has been approved.

After the configuration is in place, it is highly recommended that you set up the peering session to disallow any route modifications. Once ThousandEyes receives and approves your request, it will also approve the peering session and work with you to determine the optimal timing for establishing connections with your BGP speakers.

At this point, BGP has been configured as a test, and monitoring for prefixes is enabled. In Chapter 4, we explore how to alert on specific metrics.

Network Layer

The Network layer takes testing to a new level by allowing you to focus on traditional device monitoring using their IPs. However, where ThousandEyes truly excels is in monitoring SaaS applications. In Chapter 3, you deployed agents, and now you can utilize those agents to set up monitoring. You can position the agents anywhere globally, and you can also leverage Cloud Agents, as discussed earlier.

Agent to Agent Test

Agent to Agent tests enable you to use Enterprise Agents as well as Cloud Agents. As an example, you might need to view network and HTTP services from an on-premises Enterprise Agent to Azure or AWS. If you deploy Enterprise Agents in the cloud as well, you can use them to monitor a hybrid cloud scenario. This type of monitoring enables you to create operation awareness even across the Internet.

To configure an Agent to Agent test from the ThousandEyes UI, follow these steps:

Step 1.   Navigate to **Cloud & Enterprise Agents > Test Settings** and click the **Add New Test** button. In the New Test section, click the Layer option **Network**, and then click the Test Type option **Agent to Agent**, as shown in Figure 3-4.

Step 2.   Create a test name that will be quickly identifiable for other users when they are looking in the Views section; also include a description of the test being run.

Step 3.   On the Basic Configuration tab, choose a target agent from the Target Agent drop-down list; this agent can be an Enterprise Agent, Agent Cluster, or Cloud Agent. You can use the search bar in the drop-down list to locate a specific agent, as shown in Figure 3-5.

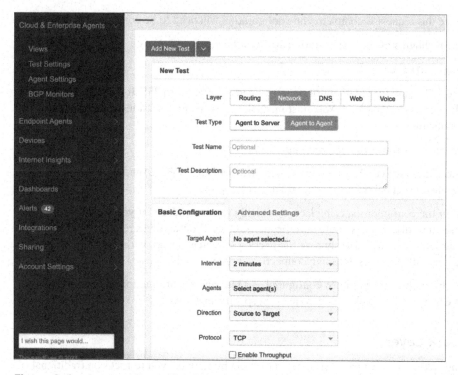

Figure 3-4 *Agent to Agent Test Setup*

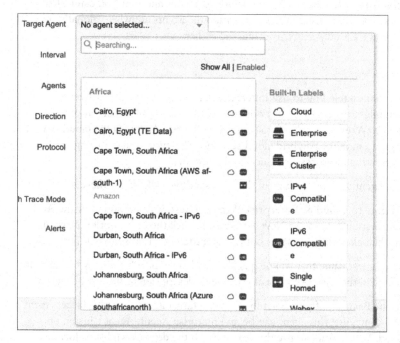

Figure 3-5 *Agent Selection*

Step 4. From the Interval drop-down list, choose how long to run the test, which can range from 1 minute to 1 hour. Best practice is to run a test for at least 5 minutes and then adjust as needed depending on the metrics for that test.

Step 5. From the Agents drop-down list, choose the source (this can be an Enterprise Agent or Cloud Agent). You can also select more than one source. If the idea is to monitor a certain destination by many other agents in other geographic areas, this would allow you to aggregate multiple sources into one test but enable you to view each source to the destination.

Step 6. From the Direction drop-down list, choose **Source to Target** (default), **Target to Source**, or **Both**. These flexible options enable you to get metrics from the destination to the source if needed, or even get metrics in both directions.

Step 7. From the Protocol drop-down list, choose **TCP or UDP**.

Note the Enable Throughput check box in Figure 3-4. Applying the throughput metric to a test requires a few things. Agent to Agent tests must be Enterprise Agents from end to end. The other gotcha is that firewalls have a tendency to drop "offset packets," packets sent from source to destination and vice versa. They do this to see if one direction has the same latency. If latency differs, this is what we call "clock sync error," and at times we have seen a firewall drop a few packets, causing this error. The expected packets received should be about 75 percent.

If you've determined that you need to use the throughput metric (and have checked the Enable Throughput check box), you can configure the duration of the throughput measurement and the rate at which the agent saturates the link with packets; you can either specify a rate or choose to use the max rate. Using the max rate will provide a better metric for throughput, but doing so can cause latency and drops in the network. If you need to use this type of metric, you should look at intervals of when the test should be run or enable it only when needed. As you'll see in the upcoming discussion of Agent to Server tests, this metric can also be used in that context, but in a different fashion.

Next, click the **Advanced Settings** tab for the Agent to Agent test, shown in Figure 3-6 and described here:

- **Server Port:** Define a specific port number to the target (port 22 is not supported).

- **Payload Size:** The use of Agent to Agent tests also enables you to monitor the payload size. You can choose between two options:

  - **Auto:** In this mode, the agent will run a test to determine the path maximum transmission unit (MTU) and select the lowest threshold as the maximum segment size (MSS).

  - **Manual:** If you select this option, specify the MSS in bytes and the agent will apply those bytes in a test to determine end-to-end metrics.

When considering payload, keep a few essential points in mind. Typically, payload is determined during the TCP 3-way handshake. If the MSS is set too low, it leads to network traffic streams being broken into numerous small packets, which can negatively impact performance. Moreover, data packets exceeding the MSS allowed over the network are simply discarded. Therefore, setting the appropriate payload value is crucial for optimizing network performance.

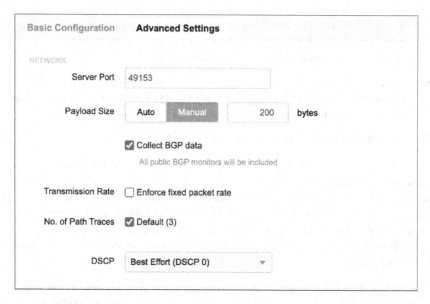

Figure 3-6 *Advanced Settings Tab for Agent to Agent Test Setup*

- **Transmission Rate:** This enables you to specify the rate at which packets are sent.

- **No. of Path Traces:** The Default entry is set to 3 packets to create a path trace for each hop. You can change this, but from a best practice perspective, it's best to leave this field at the default setting.

- **DSCP:** You can apply DSCP to the test, which is very useful when monitoring voice, video, and SDWAN underlay traffic.

> **Note**   To save the test to continue running, click Create New Test. If you need to run the test only once, click the Run Once button—this will not save the test.

Agent to Server Test

This type of test is similar to the Agent to Agent test, but the destination is a server or a URL for a specific service, such as Workday, ServiceNow, Microsoft 365, or internal applications and servers. Additionally, you can use an IP address as the destination, which can be a device other than a server. By utilizing TCP or ICMP protocols, users can test and monitor a broader range of devices beyond just servers or applications.

To configure an Agent to Server test from the ThousandEyes UI, follow these steps:

Step 1.   Navigate to **Cloud & Enterprise Agents > Test Settings** and click the **Add New Test** button. In the New Test section, click the Layer option **Network**, and then click the Test Type option **Agent to Server,** as shown in Figure 3-7.

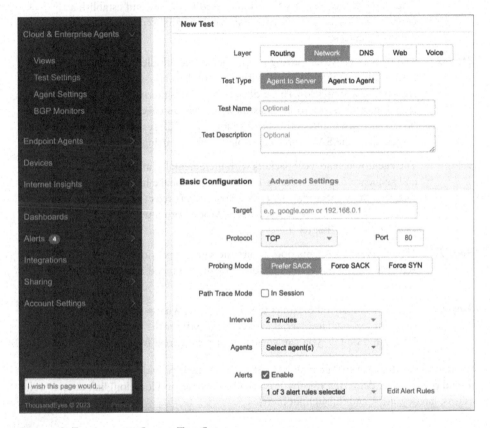

Figure 3-7   *Agent to Server Test Setup*

Step 2.   Provide a relatable test name and a test description.

Step 3.   In the Target field, enter a URL or an IP address.

Step 4.   From the Protocol drop-down list, choose **TCP** or **ICMP(Ping).** Specify a port if needed.

Step 5.   Choose one of the three Probing Mode options: Prefer SACK, Force SACK, or Force SYN.

The probing method is intriguing, particularly the use of SACK (Selective Acknowledgments), which plays a crucial role in mitigating congestion caused by retransmitting dropped packets. SACK enables endpoints to specify which parts of the data they have received, allowing for the retransmission of only the missing segments.

However, it's worth noting that not all servers support SACK. If you intend to use it, it's advisable to check whether the server in question supports this feature. By default, the entry is set to Prefer SACK, meaning the agent will utilize SACK if supported; otherwise, it will adhere to typical TCP rules.

Additionally, the Force SYN option is used to initiate and establish a connection. It serves the purpose of synchronizing sequence numbers between devices.

Step 6.   The Path Trace Mode setting is optional. Some middleboxes like firewalls or load balancers might interfere with the way the ThousandEyes platform collects path trace metrics. These devices could misinterpret the path tracing as malicious probes. To avoid this situation, you can check the **In Session** check box. This feature allows the agent to initiate a TCP session with the target server, using the SACK option enabled, before starting the discovery process.

The agent will send TCP packets with incremental Time-to-Live values (TTLs) and sequence numbers after a TCP 3-way handshake has occurred. By doing this, you can expect that the middleboxes won't reject or drop the path trace packets. We will revisit the Path Trace Mode option when we discuss path visualization in Chapter 9.

Step 7.   The Interval and Agents options are the same as previously described in the Agent to Agent test configuration; choose an interval and one or more source agents.

Step 8.   Click the **Advanced Settings** tab. This mirrors what was discussed in Agent to Agent testing. However, if you chose ICMP for the protocol on the Basic Configuration tab, you can specify to use a payload for ICMP.

Conducting both Agent to Agent and Agent to Server tests provides metrics from an end-to-end perspective, delivering hop-by-hop (BGP AS, name, and location) link data as well as loss, latency, jitter, and throughput metrics.

DNS Layer

The Domain Name System (DNS) serves as the backbone of the Internet, quietly facilitating our online interactions. It's the system responsible for translating user-friendly domain names, like www.thousandeyes.com, into the IP addresses that computers use to identify each other on the Web. DNS ensures that when you type a web address into your browser, it magically finds its way to the right server, making your Internet experience seamless. However, beneath this simplicity lies a complex network of servers, queries, and responses. In this section, we'll explore the world of DNS, how it can be monitored and troubleshooted, and essential concepts like DNS servers, tracing, and Domain Name System Security Extensions (DNSSEC). Let's uncover what ThousandEyes can do for all things DNS.

DNS Server Test

A DNS Server test is designed to monitor the availability and performance of DNS servers along with the records they contain. DNS servers can take on various roles, including serving as authoritative name servers for the relevant zone of the target record, functioning as local recursive caching DNS servers without authoritative status for the record, or being configured as nonauthoritative servers, such as pure forwarders.

DNS server testing is a pretty broad subject, so let's start off with a basic DNS Server test and build on it.

Step 1.   From the ThousandEyes UI, navigate to **Cloud & Enterprise Agents > Test Settings** and click **Add New Test.** In the New Test section, click the Layer option **DNS,** and then click the Test Type option **DNS Server,** as shown in Figure 3-8.

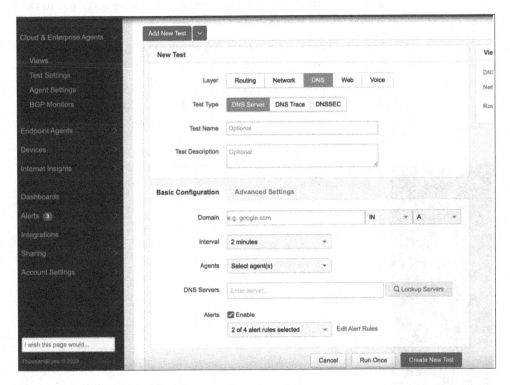

Figure 3-8   *DNS Server Test Setup*

Step 2.   Similar to the routing tests and network tests previously described, start by creating a name and description for your DNS test in the Test Name and Test Description fields.

Step 3.   On the Basic Configuration tab, enter a domain name in the Domain field (for example, thousandeyes.com).

Step 4. When it comes to specifying the test type, you have two options in the drop-down list to the right of the Domain field:

- **IN (Internet):** The IN designation is commonly used for DNS records related to the Internet. You should choose IN DNS tests when your primary goal is to ensure the correct and reliable resolution of your public domain names by DNS servers across the Internet. This is crucial for maintaining the online visibility and accessibility of your websites and services.

- **CH (Chaos):** On the other hand, choose CH DNS tests for in-depth analysis and troubleshooting of DNS server behavior. This includes assessing cache performance, query handling, and resource record validation. CH tests are valuable when you need to delve deep into the inner workings of your DNS infrastructure. This may involve examining how your DNS servers cache records, manage custom queries, or resolve issues related to DNS resolution within your network.

The distinction in test types enables you to tailor your DNS monitoring to the specific needs of your online presence and infrastructure.

Step 5. The drop-down list to the far right of the Domain field (see Figure 3-9) is used to specify the DNS record type. The UI doesn't explicitly define this entry, so we will go into a bit of detail because this option can be a little tricky if you don't know what to use.

Figure 3-9 *DNS Record Type Entry*

DNS record types are records that provide important information about a hostname or domain. These records include the current IP address for a domain.

Also, DNS records are stored in text files (zone files) on the authoritative DNS server. The content of a DNS record file is a string with special commands that the DNS server understands.

Understanding what record type to choose is crucial to ensure correct metrics. The following records are the six major record types that we usually see with ThousandEyes customers.

- **A (address) record:** This is the most important DNS record type. An A record shows the IP address for a specific hostname or domain. For example, a DNS record lookup for the domain example.com returns an IP address associated with it.

- **AAAA record:** Just like an A record, an AAAA record points to the IP address for a domain, but this DNS record type points to IPv6 addresses.

- **CNAME (canonical name) record:** This is a DNS record that points a domain name (an alias) to another domain. In a CNAME record, the alias doesn't point to an IP address. And the domain name that the alias points to is the canonical name. For example, the subdomain ng.example.com can point to example.com using CNAME.

- **NS (nameserver) record:** This DNS record type specifies the authoritative DNS server for a domain. In other words, the NS record helps point to where Internet applications like a web browser can find the IP address for a domain name.

- **MX (mail exchange) record:** This DNS record type shows where emails for a domain should be routed to.

- **PTR (pointer) record:** This is exactly the opposite of the A record and provides the domain name associated with an IP address.

Step 6. As described earlier for Agent to Agent tests, from the Interval drop-down list, choose how long to run the test, and from the Agents drop-down list, choose the source (an Enterprise Agent or Cloud Agent).

Step 7. In the DNS Servers field, specify the DNS servers that will be queried for the domain name entered in the Domain field. To automatically populate the DNS Servers field with the authoritative name servers for the specified domain, click the **Lookup Servers** button (which is functional only when a domain name is specified and won't work if a URL is provided).

Step 8. Click the **Advanced Settings** tab, shown in Figure 3-10, which has many options that were previously covered. The major field is Probing Mode, which has the same options as the Probing Mode field described earlier for Agent to Server test setup: Prefer SACK, Force SACK, or Force SYN when the protocol is using TCP.

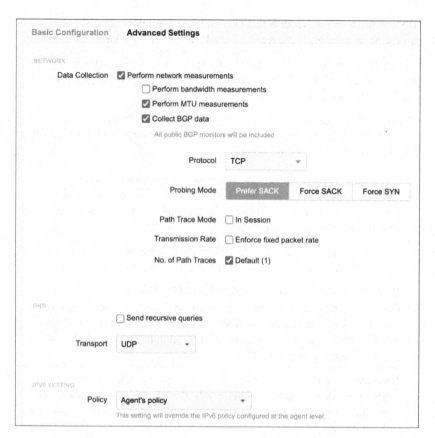

Figure 3-10   *Advanced Settings Tab for DNS Server Test Configuration*

Step 9.   Note the Send Recursive Queries check box on the Advanced Settings tab. By default, ThousandEyes does not use recursive queries. A *recursive DNS lookup* is where one DNS server communicates with several other DNS servers to hunt down an IP address and return it to the client. This is in contrast to an *iterative DNS query*, where the client communicates directly with each DNS server involved in the lookup.

DNS Trace Test

A DNS Trace test complements a DNS Server test by serving a distinct purpose. Whereas a DNS Server test is designed to assess the reachability and performance of specific servers and their associated records, a DNS Trace test is used to validate the delegation process from parent zones to child zones. Importantly, a DNS Trace test doesn't specify the precise servers to be utilized.

For instance, consider a name server that is intended to have authority over a specific zone. In this case, the parent zone correctly delegates the zone to this name server through the required records, indicating that the delegation is accurately configured. However, issues arise when the child zone is misconfigured because the name server fails to act authoritatively for the zone, resulting in what's known as a "lame delegation." When such a situation occurs, and the trace queries the lame server for the target record, a DNS Trace test would identify the error. (Theoretically, the probability of the server being selected in a given round equals $1 / n$, where n represents the number of authoritative servers for the zone as indicated by the records in the parent zone. In practice, this probability may not exhibit randomness.)

A child zone is a distinct and fully functional zone that technically operates as a subdomain of another zone. For instance, you can have both domain.com and sub.domain.com as independent zone entities, each possessing its own set of Start of Authority (SOA) records. This separation is often used to delegate control of a subdomain to another provider or entity. Child zones also enable you to grant management authority over a specific subdomain to another entity or provider.

Let's now turn our attention to the DNS Trace test.

DNS Trace test configuration (see Figure 3-11) primarily involves specifying the target domain name and record type, along with standard settings previously described, such as Interval and Agents. Refer to the previous section for a thorough discussion of the DNS record types.

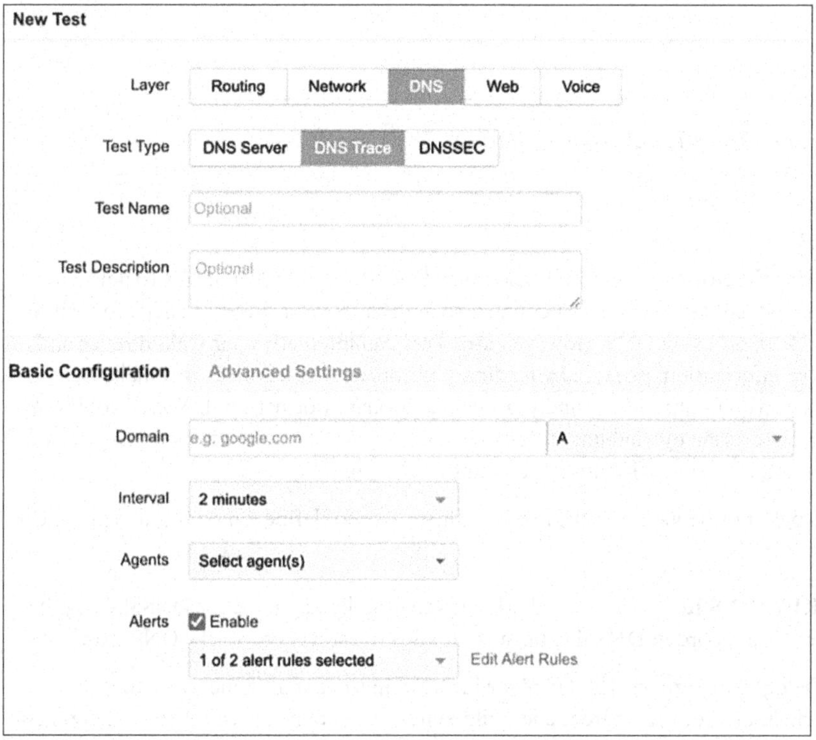

Figure 3-11 *DNS Trace Test Configuration*

The Advanced Settings tab of the DNS test has only the Transport setting, UDP or TCP, as shown in Figure 3-12.

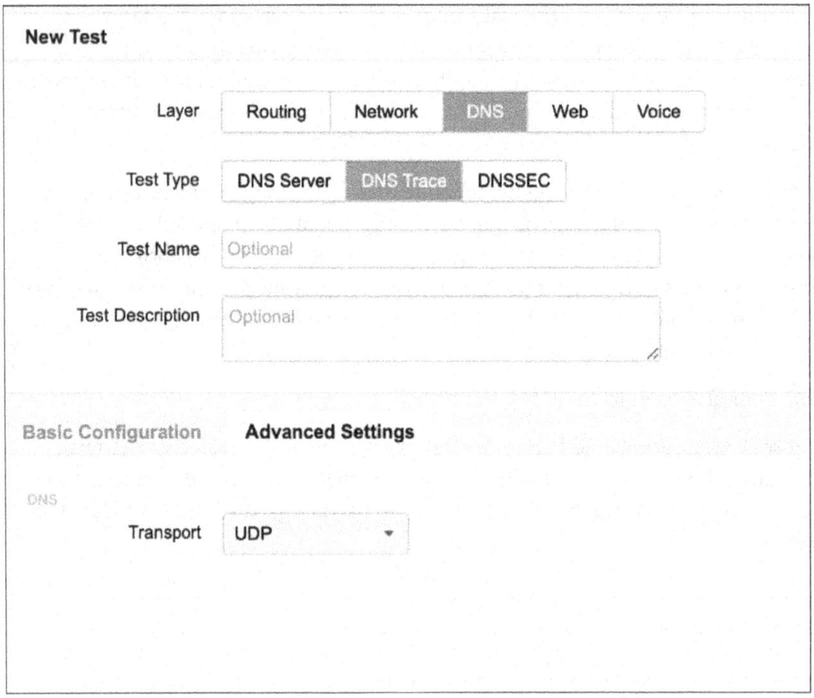

New Test

| Layer | Routing | Network | DNS | Web | Voice |

| Test Type | DNS Server | DNS Trace | DNSSEC |

Test Name   Optional

Test Description   Optional

Basic Configuration   **Advanced Settings**

DNS

Transport   UDP   ▾

Figure 3-12 *DNS Trace Test Advanced Settings*

DNSSEC Test

DNS Security Extensions, commonly known as DNSSEC, provide a means to authenticate DNS response data. When you connect to a website, your browser needs to retrieve the site's IP address using DNS. However, attackers can intercept your DNS queries and provide false information, potentially leading your browser to connect to a malicious website where you might unknowingly provide personal information. DNSSEC adds an extra layer of security by enabling web browsers to verify the accuracy and integrity of DNS information, ensuring it hasn't been tampered with.

DNSSEC might not be used widely, but it is imperative to define what record types it can provide:

- **DNSKEY (DNS Key):** This record contains the public key used for DNSSEC signing. It's a critical record in DNSSEC because it allows resolvers to verify DNS data.

- **DS (Delegation Signer):** The DS record is used in the parent zone to establish a trust chain between the parent and child zones. It contains a hash of the child zone's DNSKEY.

- **RRSIG (Resource Record Signature):** RRSIG records accompany standard DNS records (like A or MX records) and contain cryptographic signatures to verify the authenticity of those records.

- **NSEC (Next Secure):** NSEC records are used to show that a specific domain name does not exist in a zone. This helps prevent DNS amplification attacks.

- **NSEC3 (Next Secure Version 3):** NSEC3 is an enhancement of NSEC that provides better security by hashing the domain names in the NSEC records.

DNSSEC records are also associated with DNSKEY management, including RRSIGs over DNSKEYs for zone signing.

Configuring a DNSSEC test is almost identical to configuring a DNS Trace test; the sole input is a domain and record (see Figure 3-13). Also notice there is no Advanced Settings tab.

Figure 3-13 *DNSSEC Test Configuration*

The DNS trace and DNSSEC tests provide a geographical map, displaying the availability of the requested DNS record by location. They also report the average query time for the DNS record. Additionally, the DNSSEC test displays the chain of trust, either confirming successful verification up to the root or pinpointing the point of failure in the trust chain.

In DNS Server tests, the platform queries authoritative name servers from various locations. These tests reveal the availability and resolution time by location. Moreover, for DNS Server tests, you can enable network measurements, providing access to detailed network measurement information and outputs related to each authoritative name server specified in the test.

Web Layer

This set of tests touches on various web technologies, starting from the most basic HTTP measurement of availability of a web server or application all the way up to performing precision transactions (steps) within a user experience to determine those metrics and outcomes. These tests include metrics that enable you to evaluate the HTTP responses, page load time, and throughput as well as identify events happening during the loading process using waterfall charts.

HTTP Server Test

While an HTTP Server test might seem rudimentary and is the most basic test within the Web layer, it involves several critical steps. When a URL is used, DNS resolves it to an IP address. Once the connection to the web application or site occurs, a TCP negotiation follows. If SSL is involved, the necessary SSL mechanisms are also performed. Subsequently, the HTTP send and receive processes occur, culminating in a valid HTTP response code. This test is versatile because it gathers data regardless of whether the content is on-premises, SaaS, or simply a website not managed within your infrastructure. The HTTP Server test collects information from DNS, IP, SSL, and HTTP responses.

Let's start off with how to configure an HTTP Server test:

Step 1. In the ThousandEyes UI, navigate to **Cloud & Enterprise Agents > Test Settings** and click the **Add New Test** button. In the New Test section, click the Layer option **Web**, and then click the Test Type option **HTTP Server** (see Figure 3-14).

Step 2. Enter a name and description in the Test Name and Test Description fields.

Step 3. In the URL field, enter the address of the target.

Step 4. From the Interval drop-down list, choose how long to run the test.

Step 5. From the Agents drop-down list, choose an agent as the source.

The Advanced Settings tab offers various options for customization, allowing you to fine-tune the HTTP Server test according to your specific needs (see Figure 3-15). Key settings include Timeout, Target Response Time, and Perform Bandwidth Measurements. By default, the Timeout slider is set to 5 seconds and the Target Response Time slider is set to 1000 milliseconds, but you can adjust these values to meet your testing requirements.

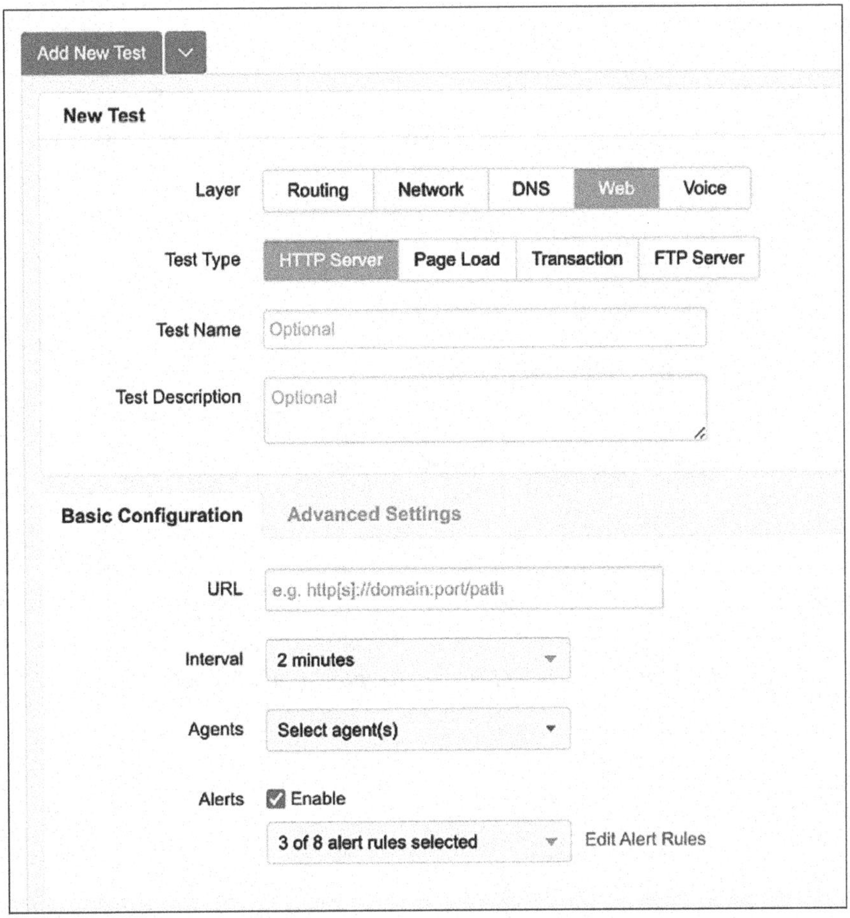

Figure 3-14 *HTTP Server Test*

Additionally, you can modify the Protocol field from the default TCP to UDP or change the Probing Mode setting from the default Prefer SACK to Force SACK or Force SYN (all three probing modes are covered in the section "Agent to Server Tests" earlier in this chapter).

For SSL-related metrics, you can choose from different SSL/TLS versions in the SSL Version drop-down list, also located on the Advanced Settings tab (see Figure 3-16). The default setting is Auto, but other options include SSLv3 and various Transport Layer Security (TLS) versions (1.0 to 1.2). When the target URL uses HTTP Secure (HTTPS), SSL negotiation occurs. Selecting a specific SSL version also enables you to adjust the TLS version. Transport Layer Security is a cryptographic protocol that ensures secure communication over a computer network. It provides privacy, data integrity, and authentication between client/server applications by encrypting the data exchanged between parties, safeguarding sensitive information from unauthorized access.

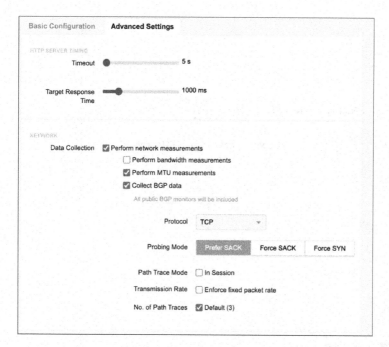

Figure 3-15 *Advanced HTTP Server Test (Timeout, Response, and Probe)*

Figure 3-16 *Advanced HTTP Server Test (SSL/TLS Version)*

Another distinction between the protocols is the port used. HTTPS typically uses port 443, while HTTP uses port 80 as the default.

You can further customize the HTTP Server test on the Advanced Settings tab by specifying the HTTP version (see Figure 3-17), which you can set to either Prefer HTTP/2 (the default) or HTTP/1.1 Only. Last, the Request Method option enables you to choose GET or POST as the request method. GET is commonly used, but you can also opt for POST when necessary.

Figure 3-17 *Advanced HTTP Server Test (HTTP Version, Request Method)*

These advanced settings provide flexibility and granularity in tailoring the HTTP Server test to your specific testing scenarios and requirements.

The HTTP Server test will return the following metrics:

- **Availability:** This indicates the percentage of time that the site is available; if you are using many source agents, this time will be averaged out and aggregated.

- **Response Time:** Also known as time-to-first-byte, this metric measures the time elapsed from the beginning of the request (before the DNS request) until the client receives the first byte of the response from the server.

- **Throughput:** Throughput is calculated by dividing the total wire size by the receive time and is expressed in MBps.

Additionally, when examining the response time, it's important to note that ThousandEyes provides data on the entire response, including DNS, Wait, SSL, and Connect times (see Figure 3-18). In Chapter 6, "Monitoring and Troubleshooting Network Performance Issues," we dive into the troubleshooting aspect of HTTP Server tests and look further into the metrics provided.

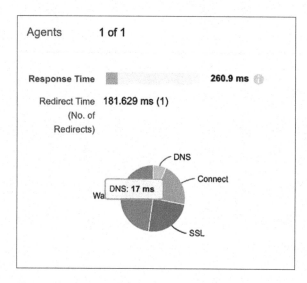

Figure 3-18   *Total Response Time Broken Out*

Page Load Tests

Page Load tests are a valuable tool for assessing the performance of web applications and websites from the perspective of a user. Whereas HTTP Server tests focus on the fundamental aspects of server response, Page Load tests dive deeper into the user experience. They are particularly useful when you want to understand how quickly a web page loads and how various page elements, such as images, scripts, and stylesheets, contribute to the overall load time.

Page Load tests offer several advantages over HTTP Server tests:

- **User-centric perspective:** Page Load tests simulate the experience of an actual user visiting a website. They measure load times, which is a critical factor for user satisfaction.

- **Comprehensive performance insights:** Page Load tests provide a comprehensive view of the web page's loading process. You can identify bottlenecks, slow-loading elements, and opportunities for optimization.

- **Document Object Model (DOM) insights:** Page Load tests can analyze the DOM, which represents the web page's structure. This lets you understand how the page is constructed and how long it takes to render.

  The Document Object Model is a programming interface for web documents. It represents the structure of a web page as a tree of objects, where each object corresponds to an element on the page (e.g., headings, paragraphs, images). Page Load tests can capture and analyze the DOM, which provides valuable insights into the rendering process.

- **Waterfall charts:** A key feature of Page Load tests is the use of waterfall charts to visually represent the sequence and timing of various page elements loading. Each element, such as images, scripts, and stylesheets, is displayed as a horizontal bar on the chart. The chart shows when each element starts loading, how long it takes, and any dependencies between elements.

  By examining a waterfall chart, you can pinpoint performance issues. For example, if a large image delays the page load, you'll see it as a prolonged bar on the chart. This visual representation makes it easier to optimize web pages for faster load times.

In summary, Page Load tests provide a user-centric perspective, offer comprehensive performance insights, analyze the DOM, and leverage waterfall charts to help you optimize web pages for a better user experience.

For each DOM component, Page Load tests use a browser bot within the deployed agent, te-chromium, a browser based on the Chromium browser, to obtain in-browser site performance metrics.

Step 1. Create a Page Load test. From the ThousandEyes UI, navigate to **Cloud & Enterprise Agents > Test Settings** and click **Add New Test.** In the New Test section, click the Layer option **Web,** and then click the Test Type option **Page Load.**

Step 2. Add a test name and test description if needed.

Step 3. Add the URL for the destination.

Step 4. For the interval, determine the test frequency. Currently, intervals are set to 1 minute.

Step 5. Select the source agent. This can be Cloud Agents or Enterprise Agents.

The Basic Configuration tab (see Figure 3-19) has a new field, Schedule, that wasn't presented for the previously discussed tests. Choosing Default does not change the normal behavior, but choosing Round-robin does. Round-robin scheduling lets you stagger the execution of tests that are run at similar intervals. In round-robin scheduling, each agent will be assigned a subinterval during which it must execute the test. Agents will be assigned to subintervals in a round-robin fashion. In Round-robin mode, a test is executed by an agent based on the Subinterval setting. The test is assigned to agents' queues with a time-based offset from the beginning of the test round to create subintervals. The offset varies by agent to evenly distribute all agents' test executions into subintervals over the time specified by the Interval setting.

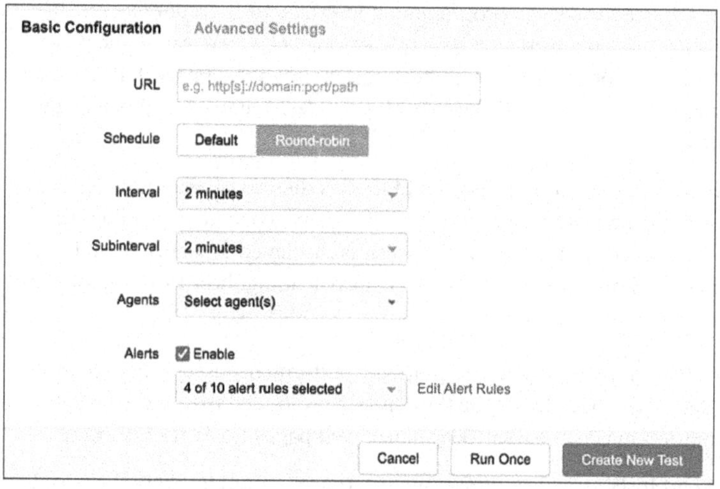

Figure 3-19 *Basic Configuration (Round-robin)*

The Advanced Settings tab for the Page Load test (see Figure 3-20) resembles that of the HTTP Server test presented in the previous section, but with a few notable differences. In particular, there are options to permit the BrowserBot to enable the microphone and camera or geolocation. By default, the Microphone and Camera field and Geolocation field are set to Block, but you can change them to Allow. There is also a unique Page Loading Strategy setting, which provides you with the flexibility to decide how long to wait before executing the **webdriver** command. You can choose whether to execute the next action immediately or wait for all elements on the page to load. For instance, you might encounter a page or application where the DOM loads rapidly, but due to JavaScript modifications or slow-loading assets, you'd typically need to wait for a prolonged period before proceeding with the next action.

The available options for Page Loading Strategy are as follows:

■ **Normal:** The test waits for the full page to load, including all subcontent, which is then loaded and parsed.

■ **Eager:** The test waits for and loads the DOM content.

■ **None:** The test returns immediately after the page has loaded and all HTML content is downloaded.

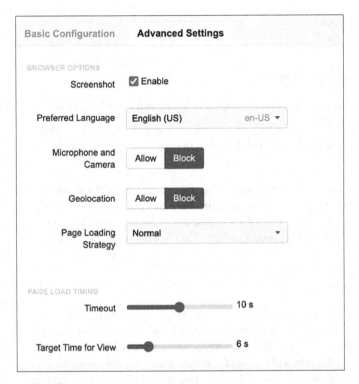

Figure 3-20 *Advanced Settings for Page Load Test*

These options enable you to fine-tune your testing approach based on the specific characteristics of the web page or application you're assessing.

In addition to showing total page load time, the Page Load test shows the load times for each of the DOM components on the page.

The view for this test includes a special Waterfall tab that only appears for Page Load and Transaction tests. The following are other metrics you will see in the views for a Page Load test:

- HTTP Server
- Overview
- Path Visualization (hop by hop)
- BGP Route Visualization (note that all Network views are optional)

Transaction Test

Transaction tests measure web user experience using synthetic browser interactions. This type of test can uncover problems that aren't always apparent from the front page.

For example, if your application relies on returning customer data from somewhere else after the user logs in, you'll need a Transaction test to evaluate this part of the user experience.

Some examples of Transaction tests include

■ **Office 365:** Log in, browse to a shared documents folder, and download a file.

■ **Shopping on Amazon:** Load the main page, search for a specific product by name, add it to a shopping cart, check out, and complete the purchase using a dummy credit card.

Transaction tests also show data for other layers of operation, such as BGP and network path visualizations. To execute commands to generate these multiple steps, we will use what's called the ThousandEyes Recorder, which is based on Selenium code. We cover this subject in depth in Chapter 7, "Scripted Synthetic User Testing with Transaction Tests."

FTP Server Test

The FTP Server test in the Web layer enhances the capabilities for network teams, allowing them to quickly assess and troubleshoot file transfer performance, whether it's with an internal or external FTP server. This test complements standard TCP/IP metrics, offering insights into network paths and routing for streamlined fault detection. It's a versatile tool that enables the validation of FTP server listings and content. Furthermore, the FTP Server test can be used for robust throughput measurements, making it an excellent choice for assessing throughput and bandwidth capacity alongside the capabilities of Web and Network layer tests.

You might be thinking that FTP is an antiquated protocol that is no longer used, but consider SFTP and FTPS, which are used all the time. FTP and FTPS have active and passive modes. In active mode, the client sends the FTP server the port it is listening on via the command channel. The server then initiates a data channel on port 20 with a TCP connection to the specified client port. However, the client might not be able to accept incoming TCP connections (e.g., it is behind a firewall). In this case, passive mode can be used to have the server designate a port (with the **PASV** command) for the client to initiate a connection to.

Next, we will create an FTP Server test. At first glance, this test might seem ordinary, but it enables you to specify the type of FTP protocol you're using, whether it's FTP, SFTP, or FTPS. It's important to note that these protocols operate on different ports: FTP on port 21, FTPS on port 990, and SFTP on port 22.

Step 1.   Navigate to **Cloud & Enterprise Agents > Test Settings** and click **Add New Test**. In the New Test section, click the Layer option **Web**, and then click the Test Type option **FTP Server**, as shown in Figure 3-21.

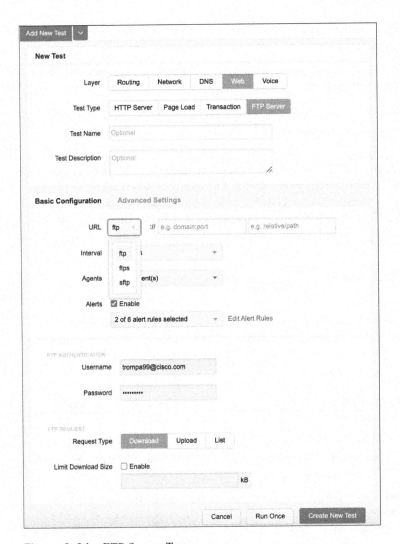

Figure 3-21 *FTP Server Test*

Step 2. As previously mentioned, ensure that the URL is added as the target, intervals have been selected, and the sourced agents have been selected.

Step 3. In the FTP Authentication section of the Basic Configuration tab, provide a username and password. If you're using an anonymous connection, use **anonymous** as the username and your email address as the password.

Step 4. In the FTP Request section, the Request Type option enables you to perform different actions to test throughput and availability:

■ **Download:** This action retrieves a file from the FTP server. You can also specify a size.

- **Upload:** This action sends a file to the FTP server. You can also specify an upload size.

- **List:** This action retrieves a listing of the files in the directory specified by your URL setting.

When performing downloads and uploads, the test uses Image (binary) transfer, while listings use ASCII transfer.

Note   The Upload setting generates a file with a random sequence of bytes as its contents. The remote filename will be taken from the URL field. You can't specify the file's contents, but you can set its size using the Upload File Size selector. The maximum recommended file size is 2,147,483 KB. Also, do not use the Limit Download Size or Upload File Size settings in combination with the Desired Reply Code setting.

The Advanced Settings tab of the FTP Server test has some great features too (see Figure 3-22):

- **Request Mode:** Choose **Passive** or **Active** to set the FTP request mode, which governs whether the client or server initiates the data channel's TCP connection:

  - Passive mode is the more common mode and is used by web browsers when retrieving files via FTP.

  - Active mode requires an inbound TCP connection to port 20 on the agent performing the test.

- **Use Explicit FTPS:** Click the box to change to active mode. FTPS is configured in passive mode, with port 21 for the initial connection and the port range of 4460 to 4500 for the data connection.

- **Desired Reply Code:** Return codes always have three digits, and each digit has a special meaning. The first digit denotes whether the response is good, bad, or incomplete. Default 2xx is checked by default, with the 2 representing the Positive Completion reply. If you need to use a non-default FTP reply code, ensure that you know what each digit represents.

Voice Layer

The Voice layer consists of two key tests: SIP Server and RTP Stream.

The Session Initiation Protocol (SIP) is a crucial signaling protocol that plays a pivotal role in enabling Voice over Internet Protocol (VoIP) services. It defines the messages exchanged between endpoints and manages various aspects of a call. SIP is versatile and supports a wide range of communication services, including voice calls, video conferencing, instant messaging, and media distribution.

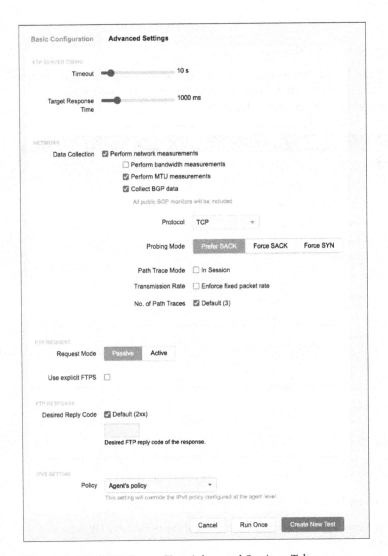

Figure 3-22 *FTP Server Test Advanced Settings Tab*

On the other hand, the Real-Time Protocol (RTP) serves as the transport protocol responsible for carrying the voice payload across the network, ensuring it reaches its intended destination in real time. This payload consists of a continuous stream of packets that traverse the network seamlessly.

Although SIP and RTP are distinct protocols with unique functions, they often work in tandem. In scenarios involving voice, video communication, and collaborative tools like Webex, the integration of SIP and RTP becomes essential to ensure a smooth and effective communications experience.

To start on this use case, let's focus on SIP, mainly when we use SIP as a way to initiate the call and a form of authentication.

SIP Server Test

To start a SIP Server test from the ThousandEyes UI:

Step 1. Navigate to **Cloud & Enterprise Agents > Test Settings** and click **Add New Test.** In the New Test section, click the Layer option **Voice**, and then click the Test Type option **SIP Server** (see Figure 3-23).

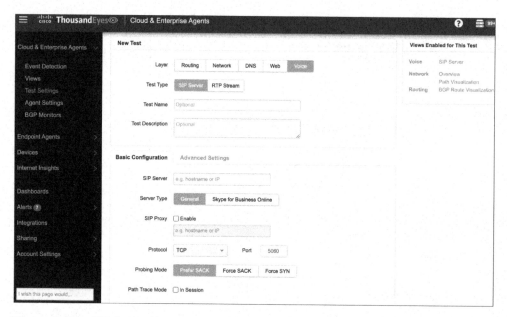

Figure 3-23 *SIP Server Test*

Step 2. On the Basic Settings tab, you'll need to configure the following:

■ **SIP Server:** This can be either a domain or an IP address.

■ **Server Type:** Typically, you can leave this at the default setting, which is General.

■ **SIP Proxy:** The SIP proxy functions similarly to other proxies, allowing packets to traverse through firewalls. Make sure to click the **Enable** check box to set the SIP Proxy Port to match the value found in the Port field for the target server.

Step 3. While the majority of the settings on the Basic Configuration tab look familiar from the discussion of previous tests, the Protocol setting has a notable difference: you can choose either TCP, TLS, or UDP. Transport Layer Security (TLS) uses TCP as a transport protocol. Choosing UDP will result in ICMP-based path discovery.

Step 4.   The Advanced Settings tab with SIP (see Figure 3-24) contains many settings that have been described previously in this chapter. The following list focuses mainly on the SIP Server Authentication and SIP Server sections:

- **Timeout:** Use the slider to set the timeout to the SIP server.

- **Perform SIP Register:** Check this box to allow the agent to attempt SIP registration with the target server using the REGISTER request.

- **Username:** The username should be unique within the ThousandEyes Account Group. This will help SIP administrators easily identify the test account and understand why it is attempting to authenticate frequently, based on the intervals set for the test.

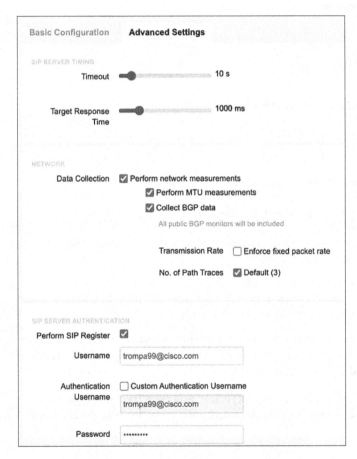

Figure 3-24   *SIP Server Test Advanced Tab*

- **Authentication Username:** By default, this optional field shows the same username as listed in the Username field, but if you want to use a different authentication username, check the **Custom Authentication Username** box and specify a custom authentication username in the field provided.

■ **Desired Status Code:** This unique entry (see Figure 3-25) enables you to specify which SIP status code returned by the target during the SIP server test is considered successful. By default, 200- and 300-level status codes are considered success. Uncheck the **Default** check box and enter a specific status code.

■ **Verify Headers:** Check the **Enable** check box if you want the headers returned by the SIP server to be matched against a configured regular expression for additional validation. ThousandEyes implements the POSIX Extended Regular Expression syntax implemented by Unix utilities such as **awk** and **egrep**.

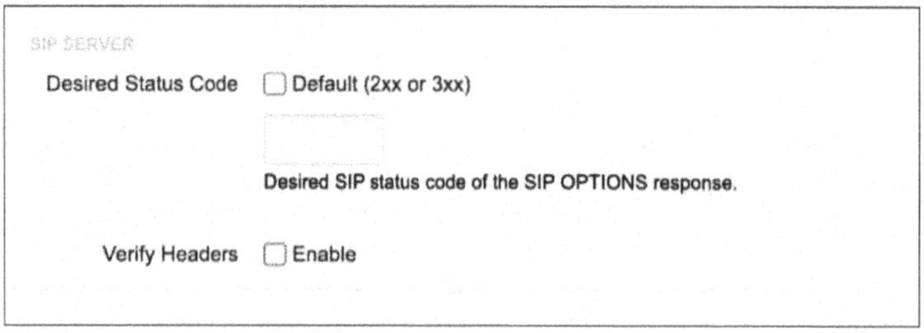

SIP SERVER

Desired Status Code   ☐ Default (2xx or 3xx)

Desired SIP status code of the SIP OPTIONS response.

Verify Headers   ☐ Enable

Figure 3-25 *SIP Server Test Desired Status Code*

The SIP Server tests enable access to the following metrics:

■ **Availability:** This represents the percentage of time that the service responds to a request, indicating its overall accessibility.

■ **Response Time:** Also referred to as "time-to-first-byte," this metric measures the duration from the initiation of the request (before DNS resolution) to when the agent receives the first byte of the response from the server.

■ **Total Time:** This metric encompasses the time required to execute the test, including DNS resolution, connect (in case of the TCP protocol), any redirects (if applicable), and the Register and Options phases of the test.

The next section within the voice layer is the RTP Test. Real-time Transport Protocol is technically a network protocol using UDP delivering audio and video over the Internet or an IP network.

RTP Stream Test

The Basic Configuration tab is pretty basic and includes nothing unique to this test, so the Advanced Settings tab (see Figure 3-26) is our focus for this test.

Step 1.   Navigate to **Cloud & Enterprise Agents > Test Settings** and click **Add New Test.** In the New Test section, click the Layer option **Voice**, and then click the Test Type option **RTP Stream.**

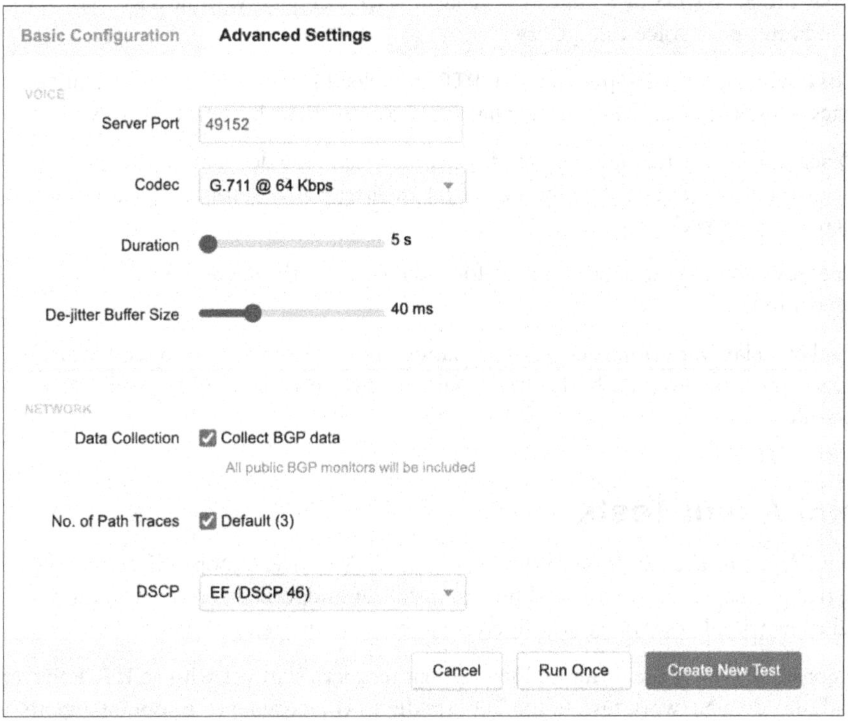

Figure 3-26   *RTP Stream Test Advanced Settings Tab*

Step 2.   Click the **Advanced Settings** tab.

Step 3.   In the Server Port field, specify the server port for the incoming RTP session to the server.

Step 4.   The Codec setting is the most important option because the codec will help you determine how well the network handles the encoding and decoding process, which will affect the quality of the voice or video. The default, G.711, is one of the most commonly used codecs, but it is worth investigating which codec is being used for this use case.

Step 5.   The de-jitter buffer stores voice data packets to eliminate the effects of delay variations. Having too small or too large a De-jitter Buffer Size value relative to network conditions can result in poor call quality. Keep in mind that buffering is latency.

RTP Stream tests enable access to the Voice Metrics, Path Visualization, and BGP Route Visualization views, which display the following metrics:

- **Mean Opinion Score (MOS):** A measurement of perceived voice quality, ranging from 1 to 5. A MOS of 5 indicates excellent voice call quality, while a MOS of 1 indicates poor voice call quality.

- **Loss:** A stream of UDP packets with RTP as payload is sent to the target agent, and packet loss is calculated from the number of packets that the target receives.

- **Discards:** Packets that are discarded when they reach the destination due to delay variations greater than the size of the de-jitter buffer setting, expressed as a percentage of packets sent.

- **Latency:** The average length of time for each packet in the stream to travel from sender to receiver.

- **Packet Delay Variation (PDV):** The variation in delay from sender to receiver. As a general rule, the de-jitter buffer size should be as large as the PDV to avoid frame discards.

Endpoint Agent Tests

Endpoint Agent tests enable you to run tests on a user's device, laptop, PC, and so on. Recall that in Chapter 2 we looked at how to install an Endpoint Agent on a laptop for individual metrics. Let's look at how to create tests from this perspective.

To demonstrate how to create an Endpoint Agent test, let's start off with an HTTP Server test and then do a Network test. In the ThousandEyes UI, navigate to **Endpoint Agents > Test Settings** and click **+ Monitor Application**. Figure 3-27 shows the path to create an Endpoint Agent test.

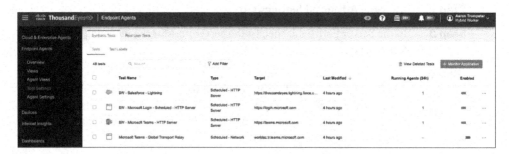

Figure 3-27 *Create an Endpoint Agent Test*

When you click Monitor Application you are brought to a Monitor Application window that provides many application choices (see Figure 3-28). The various application names are templatized so you can create a quick way to monitor popular applications.

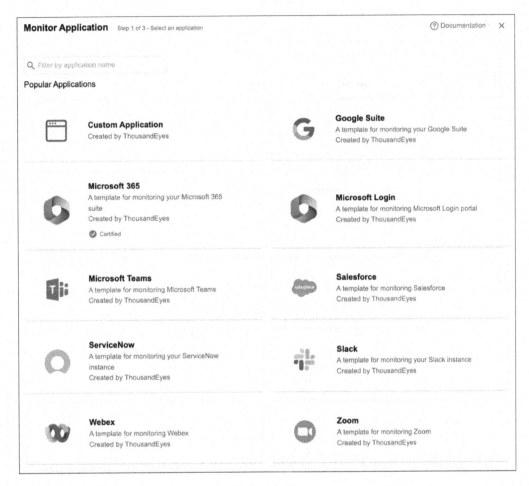

Figure 3-28 *Monitor Application for Endpoint Agents*

We dive into some of the templates later in the "Dynamic Tests" section. For this example, select **Custom Application,** and then you can create a test as seen in Figure 3-29:

Step 1. Create an application name. Here, we'll use Test Name.

Step 2. Select your agents or use the default All Agents.

Step 3. Select the interval at which to run the tests.

Step 4. Click **+ Add Test.** You can choose whether you want to use a scheduled HTTP server test or a scheduled network, as seen in Figure 3-30. For this example select **Scheduled - HTTP Server.**

Figure 3-29   *Custom Application Test*

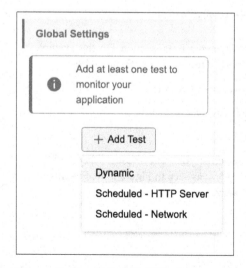

Figure 3-30   *Scheduled Test Options*

Step 5. After you select HTTP Server, notice that the test name, interval, and agents have been carried over from the previous steps, and now all that needs to be added is the URL. For this example I am using https://webex.com, as shown in Figure 3-31.

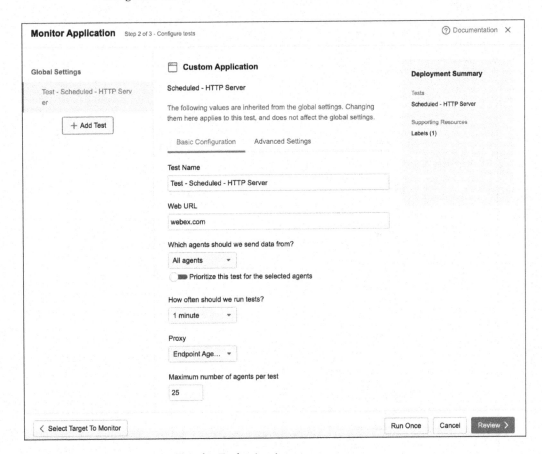

Figure 3-31 *HTTP Server Test for Endpoint Agents*

Step 6. Select the **Advanced Settings** tab to explore it. The options here are similar to the options to set up Web layer tests that utilize Enterprise Agents or Cloud Agents. These settings are all optional.

Step 7. From here, click **Review** (see Figure 3-32).

Figure 3-32 *Endpoint Agent Test Advanced Settings Tab*

Step 8.   Review the test information (see Figure 3-33). If all looks good, select **Next**. If you need to go back and make a change, select **Configure Tests**.

Step 9.   When you've completed your review, click **Next** to see the confirmation page. Click **Done** to end this configuration (see Figure 3-34).

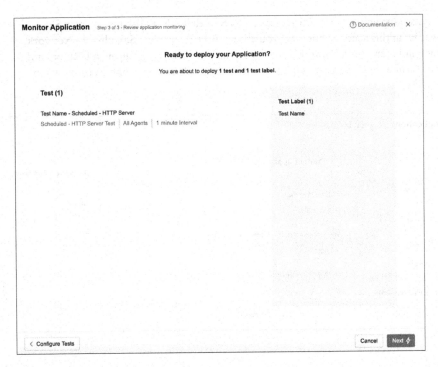

Figure 3-33 *Endpoint Agent Test Review*

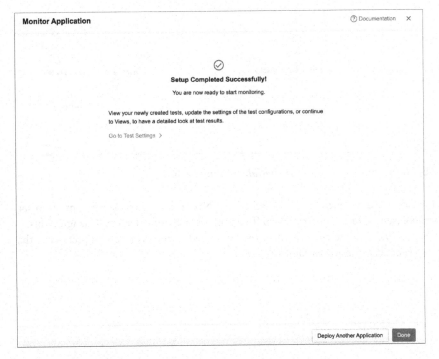

Figure 3-34 *Endpoint Agent Test Template Completion*

In this second example we will walk through a Scheduled Network test. Follow Steps 1–4 from earlier in this section, but after you click + Add Test, select **Scheduled - Network**, as shown in Figure 3-35. From this point you can select the target using a URL or an IP address. Ensure that agents are selected and the intervals are set properly, as shown in Figure 3-36.

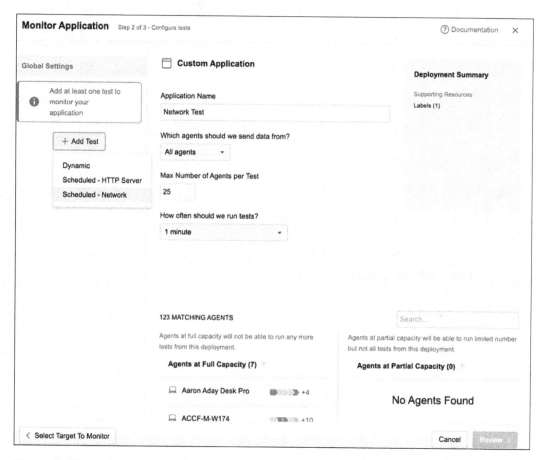

Figure 3-35   *Endpoint Agent Test—Scheduled Network Test*

From the Advanced Settings tab in the Scheduled Network test, you see an option to set the protocol (see Figure 3-37). The default setting is set to Auto-Detect. Changing this behavior is not advised unless you know the target and if there is a certain preference that needs to be statically set versus auto-detected.

Figure 3-36   *Endpoint Agent Test—Scheduled Network Test Basic Configuration*

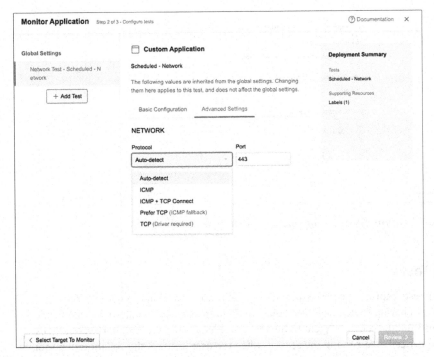

Figure 3-37   *Endpoint Agent Test—Scheduled Network Test Advanced Settings Tab*

After you've reviewed or selected the protocol, click the **Review** button and review the summary of the test, and then click **Done** to finish the test configuration.

Adding Multiple Tests to a Template

Reviewing the steps starting from Figure 3-29, the Add Test drop-down shows the options to use a Scheduled - HTTP Server test or a Scheduled - Network test. If the use case is to have multiple tests on a single template this is also feasible.

Following the earlier steps, using the Test Name template, create a Scheduled - HTTP Server test and add a Scheduled - Network test (see Figure 3-38). Follow the steps in this example to review the tests, and then click **Done**.

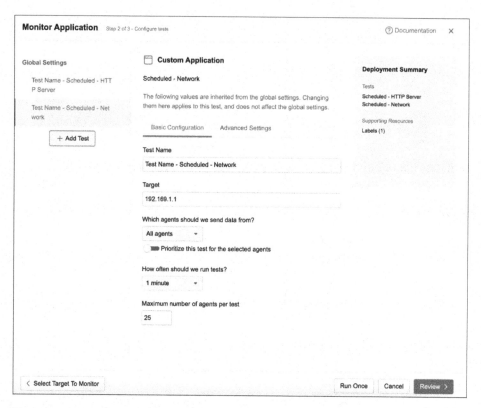

Figure 3-38 *Endpoint Agent Template Test—Multiple Tests*

Dynamic Tests

Dynamic tests capture the performance of collaboration tools like Webex or Zoom, without you having to manually configure an IP address or hostname for the application. These tests are the same as Agent to Server scheduled tests, except that ThousandEyes will automatically start to log the session when the user initiates the collaboration tool.

For example, suppose the user logs in to Webex. When the user initiates via an application or a browser, the Endpoint Agent will start to log from start to finish. This test is great to run after users complain about the experience of a video meeting. ThousandEyes will be able to see the path from the laptop to the target and, just like the agent testing with voice, the ThousandEyes admin will be able to see not just loss and jitter but laptop performance or VPN issues.

To set up a Dynamic test, navigate to **Endpoint Agents > Test Settings** and click the **+ Monitor Applications** button, as shown earlier in Figure 3-27.

From this point you have two options to explore. The first is to use the custom application that was previously explained in the Scheduled - HTTP Server test and Scheduled - Network test. The other option is to use the applications seen earlier in Figure 3-28.

Let's explore these options now, starting with using the custom application:

Step 1. Select **Custom Application**, as shown earlier in Figure 3-28.

Step 2. Create an application name, and ensure that the agents and intervals have been selected as mentioned earlier and shown in Figure 3-29. Although this is a Dynamic test, we want to ensure the agent is logging the data, so using 1-minute intervals will give the user the adequate data.

Figure 3-39 *Endpoint Agent Test—Dynamic*

Step 3.   Click **+ Add Test** and select **Dynamic**, as shown in Figure 3-39.

Step 4.   Choose the collaboration application you want to use for the Dynamic test—for this example, choose **Zoom** as seen in Figure 3-40.

Figure 3-40   *Endpoint Agent Test—Dynamic Zoom Test*

Step 5.   Click **Review**, or click the **Advanced Settings** tab as seen in Figure 3-41. The Advanced Settings will enable you to change the protocol from auto-detect to a static set protocol as previously mentioned in the Scheduled Network test, shown earlier in Figure 3-37.

Step 6.   Review the test: ensure the test is set to Dynamic, the agents have been selected, and the intervals have been properly set, as shown in Figure 3-42.

Step 7.   After your review, click **Done** (see Figure 3-43).

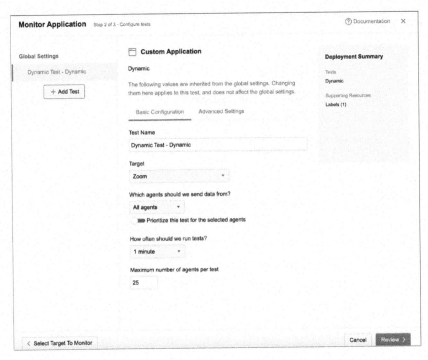

Figure 3-41   *Endpoint Agent Test—Dynamic Zoom Test Configuration*

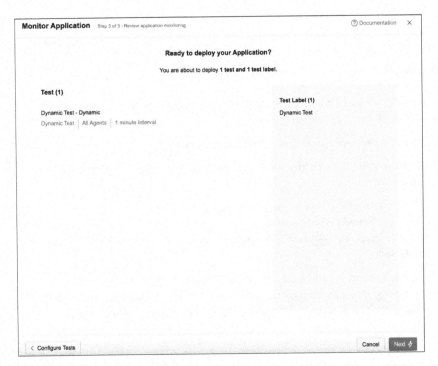

Figure 3-42   *Endpoint Agent Test—Dynamic Zoom Test Review*

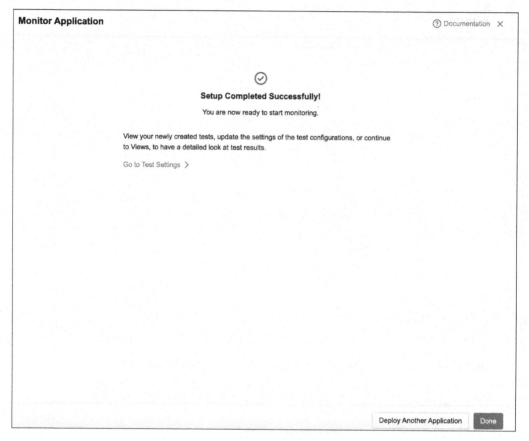

Figure 3-43   *Endpoint Agent Test—Dynamic Zoom Test Done*

The second option for the Dynamic tests is to use the application templates shown in Figure 3-44. For this example, select Webex.

Step 1.   Review the application name, interval, and agents.

Step 2.   Ensure you have a proper site ID or tenant name; for example, cisco.webex. com.

Step 3.   Under Global Settings in Figure 3-45, notice that two tests will be configured, one as a Scheduled test and the other as a Dynamic test. You can toggle either test or keep both—this will depend on the use case. Ensure that your tests are enabled.

Step 4.   Click **Review**. As previously mentioned, ensure that the tests are built properly. You may go back and make changes by clicking the **Configure Tests** button, or click **Next** if everything is good (see Figure 3-46).

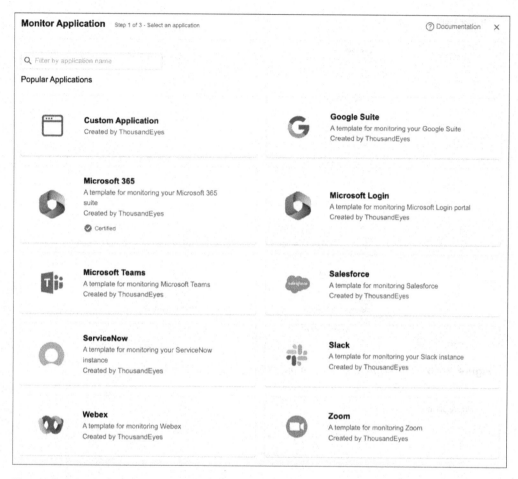

Figure 3-44   *Endpoint Agent Dynamic Test Using Application Templates*

Step 5.   Click **Done** (refer to Figure 3-43).

These application templates can be used to monitor other popular applications. Knowing just the tenant name or the site ID will enable the ThousandEyes platform to take the guesswork out of the target URL. Most of these application templates will create a test that uses the Scheduled HTTP Server test.

Figure 3-45 *Endpoint Tests—Dynamic Using Application Templates*

Figure 3-46 *Endpoint Test Webex Application Template Review*

Real User Tests

Real User tests are automatically deployed when a user visits a website within a monitored domain set. These tests enable administrators to collect valuable performance data from actual users, providing insights into how well applications and websites are performing in real-world conditions.

Monitored Domain Set

A monitored domain set consists of the domains for which you want to gather performance metrics. These domains are typically business-relevant, including tools and websites that your end users frequently access. By focusing on these domains, you can ensure that the collected data is pertinent to your organization's operational needs.

How Real User Tests Work

You can initiate Real User tests manually via the browser or set them to automatically gather data by designating groups of monitored domains. For example, monitoring a cisco.com domain would be easier to manage versus Webex.cisco.com, dcloud.cisco.com, and so on.

- **Activation:** Real User tests are triggered when a user visits a website configured by the ThousandEyes administrator.

- **Data collection:** Once triggered, the tests collect metrics on various performance aspects, such as page load times, network latency, and other critical user experience indicators.

- **Visibility:** The insights gained from Real User tests help identify performance bottlenecks, monitor service levels, and improve the overall user experience by addressing any issues promptly.

Let's configure a Real User test:

Step 1.   Navigate to **Endpoint Agents > Test Settings** and click the **Real User Tests** tab as shown in Figure 3-47.

Figure 3-47   *Endpoint Agent Test—Real User Tests*

Step 2.   Click **Add New Monitored Domain Set** as shown in Figure 3-47.

Note   Steps 3–6 use Figure 3-48 as a reference.

Figure 3-48   *Endpoint Agent Test—Real User Tests Configuration*

Step 3.   Create a domain set name. This can be any name you'd like.

Step 4.   Enter a domain or website URL; for this example, use cisco.com and cisco.webex.com.

Step 5.   Add agents or all agents to the Real User test.

Step 6.   Click **Add New Monitored Domain Set.**

From the Real User Tests tab, you can view the tests that have been configured. Figure 3-49 shows the Cisco monitored domain set and the monitored domains.

Figure 3-49 *Endpoint Agent Test—Real User Tests Review*

Review Questions

Answer the following questions. Check your answers against those provided in Appendix A, "Answers to Review Questions."

1. What would be the purpose of running a synthetic test versus monitoring?

2. What is the difference between an HTTP test versus a Page Load test?

3. What is the purpose of running a DNS Server test?

Chapter 4

Configuring Alerts

In the realm of digital experience monitoring, alerting stands as a cornerstone. ThousandEyes offers a comprehensive array of alert triggers, from web page availability to network reachability to Layer 3 metrics, ensuring that deviations or issues in performance don't go unnoticed.

The relationship between tests and alert rules is multifaceted, allowing you to assign one or more alert rules to a single test or create a common set of alert rules and apply the set to individual tests or groups of tests. If you have an agent up and running and tests underway, you're in the right place to harness the power of alerts.

In this chapter, we explore the alert notifications and how these notifications can tie into other tools that your company might use to operationalize. When it comes to thresholds, you'll find that the multitude of metrics available can lead you to select different alert triggers. We'll delve into these options to help you identify what works best for your organization. Alerting is not just a tool; it's a proactive strategy for managing performance and availability.

It's important to note that you can add as many alerts as necessary to ensure that you're notified of specific metrics' deviations. What's even more convenient is that you can apply the same alert rule to multiple metrics, streamlining your alert setup. Chapter 3, "Configuring Tests," discussed tests and their settings. Within the test settings are default alert rules already attached to the test. This chapter looks at the rules and how to change up the conditions specific to your needs.

Alert Rules

Let's explore alert rules and their conditions in more detail. Alert rules consist of simple conditions that must be met before the alert is triggered. We'll delve deeper into this shortly.

Just as the ThousandEyes UI categorizes tests, it also categorizes alert sources based on the test types and the source of the test they relate to. These categories help you to organize your alert rules effectively. The categories of alert include

■ Cloud and Enterprise Agents

■ BGP Routing

■ Endpoint Agents

Let's look at some of the default alert rules already placed on tests. For this example, we will look at an Agent to Agent test and what metrics we want to view for an alert. Figure 4-1 shows a default Agent to Agent network alert rule with packet loss as an alert condition.

Figure 4-1   *Default Agent to Agent Network Alert Rule*

Navigate to **Alerts > Alert Rules > Cloud and Enterprise Agents** and select the rule (for example, Default Agent to Agent Network Alert Rule).

As shown in Figure 4-1, the General section of the Settings tab consists of the following fields for an alert rule:

■ **Direction:** For a network test, Agent to Agent enables the user to select triggering from source to target or target to source or both.

■ **Tests:** This setting shows all tests assigned to this rule. From here you can select other tests to assign that rule.

■ **Agents:** Within this setting, specify whether all agents in the test should be associated to the alert rule or only specific agents.

■ **Severity:** This field is static. Once the alert has been triggered, it cannot be changed during the active alert process. The idea is to initially set the severity based on predefined criteria and then use metrics to associate the severity with specific conditions.

Alert Conditions

When configuring alert conditions, it's important to consider that the agent will monitor the metrics and trigger alerts. The first line of the condition depends on which agent(s) is being used for detection. Remember that multiple agents can be configured from source to target. Figure 4-2 demonstrates how to create an alert condition once specific criteria are met with the designated agents in the test.

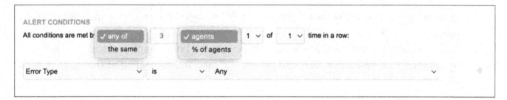

Figure 4-2   *Alert Agent Conditions*

The initial part of the condition criteria involves any of the agents (assuming there are multiple agents as a source) or the same agent. If the condition arises, all agents will need to detect the metric and report it. The second field is similar to the first, but it enables you to focus on agent numbers or percentage.

The next step is to choose the metric and apply a threshold to when the alert should occur. Figure 4-3 shows the Packet Loss metric selected with a threshold of greater than 25%. The figure also shows we are asking to alert for any agent actively running the test that has end-to-end packet loss of more than or equal to 25%.

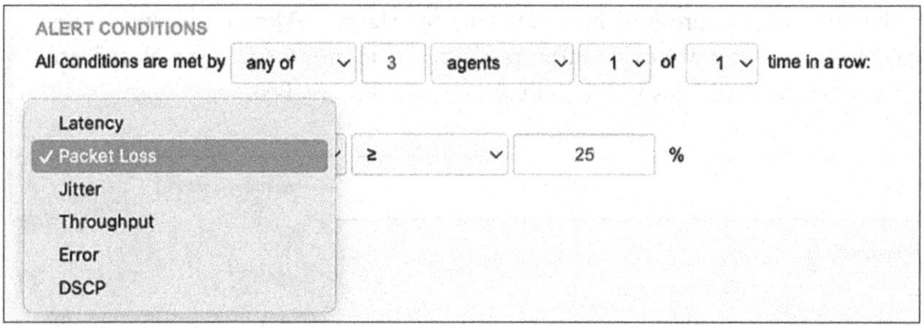

ALERT CONDITIONS

All conditions are met by   any of   ∨   3   agents   ∨   1 ∨ of   1 ∨ time in a row:

Latency
✓ Packet Loss   ≥   ∨   25   %
Jitter
Throughput
Error
DSCP

Figure 4-3   *Alert Metrics*

Now let's assume for this test that throughput and latency as a metric with certain conditions need to be added, as shown in Figure 4-4. The + button to the right of each metric enables you to add more granular criteria to the alert. Be cognizant of how you want to be alerted, and ensure you are meeting the key performance indicators (KPIs) the business needs.

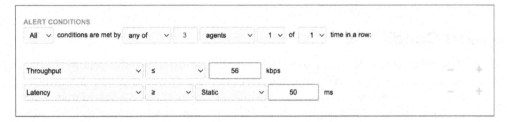

Figure 4-4 *Alert Metrics Continued*

Alerts are unique, much like tests. While default settings are useful, creating customized metrics that align with your KPIs is essential for meeting user and leadership expectations. Additionally, renaming alerts can enhance clarity. For example, renaming an alert to Campus-to-DC Throughput Alert can provide a clearer understanding of the alert's purpose.

Alert Notifications

Alert notifications enable you to choose how you want to consume the alert or be notified outside the ThousandEyes platform. Usually, ThousandEyes sends an email to a group of users, and that could suffice for your situation, but other options include using webhooks and APIs and third-party integrations that send alert data to platforms such as PagerDuty or ServiceNow.

Let's explore a few of the popular types of alert notifications. The following sections cover email and webhooks.

Email Notifications

To receive the notification through email, navigate to **Alerts > Alert Rules** and choose the alert rule for which you want to configure alert notifications. Click the Notifications tab and enter your email address in the field shown (see Figure 4-5).

Aaron-Test-PathTrace	Path Trace	Any Hop: (Delay ≥ 100 ms)

Settings   **Notifications**

EMAIL

Send emails to   [trompa99@thousandeyes... **✖**]   ▼   Edit external emails

☑ Send an email when the alert clears

Add message

Figure 4-5 *Configuring Email Alert Notifications*

Webhooks

To receive the notification via webhook, proceed to the Configure Webhooks section in the Notifications tab of the Alert Rule, as seen in Figure 4-6. To create a webhook, follow the steps for a basic/generalized webhook integration. Figure 4-7 shows the webhook fields. Additionally, there is an option to use a webhook template, which can also be found in Figure 4-6. This option enables the administrator to set up a more comprehensive webhook and ensure the payload is complete, compared to the basic webhook where control is more limited. We discuss this option in the next section, as well as in Chapter 8, "Integrations."

Step 1.   Enter a name for the webhook—we suggest you use the application name.

Figure 4-6   *Webhooks and Integration Options on the Notifications Tab*

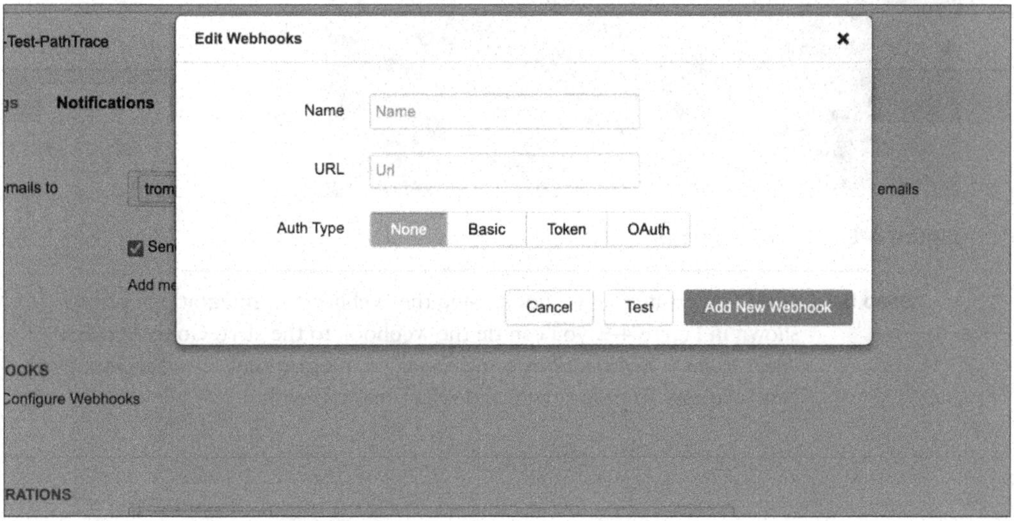

Figure 4-7   *Webhook Configuration*

Step 2.   Add the URL of the application.

Step 3.   If there is an auth type, select the appropriate method.

Step 4.   Click **Add New Webhook.**

Recall that in Chapter 3 we explored the use of application templates for the Endpoint Agents test. You also have some templates to use to assist with the webhook integrations. See the Manage Integrations link in the Alert Notification shown in Figure 4-6 or the Integrations tab shown in Figure 4-8. We can view the templates that are available to use and from here, select the application you wish to use and enter the criteria for that application and then save for Custom Webhook. This will be discussed in Chapter 8.

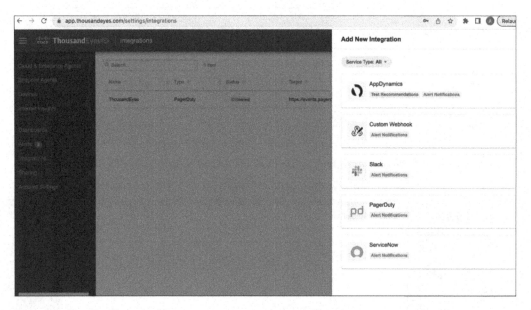

Figure 4-8   *Alert Integrations*

Step 5.   After you create the webhook using the Webhook or Integration options shown in Figure 4-9, you can tie the webhook to the alert. Go to **Manage Alert Rules > Notifications > Webhook** or **Integrations,** click the **Send Notifications To** drop-down, and select the webhook.

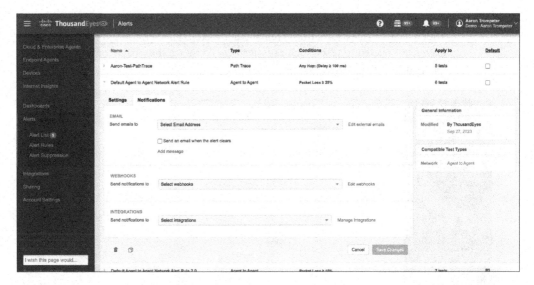

Figure 4-9 *Alert Webhook Integration*

Alert Suppression

The ThousandEyes platform offers Alert Suppression Windows (ASWs) to designate specific periods during which you want to withhold alerts, such as planned maintenance. These windows can be used either for one-time events or for recurring schedules, suitable for managing routine downtimes such as monthly maintenance activities.

When ASWs are active, tests included in the window are exempt from being evaluated against alert rule criteria. During this period, any data meeting alert conditions will not trigger alerts until the Alert Suppression Window concludes. Notifications, such as emails, webhooks, or other integrations, will not be sent during this period. However, it's essential to consider the following special cases:

- If an alert rule demands two or more consecutive data rounds to trigger, data collected during the Alert Suppression Window cannot contribute to these consecutive rounds. This means that any data collected during this suppression window will not count toward the conditions needed to trigger an alert.

- If an alert rule necessitates two or more agents to trigger in a single round, it's plausible for the Alert Suppression Window to commence or conclude within a round, where some agents have gathered data and others have not. If the suppression window starts or ends within a data collection round, agents that collect data before the window starts or after it ends will contribute their data toward the alert conditions. Conversely, agents that collect data during the suppression window will not contribute to the alert conditions.

■ Only tests associated with a New Alert Suppression Window (see Figure 4-10) are affected by its rules. Other tests remain unaffected. Furthermore, notifications for events not related to tests, such as Enterprise Agents going offline or online, remain independent of Alert Suppression Windows.

Figure 4-10 *New Alert Suppression Window Configuration*

Follow these steps to configure an Alert Suppression Window for an alert:

Step 1.   Navigate to **Alerts > Alert Suppression,** as shown in Figure 4-10.

Step 2.   In the General section, create a name for the Alert Suppression Window and then select the tests that need to be suppressed from the **Tests** drop-down list.

Step 3.   In the Schedule section, set the timeframe for the Alert Suppression Window. You can configure whether it should repeat every day, every week, or once a month in an automated fashion.

Step 4.   Click **Create New Window.**

Once the suppressed alerts are configured and the "create window" is enabled (see Figure 4-11), users can perform several actions. You can add additional tests or uncheck the Enabled check box for that specific suppressed alert. If you need to repeat a suppressed alert, the drop-down menu labeled Repeat enables you to create a schedule.

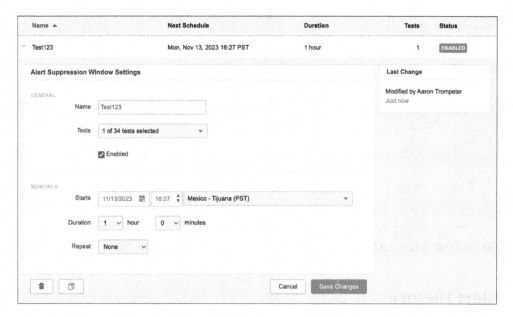

Figure 4-11 *Alert Suppression Enabled*

Finding the Source of the Alert

After you have configured an alert rule, you can view any alert that it has triggered by navigating to **Alerts > Alert List** (see Figure 4-12). On the Active Alerts tab, you can view all triggered alerts and determine the cause and type of each.

Figure 4-12 *Alert List*

Clicking any active alert takes you to a detailed page, as shown in Figure 4-13, where you can see the detailed scope and metric of the trigger. In the Scope column, clicking the hamburger icon will launch the test view. When doing so, make sure to note the time the trigger started so that you can examine the relevant historical data.

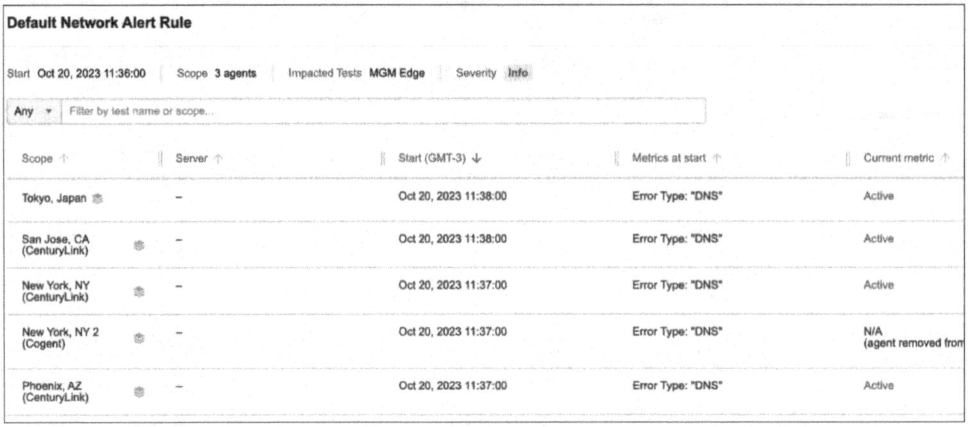

Figure 4-13   *Active Alerts*

Alert History

The ThousandEyes platform retains all alerts for 90 days. You can find them by navigating to **Alerts > Alert List** and clicking the **Alerts History** tab, as shown in Figure 4-14. This feature enables you to revisit and analyze past incidents, which facilitates post-incident analysis and retrospective evaluation.

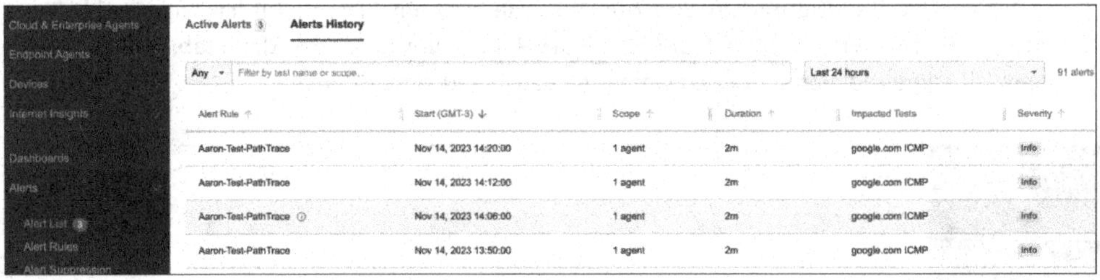

Figure 4-14   *Alert History*

Review Questions

Answer the following questions. Check your answers against those provided in Appendix A, "Answers to Review Questions."

1. Can you create a custom alert that focuses on a specific metric?

2. Can alerts be integrated into other platforms?

3. Can you change a rule to notify only if all agents met a certain condition?

Chapter 5

Dashboards

When you log in to the ThousandEyes platform, the first view that you see is the Dashboards page, containing charts and easy-to-read graphs summarizing your data. It provides dynamic and real-time insights into your network and application performance. This chapter guides you through the intricacies of ThousandEyes dashboards, helping you to harness the full potential of this essential feature.

As you enter the Dashboards page, you are greeted with live status dashboards, offering a snapshot of a specific time period (by default, 24 hours). Additionally, you have the capability to schedule and share point-in-time snapshots of a dashboard. You can organize the information derived from tests and Internet Insights into highly customized layouts. These layouts can be presented numerically, in tables, or through intuitive graphs, allowing for a comprehensive understanding of your network and application health.

A noteworthy feature of the Dashboards page is that it automatically refreshes every 2 minutes, ensuring you are consistently updated with the latest data. This not only facilitates active monitoring but also prevents automatic logouts due to inactivity. This attribute makes the Dashboards page suitable for deployment in kiosks or operations center displays.

This chapter introduces the various components, customization options, and strategies for effective utilization of ThousandEyes dashboards.

Dashboard Basics

When you log in to the ThousandEyes UI the Dashboard menu is the first page you see. By default, the dashboard uses the test data that has already been created to populate its visualizations.

As an example, Figures 5-1 and 5-2 show the defaults where the test data is represented in a basic dashboard view; we will look at how to customize for more granular specifics.

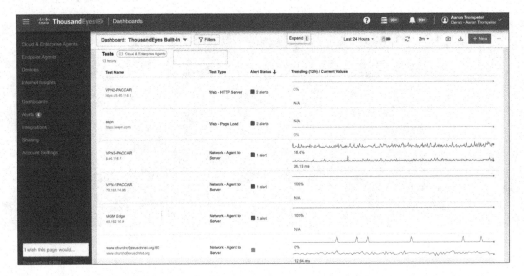

Figure 5-1 *Dashboard Defaults*

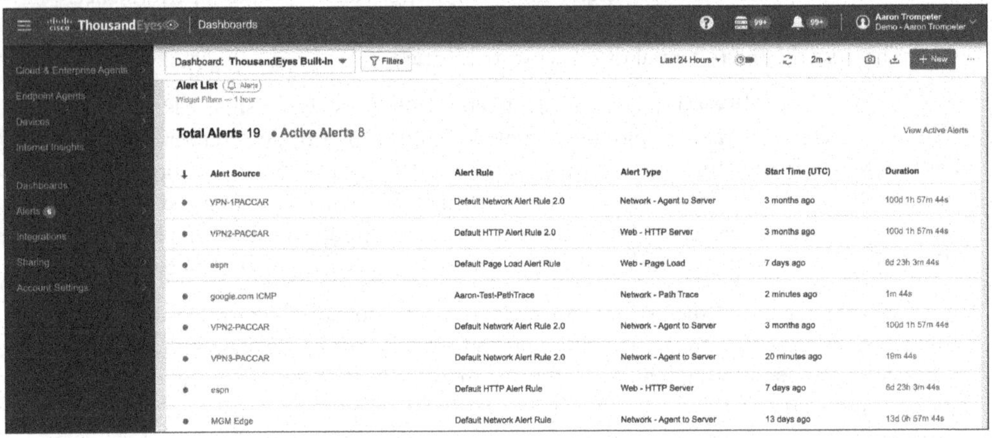

Figure 5-2 *Dashboard Defaults Continued*

When the tests shown in Figure 5-1 trigger alerts, the details of the alerts are displayed in the Alert List widget shown in Figure 5-2, including the alert rule that triggered the alert and the alert type.

You can quickly customize your Dashboards page by adding one or more of the built-in dashboards that ThousandEyes provides. From the Dashboard drop-down list, choose **ThousandEyes Built-in**, as shown in Figure 5-3, to see other built-in dashboards that might fit your needs. Notice that the dashboard categorizes the tests, so creating structure early on will help users operationalize and locate metrics more easily.

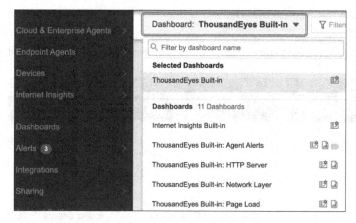

Figure 5-3 *Dashboard Built-ins*

As an example, Figure 5-4 shows the HTTP Server built-in dashboard. You can see a completely different experience versus the other default dashboard. The point of this is to show examples of what metrics can be displayed and how layouts can be presented.

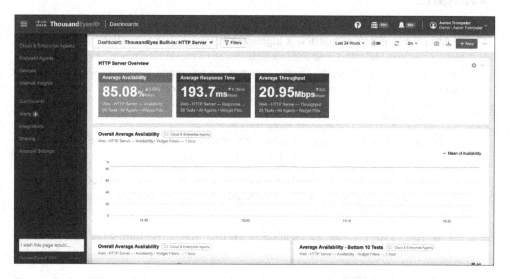

Figure 5-4 *HTTP Server Built-in Dashboard*

To help you maneuver around the dashboard, Figure 5-5 provides a quick reference for the various functions in the dashboard.

The Add Widget button and ellipsis menu shown in Figure 5-5 are the typical starting points, respectively, for adding widgets to a dashboard and creating a new dashboard, or editing or deleting an existing dashboard. These controls enable administrators to organize specific data and structure it according to a particular use case. For example, grouping Agent to Agent tests that connect to the data center enables administrators to swiftly identify issues and generate high-level reports.

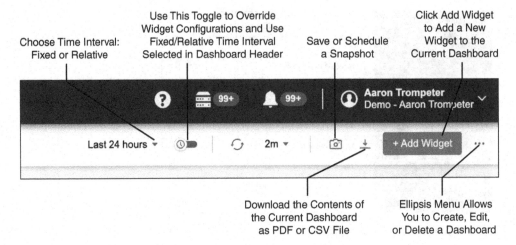

Figure 5-5   *Dashboard Built-in Controls*

Widgets

In the context of ThousandEyes dashboards, *widgets* are visual elements that represent specific types of data or metrics. Widgets can represent data from alerts, agents, and tests. They provide a dynamic and interactive way to present information relevant to your monitoring and testing needs. The following are some common types of widgets that you might encounter when expanding or customizing a dashboard:

- **Widget Type: Live Status**
  - **Agent Status:** Offers a live look at the status of your Enterprise or Endpoint Agents to give you an idea of overall agent health.
  - **Tests:** A 12-hour, live display of a list of tests configured in your account group for a one-stop glance at high-level test health. Grayed-out rows show disabled tests.
  - **Alert List:** Provides a look at the alerts that were active during the configured time interval.
- **Widget Type: Breakdown**
  - **Stacked Bar:** Provides horizontal histogram bars with multiple values, useful for composite metric data and for comparing values between multiple tests or on a per-country basis.
  - **Grouped Bar:** Represents multiple values as single bars in a group of bars, oriented either horizontally or vertically.

- **Pie:** Similar to Stacked Bar chart widgets, representing data in a circular statistical graphic. It is used to illustrate numerical proportions, which makes it easier to understand the distribution of the selected metric.

- **Widget Type:** Data Summary

  - **Table:** Allows a breakdown of numbers by rows and columns, listing by test, country, continent, or data source.

  - **Multi-Metric Table:** Can have columns with different metrics, displaying more varied information.

  - **Number:** Displays one or more cards, each showing a single scalar quantity or a number of alerts.

  - **Color Grid:** Displays an array of colored cards, where each card's color depends on the configured color scale.

- **Widget Type: Time Series**

  - **Line:** This widget displays data using a line plot, where time is represented on the horizontal axis and the selected metric or quantity is shown on the vertical axis. This type of visualization is particularly useful for observing trends and patterns over a specified time period.

  - **Stacked Area:** Line plots showing quantities over time, similar to stacked bar charts but representing values over time.

  - **Box and Whiskers:** Plots data values versus time on the horizontal axis, with the vertical axis displaying the median, minimum, and maximum data points per time value.

- **Widget Type: Maps**

  - **Map:** Displays data on a world map based on the location of testing systems, with options to show data per country, continent, or per agent. This allows the user to quickly determine whether a specific region is experiencing issues.

These widgets offer a versatile set of tools to visualize and analyze data from different perspectives, catering to various monitoring needs. To access the widgets described in the previous list, from the dashboard, click **Add Widget** to see all the widgets (see Figure 5-6).

Adding widgets to a built-in dashboard is a common practice to tailor the display according to specific needs. The purpose of each widget is to provide a clear visualization of different data metrics. In the next section, we delve into the process of creating a new dashboard, offering you the flexibility to curate your own visualizations based on the available widgets.

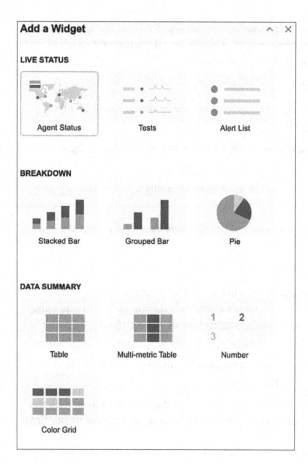

Figure 5-6   *Widgets*

Creating a New Dashboard

Creating a dashboard in ThousandEyes is as straightforward as adding a widget to a built-in dashboard. To effectively use dashboards, it's essential to understand the different widget types and the data they display. This ensures that the relevant metrics are visualized in a way that best supports your monitoring needs.

From the dashboard, click the **New** button and choose **Dashboard** (see Figure 5-7) to create a new dashboard and add widgets to it.

Figure 5-7   *Create New Dashboard Menu Selection*

In the Create New Dashboard dialog box that opens, shown in Figure 5-8, give the dashboard an intuitive name and choose which account group(s) will be able to view the dashboard. In the View Settings, you can check **Set As Private** if you don't want anyone else to be able to view the dashboard, or you can check **Set As My Default** or **Set As Default for Account Group** if you want this dashboard to be displayed by default on your own Dashboards page or the account group's Dashboards page, respectively. Click **Create Dashboard** to create the shell dashboard and return to the Dashboards page to configure it with widgets.

Figure 5-8 *Dashboard Creation*

On the Dashboards page, locate your new dashboard and click its **Add Widget** button to open the Add a Widget panel (refer to Figure 5-6). Click a widget to open a separate panel in which to configure it. As an example, Figure 5-9 shows the panel that opens when adding the Color Grid widget (Data Summary type). When creating a new widget, all the options can seem overwhelming. Focus on how you want the data to look, and experiment with the various widgets to find what suits you (click Cancel instead of Save to return to the Add a Widget panel and choose a different widget to view).

Step 1.   **Data Source:** Select a data source from the Data Source drop-down menu. Most users may use the default option, Cloud & Enterprise Agents, but it's crucial to consider other options, such as Internet Insights or Endpoint Agents.

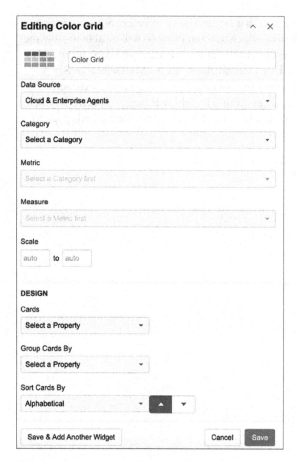

Figure 5-9 *New Dashboard Widget*

Tip   Choose a data source that aligns with the specific data you wish to visualize.

Step 2.   **Category:** Choose the category. Specify what aspect or metric you want to monitor from the selected data source. For example, if you have chosen Cloud & Enterprise Agents as your data source, you might select Web - HTTP Server as the category to display metrics related to HTTP server performance.

Note   The options available in the Category drop-down list will depend on the data source you selected.

Step 3.   **Metric:** Select the specific metric you want to monitor. You have several options to choose from, including Availability, DNS Time, or SSL Time. For the purposes of this example, let's select Availability as the metric.

Note You can select only one metric per widget. If you want to observe multiple metrics, you will need to create additional widgets for each metric.

Step 4. **Measure:** After selecting the metric, you'll need to determine how you want to measure it by choosing an option from the Measure drop-down list. The options include Median, Maximum, and Minimum.

Tip I recommend choosing Median because it provides a balanced view, avoiding the extremes that maximum or minimum values might present. There are other options such as nth percentile and standard deviations.

Step 5. **Cards:** Select Tests from the Cards field drop-down menu. If you are using categories, use the Group Cards By field to organize them accordingly. This helps in sorting and grouping specific tests or agents. Although not covered in previous chapters, labeling enables users to group specific tests or agents together. For this example, choose All to include all relevant tests or agents.

Step 6. **Set up filters:** Scroll down to the Filter By section (this section is not shown in Figure 5-9) and select Tests to filter the data. If you have numerous agents worldwide running those tests and want to focus on specific agents, add additional filters to define your data more precisely.

Step 7. **Save and view the data:** Click **Save** to apply the data and the layout to your new widget. Figure 5-10 shows the example Color Grid widget. There are additional widgets you can include: Add Agent Status and Endpoint Agents represent Real-Time Agent Status and End User Experience status in the dashboard (see Figure 5-11).

Figure 5-10 *New Widget*

Creating a dashboard allows your imagination to come alive and paint the picture of the network from many perspectives. Dashboards are fully customizable and can be created for a single use case if needed.

Another great feature of widgets is that you can duplicate a widget, change a metric or two (for example), and save the duplicate as a new widget. That way, you don't have to go through the entire process of creating a new widget every time you need one.

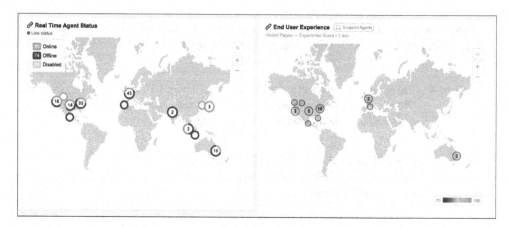

Figure 5-11 *Agent Widget Example*

The Embed Widget feature, shown in Figures 5-12 and 5-13, allows you to grab the data and use it as an iframe to insert in a web page, wiki page, or anything external that can use an iframe.

Figure 5-12 *Widget Features*

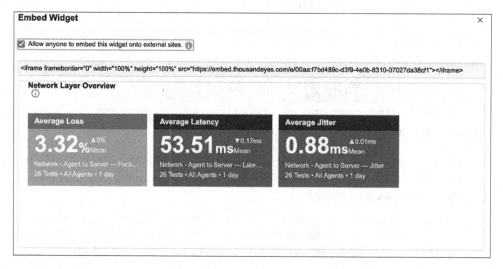

Figure 5-13 *Iframe Widget*

Returning to the dashboard widgets, if you encounter errors or issues, you can click on the widget to identify which test(s) are experiencing problems (see Figure 5-14). When you click on the widget, a window will appear to show all tests that are associated within that widget. In the next chapter, we explore how to monitor and troubleshoot network performance issues.

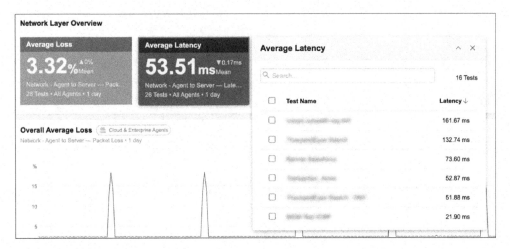

Figure 5-14 *Associated Test to Widget*

Review Questions

Answer the following questions. Check your answers against those provided in Appendix A, "Answers to Review Questions."

1. Can you create a widget that shows only alerts from Internet Insights?

2. Is there a way to extract the dashboard data to a web page?

3. When creating a widget, can you add more than one metric? If not, how can this be done?

4. What would be the best widget to use when looking at end users' wireless signal strength?

Chapter 6

Monitoring and Troubleshooting Network Performance Issues

Understanding Views

The Cloud & Enterprise Agents > Views page of the ThousandEyes UI provides an in-depth viewing platform for all test data. You can navigate between different perspectives, then drill down into the data to identify issues and determine their root cause. The Views page is where you want to go to troubleshoot network performance issues. In the previous chapters, we set up metrics for both alerts and the dashboard so that we can easily see which tests are showing issues. In Figure 6-1, you can see that the currently selected test is JIRA; however, you can go to another test by selecting one from the list.

Figure 6-1 *Select a Test to View*

After you choose the test to view, you can start to look at metrics and understand how ThousandEyes will help in troubleshooting and/or monitoring, as shown in Figure 6-2.

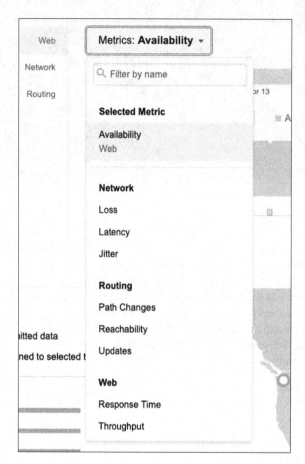

Figure 6-2   *View Metrics*

The Views page also enables you to go back in time to view past test data, as shown in Figure 6-3. The ThousandEyes UI will hold test data for up to 30 days. Moving your mouse pointer to a specific time on the timeline enables you to focus on past or present data and see what has occurred over time.

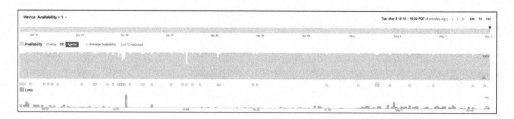

Figure 6-3   *Views History*

Understanding Network Monitoring

Now that you have learned how to configure tests (Chapter 3), alerts (Chapter 4), and dashboards (Chapter 5), you are ready to focus on the data that you get back from the tests and how this data correlates to the alerts and is viewable in the dashboard. We will explore how to monitor and troubleshoot these issues and anomalies.

Let's start with a quiz: What do LAN and WAN stand for?

Most people will answer that LAN means local-area network and WAN means wide-area network. This is technically accurate. However, for those who have spent any time working on operational issues, such as inside a network operations center (NOC), LAN could mean late at night and WAN may mean weekends and nights.

In terms of network monitoring, the following are key questions to consider:

- What is an effective way to monitor networks?

- What if you don't own or have control over the entire path?

- Is there a difference approach for monitoring LAN segments versus monitoring WAN segments?

Traditionally, leveraging SNMP and flow data, and perhaps even packet captures (when necessary), is an effective means of gathering metrics for networks (both LAN and WAN) for which you control the entire path. However, if your users are crossing the Internet, this model presents gaps in your data collection. Network engineers find themselves doing the one thing that irritates them the most, troubleshooting without data. When management asks what's causing a particular performance problem, the best they can answer is, "it's not our network." Saying this is much like saying "it's not my fault." While this is likely technically accurate, management usually leans on the network team to "figure it out" and own this issue until it is resolved, regardless of whose fault it may or may not be.

Here is the good news: ThousandEyes approaches all the different types of networks with the same troubleshooting methodology, regardless of whether it is a LAN, WAN, SD-WAN, or Direct Internet Access (DIA) network. There may be secondary tests that apply more to some network architectures than others, but the troubleshooting methodology remains very much the same.

Monitoring is very much like troubleshooting. The biggest difference with monitoring is that you begin before the problem starts.

To compare the difference between traditional troubleshooting and ThousandEyes troubleshooting, consider a scenario in which you deploy an engineer (who is proficient at protocol analysis) on site to one of your organization's branch offices to troubleshoot an issue, knowing only that users are complaining about poor performance when using several applications.

Once on site, the engineer does the following:

1. Connects to the local network to see if the issue can be duplicated by accessing the applications in question.

2. While testing the application, begins testing the network using the following methods:

   ■ Continuous ping to the URLs, noting if issues exist with DNS, latency, and loss

   ■ Traceroute to the URLs to determine the path taken

   ■ Packet captures of tests

   If the issue is intermittent, this can take time. If it is continuous, then this can take only one attempt to gather the relevant data.

3. Analyzes the packet capture and reports the results.

Instead of dispatching an engineer in this scenario, suppose that you leverage your ThousandEyes Enterprise Agent located at the site in question to troubleshoot the issue. (Ideally, this agent has already been monitoring and has established a baseline of how things were performing initially.) The following is the remote troubleshooting (or monitoring) process of the ThousandEyes Enterprise Agent:

1. Uses the local network and DNS to access the applications in question.

2. Tests the following end-to-end metrics to see how the network, server, and application are performing:

   ■ Page Load Times

   ■ Errors

   ■ Timeouts

   ■ Completions

   ■ Availability & Response Time

      ☐ DNS

      ☐ Connect

      ☐ SSL

      ☐ Wait

   ■ Throughput

   ■ Packet Loss

   ■ Latency

   ■ Jitter (note, metric is only relevant to voice/video UDP traffic, but it is collected regardless of application)

3. Performs path visualization using the same protocol as the application (e.g., TCP 443) to perform traceroute. This allows hop-by-hop analysis for metrics such as

- Forwarding Loss

- Latency

- Path MTU Discovery

- DSCP Changes

- MPLS Tunnels

4. Analyzes all packets associated with server, application, and network testing. Results are uploaded to ThousandEyes on the interval that is selected in the test configuration.

Let's spend some time looking into these metrics and understanding them better. From the Views page in the UI, select a specific test to monitor and gather metrics from, and then select a metric from the Metrics drop-down menu (shown previously in Figure 6-2).

When running a basic HTTP Server test in ThousandEyes, three tests are actually being performed.

System/Application Testing

First, there is the server/application portion where the agent initiates **curl** to access the target URL. This creates a DNS query to the configured DNS servers (ideally, the same DNS servers used by the local users) to resolve the target URL to one or more (such as with CDN) IP addresses. Then the agent creates a TCP connection (3-way handshake) to the IP address returned by the DNS server. Once the connection is established, SSL is negotiated between the agent and its target, over this same TCP connection, before any data can be sent or received. The only data sent in this scenario is an HTTP GET command, which results in the home page being returned along with the HTTP code (usually a 200/300 series). Performance is recorded for each of these steps. If the total transaction takes over 5 seconds (default), the test reports an availability error. Figure 6-4 shows the DNS response time for the Meraki Hybrid agent taking over 3 seconds to resolve. Additional DNS tests can be run to determine if there are network issues between the agent and its DNS server, or if there is a larger DNS issue upstream.

End-to-End Network Testing

The second test, which is run in conjunction with the first test, is the end-to-end network test. By default, this test runs over the same TCP port that is used to test availability and response times. When analyzing "the network" to see if it is impacting user operations/applications, focus on packet loss and latency. Those are the only two metrics that will directly impact the user experience when it comes to TCP/IP applications. When analyzing voice and video (to include collaboration applications), consider jitter as well. However, jitter has no impact on TCP performance. The test shown in Figure 6-5 adds packet loss and latency to the response time and availability metrics. This allows a very quick reference between performance degradation (increases to response time) and network spikes. If performance degrades but the network has not changed, then it is not the network impacting performance.

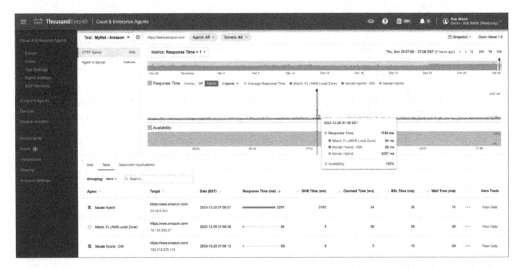

Figure 6-4 *HTTP Response Time Metrics*

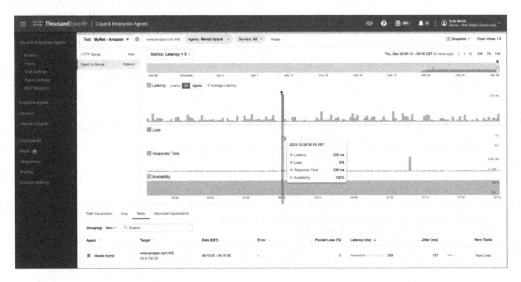

Figure 6-5 *Network and Availability Metrics*

This test consists of sending 50 packets to the target at the beginning of each test round and expecting 50 responses. Packet loss, latency, and jitter are all calculated based on these 50 packets. The results are presented on a timeline, with a timeslot representing each individual test round. Network Agent to Server tests include the ability to spread the packets out when testing at 1-minute intervals. When this interval is selected, there is an option on the Advanced Settings tab that can be enabled to provide end-to-end testing at one packet every 1 second.

Hop-by-Hop Network Testing (Path Visualization)

The third test is what ThousandEyes refers to as *path visualization*. This test shows the network path (or paths) between the agent and its target. Figure 6-6 shows the Views page with the Path Visualization tab circled for easy reference. This is accomplished by running a traceroute-style test (TTL = 1 and increments to discover Layer 3 hops along the route). By default, this test will run using the same protocol/port combination that is used to test availability and end-to-end network metrics. The only difference is that it relies on ICMP Type 11 Code 0, Time-to-Live Exceeded in Transit. This is how each Layer 3 device (router) communicates back to the sending host (agent). This is the message that tells the agent that the router sending this message discarded a packet because the TTL value of 1 would not allow it to forward the packet to the next hop in its routing table. This type of testing allows responses from routers that are not controlled by the customer. In the case of Figures 6-6 and 6-7, the Internet path is shown between a ThousandEyes Cloud Agent located in Seattle, WA, and the target for Office365 Login, login.live.com.

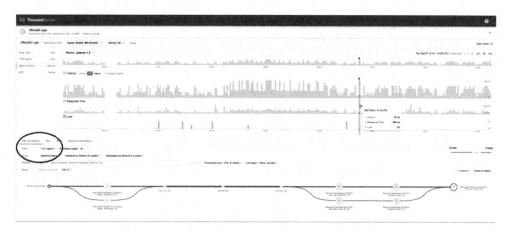

Figure 6-6   *Network Latency = 40 ms*

Figures 6-6 and 6-7 show response times and latency spiking intermittently. Figure 6-6 shows 40 ms of network latency to reach login.live.com hosted by Microsoft in Portland, Oregon, whereas Figure 6-7 shows network latency of 262 ms to reach login.live.com hosted by Microsoft in Tokyo, Japan.

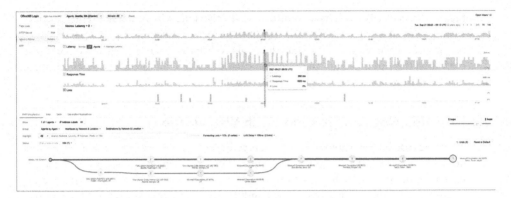

Figure 6-7   *Network Latency = 262 ms*

One tip to improve network path visualization is to increase the number of path traces from the default of 3 (see Figure 6-8). This provides the potential to discover if more than three alternative equal-cost paths exist, while also increasing the potential for witnessing where packet loss may be occurring. This option will be located either on the Basic Configuration tab or the Advanced Settings tab when configuring a test, depending on the test type being configured. Test optimization is further explored in Chapter 9, "Best Practices: Test Optimization, Collaboration, and Stories from the Field."

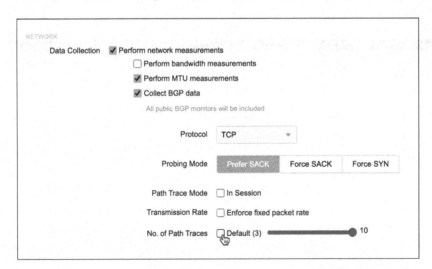

Figure 6-8   *Editing No. of Path Traces Setting*

One significant difference between end-to-end network testing and hop-by-hop (path visualization) network testing is in the way loss is reported. In the end-to-end test, packet loss is reported because replies were not received for all 50 packets sent. However, in the hop-by-hop test, forwarding loss is reported. The metric is named Forwarding Loss because the router reporting the loss was unable to forward packets to the next hop in its routing table. This could be due to several factors, including an overloaded outbound interface, a circuit down, the next hop being overloaded on its inbound interface, or the next hop being down completely. It is not uncommon to see a router start showing forwarding loss when the next hop is a firewall that has had a policy change implemented that disrupts the ability to reach the intended target.

Figure 6-9 shows end-to-end packet loss of around 15%. Note on the left side of the Path Visualization tab that the Miami agent has turned from green to orange. The router, 202.84.253.85, is reporting 32% forwarding loss. This is because it was unable to forward 12 of the 37 packets it attempted to send to its next hop for test completion in this particular test round.

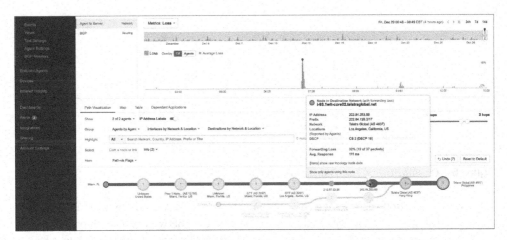

Figure 6-9   *End-to-End Packet Loss and Hop-by-Hop Forwarding Loss*

Another difference between end-to-end tests and hop-by-hop tests is in latency measurements. End-to-end tests use either Selective Acknowledgements (SACK) or the TCP 3-way handshake (SYN) to test latency. The target host will receive out-of-order data segments, forcing immediate SACK responses. If SYN is in use, then sending a SYN to the target forces an immediate SYN/ACK or RST. Any of these responses provides an accurate metric for network latency that has eliminated TCP Delay ACK as well as system/application response time issues. The hop-by-hop tests use low TTL values to force routers to discard packets and generate an ICMP response, as noted earlier. While these responses are generally produced sub-millisecond, it is possible for the ICMP response to take longer when there is a load on a given router. The end-to-end test might not be impacted, while the hop-by-hop test shows a link with higher than normal latency. The end-to-end test shows the metrics that are most related to user performance and are generally considered the benchmark for alerting. The hop-by-hop metrics can be monitored for capacity planning, but are primarily a concern only when end-to-end tests show significant loss or latency.

One area of the Views page that is often overlooked but contains additional information is the Info section (just above the network path and to the right of Click a Node or Link). The expanded Info section in Figure 6-10 shows that there are links that have Multiprotocol Label Switching (MPLS) headers associated with them as well as routers that are remarking DSCP values. While neither of these details is significant in this example, suppose you were troubleshooting a voice issue where the traffic should have been marked EF. In that scenario, the Info section would be a helpful tool that could show you how your traffic was marked all the way through the network.

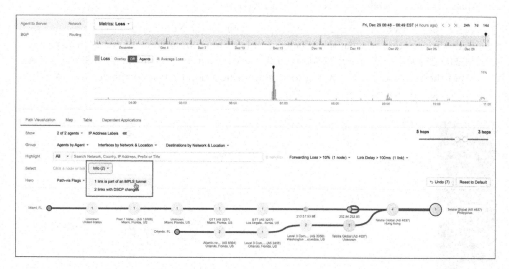

Figure 6-10   *Additional Information on Path Visualization Tab*

If for some reason you do not want to (or are unable to) use your router to mark certain test traffic with relevant DSCP values, you can configure network tests with predetermined values at the agent on a per-test basis. Figure 6-11 shows where DSCP values have changed in the network path. These highlighted sections are the result of selecting Links with DSCP Changes under Info in Figure 6-10. After you have selected an item in the Info section, you can clear it either by clicking it again or by clicking the **Clear Selection** hyperlink just to the right of the Info selector.

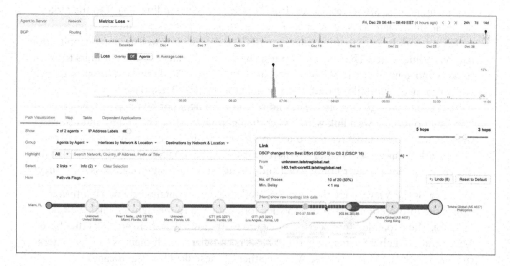

Figure 6-11   *DSCP Changes in Path*

Another way to obtain information in the Path Visualization tab is to hover your mouse pointer over individual agents in the network path, as shown in Figure 6-12. All of the information shown in Figure 6-12 is of value, but pay close attention to the TCP MSS and Min. Path MTU (Layer 3 Maximum Transmission Unit) fields. The Path MTU field shows if there are any packet-size restrictions in the path to the destination. A typical network has a 1500-byte MTU. Only when tunneling is present should the MTU be less than that. The TCP MSS value should be the MTU less the TCP and the IP headers (which are typically 20 bytes each). So, a very common MTU is 1500 bytes with a TCP MSS of 1460 bytes. As with most things networking, your mileage may vary. However, if it does vary on your enterprise network, you should understand why.

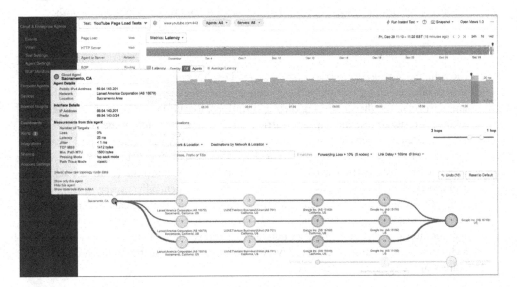

Figure 6-12 *Path Visualization Additional Details*

When delving into the analysis of data within the Path Visualization tool, consider the following pointers to expedite issue detection:

■ **Agent status:** Green signifies optimal conditions, while a gradient toward red indi-cates escalating severity of packet loss. Intermediate colors denote varying degrees of agent metric performance.

■ **Node status:** Nodes may appear light blue, indicating successful IP identification. Hovering over a node reveals details (as shown in Figure 6-9). Alternatively, white nodes are unidentifiable, often caused either by firewalls blocking ICMP type 3 or 11 or by access lists impeding data reception. The prerequisites for proper Path Visualization have been provided under the agent configuration portion of this book. Colorized nodes, like those shown in Figure 6-12, are there to help visualize the networks local to the agent and the target, facilitating swift identification of ISP handoffs. Nodes experiencing loss are outlined in red.

- **Routing anomalies:** In addition to providing insights into node-to-node loss (as shown in Figure 6-9), the Path Visualization tool exposes routing irregularities, such as potential loops.

SD-WAN Performance Monitoring

Monitoring/testing of SD-WAN traffic can be subdivided into monitoring/testing the network overlay (i.e., the path or paths users take to access data) and monitoring/testing the network underlay (i.e., the path or paths the tunnel takes). Overlay is the path the users take to access data, generally through a tunnel. Underlay is the path the tunnel takes to create the secure overlay network. ThousandEyes can and should be used to monitor both.

Network Overlay

The primary purpose of overlay testing in an SD-WAN environment (or over any type of network tunnel, for that matter) is to emulate the user's experience (both availability and performance) when accessing their applications. Recall the scenario of sending an engineer on site to test and capture traffic related to a performance issue. To properly do that, the engineer needs to test the same applications, in the same manner, and have the test traffic traverse the network the same way as the user traffic. If the users are accessing an application by a particular URL and traversing the tunnel into the cloud or back to the data center, then the test needs to do the same thing. So, generally, overlay testing can be as simple as configuring the onsite Enterprise Agent to test the critical applications the users will be accessing. Additionally, Network Agent to Server tests can be configured to only monitor loss, latency, and jitter between locations. Figure 6-13 shows an example of such a test. It is monitoring the overlay network between the Seattle data center and an IP address in the Chicago branch office.

Note that the path MTU changes between the routers, which likely is an indication that a tunnel exists.

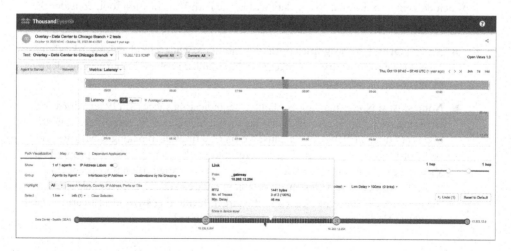

Figure 6-13 *SD-WAN Overlay Test*

Network Underlay

When performance issues (loss, latency, or jitter) are noted on an overlay network and the network is the cause, then it is important to also have end-to-end and path visualization data for the underlay network. Again, this is the network that the tunnel uses to transport data between locations (in this example, between Seattle and Chicago). If a router is dropping data in the underlay, traffic in the overlay will be impacted. If latency has increased due to an inefficient path being taken between sites, the overlay may show increased latency but will not show why the latency has increased.

Figure 6-14 shows underlay monitoring between the Seattle data center and both AT&T and Quest edge routers at the Chicago branch office. ThousandEyes is fully capable of testing any path customers are able to route traffic across. At times, specific configurations may be required such as policy-based routing (PBR) and/or static network address translation (NAT). The requirements are entirely dependent upon the customer's network architecture and how it routes traffic.

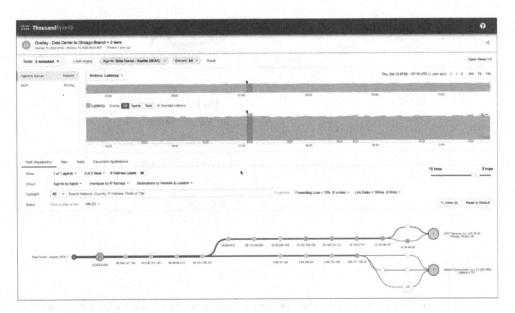

Figure 6-14 *SD-WAN Underlay Tests*

If a customer is unable to achieve underlay testing between locations, that does not mean the customer cannot monitor the most critical components associated with this path. Customers can always leverage ThousandEyes Cloud Agents to test from a location and/or provider to their site edge routers. Although this might not cover 100 percent of the underlay path, it does cover the ISPs and BGP advertisements that are absolutely critical to successful SD-WAN deployments. The Cisco and ThousandEyes solutions engineers responsible for your account are available to help you make the best choice for any particular architecture needs.

MPLS Performance Monitoring

Given that many ISPs employ MPLS, it is crucial from a network perspective to delve into the underlying structure and comprehend its impact on both employee and customer experiences. While we've discussed path visualization, it's pertinent to highlight some nuances when examining MPLS technology.

ThousandEyes has the capability to discern various MPLS tunnel types, including Explicit, Implicit, and Opaque, shown in Figures 6-15 through 6-17, respectively:

■ **Explicit tunnel:** This type of MPLS tunnel, where configurations are transparent and not obscured by router settings, is presented comprehensively. The visualization includes links between each hop in an MPLS network, showcasing label information. When an MPLS hop is detected, the quick selection link identifies links within MPLS networks, revealing label stacks upon hovering over the affected link, as shown in Figure 6-15.

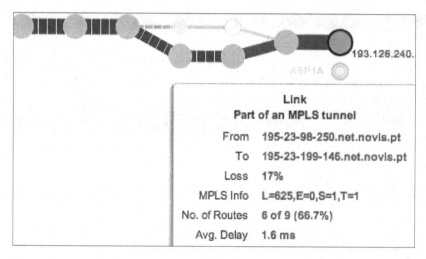

Figure 6-15 *Explicit Tunnel in Path Visualization*

■ **Implicit tunnel:** In cases where devices are set up not to transmit MPLS stack entries, ThousandEyes can still deduce that the link is part of an MPLS tunnel. It attempts to infer the hop number of the tunnel, represented in the ThousandEyes app as "Hop X in an MPLS tunnel" (e.g., "Hop 2 in an MPLS tunnel" in Figure 6-16). Although label information might be unavailable due to provider router configurations, the source IPs of the transit network can aid service providers in cross-referencing the externally visible map with internal documentation to ascertain the actual path.

■ **Opaque tunnel:** When encountering a single MPLS label but with the IP TTL (Time to Live) reset at the ingress router, ThousandEyes represents the single hop as an "X-hop MPLS tunnel" (e.g., "7-hop MPLS tunnel" in Figure 6-17). This information proves useful in diagnosing network connectivity issues during transit through a service provider's network, especially when some hops are obscured from the path visualization output, potentially leading to an incorrect inference of a one-hop transit across the MPLS network.

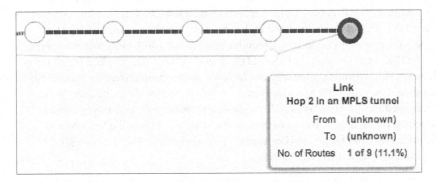

Figure 6-16 *Implicit Tunnel in Path Visualization*

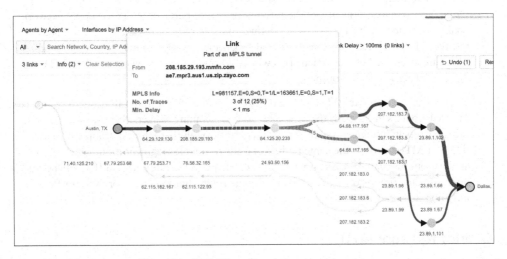

Figure 6-17 *Opaque Tunnel in Path Visualization*

MTU Best Practices

Maximum Transmission Unit (MTU) issues can lead to performance and reliability issues that are difficult to isolate. Determining the root cause of MTU issues often comes down to three things:

- Defining and standardizing MTUs in the network architecture

- Implementing those standards

- Confirming those standards were implemented properly

This is why it is highly recommended to architect MTUs by defining one consistent MTU for all overlay tunnels throughout the entire network and another for underlay networks throughout the entire network. On a single enterprise network, every tunnel should be set to the same MTU. Ideally, Path MTU Discovery (PMTUD) is operational in the environment (ICMP Type 3 Code 4 messages are allowed). Whether it is or not, a consistent MTU should be defined and built into each tunnel interface as a standard practice. As an example, if one interface requires an MTU of 1400, but another requires an MTU of 1372, then the smaller of the MTUs should become the standard for all interfaces. However, the justification for why the MTUs would require different values in the first place should be fully understood. An example might be that different encryption methods are used for different tunnels. Regardless, the smallest required value should be implemented throughout the organization as the standard. This will allow systems and applications to avoid fragmentation issues if they do not use PMTUD (DF [Don't Fragment] bit = 0) or have PMTUD blocked.

The underlay should be treated the same way. Although the underlay may require different MTUs than the overlay, all underlay links should relay on the same MTU value. If this is something other than 1500, the smallest value should be selected as the standard. Often, underlay networks utilize the Internet or a third-party provider to supply network connectivity, in which case MTUs are defined outside of your organization. In this case, testing MTUs between locations is critical. Adapting the edge routers to use the smallest MTU might be the best approach. This will avoid fragmentation when different MTUs are discovered across a common path.

If a system does not use PMTUD, then it likely has the DF bit in the IP header set to 0. This tells routers in the path that it is okay to fragment any packets that are larger than the MTU on an interface to make the packets fit through that interface/tunnel. If two different MTUs exist in the same path, this leads to double fragmentation, which some applications may fail to reassemble. Likewise, having MTU values that differ depending upon the direction of traffic can lead to strange fragmentation issues or even traffic failing to be delivered at all.

Overlay Network MTU

Figure 6-18 shows an overlay test running between Agent 1 and Agent 2. From Agent 1 to Agent 2 (source to target) the MTU is 1362. However, when testing from Agent 2 back to Agent 1 (target to source), the MTU is 1363. These MTUs should be set to the same value.

Figure 6-19 shows what happens when Agent 2 sends data, in this case ping requests, to Agent 1 at each of those MTU values. Keep in mind, Agent 2 believes (because of PMTUD) that the MTU to Agent 1 is 1363. In packets 5646 through 5718, we see pings (Echo request) with a total length (Layer 3) of 1362 being replied to with Echo replies, also with a length of 1362. However, beginning with packet 6301, we see an Echo Request with a length of 1363 being issued, which results in a fragmented reply where the first packet is 1362 in length. This is because Agent 1 believes the MTU to Agent 2 is set to 1362.

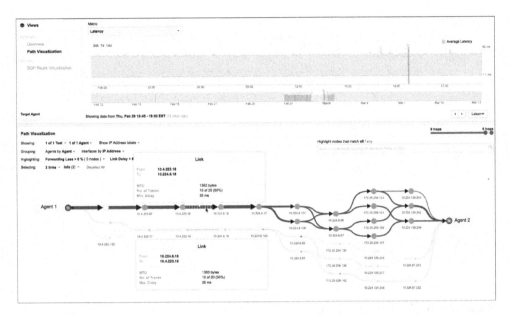

Figure 6-18 *Bidirectional Paths with MTUs*

No.	Time	Source	Destination	Protocol	IP Length	Info
5650	0.000216	10.4.220.15	10.224.96.126	ICMP	1362	Echo (ping) request id=0x7e1f, seq=20614/34384, ttl=64 (reply in 5701)
5651	0.000341	10.4.220.15	10.224.96.126	ICMP	1362	Echo (ping) request id=0xd927, seq=13503/48948, ttl=64 (reply in 5682)
5663	0.004499	10.4.220.15	10.224.96.126	ICMP	1362	Echo (ping) request id=0xd2d6, seq=55055/4055, ttl=64 (reply in 5714)
5666	0.000659	10.4.220.15	10.224.96.126	ICMP	1362	Echo (ping) request id=0x078a, seq=52147/46027, ttl=64 (reply in 5691)
5667	0.002824	10.4.220.15	10.224.96.126	ICMP	1362	Echo (ping) request id=0x6c81, seq=43735/55210, ttl=64 (reply in 5705)
5668	0.000212	10.4.220.15	10.224.96.126	ICMP	1362	Echo (ping) request id=0x2371, seq=38629/58774, ttl=64 (reply in 5718)
5670	0.000224	10.4.220.15	10.224.96.126	ICMP	1362	Echo (ping) request id=0xfb87, seq=54814/7894, ttl=64 (reply in 5706)
5682	0.028690	10.224.96.126	10.4.220.15	ICMP	1362	Echo (ping) reply id=0xd927, seq=13503/48948, ttl=55 (request in 5651)
5683	0.000342	10.224.96.126	10.4.220.15	ICMP	1362	Echo (ping) reply id=0x2307, seq=50470/9925, ttl=55 (request in 5648)
5691	0.004913	10.224.96.126	10.4.220.15	ICMP	1362	Echo (ping) reply id=0x078a, seq=52147/46027, ttl=55 (request in 5666)
5694	0.000206	10.224.96.126	10.4.220.15	ICMP	1362	Echo (ping) reply id=0xc586, seq=12862/15922, ttl=55 (request in 5646)
5700	0.001683	10.224.96.126	10.4.220.15	ICMP	1362	Echo (ping) reply id=0x7f8b, seq=26058/51813, ttl=55 (request in 5649)
5701	0.000096	10.224.96.126	10.4.220.15	ICMP	1362	Echo (ping) reply id=0x7e1f, seq=20614/34384, ttl=55 (request in 5650)
5705	0.000674	10.224.96.126	10.4.220.15	ICMP	1362	Echo (ping) reply id=0x6c81, seq=43735/55210, ttl=55 (request in 5667)
5706	0.000009	10.224.96.126	10.4.220.15	ICMP	1362	Echo (ping) reply id=0xfb87, seq=54814/7894, ttl=55 (request in 5670)
5714	0.004032	10.224.96.126	10.4.220.15	ICMP	1362	Echo (ping) reply id=0xd2d6, seq=55055/4055, ttl=55 (request in 5663)
5718	0.004172	10.224.96.126	10.4.220.15	ICMP	1362	Echo (ping) reply id=0x2371, seq=38629/58774, ttl=55 (request in 5668)
6301	4.030640	10.224.96.126	10.4.220.15	ICMP	1363	Echo (ping) request id=0xac96, seq=37050/47760, ttl=55 (reply in 6302)
6302	0.010034	10.4.220.15	10.224.96.126	ICMP	1356	Echo (ping) reply id=0xac96, seq=37050/47760, ttl=64 (request in 6301)
6303	0.000017	10.4.220.15	10.224.96.126	IPv4	27	Fragmented IP protocol (proto=ICMP 1, off=1336, ID=5094)
6304	0.000731	10.224.96.126	10.4.220.15	ICMP	1363	Echo (ping) request id=0xe2c3, seq=59386/64231, ttl=55 (reply in 6305)
6305	0.000011	10.4.220.15	10.224.96.126	ICMP	1356	Echo (ping) reply id=0xe2c3, seq=59386/64231, ttl=64 (request in 6304)
6306	0.000015	10.4.220.15	10.224.96.126	IPv4	27	Fragmented IP protocol (proto=ICMP 1, off=1336, ID=5095)
6307	0.001840	10.224.96.126	10.4.220.15	ICMP	1363	Echo (ping) request id=0xf295, seq=56394/19164, ttl=55 (reply in 6308)
6308	0.000009	10.4.220.15	10.224.96.126	ICMP	1356	Echo (ping) reply id=0xf295, seq=56394/19164, ttl=64 (request in 6307)
6309	0.000014	10.4.220.15	10.224.96.126	IPv4	27	Fragmented IP protocol (proto=ICMP 1, off=1336, ID=5096)
6310	0.000740	10.224.96.126	10.4.220.15	ICMP	1363	Echo (ping) request id=0x89c3, seq=54138/31443, ttl=55 (reply in 6311)
6311	0.000011	10.4.220.15	10.224.96.126	ICMP	1356	Echo (ping) reply id=0x89c3, seq=54138/31443, ttl=64 (request in 6310)
6312	0.000015	10.4.220.15	10.224.96.126	IPv4	27	Fragmented IP protocol (proto=ICMP 1, off=1336, ID=5097)

```
Frame 6302: 1370 bytes on wire (10960 bits), 128 bytes captured (1024 bits)
Ethernet II, Src: VMware_ab:1f:f4 (00:50:56:ab:1f:f4), Dst: 02:00:00:ff:52:10 (02:00:00:ff:52:10)
Internet Protocol Version 4, Src: 10.4.220.15 (10.4.220.15), Dst: 10.224.96.126 (10.224.96.126)
Internet Control Message Protocol
```

Figure 6-19 *Packet-Level Fragmentation*

Figure 6-20 shows the path from Agents 1 and 2 to a Microsoft Active Directory server. One path has an MTU of 1371 while the other path has an MTU of 1362. Once again, standardizing on the smallest required MTU would not only simplify the process of defining the architecture but also simplify implementing and troubleshooting it.

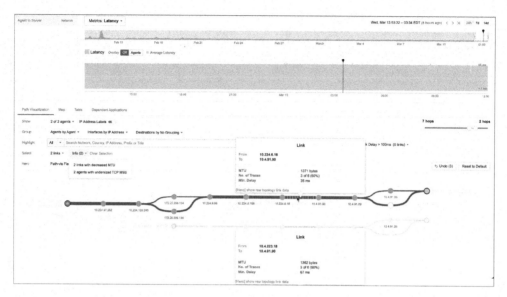

Figure 6-20   *MTU: Agents to Server*

Underlay Network MTU

Figure 6-21 shows the underlay path from Agent 1 to a public IP address on a router located at the site of Agent 2. In this path, one MTU is set to 1492 as it leaves the customer network and enters the Internet. Later, another MTU is set to 1476 as it arrives at its destination. If the underlay requires an MTU of 1476, all non-default (1500) MTU interfaces should share the value of 1476 (or whatever is the smallest required MTU for your company's underlay network).

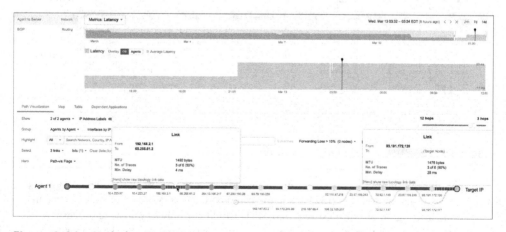

Figure 6-21   *Underlay PMTUD × 2*

In summary, it is highly recommended that these MTU values be applied consistently across both the overlay and underlay networks (each having its own value). Once standardized MTUs are in place, ThousandEyes can be configured to alert about any MTUs that are smaller than the standards chosen.

Alerting

Figure 6-22 shows an example of how an overlay alert rule could be created to identify whether any MTU other than 1362 is discovered on the network. This would be ideal to help in change validation to ensure the correct MTUs are implemented. Note that you would not want to deploy this alert rule on any test that is either running in the underlay or not going through an overlay tunnel. Make sure you only include tests and agents that will be impacted by the smaller MTU. If you have agents configured in the test that will stay at 1500 bytes, you will need to include or exclude agents from this alert, whichever is easier for your implementation.

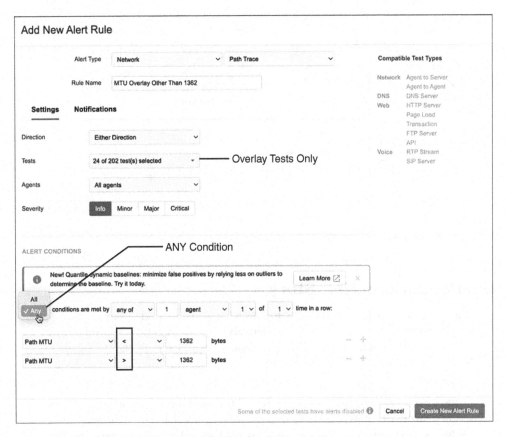

Figure 6-22 *Alert On Overlay MTU if Value Is Not 1362*

Figure 6-23 shows an example of alerting on underlay paths that have an MTU other than 1472.

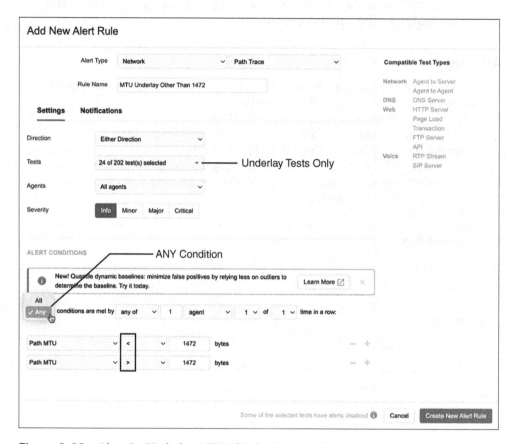

Figure 6-23   *Alert On Underlay MTU if Value Is Not 1472*

Overloaded: An NFL Story

While this story might seem dated by today's technology, we find this exact same workflow repeated in companies that we interact with on a regular basis. Although we did not have ThousandEyes technology available to us at that time, the story covers both the workflow used at the time as well as how to address this situation today using ThousandEyes.

In 2003, we were contracted to work with the IT team of a company hosting a major sports website. The objective was to help the team ensure that they were ready to begin the NFL season, as this company was hosting nfl.com at that time. A couple weeks prior to the start of the NFL regular season, we went on site to provide an assessment of their current (new) architecture and help identify any apparent risks.

The architecture they had designed consisted of four fully mesh-connected Cisco 6000 switches along with two Cisco 6500 switches to provide four 1-Gbps uplinks to their ISP. They had the capability of activating two additional 1-Gbps circuits by simply calling the ISP and asking that they be enabled.

There were somewhere in the neighborhood of 500 servers, each with a 100-Mbps FDX connection into the Cisco switches. There were 16 Brocade ServerIron load balancers, four on each of the Cisco 6000 switches. Each of these were connected by 1-Gbps FDX.

The first thing we discovered were outbound drops on the gig links, mostly on several of the ServerIron load balancers and on the active cross links between the Cisco 6000s. When we asked about how the load was being distributed across the ServerIrons, we were told four (one on each switch) hosted the company's Live Persistent Scoring (LPS) application. Additionally, all servers were spread across all load balancers, with the 140 LPS servers connecting to the four LPS load balancers. They had thought that spreading out the load would provide better redundancy. We explained that they had increased their risk profile by distributing traffic this way. If Switch 4 went down, all servers on that switch would be down, along with all servers connecting to any ServerIron on Switch 4. This was immediately corrected by reconfiguring the servers to use their locally connected load balancer.

This change resulted in lowering the outbound discards that were occurring between the switches. However, we noted an increase in discards on the uplinks to the Internet as well as on the four LPS load balancers. This was an indication that our changes not only lowered the risk profile but also increased throughput, or at least shifted the points of overload.

These output discards were interesting, because while everyone who was working on the project was busy monitoring bandwidth utilization, they were ignoring the discards until we brought them to their attention. Utilization was being measured via SNMP polling a device/interface every 5 minutes, asking "how many bytes did you see?" This is then averaged against "how many bytes could you have seen if you were 100% utilized?" The problem is that if the usage was due to spiking traffic that only occurred once every several minutes, it might not show up in the average utilization over a 5-minute period.

In this case, we were now focused heavily on the LPS application. This application showed the playing field (for every live game), the position of each team on the field, and the play that just happened. This customer had an interesting service level agreement (SLA) with the NFL that stated they would show the play on the user's application within 30 seconds of the play happening on the field. If you are not familiar with how an American (NFL) football game is executed, there is a brief flurry of activity every several minutes. On the app, that activity is pushed out to the users and then the connections go idle until the next play. Utilization on any of these switch ports was only showing up around 20 to 30 percent max. However, the discards we were seeing clearly indicated that certain interfaces were being overloaded. By the way, this is a good way to monitor for microburst traffic if you are concerned with overloading circuits.

On the opening weekend of the NFL season, we saw our discard count increase by several million. This was clearly impacting the application's capability to deliver the required data to the users. When we discussed the details of this architecture with the director of operations, he was very concerned, as he had just gotten (and used) a $2M budget to overhaul their hosting architecture, and now we were telling him the application was at (or over) capacity.

Next, we asked about slowing down the application's delivery. We pulled in the lead programmer responsible for this application. After we showed him what we were dealing with, we asked if there was a way to inject a slight delay between users so that not all 500,000+ users would be updated at once. We came up with an idea to group users. The goal was to use variables, to allow for future tuning, in the group size and in the delay between updating the groups.

This change took several weeks to build, test, and implement. After the implementation, the default values were 500 users per group and 1-ms delay between groups. Prior to this change, the four ServerIron load balancers and the four 1-Gbps uplinks to the Internet would total several million discards every Sunday afternoon during the NFL games. After the change was implemented using default values, the discarded packets on the first Sunday went down to only a few thousand.

This analysis was all done by using SNMP and packet captures. We had no way of measuring actual user performance/impact. Today, we would happily leverage a ThousandEyes HTTP Server test to monitor the effects of overloaded interfaces accessing the Live Persistent Scoring application. This would easily show us when packet loss is occurring and which applications were being impacted. ThousandEyes can even test on a 1-minute interval and have Cloud and Enterprise Agents send 1 packet per second in a continuous stream if desired. Cloud Agents could easily make these measurements from all over the United States, or even globally if needed.

As described earlier in this chapter, deploying ThousandEyes agents is like deploying engineers to various locations. The agent's job is to test, collect, and analyze the data relevant to the application and network targeted. They connect to the application and test DNS, network connectivity, SSL, and wait and receive times. They test the network both end to end and hop by hop, and they analyze their own packets throughout this effort. Then, whether the results are good or bad, they upload the report to the ThousandEyes portal, where it is *much* easier to read than packet analysis ever was.

Today, ThousandEyes lets us work smarter. We can now cover more applications, more traffic volume, and do it more often than we ever could before. Why? Because we can deploy these synthetic engineers to do the bulk of our work for us.

Review Questions

Answer the following questions. Check your answers against those provided in Appendix A, "Answers to Review Questions."

1. If an outage occurred at your company while you were on vacation, can you go back and view the data to see what transpired?

2. Can you see your network handoff to the ISP? Can you see the BGP routes?

3. Can you see latency or loss between two nodes that are not in your network?

4. What is the difference between the MSS and the MTU?

Chapter 7

Scripted Synthetic User Testing with Transaction Tests

In the landscape of testing methodologies, ThousandEyes Transaction tests carve out a distinct space, offering versatility from the fundamental to the highly intricate, tailored to the intricacies of specific use cases. This test type provides a unique feature where users can navigate from the basic to the complex. Transaction tests are scripted synthetic user interactions, from clicking a login, adding credentials, to maybe navigating through different web pages. This allows for more advanced customization to monitor the user experience compared to traditional web layer testing.

One notable feature of Transaction tests is their adaptability to different skill sets. Whether you prefer the simplicity of basic configurations or the complexity of delving into sophisticated scenarios, Transaction tests cater to a spectrum of testing needs. Transaction tests often become an admin's tool of choice because they enable comprehensive evaluations for a variety of web applications.

Furthermore, Transaction tests embrace a coding dimension, allowing administrators to wield the power of Selenium seamlessly woven into JavaScript. This integration provides a robust foundation for administrators who are inclined toward a coding-centric approach, adding a layer of flexibility and depth to their testing strategies.

However, the beauty of Transaction tests lies not just in catering to seasoned programmers but also in providing an inclusive space for non-programmers. The ThousandEyes Recorder is a user-friendly platform that beckons those who are not versed in traditional programming languages to dabble in coding. The Recorder offers an intuitive interface, breaking down barriers and making transaction testing accessible to a broader audience.

In this chapter, we journey through the intricacies of Transaction tests, exploring varied applications, code-driven capabilities, and the interactive ThousandEyes Recorder as well as the built-in Integrated Development Envionment (IDE). Whether you are a seasoned coder or someone new to the world of programming, Transaction tests unfold a realm of possibilities for enhancing your testing endeavors.

What Is Selenium?

Selenium is a scripting language that can mimic a user experience through a web page. Selenium has quite a few parts that may be useful when creating Transaction tests. Understanding the basics of Selenium will enable you to know when to use a certain function:

- **Browser automation:** Selenium is an open source automated testing framework used primarily for web, or browser, applications. It provides a set of tools and APIs that allow developers to automate web browser interactions, such as clicking buttons, filling forms, and navigating through web pages. ThousandEyes provides a wrapper for the Selenium WebDriver library that can be used in Transaction tests.

  As web applications are accessed through various browsers, Selenium's compatibility with multiple browsers ensures that Transaction tests can be conducted uniformly across different environments. Although this is true for Selenium, the ThousandEyes agents (cloud and enterprise) utilize a BrowserBot based on Chromium to run this type of test.

- **Dynamic content handling:** Modern web applications often involve dynamic content loading and interaction. Selenium's capability to wait for elements to load and handle dynamic content ensures accurate simulation of real user experiences.

- **WebDriver:** The WebDriver acts as a bridge between the Selenium scripts and the web browser. It facilitates communication and control over the browser, allowing the execution of scripted actions.

- **Element interactions:** Through the WebDriver, Selenium interacts with HTML elements on a web page. This interaction includes actions such as clicking buttons, filling forms, or navigating through different pages, replicating user behavior.

The combination of Selenium and the WebDriver in transaction testing within the ThousandEyes platform empowers teams to not only monitor the performance of web applications but also to automate and replicate user interactions effectively. This integration ensures a holistic approach to testing, covering a spectrum of scenarios that users might encounter during their interactions with the web application.

Page Load Test Versus Transaction Test

The number one question about ThousandEyes is, if we can obtain waterfall data from a Page Load test, why would we need to run a scripted test? While the Page Load test provides detailed insights into the performance of web applications and websites from a user's perspective (as described in Chapter 3), it only measures the performance of the destination URL. Page Load tests do not offer the functionality to navigate within a web page or interact with various elements inside that web page.

When end users complain about a web page hanging in a specific area, for example during login or executing a task, a Page Load test can identify whether the latency is caused by the network or by an element within the page. However, it does not provide functionality to navigate within a web page or click various widgets in a page. A Transaction test, on the other hand, enables you to create a script that can navigate just like a user would and then provide metrics back from each step that the user would do. These steps enable the administrator to look at the entire journey to see where the latency lies.

Set Up and Create a Transaction Test with the ThousandEyes Recorder

In this section we will use Cisco.com and navigate to the Solutions section and then click the Technologies section.

From the ThousandEyes UI, navigate to **Cloud & Enterprise Agents > Test Settings** and click the **Add New Test** button. In the New Test section, click the Layer option **Web**, and then click the Test Type option **Transaction**.

Figure 7-1 shows a high-level overview of the Transaction test configuration. Note that the ThousandEyes Recorder is available to download. The Recorder is a handy tool that will record the mouse and keystrokes and then turn them into code. An IDE below the recorder is also available if you want to write the code directly. (The IDE is not shown in Figure 7-1.)

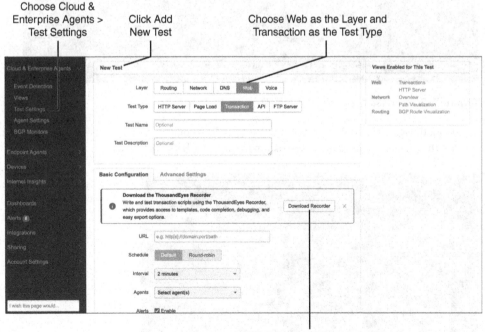

Figure 7-1 *Transaction Test Overview*

Download and open the Recorder, and you'll see quite a few options (see Figure 7-2). Here are the main features:

- **Record button:** The button with the red dot, used to start recording your actions

- **Hourglass icon button:** Enables you to add a **sleep()** method or pause in the script

- **Stopwatch icon button (marker):** Enables you to delineate steps and measure the time taken for each step by identifying where a script section starts and stops

- **Key icon button:** Used to store credentials, such as a username and password, required to log in

- **ThousandEyes icon button:** Provides access to the settings for the recording

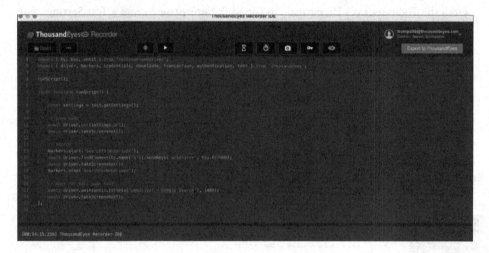

Figure 7-2 *ThousandEyes Recorder/IDE*

Click the Record (red dot) button, and the Start Recording window appears (see Figure 7-3); for this example, enter **https://cisco.com** in the Enter Base URL field.

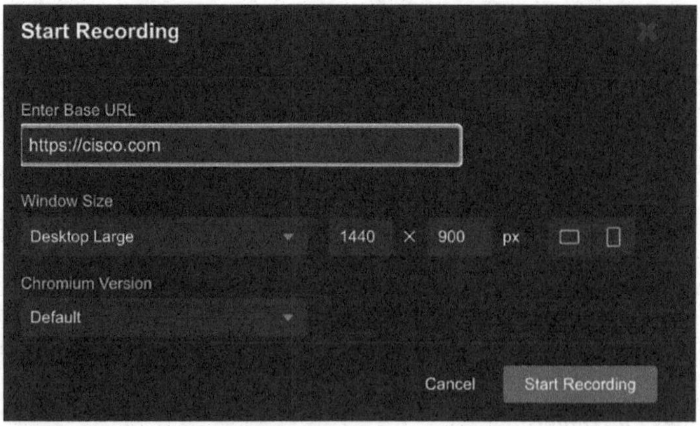

Figure 7-3 *IDE Recording Settings*

The Window Size field enables the administrator to choose the dimensions (width and height) of the browser window in which the test will be executed. It enables you to simulate how your web application behaves in different screen resolutions, which is useful for testing responsiveness and layout across various devices and screen sizes.

The Chromium Version field lets you select the version of the Chromium browser that the test will use. Different versions of Chromium can have different features, security patches, and performance characteristics.

Click the **Start Recording** button, and the Recorder will automatically take you to the website for this example, https://cisco.com, and then navigate to Solutions and then Technologies.

As you navigate through the pages in the browser, performing actions such as clicking links or entering text into input fields, the Recorder records your interactions and automatically generates the corresponding code for the Transaction Script.

Once you have completed the user journey, return to the Recorder and click Stop.

When the recording is done, you can do a couple of things. The first option is to click the Export to ThousandEyes button in the upper-right corner of the Recorder. The other option is to save the script on the local drive. To do this, click the ellipsis button in the upper left of the ThousandEyes Recorder window and choose **Save Script**. For this example, click **Export to ThousandEyes** to export the script to the ThousandEyes UI. In the Test Settings window that opens, name the test in the Test Name field and click the **Agents** drop-down arrow to add the agents that you want to use for the test, as shown in Figure 7-4. For purposes of the https://cisco.com example, name the test **Test12345**.

Click the **Export** button and the Transaction Test will show up in the ThousandEyes UI in the Test Settings (see Figure 7-4). From there, you can manage the test like any other tests. You also have the option to set the intervals and Agent Settings; if you don't, you will be able to do this from the Test Settings in the ThousandEyes UI.

Once the export has happened, notice the code appears in the Transaction Script section, below the alerts, where you can make adjustments at the same time. Reading the code comments enables you to understand the code and decide whether basic adjustments are needed. You can revise the code from the UI just as you were able to in the ThousandEyes Recorder. Figure 7-5 shows the https://cisco.com example in the Test Settings page.

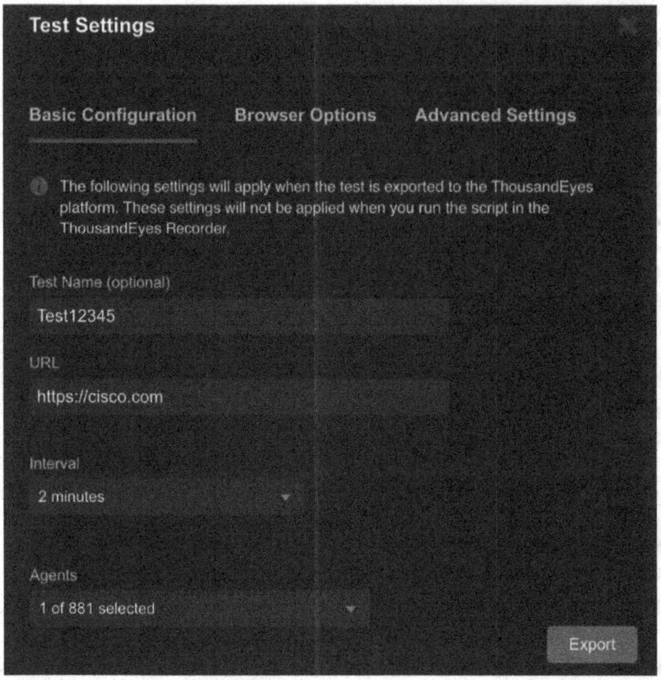

Figure 7-4 *Saving a Transaction Test*

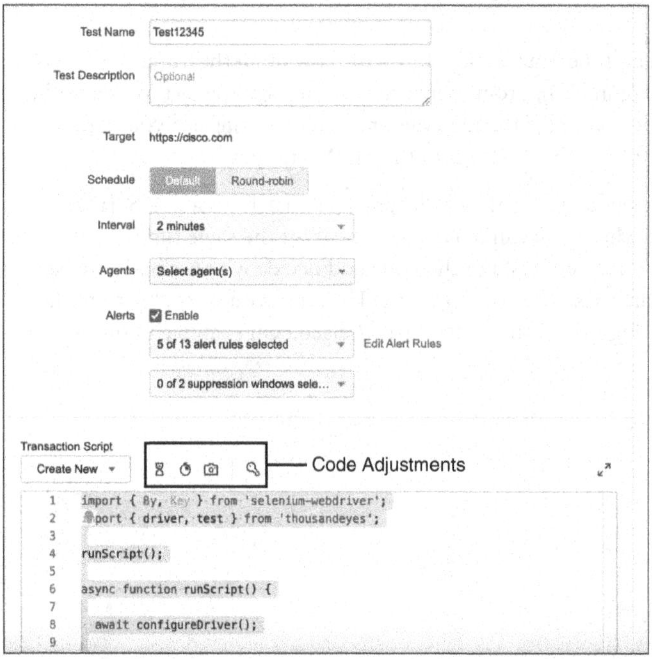

Figure 7-5 *Code Adjustments from ThousandEyes UI*

Most icons look familiar compared to the Recorder; the camera icon enables you to also take snapshots of the scripting process, as discussed in the section, "Transaction Test Script Best Practices."

Experienced coders seeking to import the code can choose **Create New > New from Template** (see Figure 7-6) and import it into the Test Settings. If you need to import into the Recorder you will need to import the script into the Recorder and click **Play** to confirm whether it produces the desired outcome.

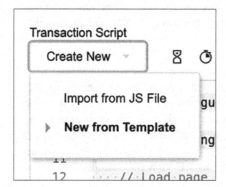

Figure 7-6   *Code Import*

If you prefer to make changes directly in the IDE, you can use the code adjustment tools to do so.

Troubleshooting and Debugging Transaction Test Scripts

We have all encountered issues with routers having incorrect configurations or code executing improperly—there are typical methods available for analysis and cleanup. The ThousandEyes platform is no exception, offering several tools to assist in troubleshooting issues and debugging transaction test scripts. Covering this extensive topic in its entirety is beyond the scope of this chapter, so we will focus on the most effective methods for troubleshooting and debugging scripts. Also keep in mind the Transaction Test is based on a BrowserBot within the Enterprise Agent or Cloud Agent, and this bot uses Chromium. Google Chrome also has developer tools to assist you.

A convenient way to troubleshoot and debug transaction test scripts is to add a function directly to the script in the Transaction Script section of the ThousandEyes IDE. You can look for issues in specific lines of code by adding a logging function. Adding additional functions into the script from the Test Settings directly into the transaction script can help in certain situations.

You can use **console.log** statements to help debug, such as printing the current line number—for example, **console.log(Line 10)**—or printing the value of a variable, such as **console.log(settings.url)**. Utilize the IDE in the recorder for this command or the Chrome Developer tools.

If the script runs successfully in the Recorder but fails during the transaction test on the ThousandEyes platform, check the Transaction Test View window. Look for any error messages displayed in the Table tab.

The **driver.sleep** function, as its name indicates, can slow down the script on certain functions or elements in the web page, enabling you to monitor at a slower rate than running a script at full speed.

Using a screenshot can be a helpful option for troubleshooting. You can add the following function to take a screenshot when you need to know the state of the screen before an action takes place. This function can also be executed using the IDE and clicking the camera icon.

```
await driver.takeScreenshot();
```

As briefly discussed earlier in the chapter, markers enable you to create a starting point and stopping point to measure timing in a specific section of the Transaction Test script. Add the following functions to your script to establish markers. At the same time, from the Views page you will be able to see this in the waterfall table to ensure this portion of the script is indeed working as usual. The waterfall aspect is covered in the upcoming section "Viewing the Transaction Test Data," in which we will view the example Transaction test and examine the metrics of this test type.

```
markers.start
markerts.stop
```

By default, the ThousandEyes Recorder uses CSS identifiers to locate HTML page elements. If you run into issues—for example, you see an error in the test view reporting "unable to locate target element"—try using developer tools to look for the XPath of the target element. (XPath is a query language for selecting nodes from an XML document.)

The following code snippet provides an example:

```
await click(By.xpath(`//*[@id="1_id1:impPost1"]/div/div[3]/input[1]`));
```

For the development tools, we recommend the Google Chrome Developer tools, keeping in mind that the agents are using the Chromium browser.

Note   If the script runs in the Recorder but the Transaction test itself is failing, look at the Transactions view and see if any error messages are displayed in the Table tab.

Transaction Test Script Best Practices

The following are ThousandEyes best practices for ensuring successful Transaction test scripts:

- **Utilize the waitFor function:** Leverage the **waitFor** function in the ThousandEyes JavaScript scripting environment. This function enables you to wait for specific conditions before proceeding with the test, enhancing synchronization.

- **Optimize element locators:** Use efficient CSS or XPath selectors to locate web elements. Prefer using unique identifiers for elements to avoid ambiguity and improve stability.

- **Leverage page initialization functions:** Implement functions for initializing pages to ensure that elements are ready before interacting with them. This helps in handling dynamic content loading.

- **Use the browser.takeScreenshot function:** For debugging purposes, utilize the **browser.takeScreenshot** function to capture screenshots during test execution. This function helps visualize the state of the web page at specific points in the script.

- **Implement logging for debugging:** Integrate logging statements using **console.log** to output information during script execution. This is particularly useful for debugging and understanding the flow of your script.

- **Create modular functions:** Break down your script into smaller modular functions to improve maintainability. This makes it easier to update and troubleshoot specific sections of the script.

- **Use the browser.pause function sparingly:** The **browser.pause** function can be used to pause script execution for debugging. However, use it sparingly to avoid unintended delays in test execution.

- **Ensure cross-browser compatibility:** Consider the cross-browser compatibility of your script. Test your Transaction tests on different browsers to ensure that they work consistently across various environments. From the Advanced Settings tab in the Transaction test, you can choose a specific browser in the User Agent field.

- **Avoid dynamically generated IDs:** Some auto-generated selectors use IDs that appear unique but are dynamically generated and might not persist over time. For example:

```
await driver.findElement(By.css('#tabZoneId278'));
```

The element ID tabZoneId278 is likely dynamically generated and might not remain consistent. CSS selectors are methods of describing elements on a web page, which can include names, categories, IDs, iframes, and so forth. Dynamically generated IDs, like the preceding example, might not provide reliable identification.

Viewing the Transaction Test Data

Assuming that you created the test named Test12345 for the https://cisco.com use case, navigate to **Cloud & Enterprise Agents > Views**, open the **Test** drop-down menu, and select **Test12345**. As shown in Figure 7-7, the Transactions view includes several metrics that should look familiar from Chapter 6. The Transactions view provides more detailed data than the HTTP Server view. You can select the Errors metric to identify any errors in your script that may require troubleshooting.

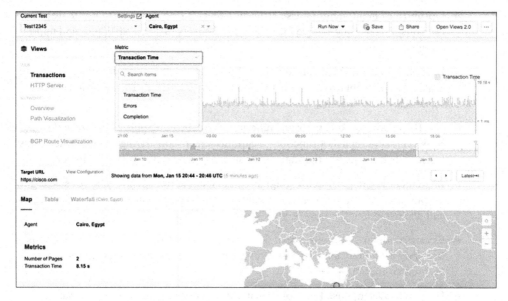

Figure 7-7   *Transactions View*

From the Waterfall tab of the Transactions view, shown in Figure 7-8, you can see the pages the script interacts with as well as the elements in the page. This tab provides a graphical representation of each network request made by the browser to the web page, as well as metrics such as DNS, Connect, and Receive, and gives a total time for the entire page load to fully render.

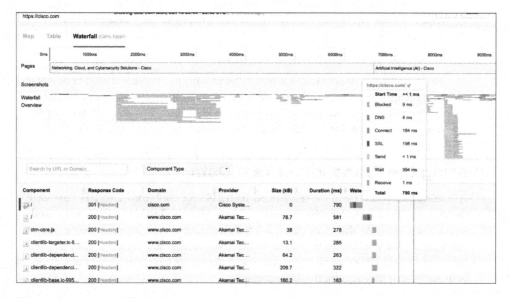

Figure 7-8   *Waterfall View*

If we dive into the Waterfall tab a little more, looking at the https://cisco.com domain, we can see certain metrics for the particular page and, if needed, click the link to follow the waterfall (see Figure 7-9), which enables you to analyze each element in the page and see if there is latency or any issues where the user experience would be elevated.

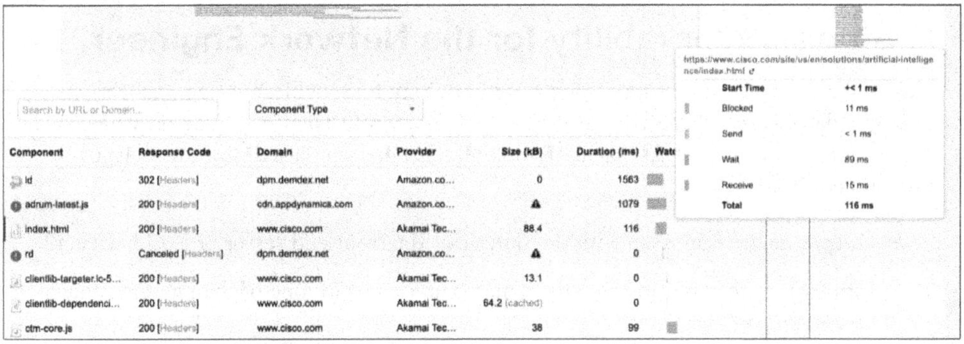

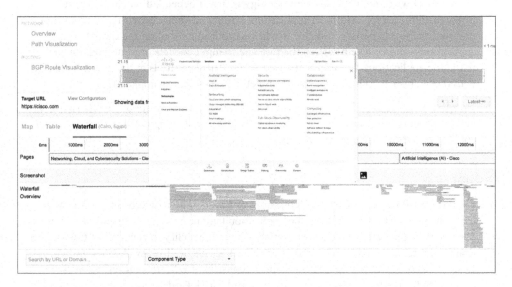

Figure 7-9 *Waterfall Components*

If you were to add a screenshot to the script, you would also see the screenshot within the script, as shown in Figure 7-10. Adding a screenshot to the script is simple: from the Test settings, click the camera icon and click the line of the script in the IDE where you want to insert the screenshot. After rerunning the test, you'll see the image.

Figure 7-10 *Screenshot Example*

So, in summary, we have conducted a Transaction test by navigating to https://cisco.com and navigating to the technologies section. Subsequently, we scrutinized the new trans-actional test, analyzing each element of the web page, including interactions, page load times, DNS resolutions, and network performance. Transaction tests enable the script to replicate user actions, facilitating the identification of latency or slowness issues on the web page. By utilizing ThousandEyes, we were able to analyze this data and pinpoint specific issues affecting user experience.

Full Stack Observability for the Network Engineer

Years ago, we worked on simplifying a methodology for troubleshooting applications inside a data center. At the core of this methodology was where to look next when an operational issue occurred. This methodology has been simplified down to Output, Input, and Processes:

- **Output:** Is there an issue with the output of the front-end server or load balancer?

- **Input:** Does the issue at the output match an issue with one of the inputs to that server/system?

- **Processes:** If the output is bad but the input is good, then look at the internal metrics for that server.

Note that each input is an output from another server. So, the process is to step back through the dependencies (web, app, DB, etc.) until the source of the issue is discovered (input is good while the output is bad).

The problem we found with this methodology is that it depended on packet captures between all the servers within an application. It required someone with a good level of protocol analysis expertise to define if/when a problem existed on the output of the application—and be able to match the timeline to input packets (output from the next tier in the application) captured at the same time. There are tools in the industry that help with these obstacles, but it remains a complex way to triage an application.

Now that we work for ThousandEyes (a part of Cisco), we went about further simplifying this process using ThousandEyes' technology. The following is a description of that application-centric triage methodology.

Output

Let's start with the output. With ThousandEyes Cloud and/or Enterprise Agents, we can now monitor the output from the application (and network as well) and view it as a consumer of that data. These agents simply give us the ability to run a client transaction against any reachable URL. This allows us to look at metrics like Availability and Page Load Times to use as our output. Availability consists of DNS resolution, network connection, SSL/TLS negotiation, Send, Receive, and HTTP Code verification. Page Load is the amount of time to download all the objects on a given page regardless of where those objects are hosted.

Let's view these metrics on a timeline. This way we can also add the network KPIs (packet loss and latency) to this same timeline and quickly spot whether it is the network causing issues. If not, then it's time to look at the inputs to the application. By leveraging ThousandEyes' reports or dashboards, we can easily create timeline views of the metrics that are important to us.

Figure 7-11 shows a problem with downloading the page (Page Load test) Cisco.com. The network (loss and latency) to and from Cisco.com is fine. However, by diving into inputs that make up this output (in this particular case, we use the Waterfall tab), we find that there is a JavaScript file hosted on Cloudflare that is taking more than 9.5 seconds to load.

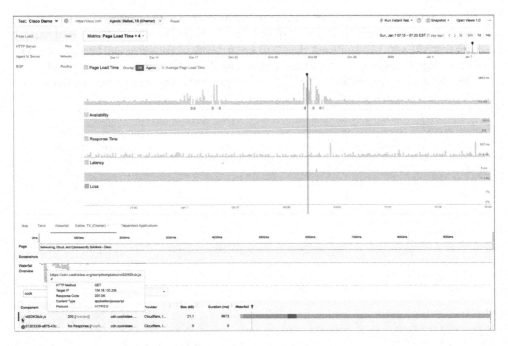

Figure 7-11 *Page Load Waterfall*

Input

Unlike the original (pre ThousandEyes) methodology previously described, where we attempted to collect packets between every server in the application's architecture and then take a single step back each time we identified the issue in an input, with the ThousandEyes methodology, we first look at the application as a whole, then simply look at any external dependency the application might have. These dependencies include any external sources of data that could impact the delivery to the end user, such as third-party APIs, DB connections to another data center, or resources located in the cloud. Whether the dependencies are internally controlled, hosted by a third party, or simply

SaaS, they should be monitored. This can be achieved with ThousandEyes locating an Enterprise Agent in the data center (or cloud if applicable) where the application is hosted. This Enterprise Agent can then be used to connect to the external resource. If the resource is web based, a Transaction test can be used to test and monitor the response time as well as provide network KPIs (and path visualization). For non-web resources, a simple Network Agent to Server test can be created that will not only test the availability of the TCP socket but also include end-to-end and network path metrics to show when the network is impacting the input to the monitored application. Also placing these metrics on a dashboard timeline along with the output shows, immediately, when the input is likely impacting the output without requiring extensive investigations.

In the example shown in Figure 7-12, a test has been created to monitor performance for api.github.com. Figure 7-12 shows a spike of about six times the normal page load time for this API, with no significant change to key network metrics (loss and latency). We do have a significant amount of wait time, indicating the application is slow to respond. The input to the application using this API is dependent on the output of api.github.com. If the API is slow, the application is also slow.

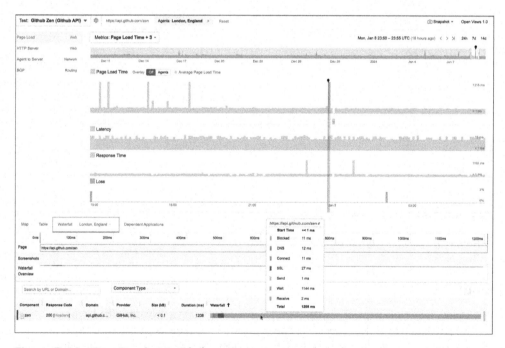

Figure 7-12   *Page Load: api.github.com/zen*

Figure 7-13 shows a Transaction test that generally takes less than a second to complete. However, when authentication takes more than 15 seconds, the Transaction time goes to more than 20 seconds. The next step for troubleshooting this application would be to have an individual test running to the API to see if there is a network issue between the application and its API or if the API is just slow in responding.

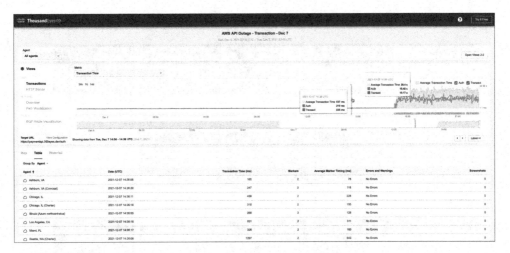

Figure 7-13   *Authentication API Impacting Transaction Time*

Processes

Now that we have looked at the application's output (and the network delivering it to the users) along with the input(s), what happens when we detect a problem with the output (with no change to packet loss or latency on the network) but observe no problem with the inputs?

This is when we need to dig into the internal processes running inside the application. The good news is that Cisco ThousandEyes has collaborated with the Cisco AppDynamics team to build some truly powerful integrations and workflows. With AppDynamics running on the application, it is easy to pivot from the peripherals (outputs and inputs) to the internals (processes) for a deep dive into what is causing the issue inside of the questionable application.

Figure 7-14 shows a dashboard that contains not only ThousandEyes performance metrics but also application health statistics pulled directly from AppDynamics. This enables an engineer to view network and application metrics without needing to jump between systems. Making views such as this a part of standard operating procedures can drastically reduce triage time when problems do occur.

Figure 7-14 *APM (AppDynamics) Application Health Inside ThousandEyes Performance Dashboard*

Review Questions

Answer the following questions. Check your answers against those provided in Appendix A, "Answers to Review Questions."

1. What is the use case for a Transaction test?

2. How do you use a Transaction test to mimic a UX with a phone?

3. What are markers?

4. What other tests are associated with a Transaction test?

Chapter 8

Integrations

Within the realm of network monitoring, ThousandEyes recognizes the significance of collaboration and interoperability. Integrations serve as the bridge that connects ThousandEyes with other essential components of an organization's technology stack. Whether it's syncing data with incident management systems, sharing insights with collaboration tools, or automating responses to identified issues, integrations enhance the capabilities of ThousandEyes. In this chapter we explore the ThousandEyes API basics, review webhooks again, and then investigate ServiceNow integration, OpenTelemetry, and Cisco Platforms.

API Basics

The ThousandEyes API is straightforward and can serve various purposes, including automation and reporting. Let's take a quick look at how we can leverage these APIs.

To interact with the ThousandEyes API, the first step is to establish authentication to the platform. In the ThousandEyes UI, navigate to the **Account Settings > Users and Roles** section, where two authentication options are available (see Figure 8-1). The Basic Authentication Token option is linked to the username. The OAuth Bearer Token option operates at the account group level, unlike Basic Authentication Token. For this example, let's use the basic authentication and copy the token.

Now that we have a token, let's use the documentation to see which GET requests we can use. We'll also make it easy by using the browser. You can find the ThousandEyes API documentation at https://developer.cisco.com/docs/thousandeyes/, as shown in Figure 8-2. For this example, let's get a list of tests using a GET request.

User API Tokens
The user tokens associated with the   profile.

Basic Authentication Token
[   ]   Regenerate

This token should be used along with your username

OAuth Bearer Token
[   ]   Revoke

Expires in: May 26, 2023 20:31:35 CST   Refresh Token:

Figure 8-1   *User API Tokens*

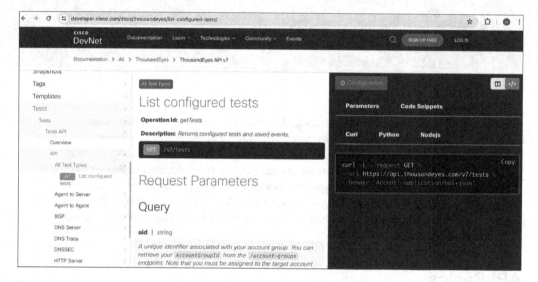

Figure 8-2   *API Docs*

From the browser, navigate to https://api.thousandeyes.com/v7/tests.json.

Log in using the username and API token supplied in the Basic Auth. I am using a JSON formatter extension in Google Chrome, so the data is easy to read.

In Figure 8-3, you can see the data provided, including details on who created the test, the test type, and the test ID. This information will be relevant when we discuss OpenTelemetry later in this chapter.

You could copy and paste the data into a text file to review all the tests and ensure intervals are set properly, but an easier approach is to send the output of the API to a file. You can use tools like Curl, Python, or any other programming language for this task. Figure 8-4 shows an example of the Curl command syntax and how to redirect the output to a file for analysis.

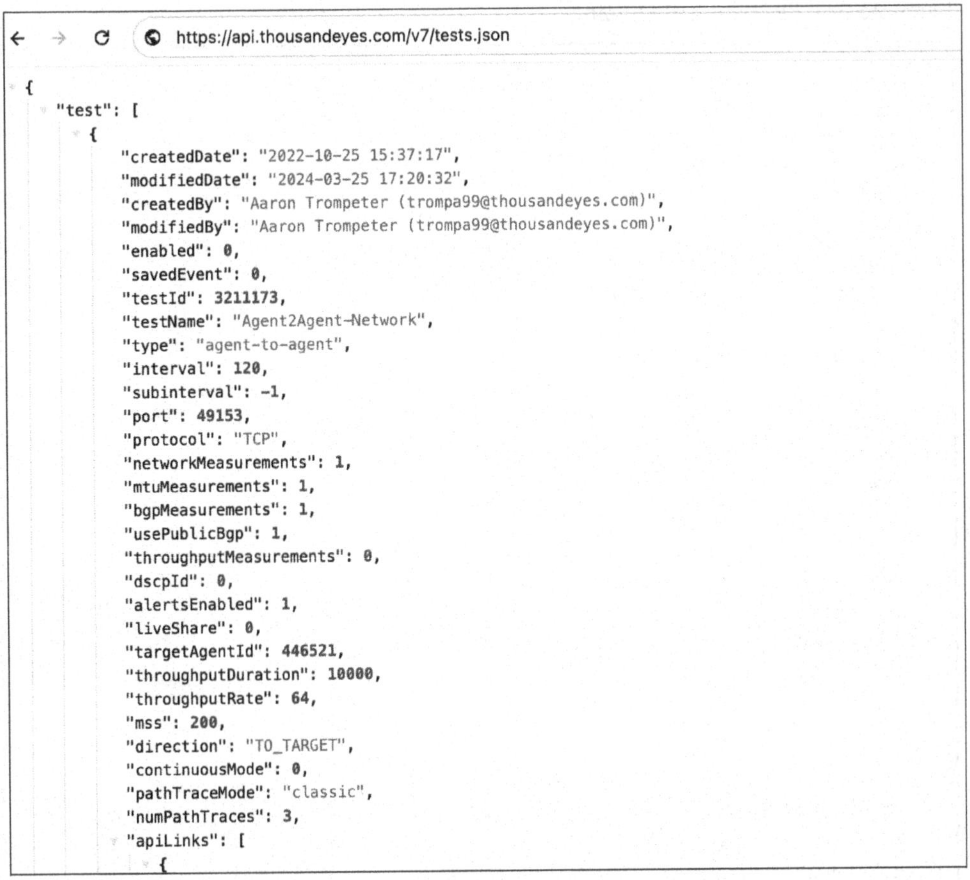

```
←  →  C    🔒 https://api.thousandeyes.com/v7/tests.json

{
    "test": [
        {
            "createdDate": "2022-10-25 15:37:17",
            "modifiedDate": "2024-03-25 17:20:32",
            "createdBy": "Aaron Trompeter (trompa99@thousandeyes.com)",
            "modifiedBy": "Aaron Trompeter (trompa99@thousandeyes.com)",
            "enabled": 0,
            "savedEvent": 0,
            "testId": 3211173,
            "testName": "Agent2Agent-Network",
            "type": "agent-to-agent",
            "interval": 120,
            "subinterval": -1,
            "port": 49153,
            "protocol": "TCP",
            "networkMeasurements": 1,
            "mtuMeasurements": 1,
            "bgpMeasurements": 1,
            "usePublicBgp": 1,
            "throughputMeasurements": 0,
            "dscpId": 0,
            "alertsEnabled": 1,
            "liveShare": 0,
            "targetAgentId": 446521,
            "throughputDuration": 10000,
            "throughputRate": 64,
            "mss": 200,
            "direction": "TO_TARGET",
            "continuousMode": 0,
            "pathTraceMode": "classic",
            "numPathTraces": 3,
            "apiLinks": [
                {
```

Figure 8-3 *API from Browser*

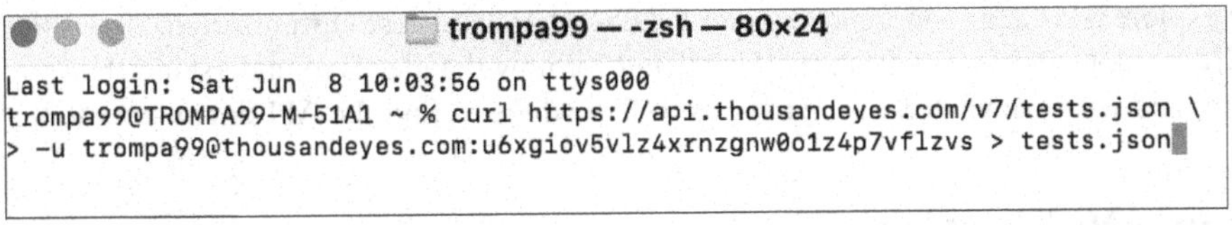

```
●  ●  ●              📄 trompa99 — -zsh — 80×24

Last login: Sat Jun  8 10:03:56 on ttys000
trompa99@TROMPA99-M-51A1 ~ % curl https://api.thousandeyes.com/v7/tests.json \
> -u trompa99@thousandeyes.com:u6xgiov5vlz4xrnzgnw0o1z4p7vflzvs > tests.json█
```

Figure 8-4 *Curl Command*

Moving on to a POST request, let's look at a basic Python script. By focusing on the documentation page, we will use the same parameters in the CURL example to POST a test. The URL we will focus on is https://api.thousandeyes.com/v7/tests/agent-to-server/new.json, as shown in Example 8-1.

From a Python perspective, notice the parameters used to create an Agent to Server test.

Example 8-1 *Python API Example*

```
import requests

url = 'https://api.thousandeyes.com/v7/tests/agent-to-server/new.json'
email = 'your_email@example.com'
auth_token = 'your_auth_token'

headers = {
    'Content-Type': 'application/json',
    'Accept': 'application/json',
    'Authorization': f'Basic {email}:{auth_token}'
}

data = {
    "interval": 300,
    "agents": [{"agentId": 113}],
    "testName": "API agent-to-server test addition for www.thousandeyes.com",
    "server": "www.thousandeyes.com",
    "port": 80,
    "alertsEnabled": 0
}

try:
    response = requests.post(url, json=data, headers=headers)
    response.raise_for_status()
    print(response.json())
except requests.exceptions.RequestException as e:
    print(f"An error occurred: {e}")
```

We explore APIs a little more in Chapter 9, "Best Practices: Test Optimization, Collaboration, and Stories from the Field," but for now the idea is to understand the basics and what parameters are needed as well as where to find the API documentation.

Custom Webhooks

We talked about webhooks only briefly in Chapter 4, "Configuring Alerts," so now we are going to revisit them in a little more detail and look at custom webhooks versus the standard or basic webhooks. The idea of the webhook is to send data (alerts, messages, events, etc.).

From the ThousandEyes UI, go to **Integrations** and click **New Integration**. From the screen shown in Figure 8-5, you can see an option to select a custom webhook. An Add Custom Webhook Integration panel opens, as shown in Figure 8-5. For this example, open the Preset Configurations drop-down menu and choose Generic. There are other options to choose from. These templates will have more context in the payload, and of course you can customize this template to include any additional payload needed, which is the reason this chapter started with a discussion of API basics.

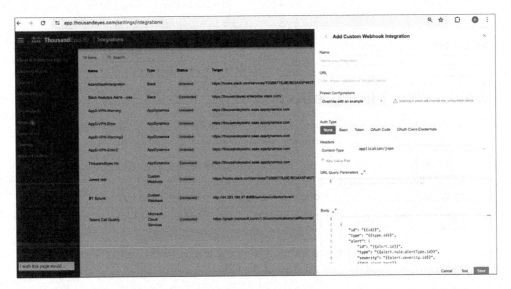

Figure 8-5 *Webhook Template*

Starting from the top of Figure 8-5, the rest of the options are as follows:

- **Name:** Provide a meaningful name for your integration.

- **URL:** Enter the URL of your destination (webhook or third-party server).

- **Auth Type:** As with ThousandEyes, you have a few options, including no authentication.

- **Headers:** You can add a key/value pair that conveys additional information about the request or the data being sent. They serve as metadata and can provide details such as the content type, authentication tokens, or any other relevant information needed for processing the request correctly.

- **URL Query Parameters:** This is also an additional feature; however, these parameters are appended to a URL to define content or actions, especially when integrating into a third-party system.

- **Body:** The body is already templatized, but you can use Ctrl-Spacebar to see these options.

Now that you have the template ready, click **Save** to save the webhook or click **Test** to test the webhook. Click **Test**, and the UI will show you the status of the test as Connected (i.e., successful), Untested, or Failure (see Figure 8-6). Failure status typically means either that the server did not respond or that the payload itself is malformed. So, again, ensure that the payload is correct; referencing the API documentation will help ensure correct context.

| AppD-VPN-Error2 | AppDynamics | Untested | https://thousandeyesinc.saas.appdynamics.com |
| ThousandEyes Inc | AppDynamics | Connected | https://thousandeyesinc.saas.appdynamics.com |

Figure 8-6   *Webhook Test*

ServiceNow Integration

ThousandEyes supports ServiceNow integration from both the incident management perspective and event management.

ThousandEyes can notify users when a test triggers an alert rule. Alert rules enable you to configure various methods of alert notification, as covered in Chapter 4, "Alerts." One of the supported methods is direct notification delivery into ServiceNow. Once the notification is delivered, ServiceNow processes it and allocates tasks based upon predefined workflows.

There are some prerequisites to address before you can create the ServiceNow integration, which are covered in the first ten steps of the following instructions:

Step 1.   Start from the ServiceNow Service Management portal (see Figure 8-7).

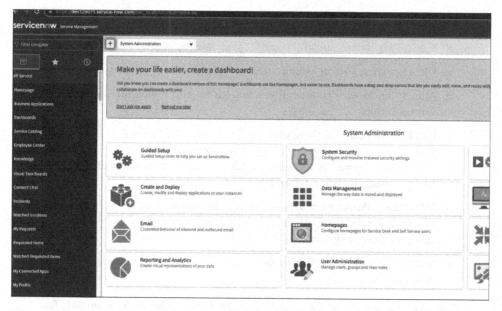

Figure 8-7   *ServiceNow Service Management Portal*

Step 2.   In the Filter Navigator field in the upper-left corner of the portal, search for Role to locate Roles under Users and Groups, and then click **Roles**, as shown in Figure 8-8.

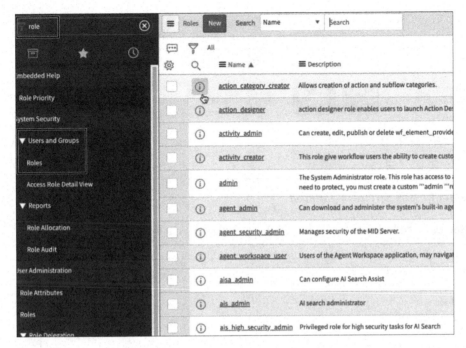

Figure 8-8 *ServiceNow Roles*

Step 3.   In the Search field, enter **web**, as shown in Figure 8-9.

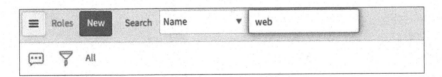

Figure 8-9 *ServiceNow Web Service Admin*

Step 4.   Locate the Web Service Admin and click the link (see Figure 8-10).

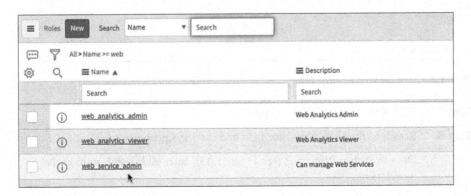

Figure 8-10 *Web Services*

Step 5.   Click **Edit** (see Figure 8-11).

Figure 8-11   *Web Services Continued*

Step 6.   Add **admin** to the Contains Roles List (see Figure 8-12).

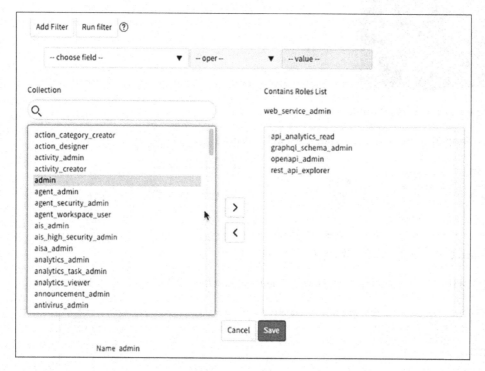

Figure 8-12   *ServiceNow Admin Role*

Step 7.   Click **Save** and then click **Update**.

Step 8.   Return to the Filter Navigator field and enter **sys.properties.list**.

Once in System Properties (see Figure 8-13), enter **glide.oauth.state** in the Search field.

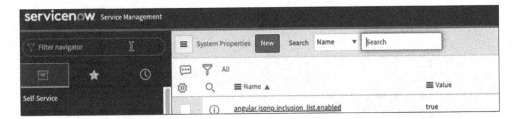

Figure 8-13 *ServiceNow OAuth*

Step 9.   From the **glide.oath.state.parameters.required** system property, change the Value field to **false** and then click **Update** (see Figure 8-14).

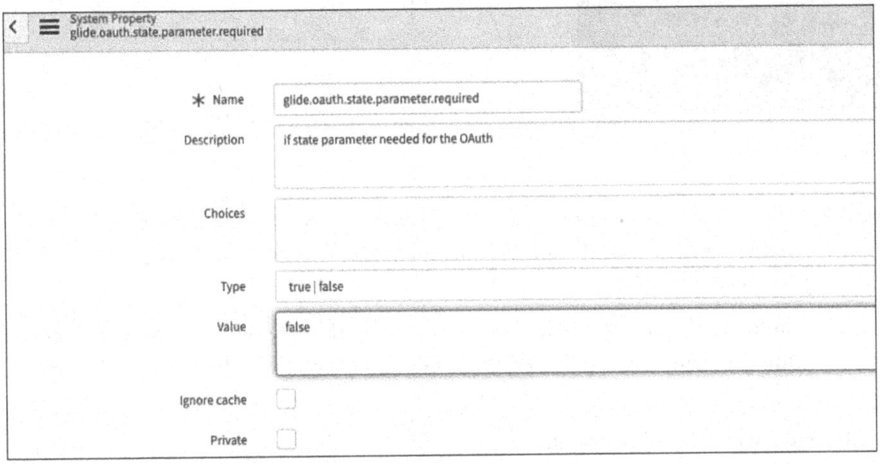

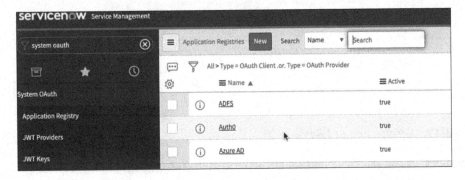

Figure 8-14 *ServiceNow False Value*

Step 10.   Return to the Filter Navigator field and enter **system oauth**.

From the OAuth Provider, click **New** (see Figure 8-15). This is where you will start the webhook integration.

Figure 8-15 *System OAuth*

Step 11. Click **Create an OAuth API Endpoint for External Clients,** as shown in Figure 8-16.

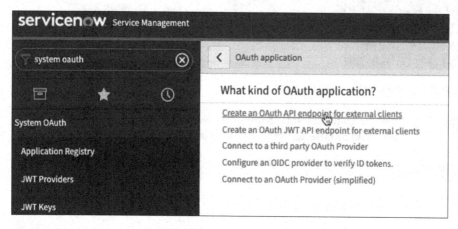

Figure 8-16 *Endpoint API*

Step 12. In the Name field, enter **ThousandEyes,** as shown in Figure 8-17. Copy the content of the Client ID field, which you will need to paste into the ThousandEyes UI.

In the Redirect URL field, enter **https://app.thousandeyes.com/namespace/ integrations/AuthCallbackPage.html.** Click **Submit** in the upper-right corner.

Note This URL will be updated again.

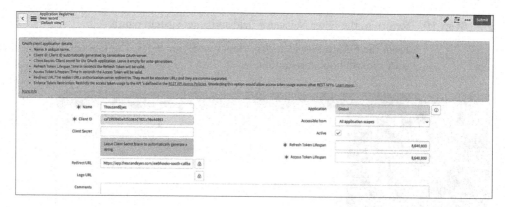

Figure 8-17 *ServiceNow API Key*

Step 13. Open the ThousandEyes UI, navigate to the **Integrations** page, and select **ServiceNow** from the **Type** drop-down menu, as shown in Figure 8-18.

Figure 8-18 *ThousandEyes and ServiceNow Integration*

Step 14.   Complete the following (see Figure 8-18):

■ **ServiceNow URL:** Enter **https://<instance-name>.service-now.com.**

■ **Auth URL:** Enter **https://<instance-name>.service-now.com/oauth_auth.do.**

■ **Client ID:** Paste the Client ID from ServiceNow (copied in Step 12).

■ **Token:** Click **Get Token.**

The expected outcome is to see an invalid redirect, as shown in Figure 8-19.

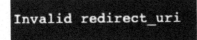

Figure 8-19 *Invalid Redirect*

Step 15.   Click **Copy** to copy the URL, as shown in Figure 8-20. If you look closely, the URL has changed from what was added in Figure 8-17 in the Redirect URL field; you can now use the specific ServiceNow instance redirect and use the URL shown in Figure 8-20 as the redirect.

Step 16.   Navigate back to **ServiceNow > System OAuth Provider** and click the ThousandEyes client (see Figure 8-21).

Step 17.   Paste the URL back into the Redirect URL field in ServiceNow and click **Update** (see Figure 8-22).

Figure 8-20   *Valid URL String*

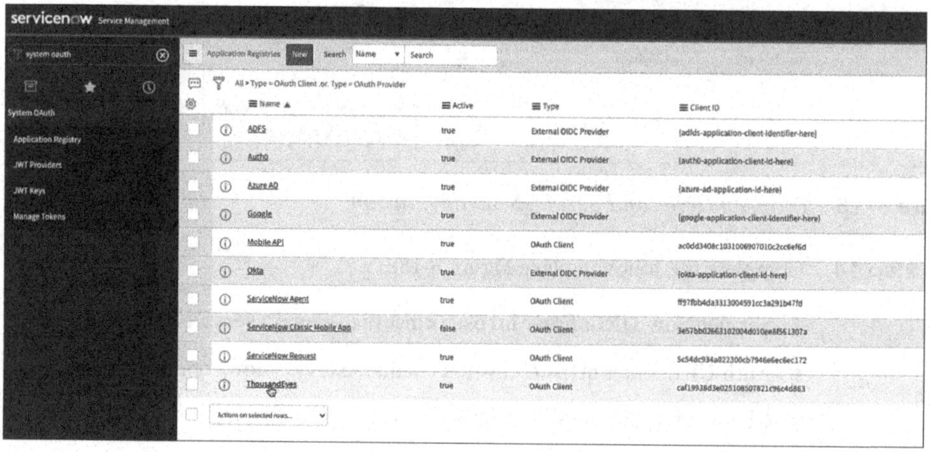

Figure 8-21   *URL Replace*

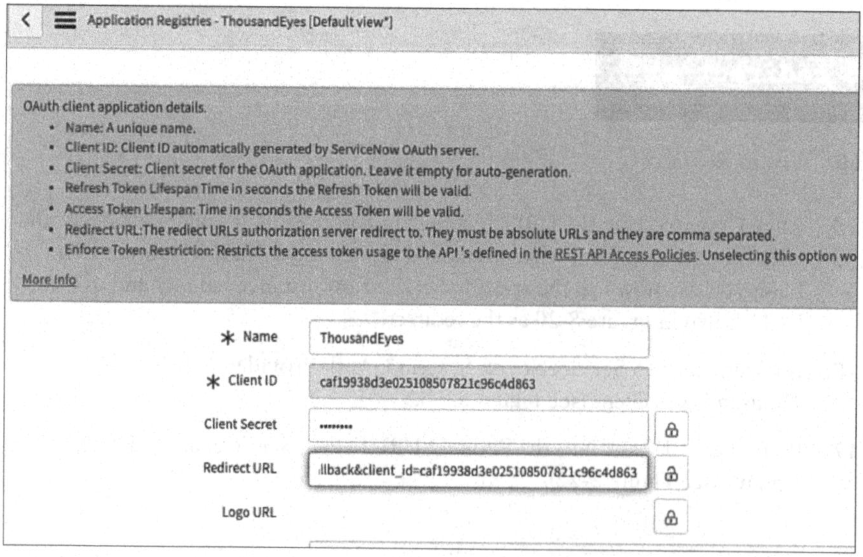

Figure 8-22   *URL Replace Continued*

Step 18.   Go back to the Edit Integrations section in ThousandEyes and click **Get Token**; you will now see that you are connected. Don't forget to click **Allow** in the bottom right, as shown in Figure 8-23. Now you can streamline alert rule notifications to ServiceNow.

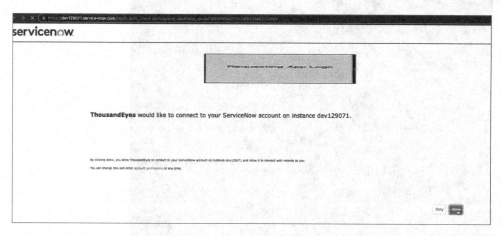

Figure 8-23   *Integration Success*

Cisco Integrations

The whole idea of integration is to streamline processes. If you are a network engineer and use a specific Cisco platform, maybe you're thinking of integrating the ThousandEyes processes into your platform, thus creating the streamlined process. This section demonstrates how to integrate some Cisco platforms with ThousandEyes and identifies which metrics can be shared.

Cisco Catalyst Center (Formerly Cisco DNA Center)

This platform is a software-defined network that can manage the enterprise network. Recall that in Chapter 2, "Agent Setup," we used the CLI method to enable application hosting on Catalyst 9000 switches. With this integration, we can deploy to many devices as well as ingest test data into the Catalyst Center controller.

The following steps demonstrate how to deploy a ThousandEyes Enterprise Agent using the controller and then ingest the test data:

Step 1.   From the Catalyst Center portal, navigate to **Provision > Services > Service Catalog** or **App Hosting for Switches**, as shown in Figure 8-24. Either option enables you to upload the ThousandEyes agent.

Step 2.   Click **Add a New Application**, click **Select**, and select the Cisco packaged application (TE agent-9k.tar file from the ThousandEyes UI). The tar file must be downloaded to the local drive to upload into Catalyst Center. After you have selected the application, click **Upload** (see Figure 8-25).

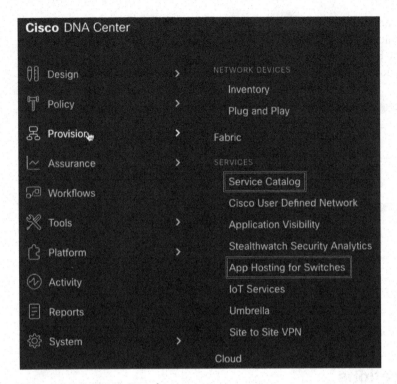

Figure 8-24 *DNA Portal*

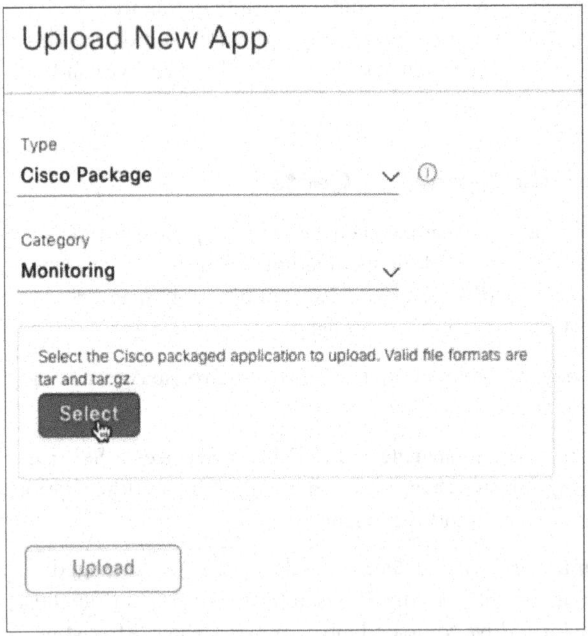

Upload New App

Type
Cisco Package ⌄ ⓘ

Category
Monitoring ⌄

Select the Cisco packaged application to upload. Valid file formats are
tar and tar.gz.

Select

Upload

Figure 8-25 *DNA ThousandEyes Upload*

Step 3.   After the application has been uploaded, you will see the ThousandEyes image shown in Figure 8-26.

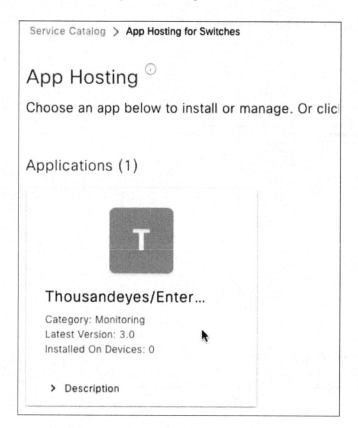

Figure 8-26   *ThousandEyes Successful Upload*

Step 4.   Click **Edit** to update the proper Docker runtime options; this is just like you did when installing the agent directly to the switch, as shown in Figure 8-27.

Ensure the token is updated as well as the hostname. The --hostname entry is using the switch hostname, but again, just like the agent template in the ThousandEyes UI, you can adjust the runtime options as needed. Click **Install** when done.

Step 5.   In the Select Switches wizard that opens (see Figure 8-28), select the switch to which you want to deploy the agent, and then click **Next**.

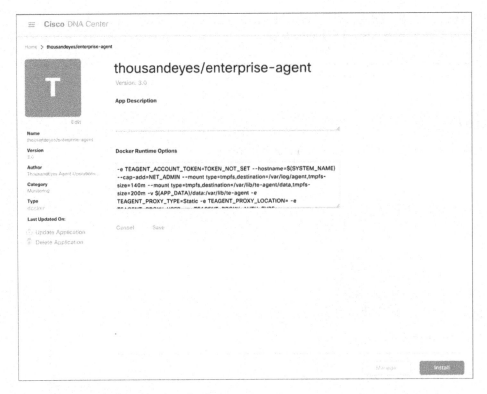

Figure 8-27 *Docker Runtime Options*

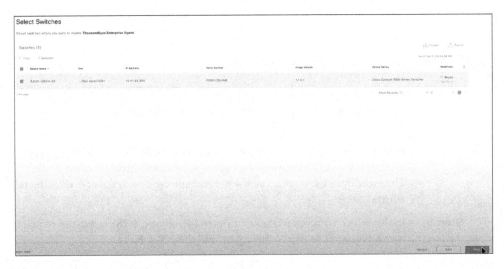

Figure 8-28 *Install ThousandEyes*

Step 6.   App Interface is the AppGigabit port. If you recall when we deployed the
Enterprise Agent on a Catalyst 9300, the AppGigabit port will connect the

agent to the physical interface. Ensure the proper device network is assigned, as well as Static or Dynamic App IP Address (see Figure 8-29). Click **Next**.

Map interfaces required by this app to available networks on selected devices.

App Interface	Device Network	App IP Address
Interface Name	Select Network	Address Type
eth0	VLAN0023	Dynamic

Figure 8-29 *Catalyst Center App Interface*

Step 7.   Review the configuration and click **Finish** (see Figure 8-30).

Home > thousandeyes/enterprise-agent > Install

✓ Select Devices   ✓ Configure App   ③ Confirm

Summary

⌄ Selected Devices
   Count: 1

⌄ Resource Profile
   Type: exact

⌄ Network Configuration
   Interface: eth0
      Interface Type: external
      Interface Hint:
      Vlan Type: VLAN0023
   Device: Cat9K-2.ebc.iseslab.cisco.com
   Interface: eth0
      Interface Type: external

Back   Finish

Figure 8-30 *Switch Options*

From the main menu in **Catalyst Center > Provision > App Hosting for Switches** click the **Agent > Manage** page. You can see that the controller is deploying the code to the switch (see Figure 8-31). When finished, a check mark will appear in the Action Status column. Then, on the ThousandEyes UI navigate to the **Cloud & Enterprise Agents > Agent Settings** page—you should see the new agent installed.

Home > thousandeyes/enterprise-agent > Manage

⊟ thousandeyes/enterprise-agent Latest Version 3.0

Devices (1) [All] Running Stopped Failed In Progress   ↻ Summary (1 Job in...)

∇ Filter Actions ⌄   ≣

☐	Hostname ▲	Device IP	App Version	App Status	Last Heard	Action Status
☐	Cat9K-2.ebc.iseslab.cisco.com	10.255.7.14	3.0	DEPLOYING	24 Mins Ago	↻ DEPLOYING

Figure 8-31 *Agent Deployed*

You need to save the token in the DNA controller by navigating to **System > Settings > External Services** and clicking **ThousandEyes Integration** (see Figure 8-32).

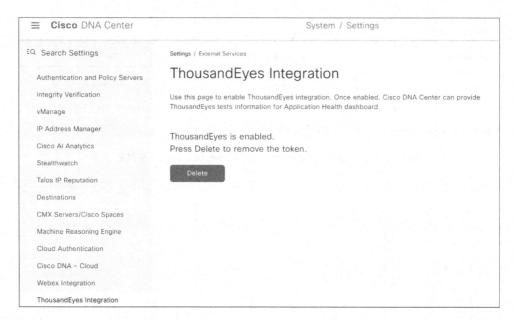

Figure 8-32   *ThousandEyes Token*

Navigate to the test data by choosing **Assurance > Dashboards > Health > Applications**. From here, you will see the test data from ThousandEyes, as shown in Figure 8-33. If you click the test name, this will cross-launch back to ThousandEyes, but metrics will be shown to indicate whether there are issues.

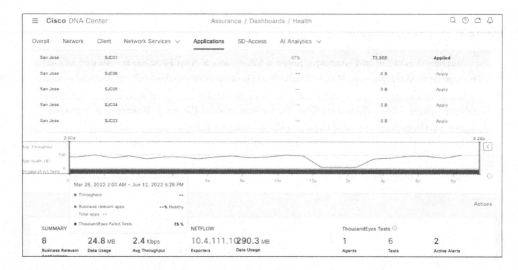

Figure 8-33   *ThousandEyes Metrics*

In the Enterprise Agent Tests section at the bottom of the page, the agents that have been deployed in DNAC will show Enterprise Agent tests. Again, notice the metrics supplied via the integration as shown in Figure 8-34.

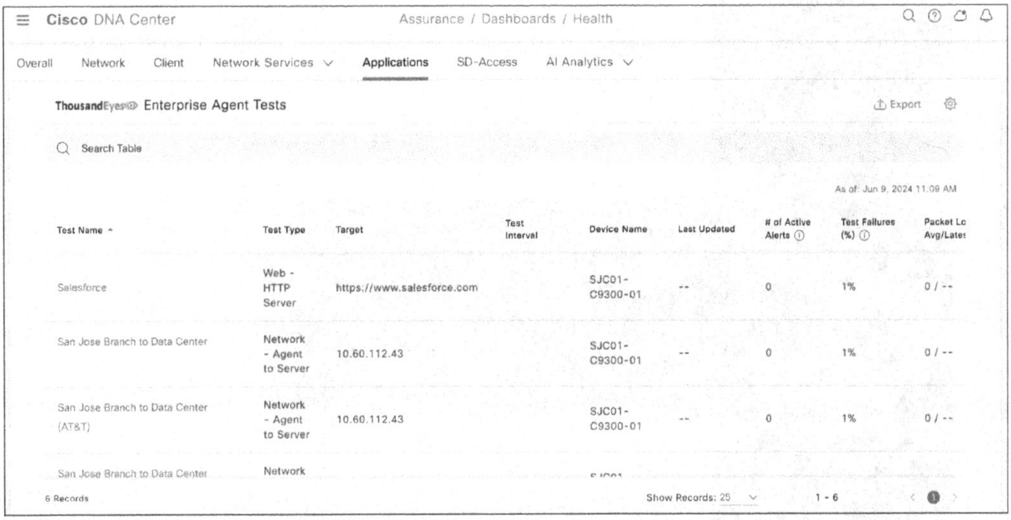

Figure 8-34 *ThousandEyes Metrics Continued*

Cisco Meraki

Like Cisco Catalyst Center, Cisco Meraki is another software-defined network that uses a controller. However, the Cisco Meraki integration with ThousandEyes is a very different experience. Recall that the ThousandEyes Agent Settings page doesn't include an option to select the Meraki MX devices. The reason is that Meraki isn't deployed via the CLI. In this section we dive into the Meraki integration setup and some caveats as well.

Within the Meraki dashboard, we can see a few new options under the Insight tab: Internet Outages and Active Application Monitoring, as shown in Figure 8-35. Let's explore these options.

Click **Internet Outages** to open the Internet Outages Overview window (see Figure 8-36), which pulls data from the ThousandEyes Internet Insights ISP Outages Catalog, showing all outages from cloud providers, SaaS, and ISPs. Moving your mouse cursor over a general area will highlight issues identified in that region. This viewpoint will update and contain outage data from the last 24 hours, but you can adjust the time scale from 24 hours down to the last 15 minutes.

Figure 8-35 *Meraki*

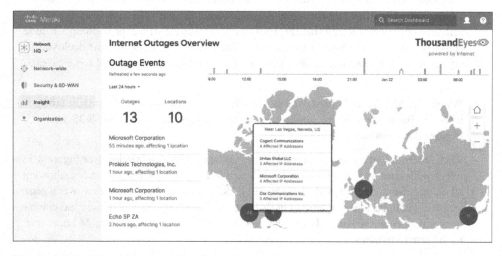

Figure 8-36 *Meraki Internet Insights*

Click **Active Application Monitoring** to launch a wizard (see Figure 8-37) that enables you to tie your ThousandEyes account directly to Meraki and then deploy agents and create tests from the Meraki dashboard. The wizard steps are as follows:

Step 1. Log in to your ThousandEyes account or create a new ThousandEyes account.

Figure 8-37 *Meraki to ThousandEyes Integration Connection*

Step 2. The next step of the wizard, shown in Figure 8-38, is to select which applications you want to monitor. You can choose one of the applications listed, click **Add a Custom Application** to choose an application that is not listed, or click **Continue Without an Application**. Click **Next** after you have made your choice.

Figure 8-38 *Selecting Applications to Monitor*

Step 3. Add your network, as shown in Figure 8-39. Notice that it lists networks, not specific MX devices. You can provision the networks today, and any MX devices added to those networks in the future will automatically have the agent deployed. This enables you to set up the networks in advance, and when you install new Meraki devices, they will automatically be included as monitoring targets.

Figure 8-39   *Network Selection*

Step 4.   After you select the network, click **Next** and Meraki will supply a summary of applications that will be monitored, the network, and the ThousandEyes account group, as shown in Figure 8-40.

Figure 8-40   *Network Review*

Once this is done, you can view the test data in ThousandEyes, which Meraki will cross-launch when you click the View Applications tab.

From the Active Application Monitoring option in the Insight category, you can also click **View** (see Figure 8-41) to see which tests are running in the Meraki network. Also, depending on which license you have, you might be entitled to free tests; click the **Get Free Tests** button in the upper-right corner to collect those free tests.

Figure 8-41 *Meraki Success*

At the time of writing, the following devices are supported for this integration:

- **Supported Meraki devices:** MX67, MX67W, MX67C, MX68, MX68W, MX68CW, MX75, MX85, MX95, MX105, MX250, MX450
- **Minimum firmware version:** 18.104
- **License type:** Eligible for customers with a Meraki Secure SD-WAN Plus license or trial; Meraki Advanced Security license

For additional information on which features are supported, check the software release notes, as features change with every release.

Cisco Webex Control Hub

When you integrate ThousandEyes with Webex, you can use the Endpoint Agents to help identify the root causes of network connection problems during meetings or conference calls. With this integration, Endpoint Agents gather network and application performance data. This data is then ingested into the Cisco Webex Control Hub, allowing Webex administrators to access and analyze the metrics directly within the Control Hub. This capability provides deeper insights into connectivity issues and improves overall meeting experience by enabling quick troubleshooting and resolution of network-related problems.

The following steps demonstrate how to integrate the Webex Control Hub and ThousandEyes platforms.

Step 1.   Navigate to **Webex Control Hub > Management > Organization Settings** and scroll down to the **ThousandEyes** section, as shown in Figure 8-42. Enable the **Allow ThousandEyes API Access** option and add the OAuth token from the ThousandEyes UI.

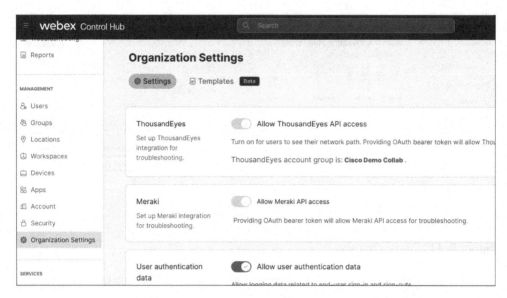

Figure 8-42   *Webex*

Step 2.   When the integration is complete, ensure that Endpoint Agents are running by using an Automatic Session Test to Webex.

Step 3.   From the Control Hub, navigate to **Site Administration Page > Troubleshooting**, where you can search for the meeting and then the user to see the user experience (see Figure 8-43). The dashed line indicates tests from ThousandEyes; also notice the metric is Network Path. Hovering on the dashes enables you to see quick metrics. To get more data, click the dash.

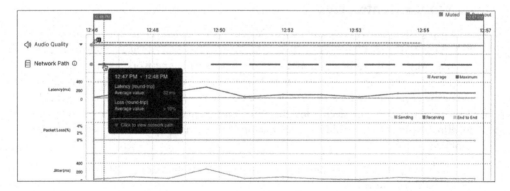

Figure 8-43   *ThousandEyes Metrics*

When you click a dash, you immediately see a path visualization of the network. Clicking each node will give you loss, latency, and jitter metrics, as shown in Figure 8-44. Notice that you can also launch ThousandEyes Dashboard to go directly to the test.

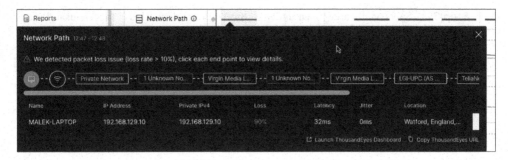

Figure 8-44 *Webex Path Visualization*

Cisco AppDynamics

Cisco AppDynamics integration with ThousandEyes can be used in two ways: for alert notifications, which are a basic webhook, and for test recommendations. Let's look at the integration.

From the AppDynamics side, add ThousandEyes API credentials in AppDynamics:

Step 1. Click the gear icon in the top-right corner of the **Home** page and select **Administration.**

Or

Navigate to **User Experience > Browser Apps > Connect to ThousandEyes** and click **Integration: Enable ThousandEyes.**

You need administration permission to access this page.

Step 2. Under **Integrations > ThousandEyes,** turn on the **Enable ThousandEyes Integration** option, as shown in Figure 8-45.

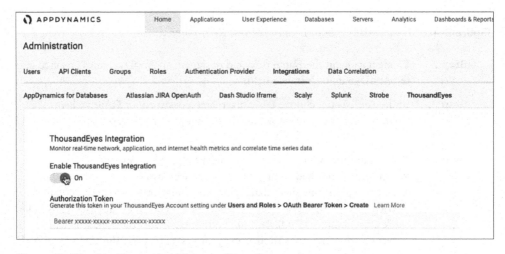

Figure 8-45 *AppDynamics ThousandEyes Integration*

Step 3.   Specify a bearer token under Authorization Token. This is the ThousandEyes OAuth Token. Navigate to **Users and Roles > OAuth Bearer Token > Create.**

From the ThousandEyes side (see Figure 8-46):

Step 1.   Navigate to **Integrations > Add Integration > AppDynamics.**

Figure 8-46   *ThousandEyes/AppDynamics Test Recommendations*

Step 2.   Create a name in the Name field and designate an AppDynamics instance in the AppDynamics Instance field.

Step 3.   Under Auth Type, choose Basic (username/password) or OAuth Client Credentials. For this example, use **Basic** and provide the username and password in the following fields.

Step 4.   This integration offers two options under Select Services: Test Recommendations and Connect to Alert Notifications Service. At a high level, these platforms share data, allowing administrators to gather detailed metrics on both the application and network, a concept that Cisco calls Full-Stack Observability (FSO). This integration facilitates the synchronization of test recommendations from AppDynamics, enhancing the administrator's visibility by ingesting ThousandEyes data. For this example, opt for Test Recommendations for the services, as shown in Figure 8-46. Click **Save**.

Step 5.   After adding the AppDynamics instance and basic parameters, ensure that the integration status is Pending or Connected from the Integrations tab in ThousandEyes (see Figure 8-47).

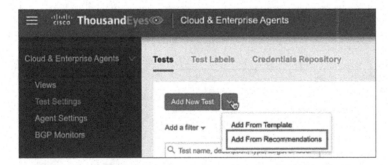

Figure 8-47   *Success*

Now, let's create a test. From the ThousandEyes UI, navigate to **Cloud & Enterprise Agents > Testing Settings > Add New Test** (use the drop-down arrow) in Figure 8-48. This integration is dynamic, sharing data with AppDynamics to recommend applications that ThousandEyes might not be testing. For instance, the first test recommendation indicates two applications in that domain that ThousandEyes isn't testing (see Figure 8-49). In contrast, the third test in the list shows 1 of 1 service monitored. For this example, let's test both suggested applications.

Figure 8-48   *AppDynamics Recommendation*

Select the applications you want to test; for this example, choose both (see Figure 8-50). Then click **Configure Tests**.

From here, as seen in Figure 8-51, you will have a template to build both tests, apply the agents, interval, and name (by default, this will use the application name). Click **Review Package**, which will show you exactly which tests and items the template is going to create. Confirm and click **Deploy Now**.

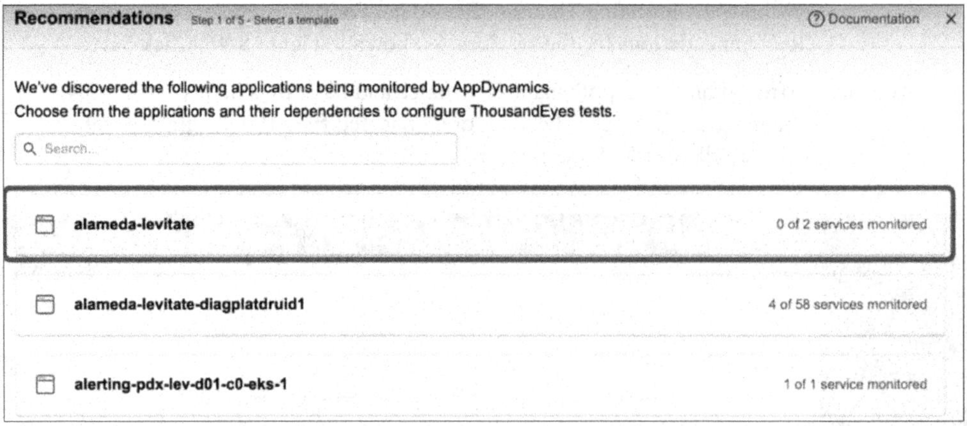

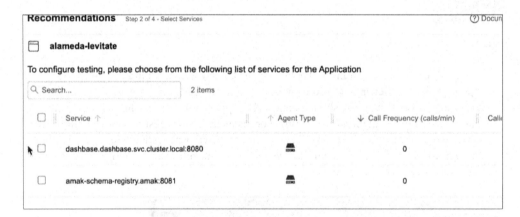

Figure 8-49 *AppDynamics Recommendation Continued*

Figure 8-50 *AppTest*

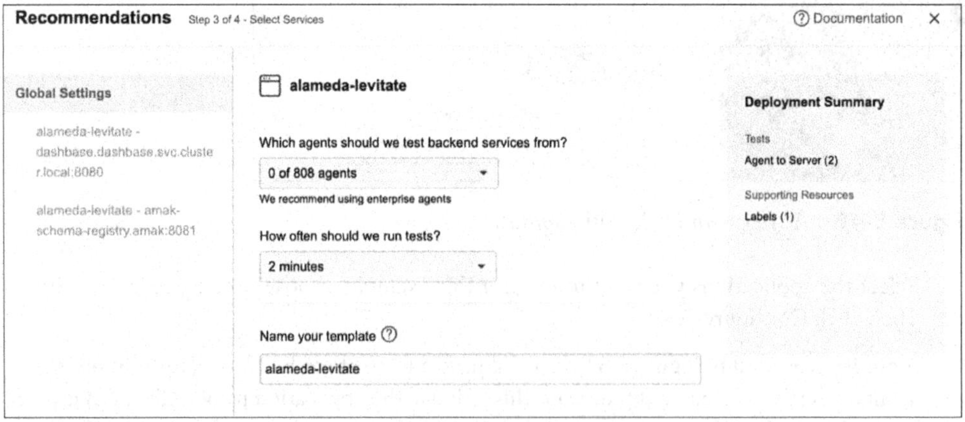

Figure 8-51 *Test Template*

Moving to **Cloud & Enterprise Agent> Views**, from the Test drop-down, find the test name. Notice the additional tab, Dependent Applications (see Figure 8-52). All other test data remains the same.

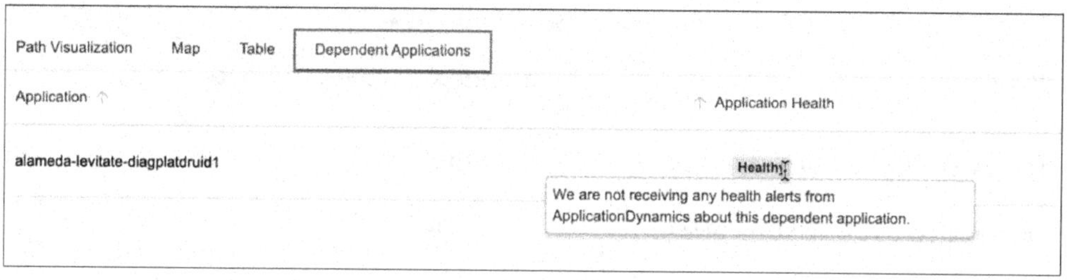

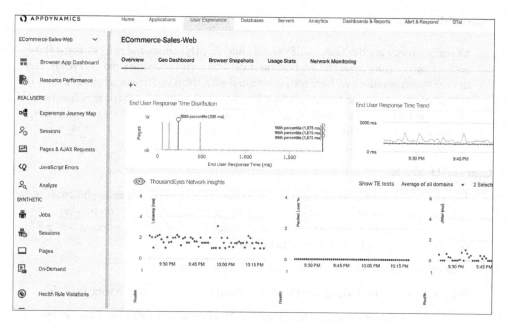

Figure 8-52 *BiDi Integration Metric*

Moving to the AppDynamics side, let's look at the integration from this perspective. From the User Experience tab, click **Browser App Dashboard**, shown in Figure 8-53. You can see the app view for this application as well as network metrics populated from ThousandEyes. Alongside all the other metrics graphs that AppDynamics normally provides, you're now seeing test data for latency, packet loss, and jitter coming directly from your ThousandEyes test.

Figure 8-53 *ThousandEyes Metrics Displayed in AppDynamics*

Navigate to **User Experience > Browser Apps** and you'll see all the different applications you have, but now you'll see the Domains Covered by TE field (see Figure 8-54).

This enables you to quickly view which applications have tests associated within ThousandEyes already created for them.

| | | Details | Add App | Actions | View Options | Sync with ThousandEyes |

Name		Requests ↓	Domains Covered by TE	Reques
ECommerce-Sales-Web Oτ SH-AAB-AAE-RPW ...		4,186	2	
ThousandEyesWebapps - TEST Oτ SH-AAB-...		14	2	
SynthRestUITests Oτ SH-AAB-AAE-SBA		0	2	
Puppetmaster-WEB Oτ SH-AAB-AAE-RPY		0	1	
TestBRUM Oτ SH-AAB-AAE-RVN		0	4	
Sreekanth_23.4.0_Web Oτ SH-AAB-AAE-RRC ...		0	2	
New App Oτ SH-AAB-AAE-SJE		0	-	

Figure 8-54 *Shared Data*

It's really easy to get the ThousandEyes data into AppDynamics and start showing those network metrics alongside the application stats. This integration also makes it really easy to view which applications have tests associated with them in ThousandEyes and view the individual stats to dive in further if you'd like. So, that's a quick look at the bidirectional integration between ThousandEyes and Cisco AppDynamics—easy to set up and start getting value on both products from the data that we can share.

Cisco SD-WAN

This integration aims to streamline the process of agent deployment through Cisco vManage for ThousandEyes and Cisco SD-WAN. This section focuses on two key aspects: enabling the upload of agents via vManage and exploring monitoring options for both underlay IP traffic and overlay tunnel traffic.

To start the process, upload the agent software into vManage:

Step 1.   From the ThousandEyes UI, download the agent.tar file to your local drive.

From the vManage UI, navigate to **Maintenance > Software Repository> Virtual Images > Upload Virtual Image** (see Figure 8-55), then select **vManage > Upload the TE_agent.tar** file (this is the agent file).

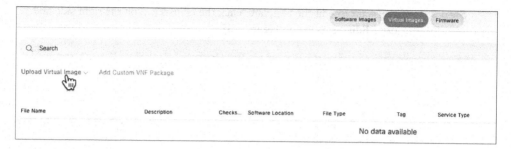

Figure 8-55 *vManage Repo*

Step 2.   Navigate to **Configuration > Templates** (see Figure 8-56). Choose the device
template you want to integrate with ThousandEyes.

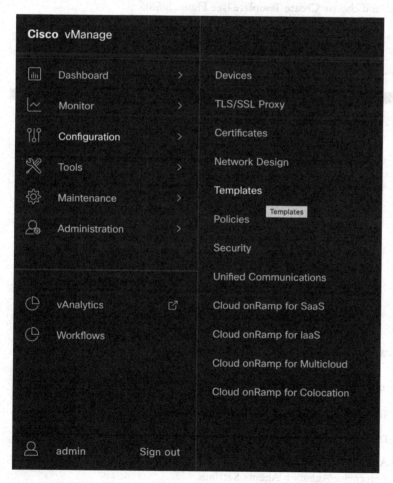

Figure 8-56 *vManage Template*

Step 3.   If you want to edit the template, click the ellipsis (...) on the right side and choose **Edit**, as shown in Figure 8-57.

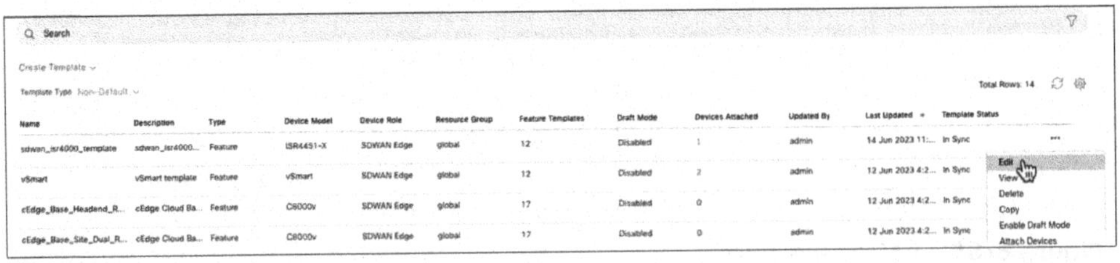

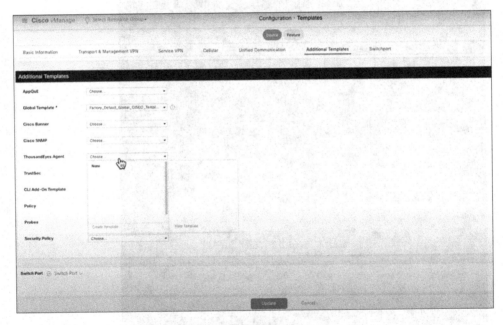

Figure 8-57   *Template Edits*

Step 4.   Navigate to **Additional Templates**, click the **ThousandEyes Agent** drop-down field, and choose **Create Template** (see Figure 8-58).

Figure 8-58   *SD-WAN ThousandEyes Agent Template*

Step 5.   Fill out the following fields (see Figure 8-59):

■ **Template Name:** Enter a unique name for the template.

■ **Description:** Enter a description for the template.

■ **Account Group Token:** From the ThousandEyes UI navigate to **Cloud & Enterprise Agents > Agents Settings.**

- **VPN:** Remains as Default (nothing is populated; this will add the agent to the transport VPN).

- **Name Server:** Enter the IP address of your preferred name server.

- **Hostname:** This field is optional.

- **Web Proxy Type:** This option does not apply for VPN 0 configuration.

Click **Save.**

Figure 8-59   *ThousandEyes Feature Template Example*

Step 6.   Once completed, ensure you add the feature template to the device template and then click **Update.** For this example, Figure 8-60 shows the template being added to the device template.

To view the configuration, navigate to **Configuration > Devices,** click the ellipsis (...) button to the right of the device, and click **Running Configuration,** as shown in Figure 8-61.

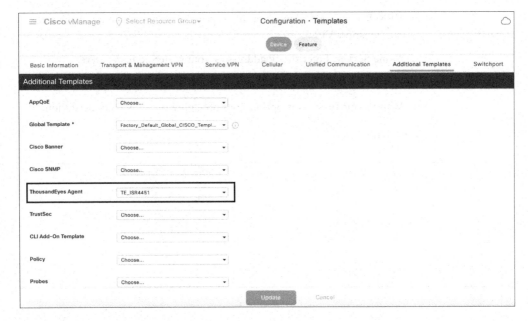

Figure 8-60 *Device Template*

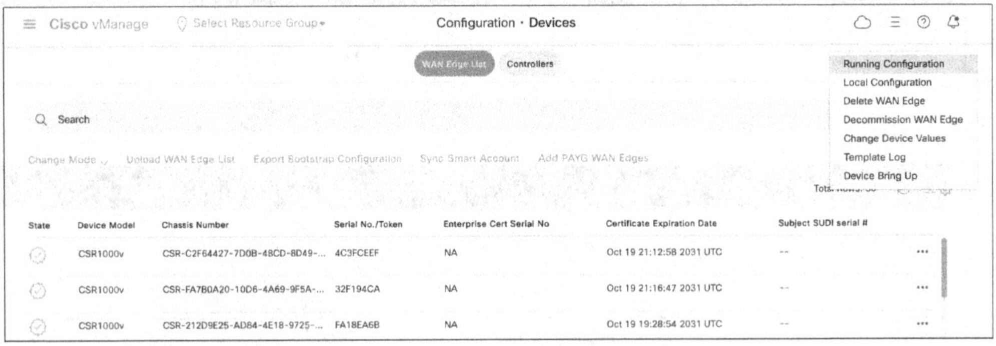

Figure 8-61 *Running Config*

The other option that might be needed, depending on use case, is to use the overlay or service VPN. In the previous steps, the agent was deployed to the Transport VPN. Recall that we did not enter data in the VPN field; this by default will use the Transport VPN.

The template will be adjusted to enable you to add the service VPN, as shown in Figure 8-62.

At this point, setting up a test from source to target will allow the user to now see the underlay or the overlay depending on how the template is configured.

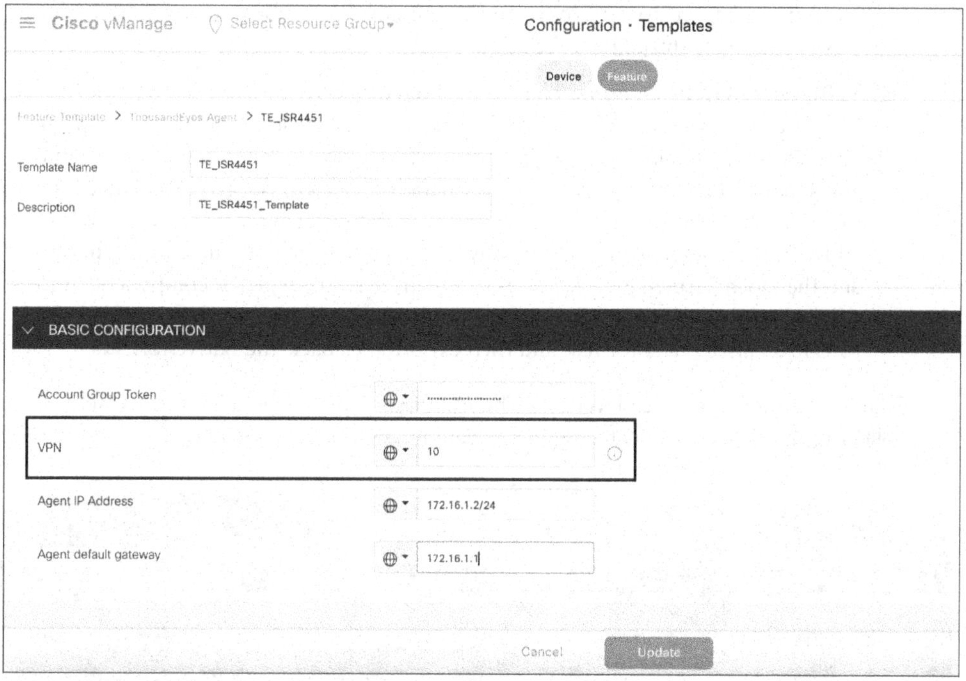

Figure 8-62 *Service VPN*

OpenTelemetry Integration

OpenTelemetry (OTel) is an open source initiative that provides a standardized, vendor-neutral framework for instrumenting, generating, collecting, and exporting telemetry data in the realm of cloud-native applications. Its purpose is to empower developers to seamlessly integrate observability into their services, thereby enhancing the monitoring, debugging, and optimization aspects of their applications.

The integration of ThousandEyes with OpenTelemetry establishes a machine-to-machine connection, allowing the export of ThousandEyes telemetry data in the widely adopted OTel format. This integration opens the door to leveraging popular observability frameworks like Splunk, Grafana, Prometheus, and Honeycomb for capturing and analyzing ThousandEyes data. Any client supporting OpenTelemetry standards can seamlessly utilize ThousandEyes for OpenTelemetry.

The components of ThousandEyes for OpenTelemetry include the following:

- **Data-streaming APIs:** These APIs enable the configuration and activation of ThousandEyes tests with OTel-compatible streams. They provide a flexible setup to define how ThousandEyes telemetry data is exported to client integrations.

- **Streaming pipelines (collectors):** These collectors actively fetch network test data from ThousandEyes, enhance the data with additional details and filters, and then push the data to customer-configured endpoints. The configuration of these collectors is achievable through public APIs.

■ **Third-party OTel collectors:** These collectors differ from the streaming pipelines. They receive, process, and export telemetry data, eliminating the necessity to run, operate, and maintain multiple agents/collectors. This approach enhances scalability and supports open source observability data formats (e.g., Jaeger, Prometheus, Fluent Bit, etc.), allowing data to be sent to one or more open source or commercial back ends. OTel collectors can be optionally deployed between instrumented applications and the OpenTelemetry backends as an OpenTelemetry pipeline component. With an OTel collector, OpenTelemetry signals can be ingested in various formats, translated to OTel's native pdata format, and then exported to back-end native formats.

Figure 8-63 shows at a high level how ThousandEyes streams the data to the OTel collector, and then the collector sends the data to any other back-end tool.

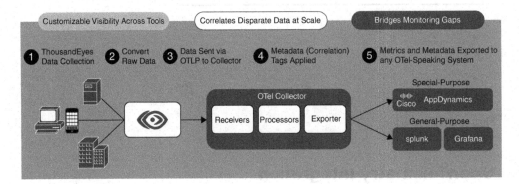

Figure 8-63 *OTel*

Configuring OpenTelemetry is easy and can only be done within the API. There are three parts to ensure that OpenTelemetry is configured properly: create a tag, assign the tag, and then create the stream.

Step 1. **Create a tag.** You should understand the concept of labels; however, we will convert this to a key/value pair instead. Figure 8-64 shows labels to key/value tags.

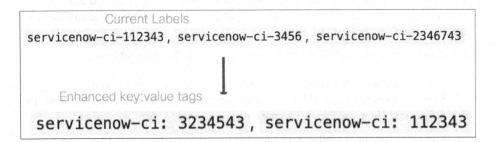

Figure 8-64 *Key/Value*

Using Python, you can see the code to create the key/value pair, as shown in Figure 8-65. The first script will create a tag. Set your tags and ensure the bearer token is added.

```
1    import requests
2
3    url = "https://api.thousandeyes.com/v7/tags"
4    headers = {
5        "Content-Type": "application/json",
6        "Authorization": "Bearer $BEARER_TOKEN"
7    }
8    data = {
9        "key": "TestKey",
10       "value": "TestValue",
11       "objectType": "test",
12       "accessType": "all"
13    }
14
15   response = requests.post(url, headers=headers, json=data)
16
17   print(response.status_code)
18   print(response.text)
```

Figure 8-65 *Script1-KeyValuePair*

Run the script and then save the output from the response. Save the following highlighted ID because it will be needed in the next script.

```
trompa99@ubuntu:~$ python3 create.py
```

```
{"id":"d582d9aa-c5f5-4a16-ae7c-
14a2c464a8c9","aid":1101061,"objectType":"test","key":
"TestKey","value":"TestValue","color":"#A7EB10","accessType":
"all","createDate":"2023-05-11T17:50:00Z"}
```

Step 2. **Assign the tag.** In the API URL, there is a place to add the ID from script1. The ID in the body of the script is the test ID where you want to place that tag. If you don't recall how to get that, run a test API call from your browser, which will show the test and test ID info. This is shown in Figure 8-66 to assign the tag.

Response:

```
trompa99@ubuntu:~$ python3 tag.py
```

```
200
{"tagId":"d582d9aa-c5f5-4a16-ae7c-14a2c464a8c9","assignments"
:[{"id":"3211173","type":"test"}]}
```

Step 3. **Stream the data.** Add the URL to the target along with the key/value. Note: ObjectType is a test field, so there's no need to change it. Figure 8-67 shows the key/value and the URL of the target to stream the data.

```
1      import requests
2
3      url = "https://api.thousandeyes.com/v7/tags/<id>/assign"
4      headers = {
5          "Content-Type": "application/json",
6          "Authorization": "Bearer $BEARER_TOKEN"
7      }
8      data = {
9          "assignments": [
10             {
11                 "id": "987654",
12                 "type": "test"
13             }
14         ]
15     }
16
17     response = requests.post(url, headers=headers, json=data)
18
19     print(response.status_code)
20     print(response.text)
```

Figure 8-66 *Script2-Assign Tag*

```
1      import requests
2
3      url = "https://api.thousandeyes.com/v7/stream"
4      headers = {
5          "Content-Type": "application/json",
6          "Authorization": "Bearer $BEARER_TOKEN"
7      }
8      data = {
9          "type": "opentelemetry",
10         "tagMatch": [
11             {
12                 "key": "TestKey",
13                 "value": "TestValue",
14                 "objectType": "test"
15             }
16         ],
17         "streamEndpointUrl": "https://example.org",
18         "customHeaders": {
19             "test": "value"
20         }
21     }
22
23     response = requests.post(url, headers=headers, json=data)
24
25     print(response.status_code)
26     print(response.text)
```

Figure 8-67 *Script3-Stream*

Response:

```
trompa99@ubuntu:~$ python3 stream.py

201
{"id":"a61e59e0-9b35-41ef-b47c-240757614cd2","type":"opentele
metry","streamEndpointUrl":"https://example.org","customHead
ers":{"test":"******"},"tagMatch":[{"key":"TestKey","value":
"TestValue","objectType":"test"}],"auditOperation":{"created
Date":1683828119844,"createdBy":1736481},"_links":{"self":
"/v7/stream/a61e59e0-9b35-41ef-b47c-240757614cd2"}}
trompa99@ubuntu:~$
```

Currently, the ThousandEyes for OpenTelemetry supports the following types of tests:

- Agent to Server
- Agent to Agent
- HTTP Server
- Web Transaction
- Page Load
- FTP Server
- DNS Server
- RTP Stream
- SIP Server
- Endpoint Agent network
- Endpoint Agent HTTP

The following test metrics are also currently supported:

- **Network:** Latency, loss, and jitter
- **Web HTTP server layer:** Availability, response time, and throughput
- **Web transactions:** Page load time, transaction time, completion, and errors
- **FTP server layer:** Availability, response time, and throughput
- **Page load layer:** Page load time and completion
- **DNS DNSSEC Trace layer:** Validity
- **DNS Domain Trace layer:** Availability and final query time
- **DNS Server layer:** Availability and resolution time
- **RTP stream tests:** MOS, loss, discards, and latency
- **SIP server layer:** Availability, response time, and total time

- **Endpoint Agent network:** Loss, latency, and jitter
- **Endpoint Agent HTTP:** Availability, response time, and throughput

Review Questions

Answer the following questions. Check your answers against those provided in Appendix A, "Answers to Review Questions."

1. What is the common theme with integrations?

2. Are there any platforms that have bidirectional integration?

3. Can ThousandEyes monitor the underlay of Cisco SDWAN?

   If so, how?

   If not, why not?

4. What data does Webex ingest from ThousandEyes?

Chapter 9

Best Practices: Test Optimization, Collaboration, and Stories from the Field

Some environments require tests to be tweaked in order to get both end-to-end and hop-by-hop components fully functional. The ThousandEyes defaults work in most cases, but sometimes a little extra configuration is needed. In this chapter we take a look at some situations where you might need to do a little extra configuration to get full value out of your testing. We also explore monitoring some of the collaboration tools customers commonly leverage in their day-to-day activities. Finally, we will share more of our stories from the field.

ThousandEyes Test Optimization

When creating tests that use TCP or even ICMP to test the network (both end-to-end and hop-by-hop testing), occasionally firewalls or other filtering devices on the network may drop ThousandEyes test traffic due to configuration or policy, which will impact the results of the test. The default settings work most of the time; however, it is always a good idea to do an operational check on any new test that is created.

ThousandEyes tests, by default, run end-to-end testing by establishing a TCP session over the destination port defined in the test setup. If the test is an HTTP Server, Page Load, or Transaction test, it will default to using HTTPS over TCP 443. While all three of these test types must use HTTP (or HTTPS), the ports can be specified by adding a colon and the application's listening port number to the end of the FQDN, such as https://notdefault.cisco.com:8443, shown in Figure 9-1, or https://notdefault.cisco.com:8080. Network tests require a port number to be entered directly into the configuration.

Note that the change shown in Figure 9-1 will impact all testing (HTTP Server, Network End-to-End, and Network Visualization) within the configured test unless the network portion (under Advanced Settings) of the configured test is modified from the default.

Path Visualization (hop-by-hop) testing will also use the same TCP port number as its destination port for the outbound packets while discovering each hop in the path. Refer to the Chapter 6 section "Hop-by-Hop Network Monitoring (Path Visualization)" for a more detailed description.

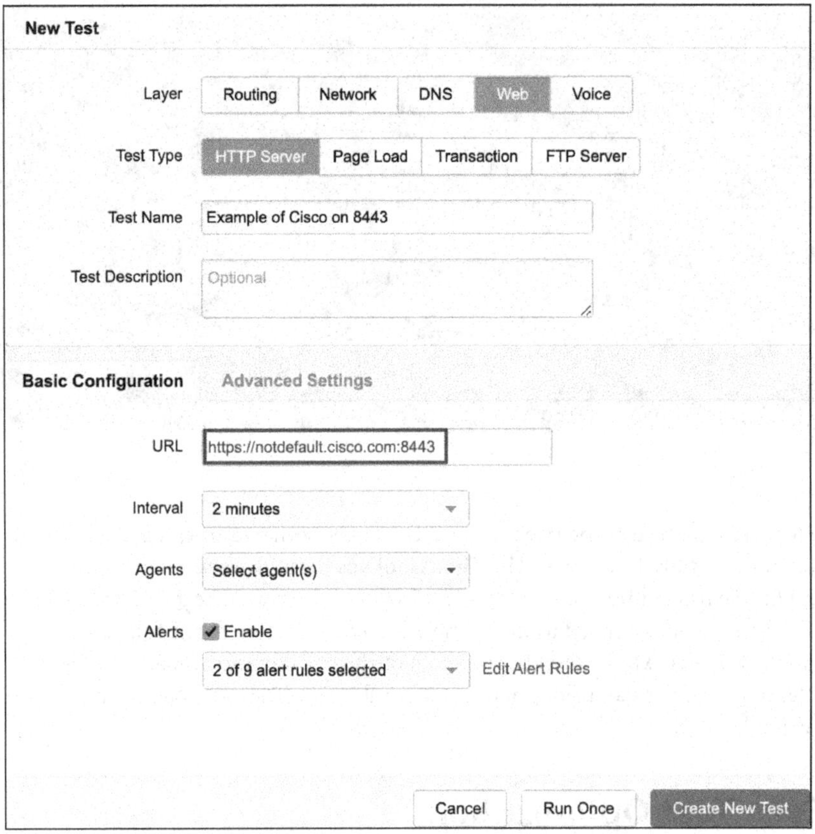

Figure 9-1 *Non-Default Port*

Note that making the protocol change shown in Figure 9-2 only impacts the network tests and not the HTTP Server, Page Load, or Transaction portions of those tests.

When network tests fail to show the expected results, it might be necessary to modify the way those tests behave in order to gain a more complete picture of the environment. Two of the most common behaviors that require network test modifications are the following:

- Consistent packet loss
- Incomplete Path Visualization

The consistent packet loss condition shown in Figure 9-3 exists due to certain firewalls dropping the first two packets out of every test run with the SACK probing method selected. Since the test uses 50 packets to test for end-to-end loss and latency, two packets equate to 8% loss...on every test round. This is simply the firewall not allowing the first two packets of the TCP session to reach the target.

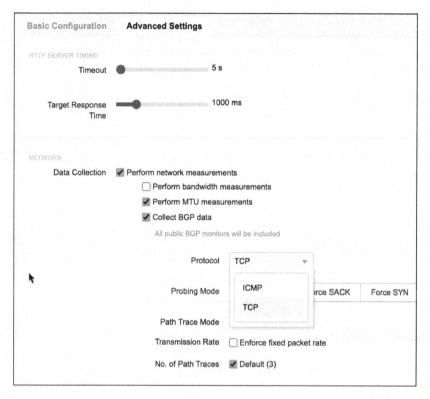

Figure 9-2 *Network Test Protocol*

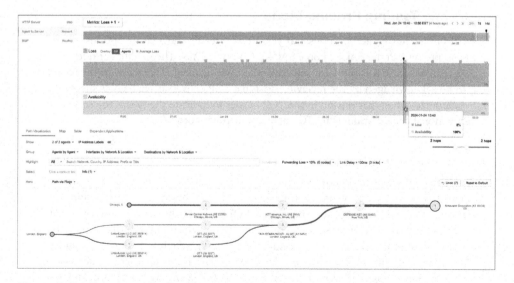

Figure 9-3 *Consistent Packet Loss*

This incomplete Path Visualization shown in Figure 9-4 is due to a firewall allowing all end-to-end packets to reach the target (packet loss = 0%) but not allowing the TCP path trace to send packets out of the network with low TTL counts on unestablished TCP sessions.

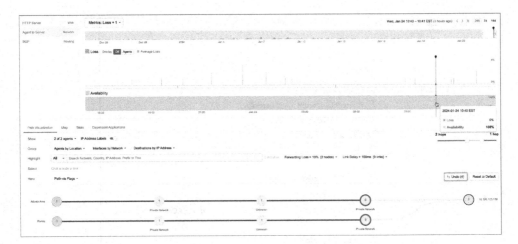

Figure 9-4   *Incomplete Path Visualization*

Let's first take a deeper look into how ThousandEyes runs these tests, which will help explain how to avoid some of these less-than-optimal situations that we occasionally run into.

End-to-End Testing: Probing Mode

As discussed in Chapter 3, ThousandEyes offers three Probing Mode options for end-to-end probing: Prefer SACK, Force SACK, and Force SYN. The default is Prefer SACK. As a reminder, SACK is short for selective acknowledgement. This refers to the way data is to be acknowledged by the receiving host in a TCP conversation. SYN is short for Synchronize, a flag that is used in the TCP header to indicate the desire to create a bidirectional conversation using TCP as the transport protocol.

Cumulative Acknowledgements

To understand selective acknowledgements (SACKs), it is helpful to first understand cumulative acknowledgements, the traditional (old school) way of acknowledging receiving TCP segments of data. Sequence (SEQ) numbers and acknowledgement (ACK) numbers keep track of bytes sent and received (TCP payload only) during a given TCP session. Most protocol analyzers (including Wireshark) default to assigning a beginning SEQ equal to 1. This is known as the *relative SEQ*. This is much easier to track visually than if the beginning SEQ were, for example, 348726702 and we started tracking bytes sent from adding onto that number. Wireshark does allow for setting the TCP SEQ tracking to the actual SEQ for anyone who prefers to see what the analyzer sees. In that case, the ACK simply tells the sender which byte it next expects to receive. So, if a sending host starts off at 348726702 and sends 1460 bytes of payload, the receiving host would acknowledge this by sending an ACK of 348726703. This informs the sender that the receiving host has received all bytes prior to 348726703 and expects 348726703 next. Using the relative SEQ, it would look more like starting off at 1, sending 1460, and seeing an ACK from the receiver for 1461. Another 1460 sent, and the receiver would ACK 2921, and so on.

Table 9-1 shows the beginning of a TCP conversation. Every TCP conversation must create a connection before any data can be transferred between hosts. TCP uses a 3-way handshake to accomplish this.

Table 9-1   *3-Way Handshake*

Client (or Agent)	Server (or Target)
SEQ = 0 no ACK (SYN only) (payload = 0)	
	SEQ = 0 ACK = 1 (SYN/ACK) (payload = 0)
SEQ = 1 ACK = 1 (ACK) (payload = 0)	

Table 9-2 shows the beginning of data moving between hosts. Most protocol analyzers today use the relative SEQ. This means that the analyzer automatically sets the beginning SEQ and ACK to zero. Then the SEQ number will increment by the number of bytes sent by the source host sending that packet. The ACK increases by the number of bytes received by the host sending the packet.

Table 9-2   *Data Transfer Without Loss*

Client (or Agent)	Server (or Target)
SEQ = 1 ACK = 1 (payload = 1460)	
	SEQ = 1 ACK = 1461 (payload = 0)
SEQ = 1461 ACK = 1 (payload = 1460)	
	SEQ = 1 ACK = 2921 (payload = 0)
SEQ = 2921 ACK = 1 (payload = 1460)	
	SEQ = 1 ACK = 4381 (payload = 0)

Table 9-3 shows what happens if the second data packet is dropped. The sender sent the following SEQs (3-way handshake remains the same).

Table 9-3   *Cumulative ACK with Loss*

Client (or Agent)	Server (or Target)
SEQ = 1 ACK = 1 (payload = 1460)	
	SEQ = 1 ACK = 1461 (payload = 0)
SEQ = 1461 ACK = 1 (payload = 1460)	
	SEQ = 1 ACK = 2921 (payload = 0)
SEQ = 2921 ACK = 1 (payload = 1460) packet/segment dropped in transit	
	SEQ = 1 ACK = 2921 (payload = 0)
SEQ = 4381 ACK = 1 (payload = 1460)	
	SEQ = 1 ACK = 2921 (payload = 0)
SEQ = 5841 ACK = 1 (payload = 1460)	
	SEQ = 1 ACK = 2921 (payload = 0)

Note that the host receiving the data (in this case, the server/target) can only tell the sending host which segment it has not received. There is no way of telling the sender that it has already received bytes 4381 through 7301. All it can do is keep telling the sender which byte it is expecting. TCP does not retransmit ACKs (no payload). Only segments with payload are monitored for delivery/reception and have a retransmit timer telling the sender when it is time to resend if the segment has not been ACK'd. In this case, it looks like the receiver/server/target is retransmitting the ACKs, but it is responding to receiving out-of-order segments. This causes the receiving host to immediately respond by notifying the sender which segment it is waiting on. Now, with cumulative ACKs, there is a good chance that the sender will eventually retransmit not only the missing segment but all the subsequent segments that were received as well. Welcome to cumulative acknowledgements.

> **Note**   TCP's congestion control algorithm is also impacted by the fast retransmit mechanism, but that topic is beyond the scope of this book. We do, however, recommend that you have a basic understanding of TCP operations because this will greatly improve your overall troubleshooting skills.

Selective Acknowledgements

Selective acknowledgements (SACKs) provide the opportunity to tell the sending host which bytes have been received and which bytes are missing. First, during the 3-way handshake, when each host sends a segment with the SYN bit set to 1, they also announce which options they are capable of using. SACK Permitted is an option that must be enabled on both hosts in order to leverage SACKs in a data transfer. The ACK still means this is what is expected next. However, now we can also see that although we are missing data starting at byte 2921, we have received bytes 4381 through 7300. Two more options become relevant at this point: SLE and SRE. SLE stands for Selective Left Edge. This is the byte that we have received. SRE is Selective Right Edge. This is what is expected next from this section of data. We are acknowledging receipt of all data between the SLE and SRE. Up to four SLE/SRE sections can be tracked in a single TCP session. If a fifth, noncontiguous data segment is missed, the TCP session will be terminated.

Table 9-4 shows what now happens when the same data packet is dropped but both hosts have agreed to use SACK instead of cumulative acknowledgements.

Table 9-4   *Selective ACK*

Client (or Agent)	Server (or Target)
SEQ = 1 ACK = 1 (payload = 1460)	
	SEQ = 1 ACK = 1461 (payload = 0)
SEQ = 1461 ACK = 1 (payload = 1460)	
	SEQ = 1 ACK = 2921 (payload = 0)
SEQ = 2921 ACK = 1 (payload = 1460) packet/segment dropped in transit	
	SEQ = 1 ACK = 2921 (payload = 0)
SEQ = 4381 ACK = 1 (payload = 1460)	
	SEQ = 1 ACK = 2921 (payload = 0) SLE = 4381 SRE = 5841
SEQ = 5841 ACK = 1 (payload = 1460)	
	SEQ = 1 ACK = 2921 (payload = 0) SLE = 4381 SRE = 7301

But the real question is, how does ThousandEyes use this in its testing strategy? Keep in mind this is all end-to-end network testing. The 3-way handshake happens just like always. The agent will set the SACK Permitted option, and if the target responds with the same option set, then they will attempt to use SACK for end-to-end tests. This is ideal because SACKs are sent immediately whenever segments are received out of order. So, all the agent needs to do is skip a segment, and then the target, if it permits SACK, will immediately respond to all subsequent segments with the appropriate SLE/SRE combinations.

Note in Table 9-5 that every subsequent byte triggers the target to respond with an updated SRE. This ensures a one-for-one match (identify when packet loss occurs) and network latency, as the response from the target is immediate (no TCP Delay ACK). ThousandEyes sends 50 packets to the target in this manner and expects 50 responses.

ThousandEyes then matches the SEQ to the SACK SRE indicating reception of that exact byte so that an accurate latency value can be assigned even when packet loss does occur. If a segment is lost between the agent and the target, SACK will start a second SLE/SRE for the subsequent received packets. However, if the SACK is dropped on the return path, the SLE/SRE would continue in the same section, but with a missing/ skipped response.

Table 9-5 *ThousandEyes SACK Testing*

Client (or Agent)	Server (or Target)
SEQ = 2 ACK = 1 (payload = 1)	
	SEQ = 1 ACK = 1 (payload = 0) SLE = 2 SRE = 3
SEQ = 3 ACK = 1 (payload = 1)	
	SEQ = 1 ACK = 1 (payload = 0) SLE = 2 SRE = 4
SEQ = 4 ACK = 1 (payload = 1)	
	SEQ = 1 ACK = 1 (payload = 0) SLE = 2 SRE = 5
SEQ = 5 ACK = 1 (payload = 1)	
	SEQ = 1 ACK = 1 (payload = 0) SLE = 2 SRE = 6
SEQ = 6 ACK = 1 (payload = 1)	
	SEQ = 1 ACK = 1 (payload = 0) SLE = 2 SRE = 7

SYN

When the Probing Mode option is set to Force SYN, the ThousandEyes agent will then use the TCP 3-way handshake to calculate end-to-end packet loss, latency, and jitter. In the example shown in Figure 9-5, the agent initiates a new TCP session by setting the SYN bit to 1 (packet no. 138). This is using a source port of 35877, thus identifying it as a unique TCP session. The response to this SYN is not seen until packet no. 149 (~7 ms later) when the target sends a SYN/ACK, both acknowledging the SYN it received and sending its own SYN in return. Packet no. 150 shows an RST where the agent immediately ends the session to free up any dedicated resources the target reserved for this TCP session. While SACK testing is preferred because it consumes less resources both from the target and the network, SYN testing is also effective and designed to have minimal impact on resources.

```
No.   Time       Delta            Source         Destination    Protocol  TTL  Info
138  *REF*       *REF* 192.168.1.73   184.84.137.34   TCP   64  35877 → 443 [SYN] Seq=0 Win=5840 Len=0 MSS=1460 TSval=101423 TSecr=0
139  0.000292    0.000292 184.84.137.34  192.168.1.73    TCP   55  443 → 41653 [SYN, ACK] Seq=0 Ack=1 Win=65160 Len=0 MSS=1400 TSval=2999324651 TSecr=95917
140  0.000423    0.000131 192.168.1.73   184.84.137.34   TCP   64  41653 → 443 [RST] Seq=1 Win=0 Len=0
141  0.001405    0.000982 192.168.1.73   184.84.137.34   TCP   64  41899 → 443 [SYN] Seq=0 Win=5840 Len=0 MSS=1460 TSval=102791 TSecr=0
142  0.001503    0.000098 192.168.1.73   184.84.137.34   TCP   2   [TCP Port numbers reused] 34639 → 443 [SYN] Seq=0 Win=62843 Len=0 MSS=1460 TSval=102859 TSecr=0
143  0.003228    0.001725 184.84.137.34  192.168.1.73    TCP   55  443 → 46233 [SYN, ACK] Seq=0 Ack=1 Win=65160 Len=0 MSS=1400 TSval=2999324654 TSecr=98673
144  0.003368    0.000140 192.168.1.73   184.84.137.34   TCP   64  46233 → 443 [RST] Seq=1 Win=0 Len=0
145  0.004067    0.000699 192.168.1.73   184.84.137.34   TCP   3   [TCP Port numbers reused] 39487 → 443 [SYN] Seq=0 Win=6302 Len=0 MSS=1460 TSval=109412 TSecr=0
146  0.004387    0.000320 192.168.1.73   184.84.137.34   TCP   3   [TCP Port numbers reused] 59713 → 443 [SYN] Seq=0 Win=19358 Len=0 MSS=1460 TSval=109698 TSecr=0
147  0.004440    0.000053 192.168.1.73   184.84.137.34   TCP   64  46957 → 443 [SYN] Seq=0 Win=5840 Len=0 MSS=1460 TSval=105853 TSecr=0
148  0.005205    0.000765 192.168.1.73   184.84.137.34   TCP   3   [TCP Port numbers reused] 59939 → 443 [SYN] Seq=0 Win=55986 Len=0 MSS=1460 TSval=108628 TSecr=0
149  0.006545    0.001340 184.84.137.34  192.168.1.73    TCP   55  443 → 35877 [SYN, ACK] Seq=0 Ack=1 Win=65160 Len=0 MSS=1400 TSval=2999324657 TSecr=101423
150  0.006688    0.000143 192.168.1.73   184.84.137.34   TCP   64  35877 → 443 [RST] Seq=1 Win=0 Len=0
151  0.006887    0.000199 184.84.137.34  192.168.1.73    TCP   55  443 → 41899 [SYN, ACK] Seq=0 Ack=1 Win=65160 Len=0 MSS=1400 TSval=2999324658 TSecr=102791
152  0.006970    0.000083 192.168.1.73   184.84.137.34   TCP   64  41899 → 443 [RST] Seq=1 Win=0 Len=0
153  0.008029    0.001059 192.168.1.73   184.84.137.34   TCP   64  53377 → 443 [SYN] Seq=0 Win=5840 Len=0 MSS=1460 TSval=109435 TSecr=0
154  0.009166    0.001137 192.168.1.73   184.84.137.34   TCP   64  34289 → 443 [SYN] Seq=0 Win=5840 Len=0 MSS=1460 TSval=110591 TSecr=0
155  0.010393    0.001227 184.84.137.34  192.168.1.73    TCP   55  443 → 46957 [SYN, ACK] Seq=0 Ack=1 Win=65160 Len=0 MSS=1400 TSval=2999324661 TSecr=105853
156  0.010536    0.000143 192.168.1.73   184.84.137.34   TCP   64  46957 → 443 [RST] Seq=1 Win=0 Len=0
157  0.011303    0.000767 192.168.1.73   184.84.137.34   TCP   64  43155 → 443 [SYN] Seq=0 Win=5840 Len=0 MSS=1460 TSval=112748 TSecr=0
158  0.013996    0.002693 184.84.137.34  192.168.1.73    TCP   55  443 → 53377 [SYN, ACK] Seq=0 Ack=1 Win=65160 Len=0 MSS=1400 TSval=2999324665 TSecr=109435
159  0.014119    0.000123 192.168.1.73   184.84.137.34   TCP   64  53377 → 443 [RST] Seq=1 Win=0 Len=0
160  0.015029    0.000910 192.168.1.73   184.84.137.34   TCP   64  40283 → 443 [SYN] Seq=0 Win=5840 Len=0 MSS=1460 TSval=116471 TSecr=0
161  0.015139    0.000110 184.84.137.34  192.168.1.73    TCP   55  443 → 34289 [SYN, ACK] Seq=0 Ack=1 Win=65160 Len=0 MSS=1400 TSval=2999324665 TSecr=110591
162  0.015245    0.000106 192.168.1.73   184.84.137.34   TCP   64  34289 → 443 [RST] Seq=1 Win=0 Len=0
163  0.016806    0.001561 184.84.137.34  192.168.1.73    TCP   55  443 → 43155 [SYN, ACK] Seq=0 Ack=1 Win=65160 Len=0 MSS=1400 TSval=2999324668 TSecr=112748
164  0.016913    0.000107 192.168.1.73   184.84.137.34   TCP   64  43155 → 443 [RST] Seq=1 Win=0 Len=0
165  0.020476    0.003563 184.84.137.34  192.168.1.73    TCP   55  443 → 40283 [SYN, ACK] Seq=0 Ack=1 Win=65160 Len=0 MSS=1400 TSval=2999324671 TSecr=116471
166  0.020565    0.000089 192.168.1.73   184.84.137.34   TCP   64  40283 → 443 [RST] Seq=1 Win=0 Len=0
```

Figure 9-5 *Force SYN (Classic Mode) Packets*

Path Visualization

The Path Trace Mode and No. of Path Traces options (both found in Advanced Settings) provide mechanisms for fine-tuning the way the hop-by-hop tests run, just as Probing Mode defines details on how the end-to-end tests run. Tweaking these test options can make a difference in seeing a complete path or not. Probing Mode has no impact on how the Path Trace tests run. However, selecting Protocol ICMP instead of the default TCP will impact both end-to-end testing and hop-by-hop discovery. In most cases, TCP is the optimal protocol when testing a TCP-based service or application. But again, some networks might not allow TCP testing to function. Another reason to use ICMP would be if traffic is going through a third-party security gateway or proxy. The TCP sessions may be terminated at that point, but ICMP would allow visualization of the path from the agent to the target. In these situations, running both a TCP test (to get the agent-to-gateway/proxy user experience) and ICMP test, to get the Path Visualization (although if a tunnel is involved, the test might not follow the same path as the tunnel), is recommended.

Path Trace Mode

The Path Trace Mode option designates how the hop-by-hop Path Visualization is achieved. The options available are classic (default) or In Session.

Classic

When running the network path trace testing in Classic mode (i.e., the In Session check box is not checked), path discovery is done by sending SYN packets with incrementing TTLs. Once a packet is sent with a high enough TTL to reach the destination (packet no. 6866 in Figure 9-6), the target responds with a SYN/ACK. Once the path is complete, the session is terminated (RST), and a new session is established (packet no. 508) for testing Path MTU.

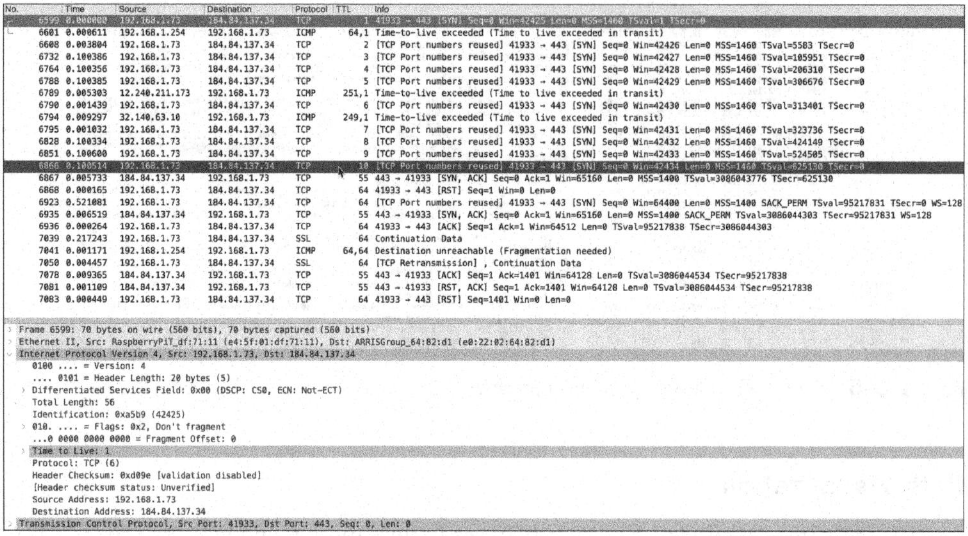

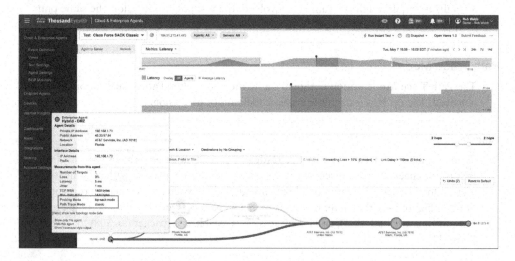

Figure 9-6   *SACK (Classic Mode) Packets*

Routers along the path that respond with "TTL exceeded in transit" will be shown in
Path Visualization (found under the Path Visualization tab, in the Agent to Server view).
Routers that do not respond will be shown on the path using white circles. Because Path
Visualization runs multiple tests (default = 3), more than one path may be shown for any
given test round.

Figure 9-7 shows Path Visualization when using SACK for Probing Mode and classic
for Path Trace Mode. By hovering your mouse pointer over the agent running the test,
ThousandEyes shows the modes used for that test interval.

Figure 9-7   *SACK (Classic Mode) Path Visualization*

Figure 9-8 shows a packet capture when the Probing Mode is set to Force SYN and the Path Trace Mode is left in classic mode.

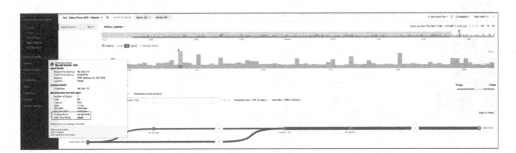

282 108.301773	0.000000	192.168.1.73	184.84.137.34	TCP	1 51509 → 443 [SYN] Seq=0 Win=11120 Len=0 MSS=1460 TSval=1 TSecr=0
284 108.302490	0.000707	192.168.1.254	192.168.1.73	ICMP	64,1 Time-to-live exceeded (Time to live exceeded in transit)
290 108.307529	0.005049	192.168.1.73	184.84.137.34	TCP	2 [TCP Port numbers reused] 51509 → 443 [SYN] Seq=0 Win=11121 Len=0 MSS=1460 TSval=7161 TSecr=0
423 108.407806	0.100357	192.168.1.73	184.84.137.34	TCP	3 [TCP Port numbers reused] 51509 → 443 [SYN] Seq=0 Win=11122 Len=0 MSS=1460 TSval=107719 TSecr=0
449 108.508262	0.100396	192.168.1.73	184.84.137.34	TCP	4 [TCP Port numbers reused] 51509 → 443 [SYN] Seq=0 Win=11123 Len=0 MSS=1460 TSval=208002 TSecr=0
454 108.608750	0.100488	192.168.1.73	184.84.137.34	TCP	5 [TCP Port numbers reused] 51509 → 443 [SYN] Seq=0 Win=11124 Len=0 MSS=1460 TSval=308442 TSecr=0
456 108.613299	0.004549	12.240.211.173	192.168.1.73	ICMP	251,1 Time-to-live exceeded (Time to live exceeded in transit)
457 108.614467	0.001168	192.168.1.73	184.84.137.34	TCP	6 [TCP Port numbers reused] 51509 → 443 [SYN] Seq=0 Win=11125 Len=0 MSS=1460 TSval=314222 TSecr=0
460 108.620011	0.005544	32.140.63.10	192.168.1.73	ICMP	249,1 Time-to-live exceeded (Time to live exceeded in transit)
461 108.620880	0.000869	192.168.1.73	184.84.137.34	TCP	7 [TCP Port numbers reused] 51509 → 443 [SYN] Seq=0 Win=11126 Len=0 MSS=1460 TSval=320651 TSecr=0
478 108.721541	0.100661	192.168.1.73	184.84.137.34	TCP	8 [TCP Port numbers reused] 51509 → 443 [SYN] Seq=0 Win=11127 Len=0 MSS=1460 TSval=421264 TSecr=0
483 108.822055	0.100514	192.168.1.73	184.84.137.34	TCP	9 [TCP Port numbers reused] 51509 → 443 [SYN] Seq=0 Win=11128 Len=0 MSS=1460 TSval=521711 TSecr=0
488 108.922329	0.100274	192.168.1.73	184.84.137.34	TCP	10 [TCP Port numbers reused] 51509 → 443 [SYN] Seq=0 Win=11129 Len=0 MSS=1460 TSval=622171 TSecr=0
491 108.935085	0.012756	184.84.137.34	192.168.1.73	TCP	55 443 → 51509 [SYN, ACK] Seq=0 Ack=1 Win=65160 Len=0 MSS=1400 TSval=647552747 TSecr=622171
492 108.935211	0.000126	192.168.1.73	184.84.137.34	TCP	64 51509 → 443 [RST] Seq=1 Win=0 Len=0
508 109.306128	0.370917	192.168.1.73	184.84.137.34	TCP	64 [TCP Port numbers reused] 51509 → 443 [SYN] Seq=0 Win=64400 Len=0 MSS=1400 SACK_PERM TSval=81900019 TSecr=0 WS=128
515 109.313377	0.007249	184.84.137.34	192.168.1.73	TCP	55 443 → 51509 [SYN, ACK] Seq=0 Ack=1 Win=65160 Len=0 MSS=1400 SACK_PERM TSval=647553128 TSecr=81900019 WS=128
516 109.313584	0.000207	192.168.1.73	184.84.137.34	TCP	64 51509 → 443 [ACK] Seq=1 Ack=1 Win=64512 Len=0 TSval=81900026 TSecr=647553128
522 110.407010	1.093426	192.168.1.73	184.84.137.34	TCP	64 51509 → 443 [PSH, ACK] Seq=1 Ack=1 Win=1424512 Len=1460
525 110.408938	0.001928	192.168.1.254	192.168.1.73	ICMP	64,64 Destination unreachable (Fragmentation needed)
531 110.411137	0.002199	192.168.1.73	184.84.137.34	TCP	64 [TCP Retransmission] 51509 → 443 [PSH, ACK] Seq=1 Ack=1 Win=1400
539 110.418677	0.007540	184.84.137.34	192.168.1.73	TCP	55 443 → 51509 [ACK] Seq=1 Ack=1401 Win=64128 Len=0 TSval=647554233 TSecr=81900026
541 110.419210	0.000533	184.84.137.34	192.168.1.73	TCP	55 443 → 51509 [PSH, ACK] Seq=1 Ack=1401 Win=64128 Len=0 TSval=647554234 TSecr=81900026
543 110.420071	0.000861	192.168.1.73	184.84.137.34	TCP	64 51509 → 443 [RST] Seq=1401 Win=0 Len=0

Figure 9-8 *Force SYN (Classic Mode) Path Packets*

Figure 9-9 shows the ThousandEyes Path Visualization when the Probing Mode is set to Force SYN and the Path Trace Mode is left in classic mode.

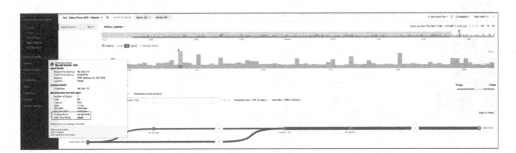

Figure 9-9 *Force SYN (Classic Mode) Path Visualization*

In Session

When the Path Trace Mode field's In Session check box is checked, the TCP session will be established prior to the network path trace being initiated. Figure 9-10 shows the TCP 3-way handshake (packets 9, 21, and 22) completing before the TTL is dropped to 1 for a trace route discovery. In this mode, Path MTU Discovery is also run from within the originally established TCP session.

When No. of Path Traces is set to the default (3), each agent configured in the test will establish four connections to the target for the network tests: one for the end-to-end network test and one for each path trace that is initiated. If the test type is HTTP Server, it will then create a fifth TCP connection on each test interval.

Figure 9-11 shows ThousandEyes Path Visualization when probing uses SACK and path trace mode is set to in-session.

```
No.  Time      Delta     Source         Destination    Protocol TTL  Info
9  0.216207  0.000000  192.168.1.73   184.51.213.41  TCP   64 57753 → 443 [SYN] Seq=0 Win=64400 Len=0 MSS=1400 SACK_PERM TSval=751619235 TSecr=0 WS=128
21 0.222473  0.006266  184.51.213.41  192.168.1.73   TCP   55 443 → 57753 [SYN, ACK] Seq=0 Ack=1 Win=65160 Len=0 MSS=1400 SACK_PERM TSval=759377428 TSecr=751619235 WS=128
22 0.222584  0.000111  192.168.1.73   184.51.213.41  TCP   64 57753 → 443 [ACK] Seq=1 Ack=1 Win=64512 Len=0 TSval=751619241 TSecr=759377428
118 0.425362 0.202778  192.168.1.73   184.51.213.41  TCP    1 [TCP Previous segment not captured] 57753 → 443 [PSH, ACK] Seq=2 Ack=1 Win=5327104 Len=1
120 0.426676 0.001314  192.168.1.254  192.168.1.73   ICMP  64,1 Time-to-live exceeded (Time to live exceeded in transit)
124 0.428188 0.001512  192.168.1.73   184.51.213.41  TCP    2 57753 → 443 [PSH, ACK] Seq=3 Ack=1 Win=5327232 Len=1
130 0.528623 0.100435  192.168.1.73   184.51.213.41  TCP    3 57753 → 443 [PSH, ACK] Seq=4 Ack=1 Win=5327360 Len=1
135 0.629023 0.100400  192.168.1.73   184.51.213.41  TCP    4 57753 → 443 [PSH, ACK] Seq=5 Ack=1 Win=5327488 Len=1
140 0.729379 0.100356  192.168.1.73   184.51.213.41  TCP    5 57753 → 443 [PSH, ACK] Seq=6 Ack=1 Win=5327616 Len=1
144 0.733751 0.004372  12.240.211.173 192.168.1.73   ICMP  251,1 Time-to-live exceeded (Time to live exceeded in transit)
146 0.734775 0.001024  192.168.1.73   184.51.213.41  TCP    6 57753 → 443 [PSH, ACK] Seq=7 Ack=1 Win=5327744 Len=1
150 0.753316 0.018541  32.140.63.10   192.168.1.73   ICMP  249,1 Time-to-live exceeded (Time to live exceeded in transit)
154 0.754702 0.001386  192.168.1.73   184.51.213.41  TCP    7 57753 → 443 [PSH, ACK] Seq=8 Ack=1 Win=5327872 Len=1
167 0.855006 0.100304  192.168.1.73   184.51.213.41  TCP    8 57753 → 443 [PSH, ACK] Seq=9 Ack=1 Win=5328000 Len=1
171 0.955307 0.100301  192.168.1.73   184.51.213.41  TCP    9 57753 → 443 [PSH, ACK] Seq=10 Ack=1 Win=5328128 Len=1
177 1.056160 0.100853  192.168.1.73   184.51.213.41  TCP   10 57753 → 443 [PSH, ACK] Seq=11 Ack=1 Win=5328256 Len=1
181 1.061531 0.005351  184.51.213.41  192.168.1.73   TCP   55 [TCP Window Update] 443 → 57753 [ACK] Seq=1 Ack=1 Win=65200 Len=0 TSval=759378267 TSecr=751619241 SLE=11 SRE=12
194 1.701670 0.640159  192.168.1.73   184.51.213.41  TCP   64 [TCP Retransmission] 57753 → 443 [PSH, ACK] Seq=1 Ack=1 Win=5328256 Len=1460
197 1.703342 0.001672  192.168.1.254  192.168.1.73   ICMP  64,64 Destination unreachable (Fragmentation needed)
203 1.708330 0.004988  192.168.1.73   184.51.213.41  TCP   64 [TCP Retransmission] 57753 → 443 [PSH, ACK] Seq=1 Ack=1 Win=64128 Len=1400
213 1.715126 0.006796  184.51.213.41  192.168.1.73   TCP   55 443 → 57753 [ACK] Seq=1 Ack=1401 Win=64128 Len=0 TSval=759378920 TSecr=751619241 SLE=11 SRE=1401
215 1.716516 0.001390  184.51.213.41  192.168.1.73   TCP   55 443 → 57753 [RST, ACK] Seq=1 Ack=1401 Win=64128 Len=0 TSval=759378922 TSecr=751619241
217 1.717465 0.000949  192.168.1.73   184.51.213.41  TCP   64 57753 → 443 [RST] Seq=1401 Win=0 Len=0
```

Figure 9-10 *SACK (In Session)—Packets*

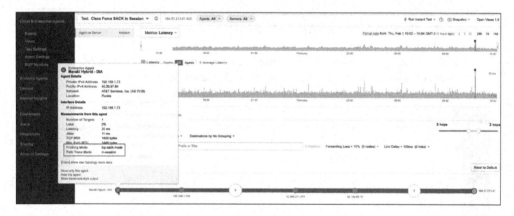

Figure 9-11 *SACK (In Session)—Path Visualization*

Figure 9-12 shows a packet capture when the Probing Mode is set to Force SYN and the Path Trace Mode is set to In Session.

```
No.  Time        Delta     Source         Destination    Protocol TTL  Info
238 108.770267 0.000000  192.168.1.73   184.25.165.31  TCP   64 43837 → 443 [SYN] Seq=0 Win=64240 Len=0 MSS=1460 SACK_PERM TSval=4089883133 TSecr=0 WS=128
244 108.788996 0.018729  184.25.165.31  192.168.1.73   TCP   53 443 → 43837 [SYN, ACK] Seq=0 Ack=1 Win=65160 Len=0 MSS=1400 SACK_PERM TSval=4279829603 TSecr=4089883133 WS=128
245 108.789182 0.000186  192.168.1.73   184.25.165.31  TCP   64 43837 → 443 [ACK] Seq=1 Ack=1 Win=64256 Len=0 TSval=4089883152 TSecr=4279829603
395 109.266165 0.476983  192.168.1.73   184.25.165.31  TCP    1 [TCP Previous segment not captured] 43837 → 443 [PSH, ACK] Seq=2 Ack=1 Win=7040896 Len=1
396 109.267210 0.001045  192.168.1.254  192.168.1.73   ICMP  64,1 Time-to-live exceeded (Time to live exceeded in transit)
401 109.271744 0.004534  192.168.1.73   184.25.165.31  TCP    2 43837 → 443 [PSH, ACK] Seq=3 Ack=1 Win=7041024 Len=1
404 109.372364 0.100620  192.168.1.73   184.25.165.31  TCP    3 43837 → 443 [PSH, ACK] Seq=4 Ack=1 Win=7041152 Len=1
408 109.473086 0.100722  192.168.1.73   184.25.165.31  TCP    4 43837 → 443 [PSH, ACK] Seq=5 Ack=1 Win=7041280 Len=1
410 109.573761 0.100675  192.168.1.73   184.25.165.31  TCP    5 43837 → 443 [PSH, ACK] Seq=6 Ack=1 Win=7041408 Len=1
414 109.674294 0.100533  192.168.1.73   184.25.165.31  TCP    6 43837 → 443 [PSH, ACK] Seq=7 Ack=1 Win=7041536 Len=1
416 109.774822 0.100528  192.168.1.73   184.25.165.31  TCP    7 43837 → 443 [PSH, ACK] Seq=8 Ack=1 Win=7041664 Len=1
419 109.792615 0.017793  32.130.16.33   192.168.1.73   ICMP  248,1 Time-to-live exceeded (Time to live exceeded in transit)
421 109.793949 0.001334  192.168.1.73   184.25.165.31  TCP    8 43837 → 443 [PSH, ACK] Seq=9 Ack=1 Win=7041792 Len=1
425 109.817140 0.023191  32.141.63.14   192.168.1.73   ICMP  246,1 Time-to-live exceeded (Time to live exceeded in transit)
427 109.818188 0.001048  192.168.1.73   184.25.165.31  TCP    9 43837 → 443 [PSH, ACK] Seq=10 Ack=1 Win=7041920 Len=1
432 109.919743 0.101555  192.168.1.73   184.25.165.31  TCP   10 43837 → 443 [PSH, ACK] Seq=11 Ack=1 Win=7042048 Len=1
435 110.020221 0.100478  192.168.1.73   184.25.165.31  TCP   11 43837 → 443 [PSH, ACK] Seq=12 Ack=1 Win=7042176 Len=1
438 110.120640 0.100419  192.168.1.73   184.25.165.31  TCP   12 43837 → 443 [PSH, ACK] Seq=13 Ack=1 Win=7042304 Len=1
440 110.137010 0.016370  184.25.165.31  192.168.1.73   TCP   53 [TCP Window Update] 443 → 43837 [ACK] Seq=1 Ack=1 Win=65280 Len=0 TSval=4279830952 TSecr=4089883152 SLE=13 SRE=14
442 110.138902 0.001892  184.25.165.31  192.168.1.73   TCP   64 [TCP Out-Of-order] 43837 → 443 [FIN, ACK] Seq=1 Ack=1 Win=64256 Len=0 TSval=4089884502 TSecr=4279830952
444 110.139344 0.000442  192.168.1.73   184.25.165.31  TCP   53 443 → 43837 [RST] Seq=14 Win=0 Len=0
449 110.155799 0.016455  184.25.165.31  192.168.1.73   TCP   53 443 → 43837 [FIN, ACK] Seq=1 Ack=2 Win=65280 Len=0 TSval=4279830970 TSecr=4089884502
450 110.156096 0.000297  192.168.1.73   184.25.165.31  TCP   64 43837 → 443 [ACK] Seq=2 Win=64256 Len=0 TSval=4089884519 TSecr=4279830970
453 110.156595 0.000499  184.25.165.31  192.168.1.73   TCP   53 [TCP Dup ACK 449#1] 443 → 43837 [ACK] Seq=2 Ack=2 Win=65280 Len=0 TSval=4279830971 TSecr=4089884502
```

Figure 9-12 *Force SYN (In Session)—Packets*

Figure 9-13 shows ThousandEyes Path Visualization when the Probing Mode is set to Force SYN and the Path Trace Mode is set to In Session.

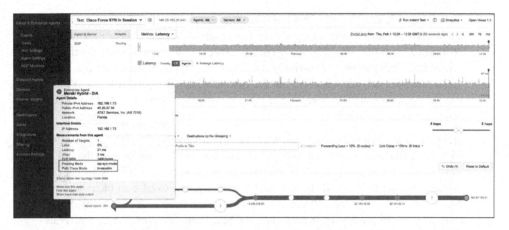

Figure 9-13 *Force SYN (In Session)—Path Visualization*

No. of Path Traces

By default, the number of traces run in a test round is set to 3 in the No. of Path Traces field. So, if more than three equal-cost routes exist to the target, only three will be discovered/shown. This is one reason it might make sense to increase this default behavior. The highest this value can go to is 10 (as shown in Figure 9-14). Increasing this value also increases the amount of time spent in each test round testing the network hops for forwarding loss and latency.

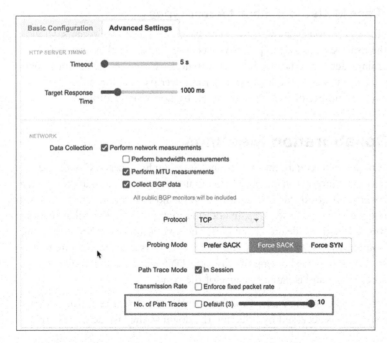

Figure 9-14 *No. of Path Traces in Advanced Settings Tab Set to 10*

Something to keep in mind is that if a customer has many locations and is testing an application or service from all those locations, each agent now has the potential of connecting 12 times (or more if browser tests are used) per test round: once for the HTTP Server test, once for the end-to-end network test, and once for each path trace (max. 10) initiated when Force SYN is used. So, if a customer has 1,000 storefronts and wants to test an application service from each, for every test round there will be 12,000 TCP connections to that service.

Figure 9-15 shows a test configured with the No. of Path Traces set to 5 (packets 352–356). This image has been filtered to show only the TTL of 3, while the full capture would show five tests for each TTL until the target is reached. Note this packet capture displays two separate rounds of testing. This test happens to have an interval set to 2 minutes. Because of the 119 seconds between test rounds, considerations should be made in terms of mission criticality, risk, and SLAs when determining test intervals.

No.	Time	Delta	Source	Destination	Protocol	TTL	Info
352	108.453473	0.000000	192.168.1.73	184.51.213.41	TCP	3	48115 → 443 [PSH, ACK] Seq=4 Ack=1 Win=2690816 Len=1
353	108.453487	0.000014	192.168.1.73	184.51.213.41	TCP	3	53487 → 443 [PSH, ACK] Seq=4 Ack=1 Win=1209600 Len=1
354	108.454743	0.001256	192.168.1.73	184.51.213.41	TCP	3	34765 → 443 [PSH, ACK] Seq=4 Ack=1 Win=7063680 Len=1
355	108.454748	0.000005	192.168.1.73	184.51.213.41	TCP	3	57503 → 443 [PSH, ACK] Seq=4 Ack=1 Win=7662208 Len=1
356	108.455388	0.000640	192.168.1.73	184.51.213.41	TCP	3	42633 → 443 [PSH, ACK] Seq=4 Ack=1 Win=4493184 Len=1
567	228.211533	119.756…	192.168.1.73	184.51.213.41	TCP	3	60641 → 443 [PSH, ACK] Seq=4 Ack=1 Win=2592256 Len=1
569	228.309509	0.097976	192.168.1.73	184.51.213.41	TCP	3	44723 → 443 [PSH, ACK] Seq=4 Ack=1 Win=7438592 Len=1
570	228.311007	0.001498	192.168.1.73	184.51.213.41	TCP	3	34177 → 443 [PSH, ACK] Seq=4 Ack=1 Win=529408 Len=1
571	228.311034	0.000027	192.168.1.73	184.51.213.41	TCP	3	44953 → 443 [PSH, ACK] Seq=4 Ack=1 Win=4023680 Len=1
573	228.312508	0.001474	192.168.1.73	184.51.213.41	TCP	3	36631 → 443 [PSH, ACK] Seq=4 Ack=1 Win=2680576 Len=1

Figure 9-15   *No. of Path Traces—Packets*

Probing and Path Trace Modes for Different Agent Types

While all the examples previously shown have been based on Enterprise Agents, Cloud Agents operate the exact same way. Endpoint Agents use a subset of these tests. The methods and meanings described here remain consistent. However, the Endpoint Agents, to minimize any risk of impact to the host system, run fewer packets for end-to-end testing and run a fewer number of path traces for hop-by-hop visualizations.

Monitoring Collaboration Meetings

Best practices for monitoring collaboration meetings leverage Enterprise, Cloud, and Endpoint Agents and use Internet Insights to help monitor access and availability from a much wider perspective. A good starting point for Cloud and Enterprise Agent tests is to use the built-in templates for these services. In addition to monitoring the collaboration services themselves, it is a good idea to also monitor how your internal DNS is servicing those queries. ThousandEyes tests will alert you to when DNS is causing a failure to a given service/test. Proper troubleshooting of why your DNS service failed requires specific DNS tests to triage and isolate the cause of the issue.

Figures 9-16 and 9-17 show adding a new Cloud and Enterprise Agent test using a preconfigured template. This is accessed by selecting the down arrow instead of selecting Add New Test.

Figure 9-16   *Cloud & Enterprise Agent Test Template*

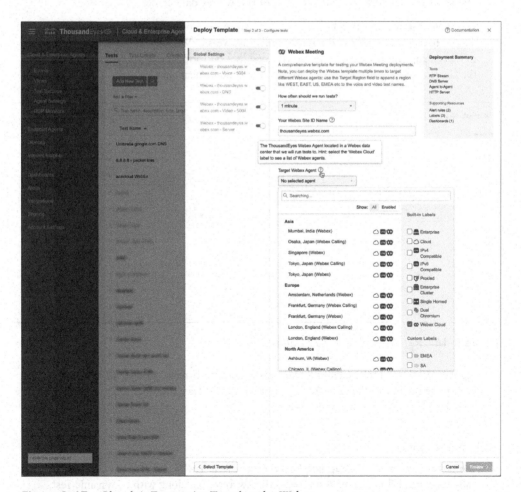

Figure 9-17   *Cloud & Enterprise Template for Webex*

Webex

Webex offers the most extensive ThousandEyes testing of all collaboration platforms. This is largely due to Webex also being a part of Cisco and the integrations that the ThousandEyes and the Webex engineers have worked on together.

Cloud & Enterprise Agents

Again, because Webex and ThousandEyes are both a part of Cisco, the respective teams have worked together to deploy Cloud Agents into Webex data centers around the world. This allows ThousandEyes customers with access to Cloud Agents to test from their corporate networks into their primary and secondary Webex data centers. Agent to agent tests can be configured using TCP or UDP. They include not only the ability to run RTP streams between locations but also the ability to run bidirectional agent to agent tests that show the network path into and out of the Webex data center.

Figure 9-18 shows a VoIP/RTP test that was set up from both Cloud and Enterprise Agents to an agent collocated with the calling servers in Webex's Dallas data center. In this example, it can be quickly determined that performance degradation is unique to the Enterprise Agent and is not impacting the Cloud Agents in that area.

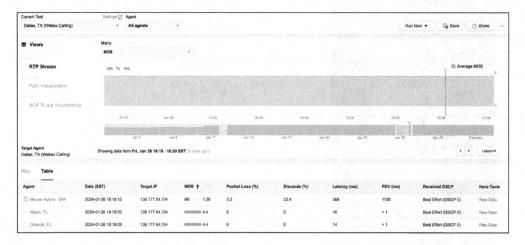

Figure 9-18 *RTP Stream to Webex Dallas*

Figure 9-19 shows the results of a bidirectional (agent to agent) test set up between an Enterprise Agent and the same Webex agent in the Dallas data center. In this case, packet loss along the return path can be seen.

Endpoint Agents

Templates now exist for Endpoint Agent tests as well. The Webex template will automatically create an HTTP Server test to <yourID>.webex.com along with a Dynamic Test.

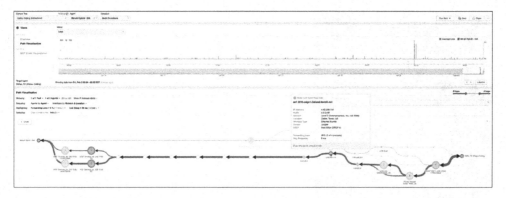

Figure 9-19 *Bidirectional Test with Webex Dallas*

To access the Endpoint Agent test templates, navigate to **Endpoint Agents > Test Settings** and click the **+Monitor Applications** button. This opens the Monitor Application wizard, as shown in Figure 9-20. Select the Webex template.

Figure 9-20 *Endpoint Agent Test Templates*

Figure 9-21 shows the Webex template for Endpoint Agents. By default, this will create two tests: one HTTP Server test and one Dynamic test. Note that you do not need to use the .webex.com domain along with the Site ID, because the template will automatically append .webex.com to whatever is entered in this field. You can change the test interval if needed. Select the Endpoint Agents you want this test applied to. Also note that the default number of agents is set to 25. You might want to increase this value to better represent the size of your deployment. Then select **Review** to confirm your selections before deploying the tests.

This Dynamic Test will activate tests directly to specific Webex servers that the client is connected to. The Endpoint Agent discovers whenever the client joins a Webex meeting and begins testing to all Webex servers it observes connection to.

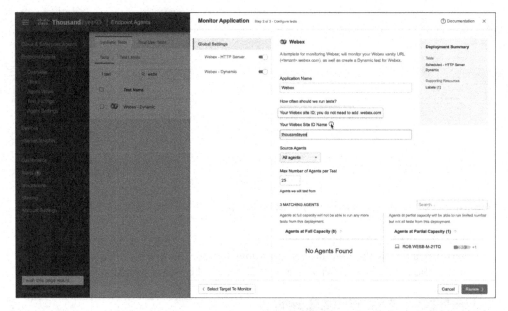

Figure 9-21   *Endpoint Agent Template for Webex*

In Figure 9-22, a Webex participant is running the Endpoint Agent with the Webex Dynamic Test configured. This test shows the participant, who is located in Florida, connecting to a server in Frankfurt, Germany. You can find this view by choosing **Endpoint Agents > Views** and then click **Dynamic Tests** and in the very top left side of the page is a drop-down menu that will list the available Dynamic tests.

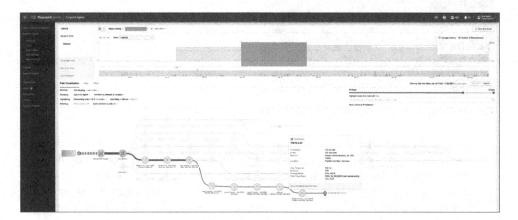

Figure 9-22   *Endpoint—Webex Dynamic Test*

Additionally, Webex Control Hub now displays information on participants who have the Endpoint Agent with the Webex Dynamic Test enabled. This adds the network Path Visualization along with latency, packet loss, and jitter to the Control Hub dashboard.

In addition to setting up synthetic and dynamic tests for Endpoint Agents, Real User tests are available and require whitelisting domains to be monitored. Figure 9-23 shows a list of domains that Webex uses. The whitelist can be accessed by going to **Endpoint Agents > Test Settings** and then selecting the **Real User Tests** tab at the top of the page. These Real User tests monitor the browser activity for Endpoint Agents that have the browser plugin (IE, Edge and Chrome) installed.

Domains and URLs that need to be accessed for Webex Services	
Cisco Webex Services URLs	
Domain / URL	Webex Apps and devices using these domains / URLs
*webex.com *cisco.com *.wbx2.com *.ciscospark.com *.webexapis.com	All
*.webexcontent.com (1)	All
Additional Webex related services - Cisco Owned domains	

Figure 9-23   *Webex Services Domains*

Internet Insights

ThousandEyes leverages test data from thousands of agents around the world to look for major outages. These outages are cataloged by service provider type: CDN, DNS, IA/400, ISP, SAAS, SECAAS, or UCAAS. Webex falls under the UCAAS catalog. Internet Insights enables you to quickly determine when your outage is part of a much larger outage, or when outages might be occurring in regions of the world where you have yet to deploy individual tests. The Internet Insights example in Figure 9-24 shows 51 major outages that have impacted multiple customers over the past 24 hours. Outages are classified as either Network or Application.

Figure 9-24   *Internet Insights Heat Map*

Network Outages

Navigating to **Internet Insights > Views** can help identify when outages impact more than just your company. For example, Figure 9-25 shows the results of setting a filter on Server Network (at the top of the page) for all Webex networks. This provides insight into any major network outage that interrupted tests to Webex. Figure 9-25 shows an Internet outage that affected networks throughout the United States and Singapore.

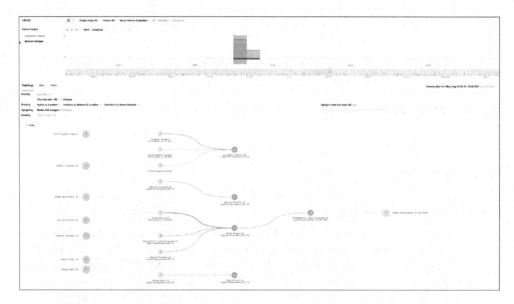

Figure 9-25   *Internet Insights—Network Outage—Webex*

Application Outages

Internet Insights can also identify when application issues are impacting multiple customers. Very quickly, a customer can determine whether their outage is part of a bigger problem or localized to them. Additionally, management can ascertain the scope of a problem by seeing more than the tests that have been configured on their own platform. Figure 9-26 shows application outages impacting Webex services.

Teams

Monitoring Microsoft Teams presents additional challenges because Teams is dependent on other Microsoft services for delivery of its collaboration platform. Fortunately, ThousandEyes is continually improving its testing capability in its Teams integration.

Cloud and Enterprise Agents

Once again, ThousandEyes provides a template for Microsoft Teams monitoring. Select the Enterprise and Cloud Agents needed, pick your interval, and away you go. Cloud and Enterprise templates are located by using the drop-down menu next to Add New Test. Figure 9-27 shows deploying the Microsoft Teams template. The Teams template is accessed the same way.

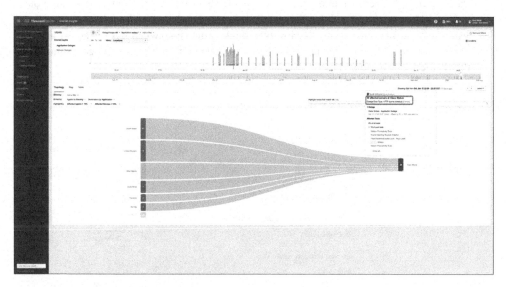

Figure 9-26   *Internet Insights—Application Outage—Webex*

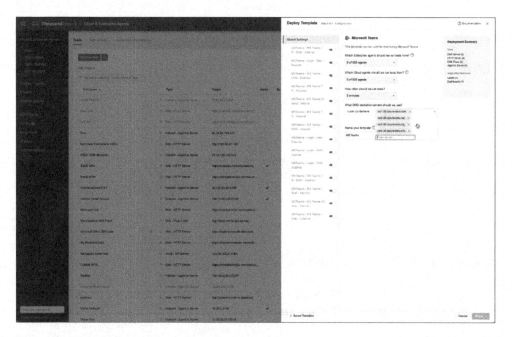

Figure 9-27   *Microsoft Teams Template*

However, there is something you should remember whenever you are using DNS Server tests. If you look at Figure 9-28 you will see a drilled-in version of Figure 9-27 that shows four DNS servers by IP address in the template configuration. Note, the tool defaults to showing the DNS server names. If you set up a DNS Server test without a template, you will have the option to Look Up Servers. This is very handy for finding the authoritative servers (SOA) for a given domain. However, think about this…when DNS is failing and you want to troubleshoot the network, how can you test to the servers if you cannot find the IP addresses because DNS is not working?

Figure 9-28   *DNS Servers by IP Address*

Every time you set up a DNS Server test, you should always look up the IP addresses of the DNS servers you will be testing to. Figure 9-28 shows the Teams DNS servers resolved to IP addresses. This way, the network test will always run to those servers, and troubleshooting DNS will not have to rely on DNS to resolve a name first.

ThousandEyes now has Cloud Agents inside the Azure region. This allows for agent to agent and RTP tests targeting inside Microsoft's data centers.

Depending on how thorough of testing you want to perform, there are additional tests that you can set up for Microsoft services. Regardless of which services we are monitoring, we usually like to monitor Microsoft's authentication by configuring HTTP Server tests to these URLs:

- aadcdn.msftauth.net

- aadcdn.msauth.net

For Teams specifically, we run network tests over TCP 443 to these URLs to monitor Teams Transport Relay:

- world.tr.teams.microsoft.com

- worldaz.tr.teams.microsoft.com

We monitor Teams Chat by setting up an HTTP Server test to teams.microsoft.com.

Based on the Microsoft document at https://learn.microsoft.com/en-us/microsoft-365/enterprise/urls-and-ip-address-ranges?view=o365-worldwide, the URLs in the following list are required to be allowed by firewalls. This provides insight into just how many service dependencies exist. Granted, this goes well beyond simply Teams. It provides some basic understanding into just how complex monitoring can become if you want to dig in that deep. This is not a list of recommended tests; instead, it is meant to highlight the complexity Microsoft has published around its application dependencies.

- Exchange Online
  - outlook.office.com
  - outlook.office365.com
  - smtp.office365.com:587
  - autodiscover.<tenant>.onmicrosoft.com
- SharePoint and OneDrive
  - <tenant>.sharepoint.com
  - admin.onedrive.com
  - officeclient.microsoft.com
  - g.live.com

- oneclient.sfx.ms
- spoprod-a.akamaihd.net
- Skype for Business Online and Microsoft Teams
  - teams.microsoft.com
  - broadcast.skype.com
  - mlccdn.blob.core.windows.net
  - aka.ms
  - mlccdnprod.azureedge.net
  - compass-ssl.microsoft.com

- Microsoft 365 Common and Office Online

  - nps.onyx.azure.net

  - office.live.com

  - ajax.aspnetcdn.com

  - apis.live.net

  - officeapps.live.com

  - www.onedrive.com

  - account.activedirectory. windowsazure.com

  - accounts.accesscontrol.windows.net

  - adminwebservice. microsoftonline.com

  - api.passwordreset. microsoftonline.com

  - autologon.microsoftazuread-sso.com

  - becws.microsoftonline.com

  - ccs.login.microsoftonline.com

  - clientconfig.microsoftonline-p.net

  - companymanager. microsoftonline.com

  - device.login.microsoftonline.com

  - graph.microsoft.com

  - graph.windows.net

  - login.microsoft.com

  - login.microsoftonline.com

  - login.microsoftonline-p.com

  - login.windows.net

  - logincert.microsoftonline.com

  - loginex.microsoftonline.com

  - login-us.microsoftonline.com

  - nexus.microsoftonline-p.com

  - passwordreset.microsoftonline.com

  - provisioningapi. microsoftonline.com

  - enterpriseregistration.windows.net

  - management.azure.com

  - policykeyservice.dc.ad.msft.net

  - compliance.microsoft.com

  - defender.microsoft.com

  - protection.office.com

  - security.microsoft.com

  - account.office.net

  - amp.azure.net

  - appsforoffice.microsoft.com

  - assets.onestore.ms

  - auth.gfx.ms

  - c1.microsoft.com

  - dgps.support.microsoft.com

  - docs.microsoft.com

  - msdn.microsoft.com

  - platform.linkedin.com

  - prod.msocdn.com

  - shellprod.msocdn.com

  - support.microsoft.com

  - technet.microsoft.com

  - ecn.dev.virtualearth.net

  - informationprotection.hosting. portal.azure.net

- o15.officeredir.microsoft.com
- officepreviewredir.microsoft.com
- officeredir.microsoft.com
- r.office.microsoft.com
- activation.sls.microsoft.com
- crl.microsoft.com
- office15client.microsoft.com
- officeclient.microsoft.com
- go.microsoft.com
- ajax.aspnetcdn.com
- cdn.odc.officeapps.live.com
- officecdn.microsoft.com
- officecdn.microsoft.com.edge-suite.net
- apps.identrust.com
- cacerts.digicert.com
- cert.int-x3.letsencrypt.org
- crl.globalsign.com
- crl.globalsign.net
- crl.identrust.com
- crl3.digicert.com
- crl4.digicert.com
- isrg.trustid.ocsp.identrust.com
- mscrl.microsoft.com
- ocsp.digicert.com
- ocsp.globalsign.com
- ocsp.msocsp.com
- ocsp2.globalsign.com
- ocspx.digicert.com
- secure.globalsign.com
- www.digicert.com
- www.microsoft.com
- www.microsoft365.com
- cdnprod.myanalytics.microsoft.com
- myanalytics.microsoft.com
- myanalytics-gcc.microsoft.com
- activity.windows.com
- ocsp.int-x3.letsencrypt.org
- admin.microsoft.com
- cdn.odc.officeapps.live.com
- cdn.uci.officeapps.live.com

Endpoint Agents

The Teams Endpoint Agent template will automatically create an HTTP Server test to teams.microsoft.com along with a Dynamic test for Teams. The Dynamic test operates the same way as the Webex Dynamic test previously described. The Endpoint Agent will begin testing while in a meeting to the servers it sees related to the Teams meeting. In addition to this, there is an integration available that allows ThousandEyes to pull Call Details from Microsoft and include them in the ThousandEyes Agent View. Figure 9-29 shows the Endpoint Test Template that is associated with Microsoft Teams tests.

Figure 9-29 *Endpoint Dynamic Test—Teams*

In addition to setting up synthetic and dynamic tests for Endpoint Agents, Real User tests require whitelisting domains to be monitored, which ThousandEyes refers to as Monitored Domains. Here is a list of domains that Microsoft uses for various services, including Teams:

- Exchange Online
  - office.com
  - office365.com
  - outlook.com
  - onmicrosoft.com
- SharePoint Online and OneDrive for Business
  - sharepoint.com
  - live.com

- trafficmanager.net
- windows.com
- onedrive.com
- microsoft.com
- sfx.ms
- sharepointonline.com
- spoprod-a.akamaihd.net
- svc.ms

- Skype for Business Online and Microsoft Teams
  - lync.com
  - microsoft.com
  - skype.com
  - sfbassets.com
  - windows.net
  - aka.ms
  - live.com
  - windows.com
  - skypeforbusiness.com
  - mstea.ms
  - skypeassets.com
  - azureedge.net
  - skype.com
- Microsoft 365 Common and Office Online
  - microsoftstream.com
  - azure.net
  - azureedge.net
  - live.com
  - office.com
  - office.net
  - onenote.com
  - microsoft.com
  - onenote.net
  - aspnetcdn.com
  - live.net
  - live.com
  - onedrive.com
  - msftidentity.com
  - msidentity.com
- windowsazure.com
- windows.net
- microsoftonline.com
- microsoftazuread-sso.com
- microsoftonline-p.net
- live.com
- msauth.net
- msauthimages.net
- msecnd.net
- msftauth.net
- msftauthimages.net
- phonefactor.net
- azure.com
- msft.net
- cloudappsecurity.com
- oaspapps.com
- akadns.net
- o365weve.com
- azure.net
- onestore.ms
- gfx.ms
- platform.linkedin.com
- msocdn.com
- office365.com
- cloudapp.net
- aadrm.com
- azurerms.com
- virtualearth.net
- sharepointonline.com
- visualstudio.com
- gfx.ms

- staffhub.ms
- msocdn.com
- aspnetcdn.com
- edgesuite.net
- c.bing.net
- msedge.net
- tse1.mm.bing.net
- acompli.net
- outlookmobile.com
- windows-ppe.net
- acompli.com
- msn.com
- getmicrosoftkey.com
- yammer.com
- yammerusercontent.com
- assets-yammer.com
- outlook.com
- sway-cdn.com
- sway-extensions.com
- sway.com
- entrust.net
- geotrust.com
- omniroot.com
- public-trust.com
- symcb.com
- symcd.com
- verisign.com
- verisign.net
- identrust.com
- digicert.com
- letsencrypt.org
- globalsign.com
- globalsign.net
- identrust.com
- msocsp.com
- officespeech.platform.bing.com
- microsoft365.com
- microsoftusercontent.com
- azure-apim.net
- powerapps.com
- windows.com
- letsencrypt.org
- cortana.ai
- cloud.microsoft

Internet Insights

Microsoft Teams, like Webex, can be monitored using Internet Insights to alert when your company's Teams tests are part of a larger outage, or to see where in the world outages are happening even without having your own tests running.

Network Outages

The example shown in Figure 9-30 uses Internet Insights to show outages across the Internet impacting tests reaching the Microsoft network. This can be seen by navigating to **Internet Insights > Views > Network Outages.** Then add a filter for an application, a domain, a server network, or whichever most accurately reflects your situation.

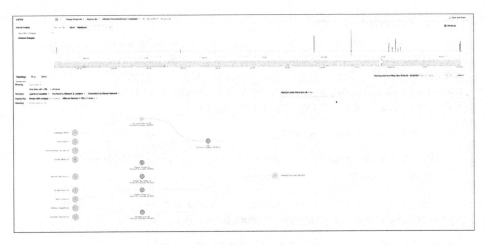

Figure 9-30 *Internet Insights—Network Outage—Teams*

Outages impacting Microsoft services can be tracked in multiple ways. In this case, domains (msauth.net, msftauth.net, and microsoft.com) filtering was in use to identify these outages.

Application Outages

Choosing **Internet Insights > Views > Application Outages** enables you to focus strictly on Teams outages or you can expand to other Microsoft SaaS services as well, depending on the filtering used. Figure 9-31 is filtered on Microsoft as being the Server Networks and shows a major Teams application outage that impacted tests worldwide.

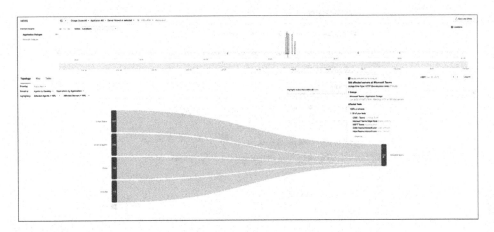

Figure 9-31 *Internet Insights—Application Outage—Teams*

Zoom

Zoom is another of the major collaboration tools that ThousandEyes has been successful in testing. Once again, there are templates to aid in the configuration and deployment of Zoom tests.

Cloud and Enterprise Agents

Zoom testing from Cloud and Enterprise Agents is very straightforward. The simplest way to begin is to use the test templates found in **Cloud & Enterprise Agents > Test Settings > Add New Test** (using the down arrow to access templates). Then choose between the simple or the comprehensive Zoom template. Each template includes the following tests as well as corresponding dashboards:

- HTTP Server: <yourID>.zoom.us

- DNS Server: (recommend changing this to the DNS Server IP Addresses) resolving <yourID>.zoom.us

It is recommended, like with most SaaS tests, to run these tests from inside your network (Enterprise Agents) and outside your network (Cloud Agents).

For more comprehensive testing of Zoom, it is recommended that you use the ThousandEyes template shown in Figure 9-32.

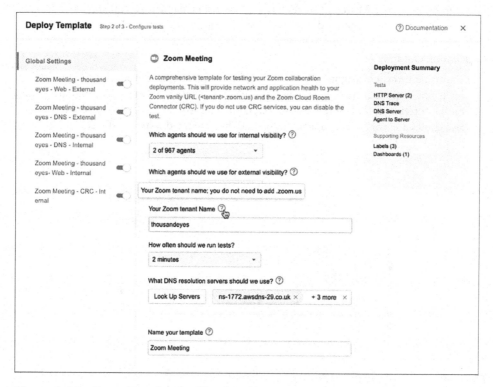

Figure 9-32   *Zoom Template for Cloud and Enterprise Agents*

Endpoint Agents

There is an Endpoint Agent test template (see Figure 9-33) available for configuring Zoom tests. It creates one scheduled HTTP Server test to <yourID>.zoom.us and one Dynamic test.

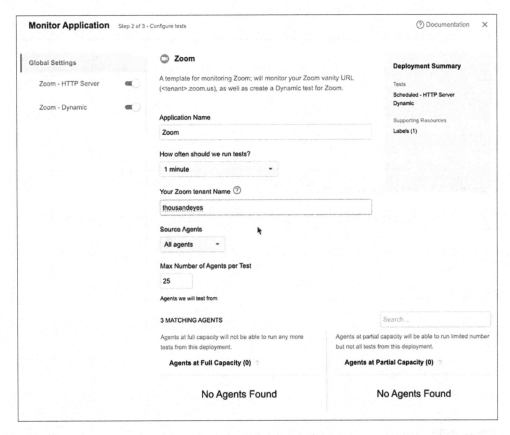

Figure 9-33 *Zoom Template for Endpoint Agents*

As with the Dynamic tests described previously, the Endpoint Agent discovers the servers being accessed and initiates tests to those servers to determine path, loss, latency, and jitter. These Dynamic tests run only while the agent has an active Zoom meeting occurring. Figure 9-34 shows an example of an Endpoint Agent running a Dynamic test to multiple Zoom servers during a meeting.

Internet Insights

Internet Insights is a great way to see the health of Zoom from a global or regional perspective. It provides information about your tests that are impacted by larger outages as well as insight into what is happening beyond the tests you have configured.

Network Outages

In Figure 9-35, a network outage in Cloudflare is responsible for disrupting services to zoom.us.

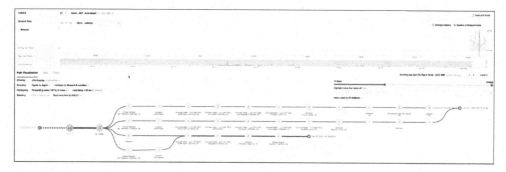

Figure 9-34   *Endpoint Dynamic Test—Zoom*

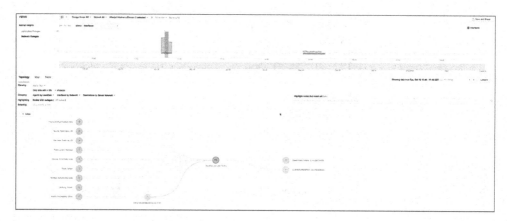

Figure 9-35   *Internet Insights—Network Outage—Zoom*

Application Outages

Figure 9-36 shows an example where the Zoom application stopped responding. The outage was seen on 293 servers and impacted users all over the world.

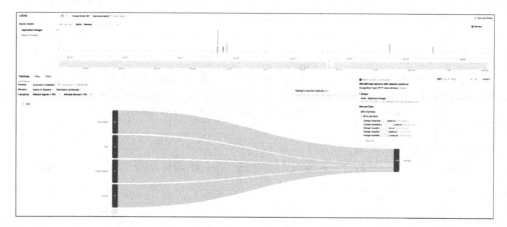

Figure 9-36   *Internet Insights—Application Outage—Zoom*

Stories from the Field

We have run into some interesting challenges—let's call them "opportunities to optimize"—over the years. We will share some of these stories here as a way of teaching from the lessons we have learned. While we may or may not have had ThousandEyes available to us when we were confronted with these issues...make that opportunities...we hope you see how leveraging ThousandEyes today could have reduced time to resolution in each of these situations.

FTP Throughput Analysis and Optimization

Performance problems are always interesting, and often challenging, when it comes to identification, isolation, and escalation. When a "very large" customer of mine planned migrating to a new mainframe on the other side of the country, they neglected to understand the protocols involved. In this case, understanding the operational characteristics of FTP, or more basically TCP/IP, was needed to appreciate the performance impact this move would have.

Although we were aware of this customer's mainframe migration effort, we were never invited to participate in the project, perhaps because we were not mainframe experts. Or perhaps because we had other priority projects to be responsible for. Or, most likely, it was because we were independent contractors and would have billed our time against a project that didn't require our expertise. Regardless, it was around 10:30 a.m. on a Friday when we got the call asking if we could drop what we were doing and join a "quick" call to share our thoughts. The migration was happening over the weekend and tests weren't going well. The level of effort and financial investment that had gone into this migration was truly impressive. Perhaps one of the most telling indicators of the impact this migration was having on our customer was in the number of non-IT managers (in addition to the IT managers) on this conference call. The move was scheduled to complete over the weekend, with all systems back up and running no later than first thing Monday morning.

We happened to be in the Washington, DC, area when we got the call. We were working primarily just outside Philadelphia at the time. One of the guys we had spent a lot of time with in the Philadelphia center asked us to join the call. By the way, never believe someone who says on a Friday that "it should only take 10, maybe 20 minutes." The customer was running FTP CronJobs from locations in Philadelphia, PA, Richmond, VA, and Columbus, OH, using HP Unix servers and retrieving files from a mainframe. The current (old) mainframe was in Columbus, but the new one was located on the West Coast of the United States. Fortunately, we had remote access to a protocol analyzer on the customer's Philadelphia network, which worked well for testing against both mainframes from their Philadelphia branch. Additionally, we had a solid reputation established with their Philadelphia IT support staff. People there took us seriously (most of the time). Most of these files were only a few megabytes, but some were considerably larger. There were a lot of them to be moved, and the jobs had to complete in a set timeframe. When the customer tested from Philly (or any other location for that matter) to the new West Coast mainframe, the jobs would run, but they would not run fast enough to complete inside the required timeframe.

The Unix admin in Philly was someone we knew. Luckily, he was willing to run tests to both mainframes while we captured packets for analysis. The TCP 3-way handshake took 72 ms (the actual measurement was from Philadelphia sending SYN until we received the SYN/ACK) to the old mainframe in Columbus. It took 170 ms for the same connection to the West Coast location. We made note of the TCP Receive Window for the HP Unix server and saw that it was set to a maximum of 56 KB and did not have the TCP window scaling (WS) option enabled. This allowed us to calculate the Maximum Theoretical Throughput (MTT) for each data transfer. Calculating the MTT as follows allowed us to determine whether a single TCP session should have been moving more data than what was observed or if a bottleneck (network, application, etc.) was preventing the through-put from approaching MTT.

Receive Window / Network Round Trip Time = Max Theoretical Throughput =

RWIN / NRTT = MTT

56 KB / 72 ms = 6.3 Mbps (from old mainframe)

56 KB / 170 ms = 2.7 Mbps (from new mainframe)

The good news was that we observed, in the TCP 3-way handshake options, that the new mainframe on the West Coast did have window scaling enabled, as WS must be enabled on both hosts to be utilized. We determined, considering the amount of latency, that the optimal RWIN should be around 192 KB. This was based on the available network bandwidth (9Mbps) the customer should be able to consume.

Available Bandwidth × Latency = Optimal Window Size

9 Mbps × 170 ms ~ 192 KB

The bad news was that this version of HP Unix did not support TCP window scaling. Additionally, almost everyone on the call thought we were idiots. After all, who would want to make changes to the Unix systems when everyone *knew* it was a network issue and needed a network resolution. Granted, 170 ms latency was well over anything reason-able for the distance covered. However, we have to focus on the things we can control. In this case, since the network was outsourced to a third party (with an enforceable SLA in place), correcting the network latency was going to be a much larger issue than tuning the Unix servers. To prove our theory, we convinced the Philly Unix admin to change the TCP Receive Window on his test server. Since window scaling was not yet an option, we settled for the maximum RWIN value you can use without window scaling, which is 64 KB:

64 KB / 170 ms = 3 Mbps

The change in performance, as calculated by the Philly admin using a stopwatch, was enough to convince him, and at least a few others on the call, that we were on the right path. This is when they reached out to their HP rep to ask them what could be done regarding activating window scaling. Fortunately, the HP rep was already participating on this immense call and started looking into options to change the TCP stack to support window scaling.

At some point in the early morning hours of Saturday, HP released a patch for this version of HP Unix that included support for window scaling. The Philly admin updated his test server, adjusted the RWIN accordingly, and ran the FTP transfer with the comment "that was faster than it ever ran using the Columbus mainframe." However, the battle was not over. His second server (the first production server to receive the update) failed to make any significant improvements. So, back to the packets we went. Capturing for this new Unix server, we noted the Maximum Segment Size (MSS) was 536 bytes. This occurs on a Unix system when Path Maximum Transmission Unit Discovery (PMTUD) is disabled. The byproduct of disabling PMTUD is that TCP Congestion Avoidance/Slow Start is seriously degraded due to the limited amount of data contained per segment sent. Joe, the Philly admin, enabled PMTUD on the system in question and retested, this time with an MSS of 1460. Success! Now it was just a matter of rolling out the new, patched, HP Unix code, adjusting the RWIN, and making sure PMTUD was enabled on the servers.

The other Unix system administrators around the country updated their HP Unix systems with the patch. But their systems failed to run FTP in a timely manner…no noticeable improvement. They swore they followed the instructions, but also added they weren't sure why they bothered (possibly implying that we were idiots). After all, everyone knows you don't fix network issues by making changes to your servers. It took us several more hours to find someone competent enough to send us a packet capture of one of those failing systems establishing their FTP job to the mainframe. Once we had the data, we could plainly see that the MSS = 536, and therefore PMTUD was not enabled as described in the instructions Joe had sent to them. After making all the changes we recommended, their FTPs ran in a timely manner and we did not hear another word from them.

If ThousandEyes had been available at the time, it would have provided the insight to avoid that last-minute call altogether. Perhaps the customer still would have asked us to determine "why" throughput was low. But they sure would have known the differences in latency along with the likely impact this would have had on performance well in advance of the migration.

In the example in Figure 9-37, ThousandEyes is showing throughput for an upload to a system from various regions. This example shows both Enterprise and Cloud Agents. In the scenario that we just related, we would have deployed Enterprise Agents to Richmond, Columbus, and Philadelphia and had them upload and download from both mainframes.

Figure 9-38 compares latency between the target and each agent. This would have provided a quick and ready mechanism to determine network latency and allowed a quick and easy calculation to determine optimal window size based on available bandwidth and latency.

Available Bandwidth × Latency = Optimal Window Size

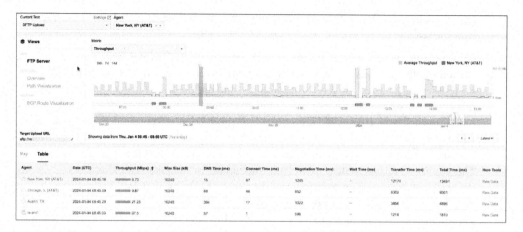

Figure 9-37   *ThousandEyes FTP Upload—Throughput*

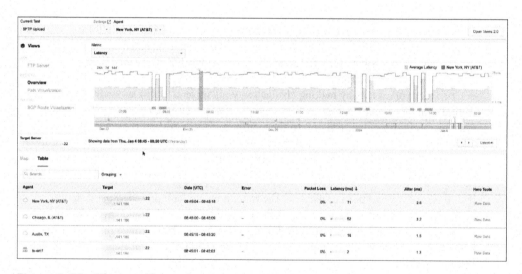

Figure 9-38   *ThousandEyes—Latency*

If you are looking to consume 25 Mbps over a circuit with 50 ms of latency, then your receive side needs a window size of about 156 KB. Anything smaller will use less bandwidth.

Keep in mind when using Maximum Theoretical Throughput that it is called *theoretical* for a reason. It is the best you can hope to obtain. Things such as packet loss or higher latency (whether due to congestion or any other network issue) or an application that has limits in the amount of data it can read or write at a time may keep you from reaching your theoretical limit.

User Experience Versus Application Performance Metric—Call Center SLA

Several years ago, we took a job working in the network operations center of a major power company in the Northeast United States. About the time we started, the company hired a new director for one of the call centers. The call centers had been struggling with customer satisfaction, the primary complaint being that customers felt they were kept on hold for too long before being connected to an agent. This new director was given a service level agreement (SLA) to shorten the hold time for callers. If she was successful, she would get a generous bonus and be considered for promotion. If unsuccessful, she would be let go.

Our NOC team included a guy who had recently transitioned from the Voice team. Now, this story predates VoIP…or at least predates it at this customer site, so it may be a little older than we let on. However, by the end we will make the story relevant to trouble-shooting user experience today, so please read it through. Back then a phone system had dedicated circuits to connect it to the outside world. It would have had inbound (DID) and outbound (DOD) circuits. The number of circuits dictated how many consecutive outside calls the system could handle. This call center had 150 DID circuits dedicated to it and 50 agents on the floor taking calls, which meant that each agent could be actively working with one customer and have two more customers on hold, each waiting their turn.

The new director saw this as an opportunity to meet the SLA. The director reduced the number of inbound circuits from 150 to 100, thus ensuring that the queue depth would be effectively one-half of what it was previously. This drastically reduced the waiting time for customers calling into the call center, and it not only allowed the director to meet the SLA but also saved the company money by reducing the number of needed circuits. However, any call volume above the 100 limit now allowed would fail at the phone company, providing the customer with what was known as a "fast-busy." Since those calls would never make it to the company's phone system, there was no way to measure the number of calls impacted by this. The director met the SLA while reducing customer satisfaction. This is because customers who would have been waiting in the queue on hold now simply receive a busy signal. This happens in the network/data world as well. Metrics and SLAs are important, but always ensure that they accurately represent the user's experience.

Improper expectations of application performance monitoring (APM) can have the same effect. Most APM systems start metrics for a user's transaction at the time the APM system receives the client's command arriving at the server. Let's say it's a simple web service and the user accessing the application is John. When the APM system sees John's GET request, it starts measuring the number of metrics, including the number of transactions, errors, and the timing of each subcomponent. However, John's experience started when he clicked the icon on his desktop that launched the application. His computer contacted his local DNS server to ask for the IP address it needs to connect to in order to launch the application. Then John's computer sends a TCP SYN to the server's IP address he received to begin the connection. Once the TCP 3-way handshake (SYN-SYN/ACK-ACK) has completed, then the SSL negotiations begin. Once SSL establishes an encrypted channel, then the GET can be sent to the server. If the server is unable to accept another TCP connection due to some limit imposed in a configuration, the GET will never be sent. This can keep the APM system from ever being aware of the failed attempts (much like running out of circuits going into the call center). In fact, the application performance could very well show performance metrics that are well within service level tolerances because the load on the application would remain limited by the number of active TCP sessions and not impacted by the number of attempted TCP sessions.

It is important to measure all aspects of a user's experience. While APM systems play an important part in monitoring and analyzing the application's health and responsiveness, the application represents only a part in the dependencies a user has in today's world of digital experiences.

In Figure 9-39, Response Time is the primary metric. This shows the Hong Kong agent is not reporting SSL or Wait times. These details can be seen in Figure 9-40, using Availability as the primary metric. The point is that if this was monitored only by an APM agent running inside the web server, this timeout would not be noticed.

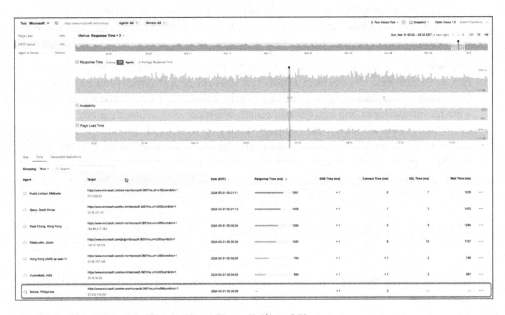

Figure 9-39   *Response Time—Hong Kong Failing SSL*

When the total response, including redirect time, exceeds the HTTP Server Timeout value (Advanced Settings, Default = 5 seconds), the test will show unavailable for that agent on that test round. It is important to watch how much time is consumed in redirects, because sometimes this is where the problem lies and an additional test (or two) may be required to uncover exactly why.

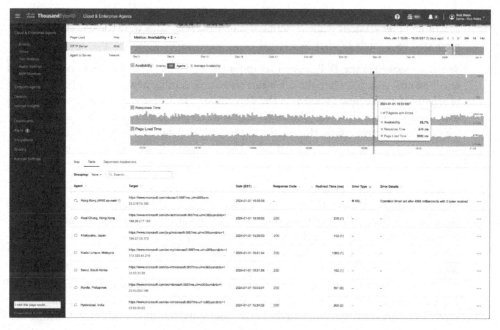

Figure 9-40 *Availability—Hong Kong Failing SSL*

Connections Failing at Load Balancer

We were once leading a monitoring and analysis training session for a company's IT department on site at their location. During the session, attendees' phones started ringing. The IT staff informed us that the company was experiencing a Severity 1 incident and would have to cancel (and hopefully reschedule) the remainder of the session.

Instead of simply packing up and leaving, we asked the manager in attendance if the class could spend 15 to 20 minutes discussing the incident and looking at the data we were already collecting to see if we could address this as a team. The IT staff happily agreed, as they saw it as getting started on the investigation immediately as opposed to everyone going back to their own desks and dialing into a conference bridge, which would likely have taken at least 30 minutes to get organized.

The company was getting a large volume of calls from a couple of their external customers reporting an inability to log into an application the company was hosting. This was a business-to-business application that was of critical importance to their largest customers. One of the company's largest customers was directly impacted and escalating the issue. It was a basic three-tier application: web, app, and database. The web tier was a cluster that was front-ended with a load balancer. The good news was that they already had packet feeds configured for the load balancer. The packet capture tool was capturing traffic from both the users to load balancer and from the load balancer to web cluster. We were able to quickly identify a lot of refused (RST) TCP sessions. The load balancer was rejecting a number of sessions as if it was overloaded. However, we saw that it was accepting other sessions while rejecting some. Most rejections were for sessions requested by a single IP address.

When we looked at the TCP session setup for the web cluster, we saw that one server was rejecting new sessions while the other servers were accepting new sessions without any problems. We were now focused on the web cluster. The tipoff was when we looked at total sessions for each server. The server that was refusing connections also had the highest number of active connections. In fact, it was hosting almost as many active TCP sessions as the other three servers combined. That indicated it was time to look back at the load balancer.

It turned out that the single IP address that was responsible for most of the refused sessions was also responsible for most of the good sessions. The company was using network address translation (NAT) for private circuits connected from its customers to its network. Each customer would receive their own unique IP address to use. They would NAT an entire customer (whether it was a few users or thousands of users) into a single IP address. The load balancer was configured to balance using Layer 3 (source IP addresses). So, the customer with the highest number of users on the application also generated the highest number of TCP sessions against a single IP address. This resulted in all users for a single customer using the same server in the cluster and, on this occasion, exhausting the number of TCP sessions available on a single server.

The customer changed the load balancer algorithm to use Layer 4 (5 tuple: protocol, source IP, destination IP, source port, destination port) for load balancing. This began allowing TCP connections to be balanced to the other servers in the cluster immediately.

Doing all of this through packet capture and analysis was difficult and time consuming. Even when you are fortunate enough to have all of the packets you need, as we were in this case, you still have to perform a lot of complex analysis. If ThousandEyes had been available to us at the time, we would have been monitoring both the load balancer (via the same URL the customers used to access it) and the individual web servers in the cluster. This would have shown

- Testing to the load balancer—depending on which server our test was sent to:
  - Balanced to the problem server, we would see connection failures (end-to-end) and no loss in the path (hop-by-hop)
  - Balanced to any other server, we would have not seen any failures (most likely)
- Testing to the individual servers:
  - A lot of connection issues with the test to that one overly busy server
  - No related network issues (loss or latency) in the path

Although that information might not have told us everything we needed to know, it would have allowed us to be alerted to the condition before it deteriorated into a customer escalation. It would also have led us to look at the architecture and how the load balancing was working from the very beginning of the situation.

Load Balancing with 20% Failure Rate

Let us share a real-world example of an issue we worked on recently. We were testing a portion of an application that was failing right around 20% of the time. All 19 ThousandEyes agents that we were using to test showed very close to 80% availability. Each round was a little different, but the overall numbers came out consistent. Unfortunately, we were not given access to test the load balancer or the servers feeding the data to the content delivery network (CDN) in use. But even without that access we could do some inferred analysis and make recommendations for next steps.

Looking at the test shown in Figure 9-41, the problem seemed to be an intermittent issue where sometimes an application returned an HTTP 404 while most of the time it returned an HTTP 200. This URL happens to be hosted by a CDN provider.

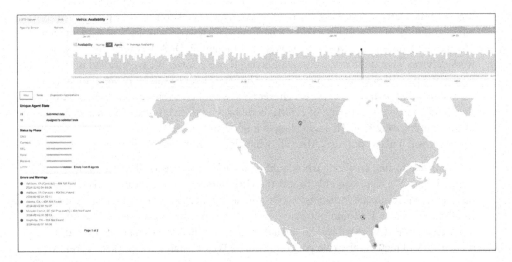

Figure 9-41   *HTTP Server Availability*

We don't need to share the IP addresses that were being accessed, but we can assure you that we looked to see if certain IP addresses failed while others did not. That was not the case. Note that all of the Cloud Agents used to test this application were failing right around 80%, as shown in Figure 9-42. That led us to believe the CDN servers were using a load balancer to access content. Checking with our customer, we determined that five servers were servicing this content through a load balancer to the CDN provider. One of those servers was problematic, causing the HTTP error to occur.

80.17 %								
82.29 Ashburn, VA	76.04 Ashburn, VA (AT&T)	82.64 Ashburn, VA (Centu...	77.43 Ashburn, VA (Chart...	79.86 Ashburn, VA (Comc...	81.25 Ashburn, VA (Cox)	83.33 Ashburn, VA (GOP ...	77.43 Ashburn, VA (Veriz...	78.82 Atlanta, GA
80.21 Atlanta, GA (AWS L...	80.9 Charlotte, NC	82.99 Louisville, KY	77.76 McLean, VA	78.47 Miami, FL	82.99 Miami, FL (AWS l.n...	81.25 Moncks Corner, SC...	78.13 Nashville, TN	81.6 Orlando, FL
79.86 Raleigh, NC								

Figure 9-42   *Availability by Agent*

When MSS Matters

Hurricane Katrina ravaged the Gulf Coast of the United States in August, 2005. I've heard many stories about the events of this storm. The story we're about to share was triggered by this storm but was not caused by it. We make that distinction because, when working on root cause analysis (RCA), you should always identify triggers and causes separately. As an example, a storm is not going to cause a roof to blow off a building. It may trigger the departure, but if the building was built to withstand the storm, then an underlying cause must be identified (poor workmanship, low-grade materials, etc.) if the roof blows off. If the building was not constructed to withstand that storm, then you are well on your way to identifying the root cause. Always look for two things, the trigger and the cause.

This story starts in the hours following the hurricane. One of our customers during that time was the Defense Logistics Agency (DLA), which is responsible for getting goods to our government entities, such as the Department of Defense and the Federal Emergency Management Agency (FEMA). So, as you might imagine, DLA was very busy and network services were quite critical to supporting those efforts. We were called in to troubleshoot a bizarre occurrence: users in the Gulf Coast states suddenly were not able to access the fuel purchase system. Whenever they would go to their URL to purchase fuel, they would receive a half page of HTML code back in their browser. Users in other parts of the country were fine. This issue began immediately after Hurricane Katrina. So, of course, it was a network issue. After all, what else could it be? Nothing else had changed.

We were able to find someone who could do a packet capture local to one of the users having issues. We were also able to test the URL ourselves and capture packets local to our location just outside Philadelphia. Of course, we were unable to duplicate the issue from our computer. It turned out that getting fuel to people in the Gulf Coast was pretty important to FEMA, so we had all the assistance (and then some) that we needed. We started by looking over the two packet captures. We compared the packet capture we took ourselves to the one we were sent from a user experiencing the issue. The only difference we originally noticed was the Maximum Segment Size (MSS) in the TCP header options. It was 1460 in our packet capture and 1380 in the other.

Well, that was to be expected. A lot of networks had to reroute traffic due to storm outages. The data from the Gulf Coast area was going through a tunnel created for this reason. Neither of these MSS values were abnormal and both met any RFC requirements for TCP/IP communications. Just for "fun," we decided to adjust the Maximum Transmission Unit (MTU) on our computer to 1420. The MTU is the largest Layer 3 packet that an interface can handle. This effectively forced our MSS to 1380 (MSS + IP header + TCP header = MTU). When we subsequently accessed the URL, we received a half page of HTML code in response. We were able to verify that the HTML we received was the first part of the code on the home page of the fuel purchase website. We were getting to the right page but not getting the whole page...and because we were not getting the entire page, what we were getting was rendering as text instead of HTML. Interestingly, we noticed that the fuel purchase server's home page (the full page) was just over 1400 bytes.

The good news was that we no longer needed to rely on someone else to test and capture data. We were able to duplicate the issue and test on demand. The bad news was that the explanation of our testing "confirmed" the application team's suspicion that this was a network issue. After all, the network was the only thing that changed. We explained that both MSS values were 100% RFC compliant. "But nothing else changed" was their argument. To us that did not matter—once we are assigned a problem to work on, there is no mean time to innocence (MTTI), only mean time to resolution (MTTR). We work it until it is resolved. So, network, application, server...it did not matter. This was our problem to figure out.

It took a bit of analysis before we realized that the TCP session, when using the MSS 1380, did not end properly. Both the good (MSS 1460) and bad (MSS 1380) TCP sessions shut down using the FIN bits. The response the MSS 1460 session provided from the fuel purchase server was in a single data segment (the TCP equivalent of a packet) that included the data payload as well as the FIN bit set in the TCP header, whereas the MSS 1380 session contained two data segments, with the FIN bit set in the first of the two segments. The FIN indicates the sender has nothing more to say. This is not the same as immediately terminating the session, as an RST does. The FIN only indicates that the host sending the FIN (in this scenario, the fuel purchase server) has no more data to deliver in this session. So, no more segments with payload from that host should follow the FIN. Think of it like arguing with your significant other. There are times when you are better off not saying a word. The side of the conversation that sends the FIN is saying "I'm going to stop talking now...but I'm still listening to anything you have to say." Also, the FIN bit can be sent with a payload. This is perfectly acceptable behavior, provided it is sent with the last segment of data. So, seeing the one segment containing data (MSS 1460) with the FIN bit set was fully RFC compliant. However, seeing two segments of data, with the FIN bit set in the *first* of the two, was not compliant.

Now the question was, "Who sent the premature FIN"? We suspected it was from the server, which was not a popular opinion, since "nothing had changed" at the data center. The only way to be certain was to take a packet capture inside the data center and compare it to the data we were receiving when we tested with the MSS 1380 setting. The question was, as it was leaving the server, did the TCP session contain two data segments and then a FIN? Leaving the firewall at the data center, the TCP session contained a data segment with a FIN and then another data segment. It should be noted that the IP ID and TCP SEQ numbers proved these were not out-of-order packets. Now we had the data we needed. It turns out there was a bug in the firewall code. An updated version of code had been released for this firewall but not implemented. An emergency change was enacted, taking down the data center. When it came back online, everyone was able to use the fuel purchasing application once again no matter where in the country they were located or what their MSS was set to.

The routing change was the trigger. It caused the MSS value to change (a secondary trigger). The root cause was the bug in the firewall...but even more so, the root cause was the fact that the firewall had not been kept updated in the newest release. True root cause remediation was to implement periodic scheduled maintenance checks that went on a calendar (weekly, monthly, quarterly, etc.) that would include a firewall version review. What we ultimately identified as the root cause was a process deficiency, not a network issue after all. It was simply something triggered by a network incident.

This story still amazes us when we think back on it. It was one of the strangest occurrences we've run into. We don't recall how many hours we had worked on this. We do know that most of the time spent was just waiting for tests and data captures to be sent to us. We've never liked relying on others to capture packets…we are never 100% sure of what is being captured, what is filtered, or if we will need another capture. Also, protocol analysis is very time consuming—reading a packet capture takes a lot longer than reading a story.

So, how would we handle something like this scenario today with ThousandEyes available to us? Assuming that we had already been monitoring with ThousandEyes, we would have multiple locations we could analyze data from. Not only that but leveraging Transaction tests would allow us to collect screenshots such as shown in Figure 9-43. While this is not the actual application we were troubleshooting in the preceding story, it does provide a visual reference as to the effectiveness this type of information would have had in aiding our analysis.

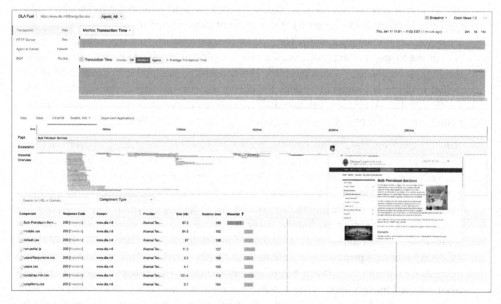

Figure 9-43   *Transaction Test with Screenshots*

Additionally, with ThousandEyes we could easily see the MSS values that have been negotiated between the agents and the target server. This would allow us to see within minutes which agents were showing the issue and what their respective MSS values were. Figure 9-44 shows an Enterprise Agent accessing Netflix.com while Figure 9-45 shows a Cloud Agent doing the same MTU/MSS values. Note the MTU and MSS values change based on the network path.

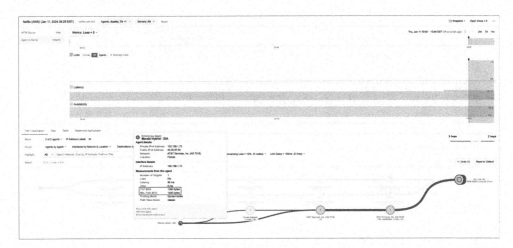

Figure 9-44   *MSS = 1380*

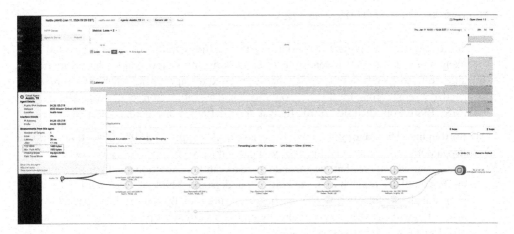

Figure 9-45   *MSS = 1460*

Figure 9-46 shows a packet capture with a TCP handshake taking place in packet numbers 2993 and 2999. During the handshake, TCP hosts announce the options they can support. In this example, host 45.20.97.84 has a maximum segment size, MSS, of 1460, while host 54.237.226.164 has an MSS of 1440. Both systems will use the smaller of the MSS values, 1440, when exchanging data in this TCP session.

Now, even with this data from ThousandEyes, we would only be able to see the data after it went through the firewall. Root cause analysis would still require a packet capture between the server and the firewall. We could deploy an Enterprise Agent inside the firewall (between the server and the firewall) to test. However, we would need a way of managing the MSS to test both 1380 and 1460 in order to adequately test this way.

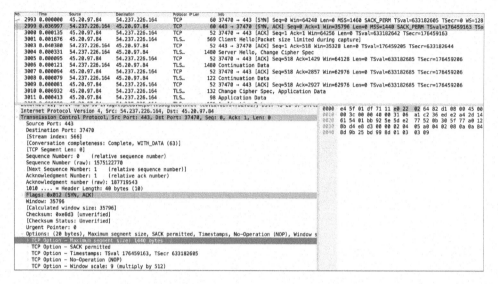

Figure 9-46 *Path MTU Discovery Packets*

So, for the fuel purchase system situation, having ThousandEyes to test with would have likely reduced a couple of weeks' worth of work down to a few hours. This would have allowed us to specify very quickly what we needed to capture and where that capture needed to come from. Ideally, we would have had a capture from one of the failing tests (MSS 1380) from each side of the firewall for a definitive one-to-one comparison.

Bottom line: ThousandEyes might not replace packet captures 100% of the time, but even if you don't replace them completely, you can reduce your dependency on packets and focus your efforts on what, when, and where to capture. Additionally, Path Visualization in ThousandEyes is much easier to read and understand. Think of ThousandEyes as a packet analysis tool as opposed to a packet capture tool. By analyzing the packets associated with synthetic tests, it already knows exactly what packets it is sending and therefore knows what to expect back.

Bizarre Failure Is Not Adding Up

Several years ago, before knowing anything about ThousandEyes, a long-standing customer called us one evening to ask for help. This customer had come to know that we have a very particular set of skills, skills we have acquired over a very long career. They found themselves in need of those skills and reached out to see if we could help them with the nightmare they were experiencing. They had an issue that had been going on for two weeks and they were no closer to explaining it, let alone resolving it, than they were the day it started.

Problem Description

The customer had multiple applications running virtually, hosted on multiple IBM iSeries AS/400s. Every evening around 6 p.m. (Eastern), all the applications would show severe performance degradation. Our first step was to identify what all of these applications had in common, so we asked the following questions and received the corresponding answers:

■ Are all of the impacted AS/400s connected to the same switch? No.

■ Are they on the same subnet, using the same gateway? Yes.

So, we looked at the gateway. It showed an increase in traffic volume around 6 p.m., but no increase in errors or discarded packets. Also, we could see that the main issue was that the servers/applications were slowing down, not that the delivery was problematic. This was looking more like an application issue than a network issue, prompting the following questions:

■ Do they use a common DB server? No.

■ Do they share an API? No.

Now it was getting interesting, enough so that we started joining the customer's 6:00 p.m. calls. The problem continued until morning. The calls would as well.

We came up with a few more questions to help us focus on this behavior.

■ When do backups run? Nightly, and they are not allowed to start before 6 p.m. and must be completed by 6 a.m.

■ Do all these applications get backed up on the same days and at the same times? No, the backups are staggered.

First Progress

The first real clue we received was when one of their network engineers shared SNMP data he had for the switch ports connected to the AS/400s. This data showed traffic volume increases outbound starting at 6 p.m. nightly. We now constructed a list of things that "could" be related even if they did not make sense to us at the time:

■ Backups

■ Subnet

■ Gateway

■ Traffic

We asked about the router interface for that subnet:

■ What did the traffic volume look like on it? Outbound traffic volume increased at 6 p.m. entering the subnet.

■ What did the traffic look like on any other active interfaces on the same subnet? The switch ports, whether connected to the AS/400s or not, also showed the outbound volume identical to the AS/400s.

Hypothesis

Now we had a theory: traffic was being flooded across the VLAN. The traffic (as confirmed via packet captures) was backup traffic destined to the backup server. This was not broadcast or multicast traffic. We asked for a packet capture without a SPAN setup—meaning, plug in your packet capture system on an open interface on that VLAN and capture data. We wanted to see what traffic was flooded out all switch ports. Sure enough, this was TCP traffic destined to the backup server. TCP traffic should never be flooded, except when the switch does not recognize the destination MAC address. The MAC address is then learned as soon as the switch sees a packet with that MAC as a source address. Then the switch updates its CAM table so it can forward traffic to that MAC on that one port and filter that destination MAC from all other interfaces. Using this capture method, TCP should very rarely be seen unless it is directed to or from the system plugged into that switch port. This is because TCP is a connection-oriented protocol and should never have a broadcast or multicast address associated with it. Broadcast and multicast packets are normally flooded by a switch, but TCP should be quickly learned and filtered accordingly. This obviously was not happening.

Two questions remained to be answered:

- Why was this subnet flooding all traffic addressed (IP and MAC) to the backup server?

- Why was traffic with a destination address of the backup server impacting performance of the applications running on the AS/400s?

First Significant Finding

Because this traffic had a unicast MAC address not associated with any AS/400 NIC, the systems should have ignored the packets. Evidently the systems were processing the packets instead of ignoring them. The only times an Ethernet network interface card should process packets past the first 8 bytes (which is the destination MAC address) is when the packet contains the following:

- The destination address is that of the NIC receiving the packet. This was not the case.

- The destination address is a multicast and the system receiving the packet is listening due to an application running on it that directs the NIC driver to accept packets to a multicast group. This was not the case.

- The destination address is a broadcast address, telling all NICs receiving the packets to process, at least, the Ethernet headers. This was not the case.

- The NIC receiving the packets is running in promiscuous mode (that is, accepting all inbound packets regardless of the destination address). This was what we found to be occurring.

Turns out the AS/400s were running in promiscuous mode. That explained why flooded traffic was impacting all those applications. It did not, however, explain why the traffic was reaching them. The flooding was caused by something else. Our theory was either a blown CAM table (more addresses on the network than the switch can support) or the use of asymmetric routing. We were suspecting the latter.

Eureka!

We started looking closely at the backup server at this point. If the backup server had a second NIC on a different subnet, it might be sending all outbound traffic through the second interface. Sure enough, about the time this issue started, the backup team had added a 10-Gbps NIC to the backup server and attached it on a different subnet. This NIC was in addition to the existing 1-Gbps NIC on the subnet we had been troubleshooting. Now we understood what was going on:

1. When backups kicked off, the backup server would receive packets on the 1-Gbps NIC that it had always used. This was the 1-Gbps NIC on the same subnet as the AS/400s.

2. The router connected to the local subnet would ARP for the IP address of the backup server. The router would update its ARP table to include the IP address and MAC address of the backup server.

3. The server would respond. This ARP response would contain a source address of the backup server's 1-Gbps NIC and would be received on the switch port where the backup server was attached. As the response crossed other switches on the subnet, they would all "learn" the port that was closest to the backup server and update their CAM tables accordingly.

4. The router would then forward any packets destined to the backup server to the switch port it was connected on. The switches would look into their CAM tables for the MAC address of the backup server and forward the packets accordingly, filtering them out of all other ports to keep from flooding the network with unnecessary traffic.

5. The backup server would send its IP responses from its new 10-Gbps NIC. So, the subnet where the AS/400s reside never saw a TCP response from the backup server out to the servers it was backing up. This means the switches did not see packets to use for updating/refreshing their CAM tables—at least not until the router's ARP table expired and forced it to ARP again on that subnet.

The important thing to understand is the relationship between the CAM table, which focuses on Layer 2 addressing, and an ARP table, which maps Layer 2 to Layer 3. A CAM table will expire an address (by default) after 300 seconds (5 minutes), whereas a router's ARP table will retain an entry for 4 hours. This means that 5 minutes after the initial packet is sent from the router to the backup server (this initial packet requiring the ARP and updating the CAM table), the CAM table will expire the entry. Then, when the router sends packets against its ARP table (still active for another 3 hours and 55 minutes), they contain a destination MAC address that no longer exists in the switching CAM tables. This forces the switches to flood any packet (TCP or otherwise) destined to the backup server until they receive a packet from the backup server's NIC, which likely will not occur until the router's ARP table expires.

This was not the first time we had seen asymmetric routing cause packet flooding. It was the first time we had witnessed it having this level of impact in a customer's environment. The combined effects of asymmetric routing and promiscuous servers created a very interesting storm of events.

The customer disabled the second (10 Gbps) NIC in the backup server immediately. This resulted in an immediate decrease to all traffic levels outbound on the switch ports (other than to the backup server) and a definite improvement in the server/application response times. Using a second NIC in a backup server should not be a problem. However, when multiple NICs are involved, the routing table in that system should be architected by design and not by default. If the customer had defined which subnets would use which NIC and ensured inbound and outbound traffic matched the same route in and out of the backup server, they would not have run into this issue.

Of course, the customer started asking about monitoring for this and what they could do in the future. That was a much harder problem to solve at the time. Today, we could recommend using ThousandEyes, as it could help detect this type of situation. With ThousandEyes, the customer could choose the applications to alert on and also build dashboards using application labels. A best practice would be for the customer to run tests to all the applications in question and then group them according to the AS/400 they are hosted on, which would allow them to easily identify when multiple applications within a single AS/400 are showing performance issues such as long wait times or perhaps long SSL times (depending on where the SSL is handled). Additionally, we would recommend having a dashboard comparing response times for all applications in each AS/400 (comparing AS/400 to AS/400). All of these would be on a timeline so that the customer could quickly determine whether the same condition was impacting all the systems at the same time.

In Figure 9-47, we have created four application labels, one for each of the AS/400s hosting the applications. There is a total of ten application hosts among these four AS/400s. We are watching for patterns. If the situation described in this use case were to occur, we would see the same pattern (likely for both availability and response times) emerge on multiple AS/400s. We added a widget to this dashboard to report on alerts associated with the tests we are monitoring on this page. There are other things that could cause multiple applications to experience performance degradation at the same time. One item that was not listed here is DNS. If applications are dependent on resolving names and using the same DNS server, DNS performance issues could inflict degraded user experiences across multiple applications. Again, ThousandEyes can help monitor and alert on these conditions.

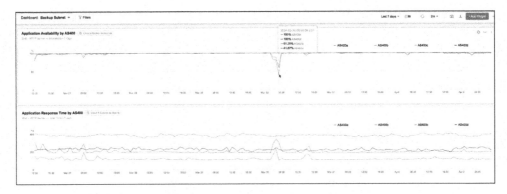

Figure 9-47   *Dashboard Comparing AS/400s*

Review Questions

Answer the following questions. Check your answers against those provided in Appendix A, "Answers to Review Questions."

1. Probing Modes apply to which type of network test, end-to-end or hop-by-hop?

2. Path Trace Modes apply to which type of network test, end-to-end or hop-by-hop?

3. When monitoring collaboration calls, Dynamic tests are associated with which type of agent?

Chapter 10

Device Monitoring

ThousandEyes understands that while gaining visibility across the Internet is important, the need for visibility within an enterprise network has not diminished. Leveraging Enterprise Agents can provide end-to-end metrics and path visualization; however, this is no substitute for device level monitoring. To this end, ThousandEyes can collect metrics directly from devices inside your network and add these metrics to the path visualization you already have. In this chapter we explore this feature that can be deployed from any Enterprise Agent in your environment.

ThousandEyes Device Monitoring

ThousandEyes device monitoring is accomplished by what ThousandEyes refers to as Device Layer. ThousandEyes Device Layer enables organizations to monitor the performance and availability of network devices, such as routers, switches, firewalls, and load balancers, from multiple vantage points across their network infrastructure. Here's a breakdown of how ThousandEyes Device Layer works and its key features:

- **Agent-based monitoring:** ThousandEyes utilizes lightweight software agents deployed across different locations within the network to continuously monitor the devices. These agents collect SNMP data on device performance, including metrics such as CPU utilization, memory usage, interface status, and routing protocol status.

- **Alerting and notifications:** ThousandEyes offers customizable alerting capabilities to notify IT teams of any deviations from normal device behavior. Alerts can be configured based on predefined thresholds for key metrics, ensuring that IT teams are promptly notified of any issues that may impact network performance.

- **Historical data analysis:** ThousandEyes stores historical data on device performance, allowing organizations to analyze trends over time and identify recurring issues. This historical data can be used for capacity planning, performance optimization, and troubleshooting purposes.

■ **Integration with other tools:** ThousandEyes integrates with existing network management and monitoring tools, allowing organizations to consolidate monitoring data and streamline operations. Integration with tools such as SNMP-based monitoring systems and ticketing platforms enhances visibility and enables more efficient incident response.

■ **Visualization and reporting:** Similar to other monitoring data, SNMP data collected by ThousandEyes can be visualized through dashboards, charts, and reports. Users can monitor trends, track device performance over time, and identify potential issues or anomalies.

Figure 10-1 shows at a high level how ThousandEyes can also monitor devices within your infrastructure.

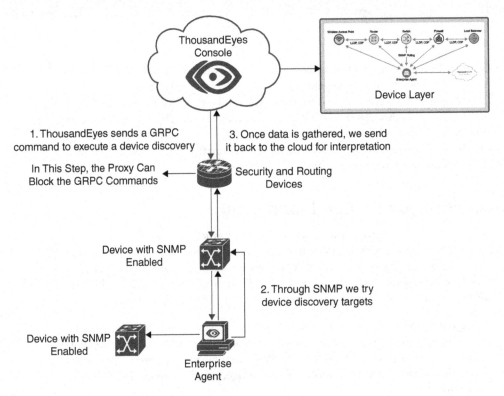

Figure 10-1   *High-Level Design for Device Monitoring*

Before we begin the process, there are prerequisites:

■ Verify that each device will answer SNMP queries.

■ Obtain the following from each device:

   ■ The version of SNMP enabled

   ■ The community string (SNMPv2c) or authentication and privacy settings

■ Ensure that SNMP queries are allowed from the Enterprise Agent IP addresses to each device.

If your target or other network devices (firewalls and other security devices) restrict SNMP queries from Enterprise Agents to your target network devices using access control lists (ACLs), add the Enterprise Agents' IP addresses to the ACLs.

■ Allow SNMP queries destined to port 161/UDP.

The following MIBs are supported:

■ Discovery:

  ■ SNMPv2-MIB

  ■ IF-MIB

■ Interface metrics:

  ■ IF-MIB

■ Device metrics:

  ■ HOST-RESOURCES-MIB

  ■ CISCO-PROCESS-MIB

  ■ JUNIPER-OPERATING-MIB

■ Topology:

  ■ LLDP-MIB

  ■ CDP-MIB

To use Device Monitoring, you must first discover the devices to be monitored:

Step 1.   Device Layer requires your devices' SNMP credentials to discover the devices. In the ThousandEyes UI, navigate to **Devices > Device Settings > Device Credentials** tab (see Figure 10-2). Click **Add New Credentials** to add a new set of credentials.

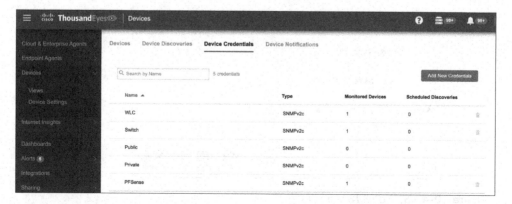

Figure 10-2   *SNMP Device Credentials*

Step 2.   Depending on which version of SNMP you choose, certain criteria are needed. SNMPv2 requires a community string, which serves as a plain-text password. Figure 10-3 shows the SNMP Type field set to SNMPv2c and the corresponding Community String field that must be filled in. Ensure you have a device name in the name section.

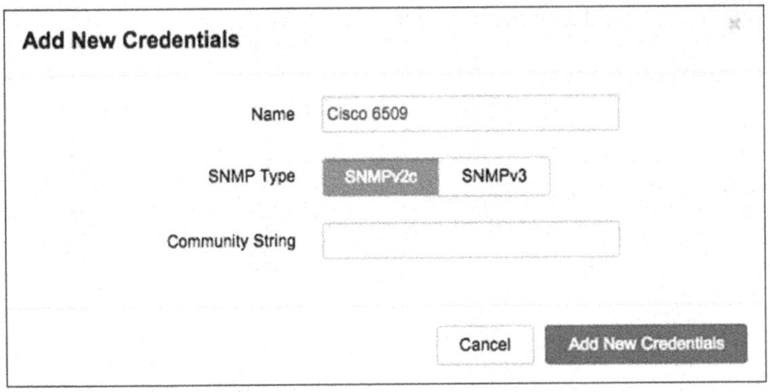

Add New Credentials

Name	Cisco 6509
SNMP Type	**SNMPv2c** SNMPv3
Community String	

Cancel   **Add New Credentials**

Figure 10-3 *SNMPv2 and the Community String Field*

Choosing SNMPv3 requires a few other parameters (see Figure 10-4):

- Security Name
- Context Name (optional)
- Authentication Protocol and Key (optional)
- Privacy Protocol and Key (optional; displayed only if using an authentication protocol)

Add New Credentials

Name	Cisco 6509
SNMP Type	SNMPv2c **SNMPv3**
Security Name	
Context Name	Optional
Authentication Protocol	None ▾

Cancel   **Add New Credentials**

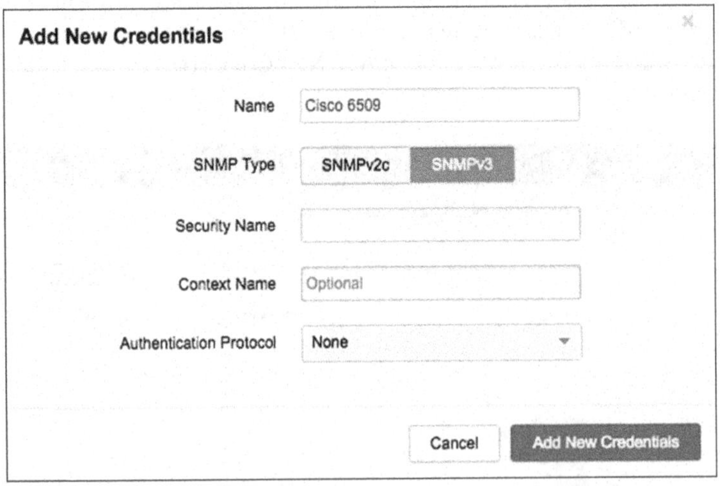

Figure 10-4 *SNMPv3 Parameters*

Step 3.   For either SNMP option, click the **Add New Credentials** button to save the changes. If you have gathered different sets of credentials for different network devices, repeat the process for each set of credentials you have gathered.

Device Discovery

With at least one device credential configured, you can configure one or more device discoveries. From the ThousandEyes UI, navigate to the **Devices > Device Settings > Device Discovery** tab. Device discovery can be performed manually or can be scheduled at regular intervals ranging from 5 minutes to 24 hours.

Device discovery will poll targets specified in the discovery configuration. Polled devices may report interfaces on additional networks not specified in the targets. The Enterprise Agent can perform discovery on any additional networks, and it polls discovered devices for further additional networks. This recursive process will continue until no new networks are found. In this way, the maximum number of pollable devices across all networks can be discovered without needing to manually configure polling for all devices. You can control the depth of the recursion to reduce the time or network traffic levels of the discovery process.

Step 1.   To start the device discovery from the ThousandEyes UI, navigate to the **Devices > Device Settings > Devices** tab and click **Find New Devices**. A discovery configuration form appears, as shown in Figure 10-5.

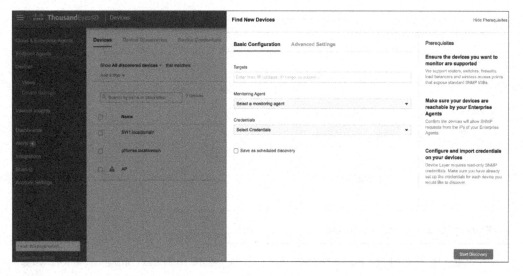

Figure 10-5   *Device Discovery*

From the **Basic Configuration** tab:

- **Targets:** Specify which devices the Enterprise Agent should attempt to discover. Enter the hostname, IP address, IP address range (e.g., 192.168.1.1–192.168.1.10), or subnet using CIDR notation (e.g., 192.168.1.0/24).

- **Monitoring Agent:** Select an Enterprise Agent that will handle the discovery and SNMP collection.

- **Credential:** Select the credentials needed for the specific device(s).

- **Save as Scheduled Discovery:** If checked (optional but recommended), this allows the platform to run scheduled discovery at intervals that you choose in the following step. If not checked, this is a one-time discovery. We will look at both options in this chapter.

Step 2.　Check the **Save as Scheduled Discovery** check box (again, optional but recommended) and complete the following parameters (see Figure 10-6):

- **Discovery Name:** Enter the name of the saved discovery configuration, which will be listed on the **Device Discovery** tab (discussed in the next section).

- **Interval:** Choose the time interval between automatic runs of this discovery.

- **Notification Rules:** Choose the names of device notifications assigned to this discovery.

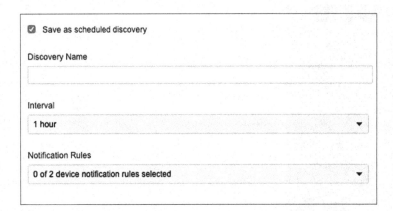

Figure 10-6　*Configuring Scheduled Discovery*

Step 3.　Click the **Advanced Settings** tab (see Figure 10-7) and configure the following:

- **Whitelist:** Specify devices (either listed in the Targets field of the Basic Configuration tab or identified via discovery) that the Enterprise Agent should attempt to poll. Enter the IP address, IP address range (e.g.,

192.168.1.1–192.168.1.10), or subnet (CIDR notation; e.g., 192.168.1.0/24). Hostnames are not permitted.

- **Blacklist:** Specify devices within the Targets field or via discovery that the Enterprise Agent should *not* attempt to discover. Enter the IP address, IP address range (e.g., 192.168.1.1–192.168.1.10), or subnet (CIDR notation; e.g., 192.168.1.0/24). Hostnames are not permitted. If the lists overlap, the blacklist (aka *deny list*) takes priority over the whitelist (aka *allow list*).

- **Maximum Hops:** Limit the number of additional discovery attempts to perform, based on information returned by the discovered devices. The default is 0, which results in polling only the devices in the Targets field (no additional discovery attempts).

- **Connection Attempts:** Set the number of connection attempts per device. Heavily utilized devices or saturated networks may require multiple SNMP connection attempts per device.

- **Connection Timeout:** Set the timeout on each connection attempt.

- **Discovery Timeout:** Set the total time allowed for discovery. When the Maximum Hops setting is greater than 0, this setting can be useful to limit the discovery if discovered devices return large numbers of additional targets.

- **Query Mode:** Select **Fast** or **Compatible**. Fast mode attempts to gather multiple separate object identifiers, which results in fewer queries to the device. Compatible mode requests one object identifier but expects multiple results.

After you've reviewed the advanced settings, click **Start Discovery**.

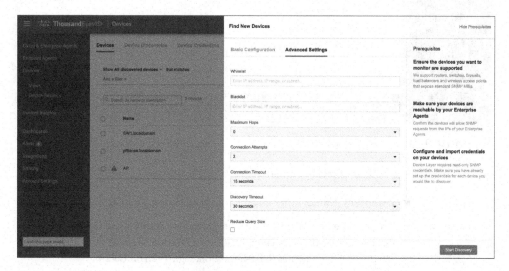

Figure 10-7 *Find New Devices Advanced Settings*

Scheduled Discovery

When we set up this process, there was an option to check **Save as Scheduled Discovery** (refer to Figure 10-5). Let's delve into this a little bit more.

Step 1.   To start a scheduled device discovery, navigate to the **Devices > Device Settings > Device Discoveries** tab. Click **Schedule Discovery** (see Figure 10-8).

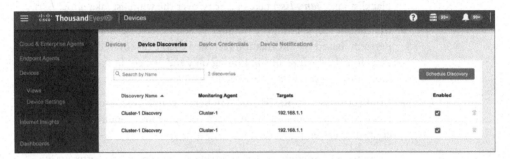

Figure 10-8   *Schedule Discovery*

Step 2.   A discovery configuration form appears, as shown in Figure 10-9.

Figure 10-9   *Scheduled Discovery*

The following settings are available:

■ **Discovery Name:** Enter a name for this discovery configuration.

■ **Targets:** Specify which devices the Enterprise Agent should attempt to discover. Enter the hostname, IP address, IP address range (e.g., 192.168.1.1–192.168.1.10), or subnet (CIDR notation; e.g., 192.168.1.0/24).

- **Credentials:** Select all the credentials used by devices in the Targets field. These are the credentials that you entered in the Configuring Device Credentials tab (refer to Figure 10-2).

- **Monitoring Agent:** Select the monitoring agent that will perform the device discovery. This can be an Enterprise Agent or an Enterprise Agent cluster.

- **Interval:** Specify the frequency at which the discovery will be performed.

- **Notification Rules:** Select one or more device layer notification rules to be notified when discovery produces new information, such as discovery of a new device or new interface on an existing device, or if an existing device is no longer contactable.

Step 3. Click the **Advanced Settings** tab (see Figure 10-10) and configure the following:

- **Whitelist:** Specify devices within the Targets field and from discovery that the Enterprise Agent should attempt to poll. Enter the IP address, IP address range (e.g., 192.168.1.1–192.168.1.10), or subnet (CIDR notation; e.g., 192.168.1.0/24). Hostnames are not permitted.

- **Blacklist:** Specify devices within the Targets field and from discovery that the Enterprise Agent should not attempt to discover. Enter the IP address, IP address range (e.g., 192.168.1.1–192.168.1.10), or subnet (CIDR notation; e.g., 192.168.1.0/24). Hostnames are not permitted. If the lists overlap, the deny list takes priority over the allow list.

- **Maximum Hops:** Limit the number of additional discovery attempts to perform, based on information returned by the discovered devices. The default is 0, which results in polling only the devices in the Targets field (no additional discovery attempts).

- **Connection Attempts:** Set the number of connection attempts per device. Heavily utilized devices or saturated networks may require multiple SNMP connection attempts per device.

- **Connection Timeout:** Set the timeout on each connection attempt.

- **Discovery Timeout:** Set the total time allowed for discovery. When the Maximum Hops setting is greater than 0, this setting can be useful to limit the discovery if discovered devices return large numbers of additional targets.

- **Reduce Query Size:** Check this box to instruct the device to limit the number of fields it includes in its response, instead of sending as many as it can accommodate. While this means more queries are sent to retrieve the same amount of data, it aids in keeping UDP packets within the network's Maximum Transmission Unit (MTU).

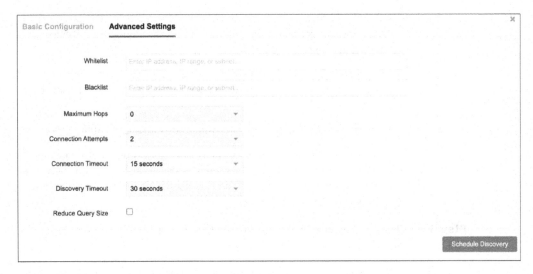

Figure 10-10 *Scheduled Discovery Advanced Settings*

Discovered Devices

To view the new devices that were discovered, navigate to the **Devices > Device Settings > Devices** tab (see Figure 10-11).

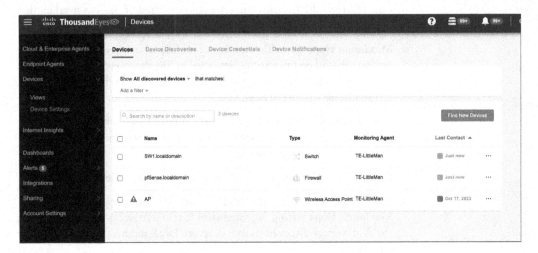

Figure 10-11 *Discovered Devices*

You can see a few details from the name that was supplied in the SNMP query. Also notice that the Monitoring Agent column lists the agent collecting the SNMP data and sending it to the ThousandEyes platform.

Device Details

Click the device name in the Devices tab to view the following details (see Figure 10-12).

Figure 10-12 *Device Details*

- **Name:** The SNMP name of the device. This view shows that it can't be changed; however, if you change from the source of the object, ThousandEyes will use that name convention.

- **Type:** Ensure the device is labeled properly—for example, switch or router.

- **IP/Hostname:** This is another hard-coded object that cannot be changed from the ThousandEyes platform.

- **Monitoring Agent:** If you need to move the SNMP query to another agent, you can use this drop-down menu to do so.

- **Monitored Interfaces:** By default, the platform should monitor all ports; however, in this example some instances are not being monitored, such as app-gigabit. Ensure that all ports have been checked.

- **Interval:** This is the interval set from the previous configuration in the "Scheduled Discovery" section.

- **Credentials:** The credential that is used to poll this device. The credential can be changed via this drop-down menu.

- **Alert Rules:** Select the alert rules you want to use for device events. You may need to create a new alert rule.

- **Notification Rules:** Select the notification rules you want to use for device events. You may need to add a notification to the alert.

- **Discovery Information:** This section displays the discovery configuration, monitoring agent, and credentials used to discover this device. You can click the discovery name to view the saved discovery configuration.

- **General Information:** This section displays the System Name, Vendor, Platform, and Description fields obtained from the device through the SNMP process.

- **Device Uptime:** The device is polled every 5 minutes. If the device can respond to any SNMP queries, the device is considered up.

- **Monitoring Support:** Displays whether interface list, IP address list, and topology discovery are supported for this device.

- **Stop Monitoring:** This button stops the agent from polling the device via SNMP. Once stopped, the Test button is replaced with a Monitor Device button, which restarts monitoring.

- **Cancel:** Use this button to cancel any changes you've made to this device's configuration.

- **Test:** If you make changes to the configuration, the Test button becomes clickable. Click **Test** to test the configuration.

- **Save:** Click **Save** to save any changes.

Device Alerts

By default, the alert rules have not been created. Let's review device alerts.

Step 1.　Navigate to the **Alerts > Alert Rules > Devices** tab (see Figure 10-13).

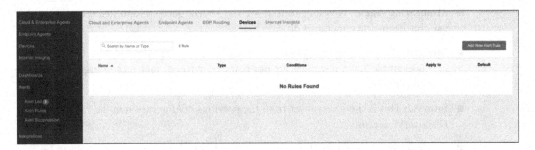

Figure 10-13　*Device Alert Rule*

Step 2.　Click **Add New Alert Rule** to open the window shown in Figure 10-14, which has the following settings:

Figure 10-14 *Device Alert Rule Creation*

- **Alert Type:** Choose **Device** to monitor the entire switch, including all interfaces, or choose **Interface** to select specific ports on the switch.

- **Rule Name:** Enter a rule name that is easily understood.

- **Devices:** Select the devices that will be grouped to this ruleset.

- **Alert Conditions:** Create a condition that will meet the SLAs of the organization. The following conditions can be retrieved and notified using the options in the Alert Conditions section:

  - Throughput

  - Discards

  - Errors

  - Operational Status (offline or online)

  - Admin Status (enabled or disabled)

  - State (changed or unchanged)

Once the conditions have been created, click the **Notifications** tab (see Figure 10-15). Add how a user or team needs to be notified once a condition has been met. Once done, click **Create New Alert Rule.**

Figure 10-15   *Device Notification*

Add the new alert rule in the device configuration:

Step 1.   Navigate to **Devices > Device Settings > Devices** and select a device.

Step 2.   On the Basic Configuration tab, scroll to the **Alert Rules** section and select the rule (see Figure 10-16).

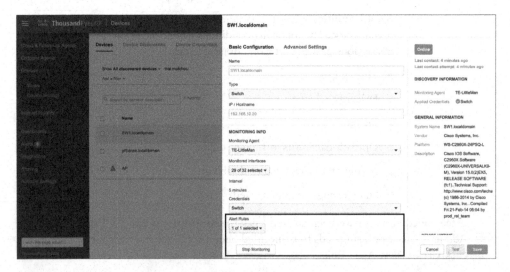

Figure 10-16   *Alert Rule Device Monitoring*

While we did select a notification inside the Alert Rule, notice that nothing is available under Notification Rules (see Figure 10-17). Within the **Devices** tab, there is an additional Notification setting.

Figure 10-17   *Device Notification*

Device Notifications

From the ThousandEyes UI, navigate to the **Devices > Device Settings > Device Notifications** tab and click **Add Notification Rule** (see Figure 10-18).

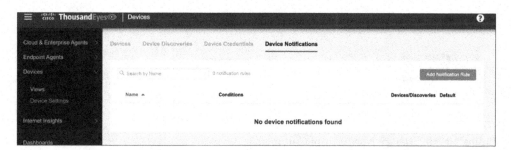

Figure 10-18   *Device Notification Rule*

When adding a new notification rule, you have two options for the Notification Type field, **Devices Status** or **New Devices**, as shown in Figure 10-19.

For this example, choose **Devices Status**, enter a name in the Notification Name field (e.g., **Test**), select devices in the **Devices** drop-down menu, and select a condition in the Conditions section.

Click the **Notifications** tab and use the same options you used on the Notifications tab in the Add New Alert Rule window (refer to Figure 10-15).

Device Views

Now that you have devices configured, take a look at the **Devices > Views** page (see Figure 10-20) and see what data you have—just like running tests, you can dive into the views and look at the metrics. You can add a filter, choose a metric, and navigate between the Topology, Interface Table, and Device Table tabs.

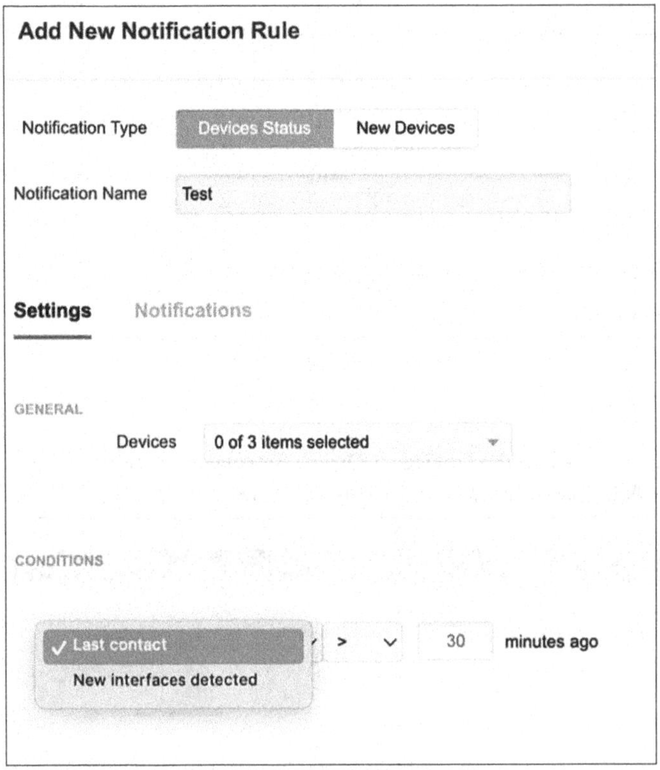

Add New Notification Rule

Notification Type   Devices Status   New Devices

Notification Name   Test

Settings   Notifications
_____

GENERAL

Devices   0 of 3 items selected   ▼

CONDITIONS

✓ Last contact   > ∨   30   minutes ago

New interfaces detected

Figure 10-19 *Device Notification Config*

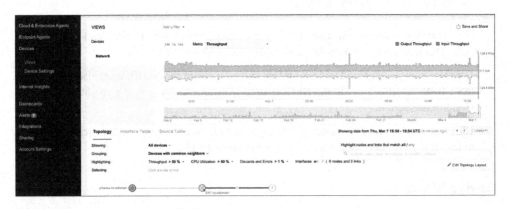

Figure 10-20 *Device View Overview*

As an example, Figure 10-21 shows device SW1.localdomain (switch) with the Metric drop-down menu option **Throughput** selected.

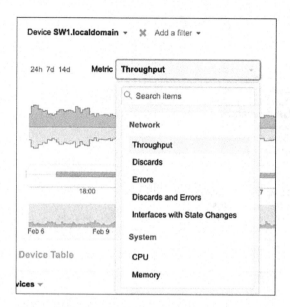

Figure 10-21   *Device View Specifics*

Figure 10-22 shows the Topology tab for this example, which shows whether any anomalies exist, just like a path visualization when inspecting a test.

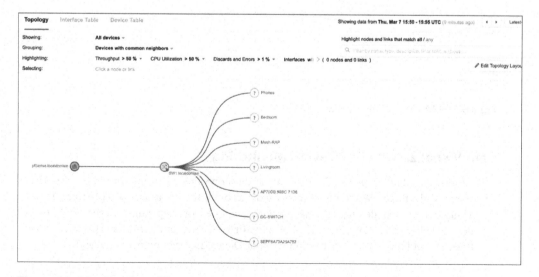

Figure 10-22   *Topology View*

By selecting a link between devices, as shown in Figure 10-23, you can also gather metrics on those two devices.

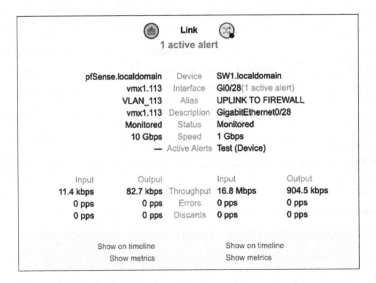

Figure 10-23   *P2P Link Metrics*

Moving to the next tab, **Interface Table** (see Figure 10-24), you can inspect each interface from VLAN, throughput, or discards.

Status	Interface	Device	MAC Address	IP Address	Speed (bps)	VLAN	Throughput (bps in/out)	Discards (pps in/out)	Errors (pps in/out)	Last Changed (UTC)
	Gi0/28	SW1.localdomain	c4:72:95:77:2d:1c	—	1G	Trunk	20.0M / 1.30M	0	0	2023-11-04 00:23:50
	Gi0/1	SW1.localdomain	c4:72:95:77:2d:01	—	1G	Trunk	244k / 16.0M	0	0	2023-10-19 04:26:22
	Gi0/13	SW1.localdomain	c4:72:95:77:2d:0d	—	1G	Trunk	867k / 3.38M	0	0	2024-03-04 15:44:54
	Gi0/5	SW1.localdomain	c4:72:95:77:2d:05	—	1G	Trunk	175k / 647k	0	0	2023-11-15 04:41:28
	Gi0/2	SW1.localdomain	c4:72:95:77:2d:02	—	1G	Trunk	11.3k / 34.6k	0	0	2023-10-19 04:17:22
	Gi0/6	SW1.localdomain	c4:72:95:77:2d:06	—	1G	Trunk	3.28k / 31.0k	0	0	2023-10-19 04:03:16

Topology   **Interface Table**   Device Table   Showing data from Thu, Mar 7 15:50 - 15:55 UTC (9 minutes ago)   ◀ ▶   Latest ▶|

Figure 10-24   *Interface Metrics*

Path Visualization with Device Monitoring

As introduced in Chapter 6, Path Visualization shows the traceroute from the Enterprise Agent to the target. When you discover a device with the ThousandEyes platform, Path Visualization then identifies the device with a unique icon, depending on the type of device. For example, Figure 10-25 shows the firewall icon for the firewall that was added. Keep in mind that Path Visualization without Device Layer only shows Layer 3.

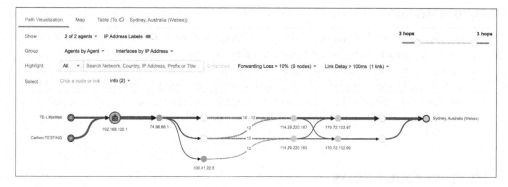

Figure 10-25 *Device Monitoring in Path Visualization*

Operational Insights

In this section, we offer practical insights and guidance to navigate various operational challenges effectively. From device replacements to optimizing polling and enhancing topology views, these tips and tricks can be invaluable in ensuring smooth network operations.

Replacing a Device with a New Piece of Hardware

Devices are uniquely identified using the Engine ID, which is the enterprise number and MAC address. This ID is significant if a device is replaced in an environment. If that occurs, an old device is preserved in the Device Layer listing as offline. The new device is discovered as a uniquely different device.

If a user asks why a new device cannot be integrated into the existing listing, the uniqueness of the Engine ID is why that is the case. The Engine ID is under SNMPv3.

Polling

At the time of writing, ThousandEyes does not support polling of virtual interfaces, tunnel interfaces, or subinterfaces via SNMP. Check the latest release notes, as features are constantly being added or updated on a monthly basis.

Topology

For the topology view to function optimally, it's essential to have Cisco Discovery Protocol (CDP) or Link Layer Discovery Protocol (LLDP) enabled on all devices that are to be discovered by ThousandEyes. While Enterprise Agents retrieve Layer 2 information via SNMP, neighbor data must already exist on these devices, obtained through CDP or LLDP. When discussing this, it's helpful to request the results of CDP/LLDP to ensure proper data collection.

Agent Clusters

The Device Layer does support Enterprise Agent clusters. Previously, only individual Enterprise Agents could be configured for Device Layer testing. With this enhancement, testing can be conducted by a single cluster member, during cluster setup. If an Agent performing Device Layer testing is moved into a cluster, testing responsibilities will be automatically reassigned to another cluster member. It's important to note that any data collected by an individual Enterprise Agent before joining a cluster will no longer be accessible.

Review Questions

Answer the following questions. Check your answers against those provided in Appendix A, "Answers to Review Questions."

1. Can ThousandEyes Device Monitoring use SNMPv2 or v3?

2. Do you need CDP/LLDP turned on?

3. How can you find throughput for an individual port?

Chapter 11

Account Administration

This chapter provides information on how to manage users, accounts, account groups, and usage; view user activity; implement authentication with single sign-on (SSO); and assign permissions with role-based access control (RBAC).

Adding a New User

Adding a new user to the ThousandEyes platform requires Administrative or Organizational rights and is accomplished as follows:

Step 1.   Navigate to the **Account Settings > Users and Roles > Users** tab.

Step 2.   Click the **New Users** button (see Figure 11-1) to open the New Users dialog box shown in Figure 11-2.

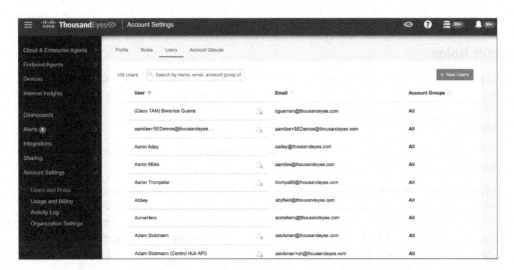

Figure 11-1   *New Users Button*

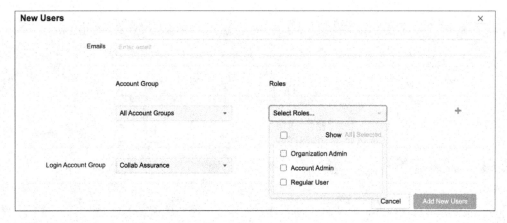

Figure 11-2 *New User Role(s) Assignment*

Step 3.   Configure the following options:

- **Emails:** Add the user's email address. The ThousandEyes platform will send an email to the user to verify the address and will enable the user to create a password.

- **Account Group:** If the organization has account groups, select an account group or **All Account Groups.** Account groups are discussed shortly.

- **Roles:** Choose one or more default roles, as discussed next.

Note   Each user's password must be at least eight characters long and contain at least three of the following types of characters: digits, symbols, uppercase letters, and lowercase letters.

Default Roles

As just discussed, when adding new users to the platform, you must assign each user to an account group and a role. The ThousandEyes platform follows a role-based access control (RBAC) model, where users' roles dictate their permissions within the platform. Administrators can use the default built-in roles or create custom roles.

As shown in Figure 11-2, the built-in roles consist of Organization Admin, Account Admin, and Regular User.

Assigning a user the Organization Admin role grants full permissions, including managing usage, users, and account groups. It is recommended to reserve this role for administrators who are fully trained in ThousandEyes account setup. In ThousandEyes, an organization represents the top-level entity that encompasses all account groups, tests, agents, and other resources associated with a company. It serves as the primary container for managing and organizing all aspects of ThousandEyes usage within a company.

The Account Admin is similar to the Organizational Admin, with the exception of viewing billing information.

The Regular User role is for read-only access and carries no administrative permissions.

Users needing access between Organization Admin and Regular User levels can hold the Account Admin role.

To view the default permissions, navigate to the **Account Settings > Users and Roles > Roles** tab, where you can see what permissions are available for each of the roles provided, as shown in Figure 11-3. The upcoming section "Role-Based Access Control" covers how to configure the proper RBAC permissions for your organization.

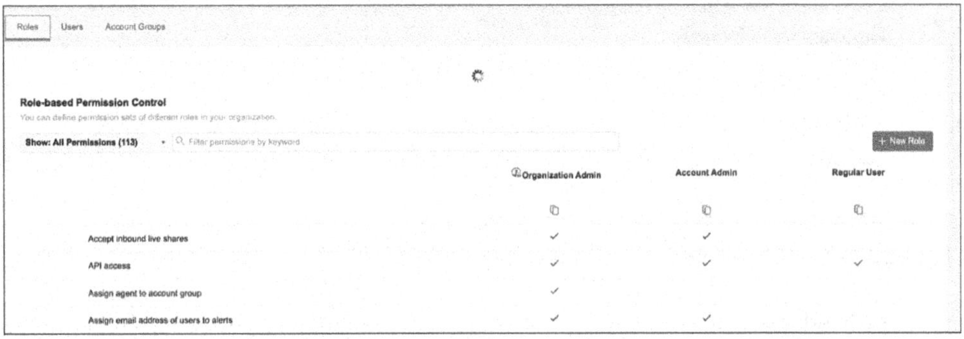

Figure 11-3 *User Roles*

Account Groups

Every ThousandEyes user is associated with an organization, which represents the customer's billing entity. When licenses are purchased, they are applied to an entire organization and then shared among its account groups. An *account group* is a way to divide the organization into functional groups. For example, Network, Security, and Applications teams all would have a separate space to conduct their own tests, create dashboards, and so forth, which allows each team to focus on their needs and create specialized data based on those needs.

Although billing is shared across account groups, users within one account group cannot access data from other account groups unless the permissions are set to allow that user to do so.

A user can belong to multiple account groups and switch among them seamlessly without reauthentication. In the example shown in Figure 11-4, user Super User has access to three account groups within the ThousandEyes Internal organization and is currently logged into the Engineering account group. When logged in your username will appear in the top-right corner. Clicking the drop-down window will show all available account groups.

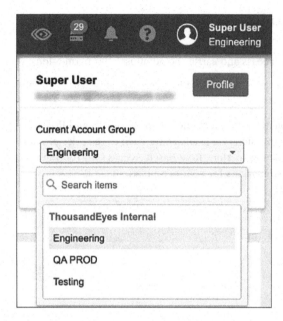

Figure 11-4 *User's Current Account Group Options*

It's advisable to plan how you'll utilize account groups based on your company structure. There's no limit on the number of account groups.

To create an account group in the ThousandEyes platform, follow these steps:

Step 1. Navigate to **Account Settings > Users and Roles > Account Groups**.

Step 2. Click the **New Account Group** button, as shown in Figure 11-5.

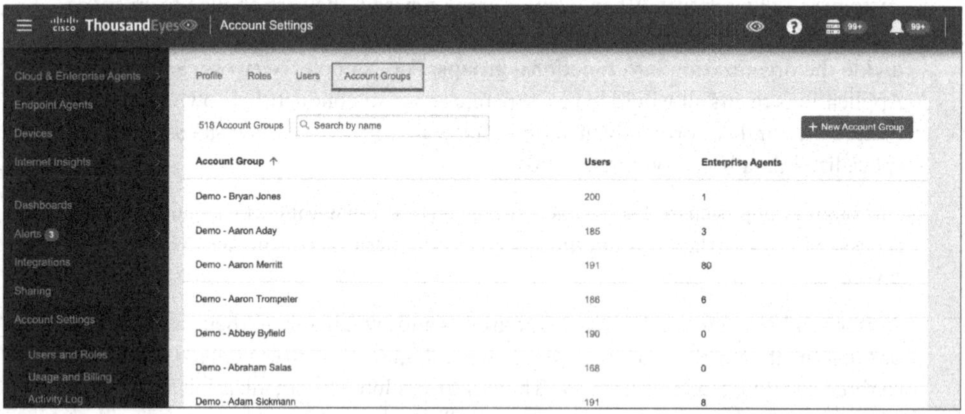

Figure 11-5 *New Account Group Button*

Step 3.   Create a name for the account group and then click **Add New Account Group**, as shown in Figure 11-6.

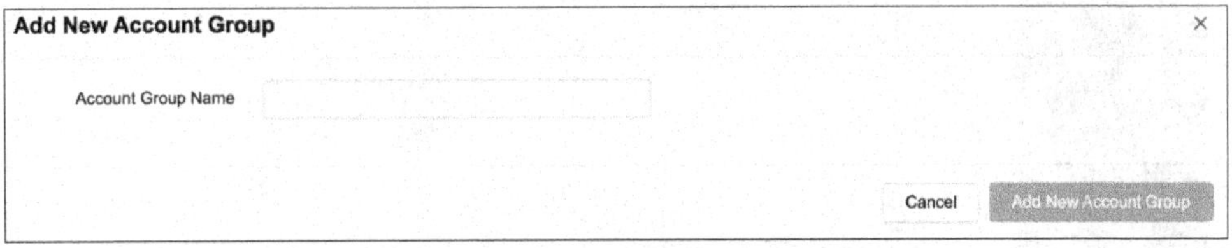

Figure 11-6   *Adding a New Account Group*

To view the account groups in the organization, review Figure 11-5.

Role-Based Access Control

Previously, a user who needed to administer their company's ThousandEyes users across multiple accounts had to be assigned the Organization Admin role. This role provided permissions not only to manage all users in every account but also to access billing information for all accounts. With RBAC, you can now assign roles that are restricted to specific user administration tasks within only the necessary account groups, without granting permissions for billing or other unrelated tasks. Let's dive into the RBAC permissions and the process of creating a new role.

Step 1.   From the ThousandEyes UI, navigate to the **Account Settings > Users and Roles > Roles** tab. Click **New Role**, as shown in Figure 11-7.

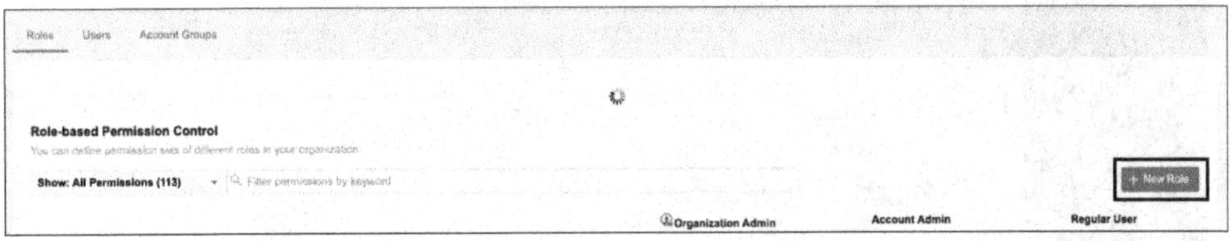

Figure 11-7   *RBAC*

Step 2.   Create a role name and select the permissions needed for that role from the list shown in Figure 11-8. Then click **Save**.

The ThousandEyes platform has a few ways to select permissions. At the time of writing, there are 113 permissions, so scrolling through all of them would be a daunting task. The platform has a filter, and groups many of the permissions together. From the drop-down menu, select All Permissions, Management Permissions, or Related Component, as shown in Figure 11-9.

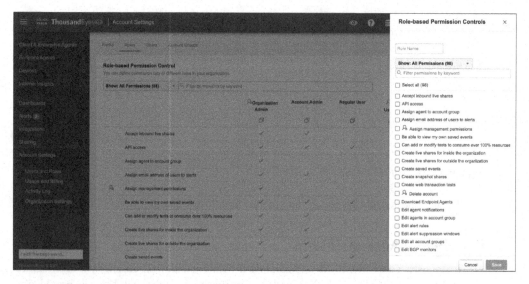

Figure 11-8 *RBAC Permissions*

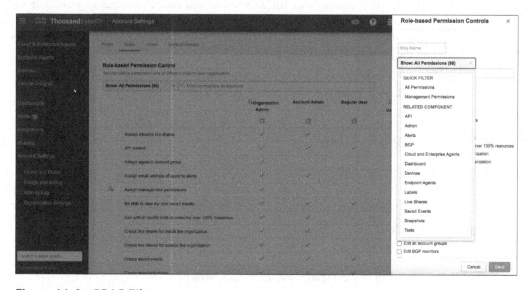

Figure 11-9 *RBAC Filter*

Step 3. Once the role has been created, switch back to the Account Settings, click
Users and Roles, and then **Users**. You can either edit the user role or, when
adding a new user, select the appropriate role (see Figure 11-10).

Figure 11-10   *RBAC User*

Single Sign-On with ThousandEyes

To enhance the security of your cloud-based infrastructure and streamline user access, ThousandEyes offers single sign-on (SSO) login capability. SSO in ThousandEyes supports both service provider–initiated logins and identity provider–initiated logins and is based on Security Assertion Markup Language (SAML) version 2.0.

Setting up SSO involves two main steps:

- **Identity provider (IdP) configuration:** This is done within your chosen SSO system. There are a number of them, such as ADFS, Azure AD, and Okta, and they can be either on-premises (ADFS) or in the cloud (Cisco DUO, Azure AD, Okta).

- **ThousandEyes configuration:** This is done within the ThousandEyes platform.

Before you begin setup, ensure you have the following:

- A ThousandEyes account with the necessary permissions

- An account or subscription with your chosen IdP

- Configuration details for both the service provider (ThousandEyes) and the IdP

Identity Provider Setup

Log in to your IdP and configure a new service provider (SP). Instructions will vary depending on your IdP, but the common steps include

- Finding and selecting ThousandEyes within the IdP's application/SP directory

- Configuring SSO settings and parameters

- Downloading verification certificates or metadata files

- Configuring ThousandEyes details

The following are some more specific details for the preceding common steps:

- **Finding ThousandEyes:** Within the IdP's application/SP directory, you'll search for ThousandEyes by name. Depending on the IdP you're using, ThousandEyes may be listed by default, or you may need to manually add it to your directory, as described next.

- **Adding ThousandEyes to your IdP:** If ThousandEyes isn't already listed, some IdPs offer the option to manually add custom applications or service providers. In this case, you'll typically need to provide some basic information about ThousandEyes, such as its name, description, and logo.

- **Configuring SSO settings:** Once you've located (or added) ThousandEyes within the IdP's directory, you'll proceed to configure the specific SSO settings and parameters required for integration. This includes things like SAML endpoints, assertion formats, and encryption settings.

- **Uploading verification certificates or metadata:** As part of the configuration process, you may need to upload verification certificates or metadata files provided by ThousandEyes. These files contain cryptographic keys and other information necessary for secure communication between ThousandEyes and your IdP.

Overall, the process of finding and selecting ThousandEyes within the IdP's application/ SP directory involves locating ThousandEyes as an available integration option, configuring its SSO settings, and ensuring that the necessary cryptographic keys and metadata are exchanged between ThousandEyes and your IdP for secure authentication.

ThousandEyes Setup

Here are the specifics you need for ThousandEyes configuration:

- **Configuration Type:** Choose Static, Metadata File, or Dynamic, as shown in Figure 11-11:

  - **Static:** This option requires you to manually enter the SSO configuration details such as the identity provider (IdP) URL, entity ID, and X.509 certificate. You input all the necessary information directly into the ThousandEyes SSO settings.

  - **Metadata File:** With this option, you upload an XML metadata file provided by your IdP. The metadata file contains all the necessary configuration details, such as the IdP URL, certificates, and other parameters. ThousandEyes will automatically extract the required information from the file.

■ **Dynamic:** This option typically involves providing a URL from which ThousandEyes can dynamically fetch the IdP metadata. This enables ThousandEyes to automatically retrieve and update the SSO configuration details, ensuring that any changes on the IdP side are reflected without manual intervention.

■ Login URL for your SAML provider

■ Logout URL for your SAML provider (optional)

■ Identity Provider Issuer

■ Service Provider Issuer

■ Verification certificate(s)

Set Up Single Sign-On (SSO) Authentication
Set up access to ThousandEyes using your identity provider (IdP) Learn more about SSO

Enable SSO ⑦
Force SSO ⑦

Configuration Type   Static   Metadata File   Dynamic

CONFIGURATION

Login Page URL

Logout Page URL

Identity Provider Issuer

Service Provider Issuer
Your IdP configuration needs to use this exact value. In some IdPs, this value is called "Audience Restriction".

Verification certificates   Choose file No file chosen

Discard Changes   Run Single Sign-On Test   Save

Figure 11-11 *SSO Configuration*

With that information at hand, follow these steps to set up SSO for ThousandEyes:

Step 1.   Navigate to the **Account Settings > Organization Settings > Security and Authorization** tab. Scroll down to the Set Up Single Sign-On (SSO) Authentication section.

As shown in Figure 11-11, you can choose **Enable SSO** or **Force SSO** for your organization. Enabling SSO allows users to choose between local login and SSO, while forcing SSO mandates SSO authentication for all users.

Step 2.   After you have configured access to ThousandEyes using your IdP, it's essential to test SSO to ensure that it works correctly. ThousandEyes provides a single sign-on test feature to verify the setup's success. Click **Run Single Sign-On Test**, as shown in Figure 11-12.

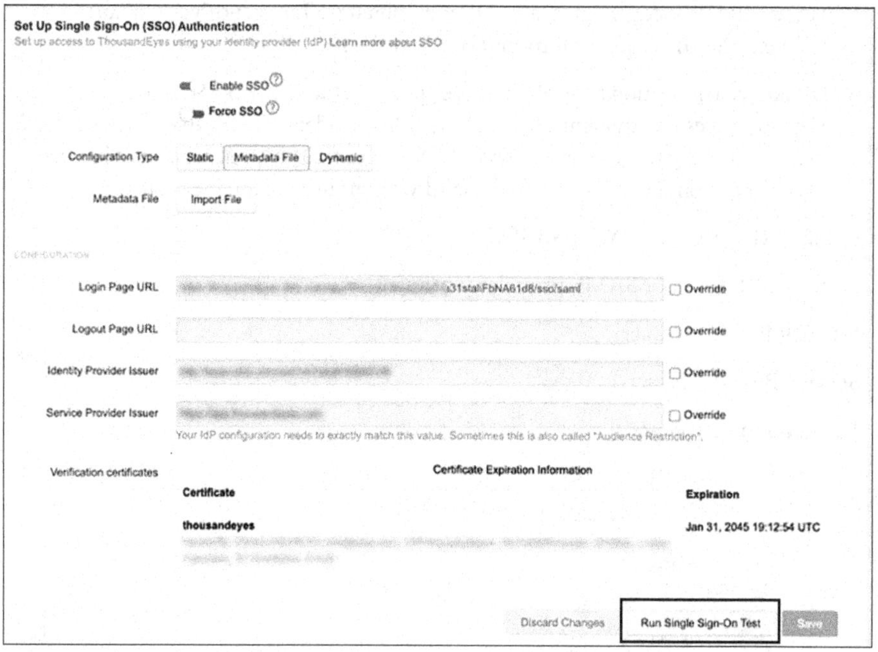

Figure 11-12 *SSO Test*

If the test is successful, you'll receive a confirmation message.

Additionally, you can test SSO login from your IdP's site or use the SSO login link provided on the ThousandEyes login page.

> **Note**   For a user to log in using SSO, they must be assigned a role with the Login via Single Sign-On permission. As another way of restricting users to log in only via SSO, you can remove the Login via ThousandEyes login page permission. This is useful for managed service providers, for example, who may not want to force SSO for all the organizations they manage.

Imported Metadata Configuration

Imported metadata configuration refers to a method where ThousandEyes retrieves the necessary SAML configuration details directly from a metadata XML file provided by your IdP. To use this method while still in the Set Up Single Sign-On (SSO) Authentication section, proceed as follows:

Step 1.   For the Configuration Type option, click **Metadata File**, as shown in Figure 11-13.

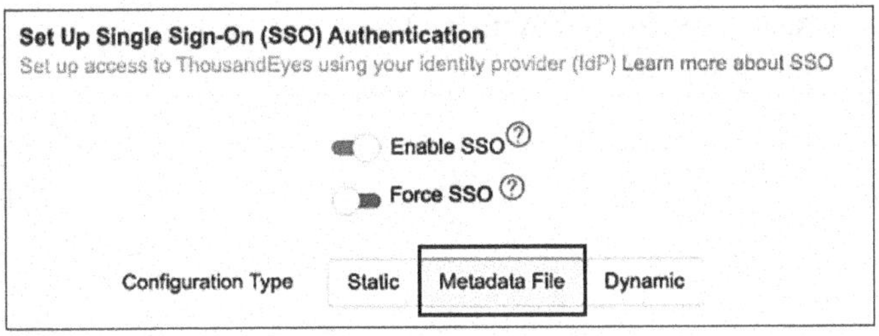

Set Up Single Sign-On (SSO) Authentication
Set up access to ThousandEyes using your identity provider (IdP) Learn more about SSO

Enable SSO ⑦

Force SSO ⑦

Configuration Type   Static   Metadata File   Dynamic

Figure 11-13   *SSO Metadata File Configuration Option*

Step 2.   Click **Import File**, as shown in Figure 11-14.

Metadata File   Import File

Figure 11-14   *SSO Metadata File Import Option*

In the new window that opens, shown in Figure 11-15, click **Choose File** to navigate to the metadata file downloaded from your IdP.

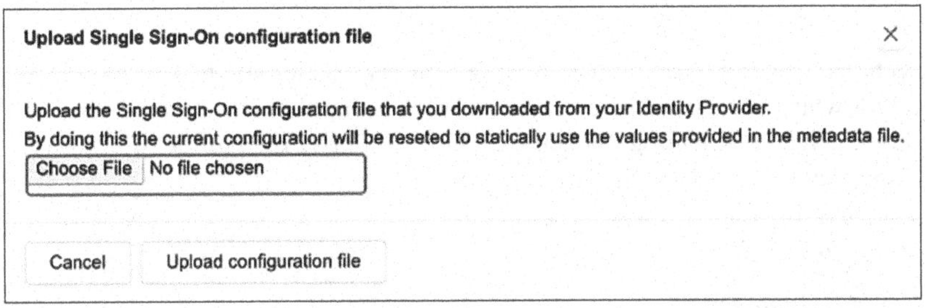

Upload Single Sign-On configuration file   ✕

Upload the Single Sign-On configuration file that you downloaded from your Identity Provider.
By doing this the current configuration will be reseted to statically use the values provided in the metadata file.

Choose File │ No file chosen

Cancel   Upload configuration file

Figure 11-15   *Choosing and Uploading SSO Metadata File*

Step 3.   After you have chosen the metadata file, click **Upload Configuration File**. The configuration file will then update the verification certificate.

Activity Log

This feature provides organizations with a comprehensive overview of user activities within the ThousandEyes platform. From login events to configuration changes, the Activity Log offers transparency and accountability, allowing administrators to track and analyze user behavior, identify security incidents, and ensure compliance with organizational policies. With detailed timestamps and event descriptions, administrators can easily monitor user actions, detect anomalies, and take proactive measures to safeguard their network infrastructure and sensitive data.

The Activity Log is located at **Account Settings > Activity Log**, as shown in Figure 11-16. The options are described next.

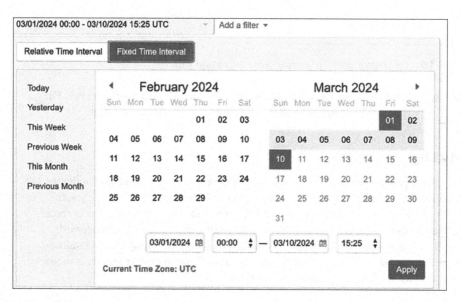

Figure 11-16   *Activity Log*

Time Selector

The time selector drop-down menu in the upper-left corner enables you to select a time and/or period for which you want to view activity. When using the time selector, you have a few options, such as selecting a specific time or looking at the past month. Figure 11-17 shows the Fixed Time Interval tab options.

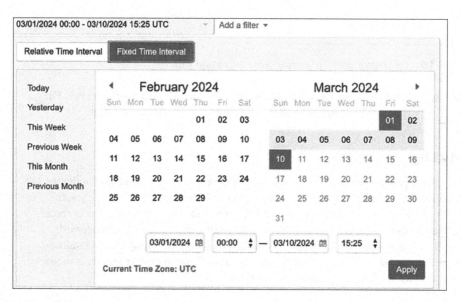

Figure 11-17   *Fixed Time Interval Options*

The other tab is Relative Time Interval (see Figure 11-18), which enables you to go back in time and look at logs for the last 1 hour or all the way back to logs for the past 60 days.

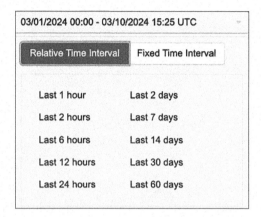

Figure 11-18   *Relative Time Interval Options*

Add a Filter

After choosing a time interval option, you can also use filters to quickly find specific activities. As shown in Figure 11-19, the Add a Filter drop-down menu offers the following filters: Event Type, Component, Account Group, User, IP Address, and Event.

Figure 11-19   *Log Filter*

As an example, selecting the Component filter allows you to see specifics regarding the components configured in the ThousandEyes platform, as shown in Figure 11-20, where Test is selected to see all the tests that have been created.

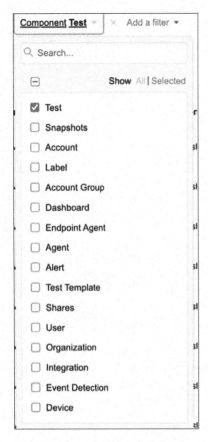

Figure 11-20   *Test Component*

After selecting Test under the Component filter, all tests created during the specified time period are displayed, including a description of each test, which user created the test, and the account group to which the user belongs, as shown in Figure 11-21.

Time (UTC)	Account Group	User	Event Type	Component	Description
2024/03/09 10:38 PM	Demo - Sha...		IP Address: ▓▓▓▓ ⓘ Operation	est	Test Synopsys - Community Login alert rules upda...
2024/03/09 10:38 PM	Demo - Sha...		Operation	Test	Test Aldine - Destiny Discover (Azure) alert rules u...

Figure 11-21   *User Activity Log with Test Component of Component Filter Applied*

Download Logs

You can also use the Download option to export the log files to your computer and save them as a CSV file (see Figure 11-22). If there was a need to use an API and gather the logs automatically, this can also be an option.

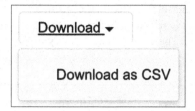

Figure 11-22   *Download Log*

Usage

Understanding usage can often be tricky, and a consumption-based model might seem complicated at first glance. However, it's crucial to grasp how this model works, as it directly affects how ThousandEyes bills for services. The key is to understand the use cases, determine the number of tests needed, and anticipate future requirements.

ThousandEyes operates on a consumption-based model, where organizations are billed based on the usage of the platform. This usage is measured in units. Each test, whether it's a network test, a transaction test, or a page load test, consumes a certain number of units. Therefore, understanding how many units your organization will need is essential for accurate billing and budgeting. This matters because, with a clear understanding of consumption, organizations can optimize their usage, avoid unexpected costs, and ensure they have sufficient capacity to meet their monitoring needs. By planning ahead, you can better manage your resources and get the most value out of the ThousandEyes platform.

Let's break this down using the unit calculator in the ThousandEyes platform:

Step 1.   Navigate to the **Account Settings > Usage and Billing > Usage** tab and click **Calculate the Units You Need for This Account Group** (see Figure 11-23). The Usage tab is accessible only to Organization Admins or an RBAC permission allowing users to access the Usage and Billing section.

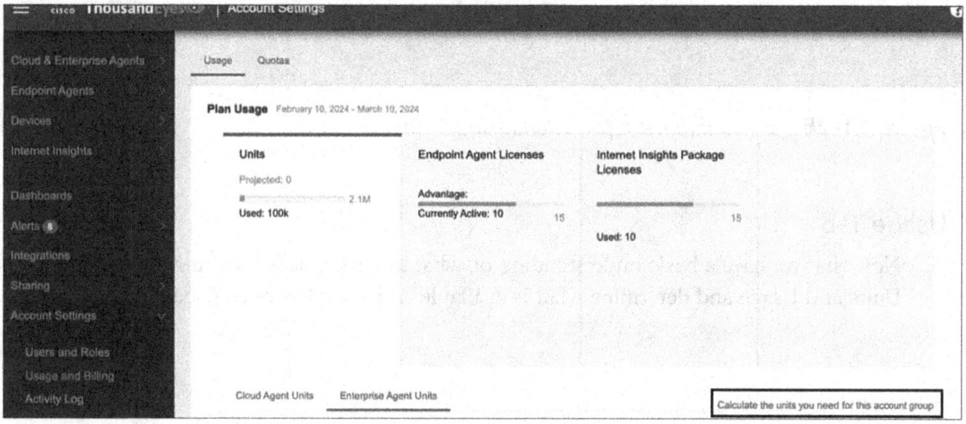

Figure 11-23   *Unit Usage Overview*

Step 2. From the calculator view, click **Add Row** and select a test. In the example shown in Figure 11-24, an HTTP Server test is selected, the Interval is set to 5 min, and one Enterprise Agent is selected. The approximate monthly usage for this test is 22,320 units.

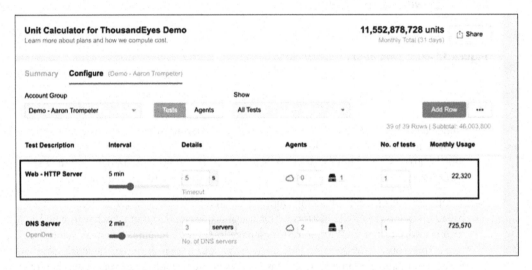

Figure 11-24   *Unit Calculator*

All of these parameters will change if you add more agents or change the interval. The equation in Figure 11-25 is a basic formula for calculating units, but using the unit calculator allows a more accurate count when looking at many tests and aggregating the unit counts.

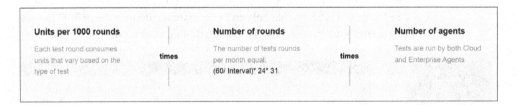

Figure 11-25   *Basic Equation for Calculating Units*

Usage Tab

Now that we have a basic understanding of what *units* are, let's look at an example of the Units and Usage and determine what is available and what has been used.

From the ThousandEyes UI, navigate to **Account Settings > Usage and Billing.** The Usage tab is displayed by default. As shown in Figure 11-26, the Usage tab has three sections, described next for this example:

- **Units:** This example shows 100k units used and 2.1M total units available. Using the unit calculator would help the administrator understand how many tests they can use before hitting the threshold of 2.1 million units.

- **Endpoint Agent Licenses:** This example shows 10 EPAs active now, with 5 more licenses available to use.

- **Internet Insights Package Licenses:** This example shows 10 packages have been used and 5 are available. Each package represents a geographic area and specific domain; for example, ISP North America or EMEA CDN providers.

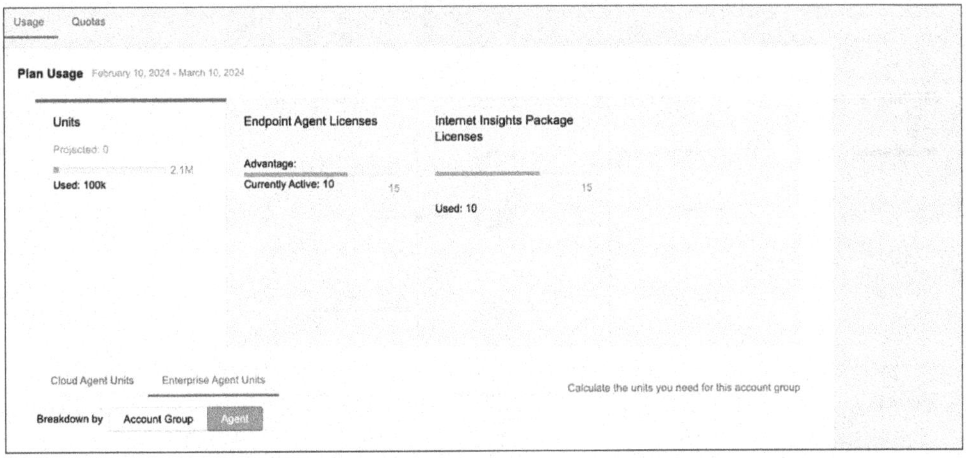

Figure 11-26   *Usage Tab Showing Plan Usage*

Quotas Tab

Quotas in ThousandEyes are predefined limits or thresholds set for account groups within the platform. These quotas ensure that users adhere to allocated usage limits, preventing overutilization of resources and potential service degradation. Quotas are very important to administrators because they directly impact their ability to utilize ThousandEyes effectively and efficiently. Here's why:

- **Resource management:** Quotas help organizations manage their resources effectively by setting limits on the number of tests, agents, or other resources they can use. This ensures fair allocation of resources among account groups and prevents any single group from monopolizing resources to the detriment of others.

- **Cost control:** Quotas can also help control costs by preventing excessive usage that could lead to unexpected charges or overages. By adhering to quotas, organizations can better predict their usage and budget accordingly, avoiding unnecessary expenses.

■ **Performance optimization:** By enforcing quotas, ThousandEyes helps maintain platform performance and stability. By preventing excessive usage, ThousandEyes ensures that resources are available to all users and that the platform operates smoothly for everyone.

As you likely noticed in the previous section, the Quotas tab is next to the Usage tab (**Account Settings > Usage and Billing > Quotas** tab). As shown in Figure 11-27, the Quotas tab provides a summarized view of the organization's plan and usage details at the top, followed by a breakdown of the account groups, their current usage rate, and tools to manage their quotas.

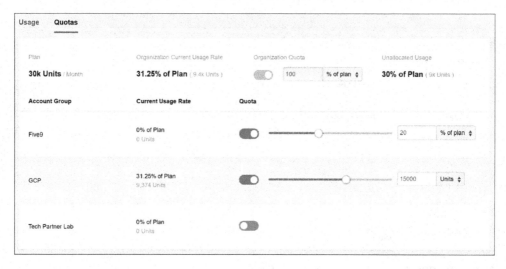

Figure 11-27 *Quotas Tab*

The following are all the components of the Quotas tab:

■ **Plan:** Total units allocated to the organization per billing cycle.

■ **Organization Current Usage Rate:** The organization's total current usage rate for the billing cycle.

■ **Organization Quota:** The total units the organization may utilize per billing cycle. The Organizational Admin can specify a desired usage limit by toggling the setting on and setting the value to what is appropriate.

■ **Unallocated Usage:** The percentage and number of monthly units not allocated to any account group.

■ **Account Group:** This column lists the names of account groups defined.

- **Current Usage Rate:** This column displays the current usage rate for each account group as a percentage of the plan.

- **Quota toggle:** This toggle enables or disables the option to assign a fixed percent of total plan units for an account group. When disabled, the account group can utilize any number of units up to the total plan amount. When enabled, an admin can use the slider bar to select a value for that account group. For example, in Figure 11-27, the Five9 account group is allocated to 20% of the plan usage.

Note When an organization exceeds or comes close to 100% of plan usage, the ThousandEyes platform will notify all organizational users via email of the usage.

Review Questions

Answer the following questions. Check your answers against those provided in Appendix A, "Answers to Review Questions."

1. Is it possible to create a user that can make agent changes but not tests?

2. Can you segment two business units and allocate a certain number of test units per business unit?

3. How can you determine how many units ten tests would consume?

Chapter 12

Automation—Use Cases and Case Studies

When looking at automation, obviously we can go in many different directions, from agent deployment and test creation to general maintenance. The most common ThousandEyes automation question is, can we tie ThousandEyes into Kubernetes and automate the testing? The second most common question is, can ThousandEyes be added to a CI/CD pipeline or a DevOps pipeline? Let's look at some ideas on how we can achieve a few automation use cases. We are going to look at other ways to utilize the API to streamline the ThousandEyes and the process.

Use Case 1: Automated Testing Basics

Many ThousandEyes customers seek the help of the ThousandEyes Professional Services team to help them set up automated testing. This section presents and describes a few example scripts that the Professional Services team has created to help customers automate ThousandEyes tasks.

The script presented in Example 12-1 does a few things. First, it can read from a CSV file to determine the Test Type, Interval, and Agent ID. The idea is to allow the ThousandEyes administrator to use a CSV file where other ThousandEyes users can add what they need tested and enter the variables needed, and the Python script can run it.

Example 12-1 *Python Read from CSV File*

```
import csv

def create_tests(api_token, csv_file):
    with open(csv_file, 'r') as file:
        reader = csv.DictReader(file)
        for row in reader:
            # Access data from the CSV file
            test_type = row['test_type']
```

```
        agent_id = row['agent_id']
        interval = row['interval']
        test_name = row['test_name']
        target = row['target']

        # Use the data to make API calls to create tests in ThousandEyes
        # (Replace the following line with your actual API calls)
        print(f"Creating test: {test_name} ({test_type}) with target {target} on
agent {agent_id} with interval {interval}")

# Example usage
create_tests('your-api-token', 'path/to/your/file.csv')
```

Webhooks on GitHub

GitHub enables you to set up webhooks to notify external services when certain events occur. You can configure a webhook to trigger your ThousandEyes tests whenever there's a new commit or a pull request.

Step 1. Go to GitHub.com and access your GitHub repository.

Step 2. Navigate to **Settings > Webhooks** and click **Add Webhook**.

Step 3. In the Payload URL field, enter the endpoint where your ThousandEyes test trigger script is hosted.

Step 4. Click the **Let Me Select Individual Events** radio button and choose **Push** or other relevant events.

Step 5. Click **Add Webhook** and save the webhook.

Step 6. Write a script that triggers your ThousandEyes tests. This script can be hosted on a server or a cloud service, and the URL of this script will be used as the Payload URL in the GitHub webhook settings.

Example 12-2 shows a simplified example script using Python and Flask.

Example 12-2 *Python GitHub Example*

```
from flask import Flask, request
import subprocess

app = Flask(__name__)

@app.route('/run_thousandeyes_tests', methods=['POST'])
def run_thousandeyes_tests():
```

```
    try:
        # Run your ThousandEyes tests using the appropriate command or script
        subprocess.run(['python', 'run_thousandeyes_tests.py'])
        return "Tests triggered successfully", 200
    except Exception as e:
        return str(e), 500

if __name__ == '__main__':
    app.run(debug=True, port=5000)
```

This script creates a simple Flask web server. When GitHub sends a POST request to the run_thousandeyes_tests endpoint, it triggers your ThousandEyes tests. Make sure your Flask app is accessible from the Internet. You might need to deploy it on a server or use a service like Ngrok for testing. This way, whenever there's a check-in on GitHub, GitHub will send a webhook event to your Flask app, triggering the ThousandEyes tests.

Remember to secure sensitive information like API tokens and secrets and consider implementing proper error handling and logging in your automation scripts.

Use Case 2: Jenkins

Jenkins is an open source automation server to enable continuous integration and continuous delivery (CI/CD), automating each stage of software development such as test, build, and deployment. Using plug-ins is the best way to integrate the ThousandEyes APIs. For this example, we will look at the Jenkins DSL plug-in.

Jenkins Domain-Specific Language (DSL) is a scripting language that allows you to define Jenkins jobs and configurations as code. Instead of configuring Jenkins jobs through the graphical user interface, you can use DSL scripts to define job configurations in a text-based format.

First, install the Jenkins Job DSL plug-in:

Step 1.   In your Jenkins instance, go to **Manage Jenkins > Manage Plugins.**

Step 2.   Click the **Available** tab and search for **Job DSL.**

Step 3.   Install the Job DSL plug-in.

Next, create a seed job. A seed job is a normal Jenkins job that runs the Job DSL script.

Step 1.   Create a new Jenkins job and select **Freestyle Project.**

Step 2.   In the job configuration, under the Build section, add a build step of type Process Job DSLs.

Step 3.   In the **DSL Scripts** section, you can either enter your DSL script directly or provide a link to a script in your version control system.

Step 4.   Save and run the job.

Example 12-3 provides a simple DSL script that creates a ThousandEyes HTTP Server test.

Example 12-3 *Jenkins DSL Script*

```
// Jenkins DSL script for creating ThousandEyes HTTP Server test

job('Create-ThousandEyes-Test') {
    description('Automated job to create ThousandEyes HTTP Server test')

    steps {
        script {
            // Define variables
            def TE_API_URL = 'https://api.thousandeyes.com/v7'
            def TE_API_TOKEN = 'your_api_token'

            // ThousandEyes API request to create HTTP Server test
            def createTestRequest = '''
                {
                    "test": {
                        "testType": "http-server",
                        "interval": 300,
                        "target": "https://example.com",
                        "agents": [
                            {"agentId": 1},
                            {"agentId": 2}
                        ],
                        "alerts": [
                            {
                                "type": "http-server",
                                "threshold": 5000
                            }
                        ]
                    }
                }
            '''

            // Execute ThousandEyes API request to create the test
            def response = httpRequest(
                acceptType: 'APPLICATION_JSON',
                contentType: 'APPLICATION_JSON',
                httpMode: 'POST',
                requestBody: createTestRequest,
                url: "${TE_API_URL}/tests.json",
                headers: [
                    Authorization: "Bearer ${TE_API_TOKEN}"
```

```
            ]
        )

        // Print the API response
        echo "ThousandEyes API Response: ${response}"
    }
  }
}
```

The following are several benefits of using Jenkins DSL:

■ **Version control:** DSL scripts can be version-controlled using tools like Git, enabling better collaboration and change tracking.

■ **Reusability:** You can reuse DSL scripts for different jobs, making it easy to manage configurations consistently.

■ **Automation:** Changes to your ThousandEyes configurations trigger automatic updates in Jenkins, ensuring synchronization between your testing and deployment processes.

Among the many other plug-ins that Jenkins offers is URLTrigger, python, and HTTPRequests.

The URLTrigger plug-in makes it possible to check the last modification date response and the response content of a URL invocation. For the response content, you can check the following:

■ A simple response content (the content nature is not interpreted; an MD5 is used)

■ A TXT response content (the returned values from the evaluation of regular expressions are checked)

■ An XML response content (the returned values from the evaluation of XPath expressions are checked)

■ A JSON response content (the returned values from the evaluation of JSONPath expressions are checked)

Jenkins plug-ins also exist for Ansible, Docker, Puppet, Chef, and Terraform to tie these tools into Jenkins.

Use Case 3: Ansible Playbook

Using Ansible (or Terraform) is a great way to create a structured repository for cataloging scripts. One of the best features of Ansible is its capability to create reusable playbooks. Within a playbook, you can define multiple plays and execute them individually. This flexibility enables you to deploy agents, create tests, and add them to a dashboard efficiently.

Example 12-4 shows an example of a YAML file to create a ThousandEyes test that can be incorporated into other plays. Using Ansible Tower can also help with the automation process as well.

Example 12-4   *Ansible Example Test Creation*

```yaml
---
- name: Create Test in ThousandEyes
  hosts: localhost
  gather_facts: false
  vars:
    te_api_url: "https://api.thousandeyes.com/v6/tests"
    te_api_token: "YOUR_API_TOKEN"
  tasks:
    - name: Create Test
      uri:
        url: "{{ te_api_url }}"
        method: POST
        headers:
          Content-Type: "application/json"
          Authorization: "Bearer {{ te_api_token }}"
        body: |
          {
            "testName": "YourTestName",
            "type": "http",
            "agentGroupId": YOUR_AGENT_GROUP_ID,
            "url": "https://example.com",
            "httpServerTest": {
              "httpServer": "example.com",
              "verifyCertificate": true
            }
          }
        body_format: json
        status_code: 200
      register: response

    - name: Display API Response
      debug:
        var: response.json
```

Use Case 4: Kubernetes

The Cisco DevNet team created the ThousandEyes Kubernetes Operator to manage ThousandEyes tests deployed via a Kubernetes cluster. Using Kubernetes Operator, you can automate the tests as a resource within Kubernetes. For more information about this type of automation, visit https://github.com/CiscoDevNet/thousandeyes-kubernetes-operator.

Scaling ThousandEyes via Automation

We were collaborating with a major entertainment provider on a proof of concept (PoC) to assess how ThousandEyes could measure customer and user experience. Our task involved deploying approximately 200 tests across 53 locations, with the primary goal being to validate the PoC and the key performance indicators (KPIs) the customer's leadership was concerned with.

Given the complexity of the entertainment provider's network, we took a modular approach to design its infrastructure to help automate certain processes. By developing and templating reusable components, the ThousandEyes team enabled the customer to automate and manage the deployment in an agile fashion. The automation process broke each component down, to agents enabled/deployed, creation of tests, dashboards, reports, alerts, and alarm rules.

To simplify the deployment within the customer's network infrastructure, we used a tool that would automate configuration management and provisioning. We found the solution with YAML files, which we used to deploy agents in their corporate environment on a semiautomated or fully automated basis.

We also used the ThousandEyes API to ensure that deployed agents remain configured, secure, and compliant.

We worked with the customer's application team to determine how they could add new tests as new applications go online in the future and how, if changes occur, they can measure the waterfall as a comparison of before and after the changes.

Once we found how we would insert ourselves in the pipeline, we were able to push the tests out to the various agents and knowing we also had automated the function to keep the agents up to date, we left the customer the tools to have this process running automatically.

Operationalizing

Customers often ask how best to operationalize ThousandEyes tests. This is where dashboards can be leveraged to combine metrics, tests, agents or almost any other combination of data available in the ThousandEyes platform.

Dashboards for Comparisons

As a deliverable in a proof of concept, customers occasionally ask if ThousandEyes can help them visually compare things like Internet performance versus enterprise network performance or in-office user experience versus outside-of-office user experience.

One of the best questions was whether the ThousandEyes platform can be used to determine which zones in a building are being problematic. Having a dashboard prepre-pared aids in being able to rapidly distinguish between an event inside your network and an event on the Internet.

Inside Your Network vs. Outside Your Network (the Internet)

A customer was operating from two buildings in London. We deployed an Enterprise Agent to each building. Additionally, we selected three Cloud Agents that were in the same geography as the offices. We created tests from all five agents to test the SaaS appli-cations identified as being critical to the users. Then we built a ThousandEyes dashboard to provide a side-by-side comparison of the metrics reported by the Enterprise Agents (corporate network) and Cloud Agents (Internet). Figures 12-1 and 12-2 compare metrics for inside and outside the enterprise network. This type of dashboard can make problems such as DNS issues very apparent without the need to dive into individual tests. In the example shown in Figure 12-1, most of the errors were due to the HTTP Server test tim-ing out (receive errors), which is most likely caused by the application not responding. In this example, these errors were generally impacting tests running from both inside and outside the corporate network.

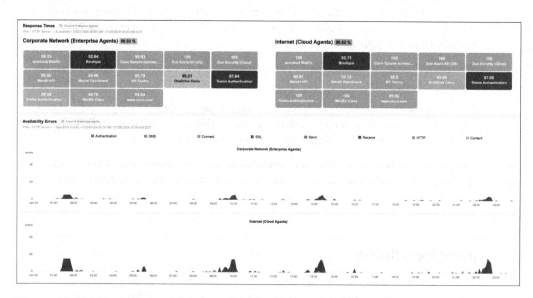

Figure 12-1   *Comparison: Corporate Network Versus Internet*

By leveraging ThousandEyes agent labels (as shown in Figure 12-2), the agents were grouped into either Corporate Network (Enterprise Agents) or Internet (Cloud Agents). Then the tests were grouped by agent labels. Then, a filter was implemented to ensure only the desired agent labels were displayed in each widget.

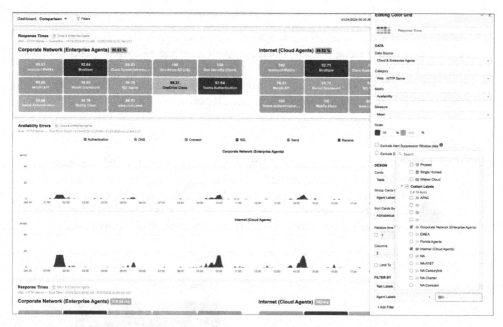

Figure 12-2 *Dashboard Labels and Filters*

Figure 12-3 is another example of how metrics can be displayed for comparison purposes. In this example, Response Time, Packet Loss, and Latency metrics are all shown on a timeline comparing inside the corporate network (Enterprise Agents) to outside the corporate network (Cloud Agents).

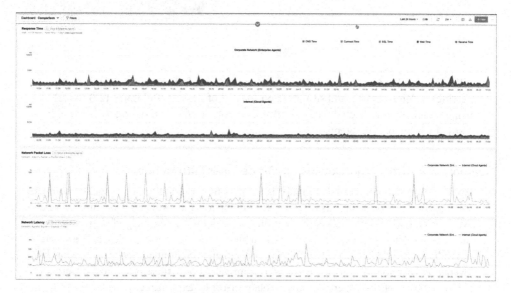

Figure 12-3 *Comparison: Response Time, Packet Loss, and Latency*

Results

The results of these dashboards allowed the customer to quickly determine that issues its users were experiencing with the Boutique application and Microsoft Teams were not unique to their corporate network. Instead of having to waste time troubleshooting issues outside their network, they were able to provide their management with immediate visual proof that the issues were not on the corporate network.

Comparing ISPs

Figure 12-4 shows an example of comparing the performance of four ISPs in North America. Customers often do this to test the availability and performance of data to their VPN gateway for their remote employees. This way, if systematic issues transpire on a particular ISP, it becomes rapidly apparent. One option is to label ISPs based on the region they are in, such as East/West, in addition to the individual ISP breakout.

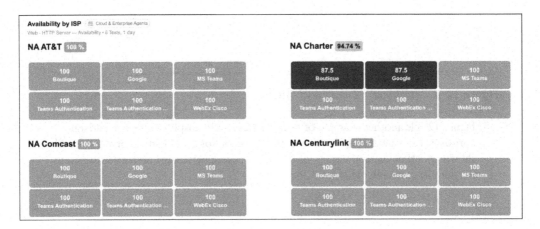

Figure 12-4 *Comparison: North American ISPs*

ISP labels can be easily created by navigating to **Cloud & Enterprise Agents > Agent Settings > Agent Labels** and searching on the ISP of interest. In Figure 12-5, AT&T is being searched and selected with the IPv4 Compatible filter (on the right) set to only show IPv4-compatible agents.

Comparing In-Office and Outside-of-Office User Experience

Another common comparison to make is to show how users (Endpoint Agents) compare working from inside a campus or office environment versus working from anywhere else. We've used dashboards such as the one shown in Figure 12-6 to help IT departments quantify in-office user experience versus outside-of-office user experience. We've successfully identified issues such as DNS (in-office) and SSL (outside-of-office) issues by leveraging dashboards that first show who is impacted or if there is any real difference between the in-office experience and outside-of-office experience.

Figure 12-5 *Cloud and Enterprise Agents—Agent Labels*

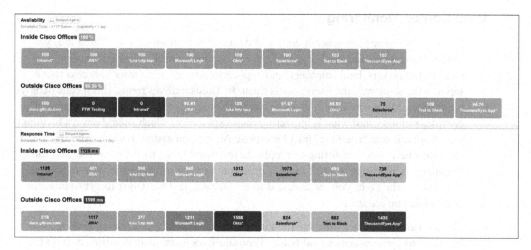

Figure 12-6 *Comparison: Users in Office Versus Users Outside Office*

Comparing Inside a Building by Floors and Zones

Labels can be created using networks, gateways, SSIDs, or even BSSIDs to define where in a building users are connecting. Which you choose will depend largely on your network architecture. When this feature is leveraged in terms of physical architecture, issues such as equipment failures impacting portions of a building can be quickly isolated. For example, if a switch or cabling issue is occurring in Building A, Fifth Floor, South closet (upper-right section of Figure 12-7), the dashboard tile for that area would rapidly go red. Packet loss, latency, and jitter are additional key metrics worth showing for this type of comparative data. Ideally, this dashboard would be built for each floor of the office building. Separate dashboards (copied from the original and updated with other labels) can then be created for each building. Figure 12-7 shows the fourth and fifth floors of a building with agents labeled based on where on each floor they are connected.

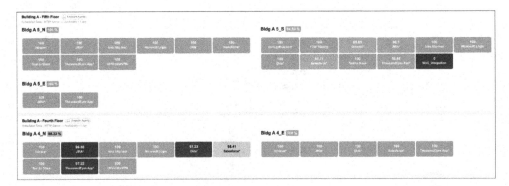

Figure 12-7   *Comparisons: Building Floors and Closets*

Data Center Monitoring

There are two strategies when it comes to data center monitoring with ThousandEyes. Both are important and neither provides a full picture by itself. The first strategy is to monitor the servers, load balancers, and applications by creating tests to access those services the same way the users access them. In ThousandEyes terms, this means deploying agents local to where your users are when they access the data center resources. This provides visibility into what is impacting their experience, which should always be your top priority. If that "engineer" (aka Enterprise Agent) you assign to work from the remote location where users are sitting can replicate the users' issue, the value of the data the "engineer" is analyzing is much more significant than any top-*n* metrics that may or may not relate to the event you are assigned to analyze and resolve. Don't forget to monitor DNS while you are at it.

The second strategy is to analyze the infrastructure. This includes testing from remote locations to the data center (and back). ThousandEyes is uniquely positioned to do this using Network Agent to Agent bidirectional tests. Routing can be, and often is, asymmetric. Therefore, testing in both directions is important to understand the path your traffic is taking. Additionally, activating Enterprise Agents inside the data center provides insight into how applications are performing locally. These same Enterprise Agents can then be leveraged to show how APIs are delivering content to the applications hosted in that data center.

VXLAN Versus Traditional Layer 2/Layer 3

Data centers are a critical focus area when considering ThousandEyes. The reason lies in understanding the true data and control planes, especially in contrasting technologies like VXLAN versus traditional Layer 2 and Layer 3 architectures. While simplicity characterizes Layer 2 or Layer 3 setups, the move away from Layer 2 is largely due to concerns such as spanning tree. The evolution toward VXLAN aims to scale past these limitations. However, it's essential to grasp the differences between these architectures.

First, let's examine the data plane. Is it managed by IP? This consideration dictates the placement of ThousandEyes agents within the data center. Because ThousandEyes can collect data only down to a Layer 3 perspective, it's crucial to ensure compatibility with the data plane's configuration.

Beyond traditional architectures, there are newer approaches, such as Cisco Application Centric Infrastructure (ACI), which utilize technologies such as Intermediate System-to-Intermediate System (IS-IS). In such cases, while the control plane might be VXLAN, the data plane may not be IP based. This highlights the importance of understanding both the control and data planes to ensure compatibility with ThousandEyes.

Active-active data center scenarios, where synchronized databases or messaging systems are critical, can benefit from ThousandEyes agents deployed on Cisco Nexus devices running NX-OS mode. These agents can monitor the network from one edge of the data center to another, complementing analytics provided by platforms like Nexus Dashboard. Additionally, ThousandEyes can bridge gaps in multisite architectures, as seen in SD-WAN deployments, by providing insights into each hop beyond the edge.

Similarly, deploying ThousandEyes agents within VMware infrastructure is feasible, provided compatibility with the underlying infrastructure is ensured. For instance, in Cisco ACI environments, monitoring latency to another data center reveals insights up to the border leaf, but not the spine and leaf architecture in the underlay due to its non-IP nature. Thus, understanding the nuances of data and control planes is crucial for effective monitoring.

Agent Placement

When considering agent activation in the data center, several factors come into play. In legacy three-tier architectures, comprising access, aggregation, and core layers, agents can be strategically used in either the aggregation or core layers. However, scalability concerns may arise when considering activating agents on every access switch. In such cases, careful consideration is required to balance scalability with data-gathering requirements. Agents can be clustered to extend scalability in terms of the number and frequency of tests being run.

Automation plays a crucial role in agent deployment, especially in scenarios where quick deployment is necessary to address user experience issues. By automating agent deployment, administrators can swiftly address monitoring needs and ensure adherence to SLAs. Additionally, many Cisco routers and switches are now shipped with agents already installed on them as Docker containers. In these situations, all that remains is to activate them and add them to ThousandEyes tests.

Moving toward next-generation data centers, it's essential to understand the data plane's nature. If uncertain, starting with edge deployments and gradually moving closer to the data center allows for incremental data gathering and better insights into network metrics.

Additional Note for Cisco Nexus Devices

If the data center is using Cisco Nexus devices, it's worth noting that these devices also support the application framework and can be installed just like a Cisco Catalyst switch. However, at the time of writing, ThousandEyes is supported only on Cisco NX-OS images.

Review Questions

Answer the following questions. Check your answers against those provided in Appendix A, "Answers to Review Questions."

1. Is it possible to create a process to install an agent and then test?

2. What is the benefit to using a GitHub webhook?

3. Can Endpoint Agent Labels be created to only show agents connected to specific BSSIDs?

4. Which is the preferred method of monitoring a data center using ThousandEyes?

   ■ Test to the applications hosted in the data center

   ■ Monitor the infrastructure connecting remote locations to the data center

   ■ Both

Chapter 13

Business Strategy for Engineers

Business strategy discussions often focus on operational expenses, capital expenses, or net present value. But what does this mean for an engineer? Conversely, how do technical capabilities translate into business value? This is where a gap often exists—understanding business outcomes and aligning them with technical features and functionalities.

This chapter explores business strategy from a different perspective, illustrating this with a story involving a customer engagement. In this story, ThousandEyes data was used to bridge the understanding of business objectives, leading to a successful alignment of technical and business goals.

Bridge the Divide: Aligning Technical Expertise with Business Strategy

During customer demonstrations, the focus is often on external applications or websites used by the customer's users. Cloud Agents are set up to monitor these applications or web pages, aiming to detect anomalies or issues across the Internet or local to the web server. In one particular demo, a DNS issue was identified in a specific area of the United States, associated with a particular carrier. As this was being explained, an executive vice president inquired, "What does this mean to me?"

Initially, the ThousandEyes team realized the need to frame the results from a business perspective. The response was re-articulated to address the executive's concerns: "How many locations are there in this region? How many stores or remote locations are reporting connectivity issues with this application?" Consider the frequency with which staff members investigate these issues and reflect on the potential business losses due to poor user experience.

The outage lasted for approximately 2 hours, confirming a DNS issue during that period. By asking pertinent questions, the conversation shifted to the business impact: "How much money did the business lose during this outage?" Although most vice presidents do not share specific figures, they typically know the cost of downtime per minute. Another critical question was, "How much time does your staff spend investigating these issues?"

The goal is to quantify the issue accurately: Is the problem real? Is it within the network, the application, the user, or another third-party dependency? By identifying these factors, the question arises: Does this approach accelerate the resolution process compared to previous methods?

As engineers, there is a tendency to focus exclusively on the technology itself. However, it's equally important to step back and assess the business value of this technology. While the value of ThousandEyes is evident to us, understanding its benefits from a C-level executive's perspective is crucial. Essentially, ThousandEyes helps in pinpointing the root cause of issues, which is a significant value proposition.

Most network and software engineers tend to look only within their domain. But it's important to consider what executive leadership needs to know during an outage: How did it happen? When did it happen? How long did it last? And how can future occurrences be prevented?

As engineers focus on their specific domains, how often do we hear statements like, "It's not a network problem," or "I don't see any issues with the application"? In the DNS use case, the issue was related to a service provider. With a focus solely on their own on-premises network, the network team might conclude, "It's not the network," but how long would it take to identify the DNS issue?

Application monitoring tools only track the application. If there's a DNS problem, these tools might not detect it because, as far as they are concerned, the application is functioning correctly. This highlights a significant gap: one set of tools can identify and narrow down the issue across different domains.

In outage situations, how often do we join Zoom or Webex meetings with numerous participants, each looking at their own tools and separate data, without a unified view? The value of using a comprehensive tool like ThousandEyes is that it enables us to pinpoint issues quickly and provides a common ground for all stakeholders, facilitating faster and more effective resolution.

Returning to the business perspective, imagine being in an outage situation and having a bunch of people on a conference call. The call begins with the report that the ThousandEyes team has identified the issue before customers even called, determining that it is outside the organization's own network, and that a trouble ticket has been set up to expedite resolution. From a leadership perspective, this provides clear information on the issue's location, reassures that the network staff is not scrambling to fix the problem internally, and identifies which vendor or provider to work with to set expectations and mitigate future issues.

When articulating the value of ThousandEyes in a business context, it's crucial to emphasize the tangible benefits it can bring to your company's operations, performance, and overall bottom line. Here's a structured approach to help you convey the value proposition effectively:

- **Identify pain points and challenges:**
  - Highlight existing challenges your company faces in terms of network visibility, performance monitoring, and troubleshooting.
  - Discuss any recent incidents or outages that have impacted business operations or customer experience.

- **Explain how ThousandEyes addresses these challenges:**
  - Describe how ThousandEyes provides comprehensive network visibility across both internal and external networks, including cloud and Internet service providers.
  - Emphasize its ability to monitor network performance in real time, detect issues proactively, and provide actionable insights for troubleshooting and optimization.

- **Quantify the benefits:**
  - Quantify the potential impact of improved network visibility and performance on key business metrics such as uptime, mean time to resolution (MTTR), and customer satisfaction.
  - Estimate cost savings from reduced downtime, improved productivity, and more efficient use of IT resources.

- **Highlight key features and capabilities:**
  - Highlight specific features of ThousandEyes such as network path visualization, application performance monitoring, and cloud agent deployment.
  - Illustrate how these features enable your team to quickly identify and resolve issues, optimize network performance, and ensure a seamless user experience.

- **Demonstrate ROI:**
  - Present a compelling ROI analysis that compares the cost of implementing ThousandEyes against the potential benefits and cost savings it can deliver over time.
  - Include both quantitative metrics (e.g., cost savings, productivity gains) and qualitative factors (e.g., improved customer satisfaction, reduced risk of reputation damage).

- **Address security and compliance considerations:**
  - Discuss how ThousandEyes helps enhance security posture by detecting and mitigating threats such as DDoS attacks, data breaches, and unauthorized access.
  - Highlight any compliance requirements (e.g., GDPR, HIPAA) that ThousandEyes helps address through its monitoring and reporting capabilities.

- **Provide customer success stories and case studies:**
  - Share examples of how other companies in similar industries have successfully implemented ThousandEyes and realized significant benefits.
  - Highlight specific use cases and outcomes relevant to your company's objectives and challenges.
- **Outline implementation and support:**
  - Provide details on the implementation process, including deployment options, integration with existing systems, and training for your IT team.
  - Discuss ongoing support and maintenance services offered by ThousandEyes to ensure continued success and maximum ROI.

Some of the benefits your business can measure include:

- Revenue assurance from faster resolution of disruptive incidents and outages impacting operations.
- Reduce customer churn and increase satisfaction through improved digital experiences.
- Engage employees and make them more effective with better application experiences.
- Hold service providers accountable to their SLAs to eliminate disruptions to your operations.

Another way to support your value proposition is to reference reports about the benefits of using ThousandEyes, such as the white paper "The Total Economic Impact Of Cisco ThousandEyes End User Monitoring." In 2022, ThousandEyes hired Forrester Consulting to survey current ThousandEyes customers to determine the potential ROI of using ThousandEyes End User Monitoring. Forrester Consulting interviewed five ThousandEyes customers who were monitoring enterprise networks and then combined the results to form a single, composite organization. The study found many benefits over a three-year period, including the example shown in Figure 13-1.

Figure 13-1 highlights several key findings from the report:

- **Reduced downtime:** The composite organization experienced a significant reduction in network downtime, resulting in improved business continuity and productivity.
- **Cost savings:** There were substantial cost savings due to more efficient trouble-shooting and faster resolution of network issues.
- **Improved user experience:** End-user satisfaction improved as network issues were identified and resolved more quickly, leading to fewer disruptions.
- **Increased operational efficiency:** The network teams were able to operate more efficiently with better visibility into network performance and issues, reducing the time spent on diagnostics and repairs.

Figure 13-1 *Forrester Consulting Statistics*

You can read the full report by filling out a simple form and clicking **Read the Study** at the following page:

https://www.thousandeyes.com/resources/total-economic-impact-cisco-thousandeyes-end-user-monitoring

By following the structured approach presented in this section, you can effectively articulate the value of ThousandEyes in a business context and secure buy-in from key stakeholders within your company.

Answers to Review Questions

Chapter 1

1. Where is the most likely fault domain when a device is showing inbound discards on an interface?

   Answer: The most likely fault domain is the device reporting the discards.

2. Of the five sources of network latency, which is most likely the largest contributor to latency over a WAN?

   Answer: Distance delay is likely the largest contributor to latency over a WAN.

3. What should the expected result be of placing an application in a higher priority queue (DSCP)?

   Answer: More consistent performance metrics (less variation) should be expected.

Chapter 2

1. What are the three main types of agents in ThousandEyes, and what are their primary use cases?

   Answer: In ThousandEyes, the three main types of agents are the following:

   - **Enterprise Agents:** These agents are deployed within your organization's network infrastructure, typically behind your firewall. They provide visibility into internal network performance, helping you monitor and troubleshoot issues affecting user experience and application performance within your network.

   - **Cloud Agents:** These agents are deployed in various locations around the world, typically within major cloud service providers' data centers or Internet exchange points. Cloud Agents offer insights into Internet and cloud service provider performance, allowing you to monitor the performance of your applications and services as accessed by users from different geographical locations.

- **Endpoint Agents:** These agents are installed on end-user devices, such as laptops, desktops, or mobile devices. Endpoint Agents provide visibility into the end-user experience, allowing you to monitor network performance and application behavior from the perspective of individual users. This can be particularly useful for trouble-shooting issues specific to certain devices or locations.

2. How do you install an Enterprise Agent on a Cisco device using the Cisco Application Framework?

Answer:

- Download the tar file by using the command **app-hosting install**.

- Ensure AppGigabitEthernet is configured and tied to the app-vnic using the command **app-vnic AppGigabitEthernet**.

- Ensure Token is added as a run option and Name server added, once done.

- Use the **show app-hosting list** or **show app-hosting detail** command to ensure the container is up and running.

3. What are some prerequisites for installing an Enterprise Agent?

Answer: Ensure that the firewall rules are configured properly, because all Enterprise Agent flavors depend on communication to AWS and other dependencies. You can also ensure that proper code on devices is up to date for IOS-XE devices 17.6.1 and Nexus 10.3.3.

4. What are the key differences between Cloud Agents and Enterprise Agents?

Answer: Cloud Agents are owned by Cisco and managed by Cisco ThousandEyes. Enterprise Agents live on premises and are managed by the owner. Cloud Agents live in ISPs and cloud service providers.

5. When might you choose to use an Endpoint Agent instead of an Enterprise Agent?

Answer:

- You need to monitor network performance and application behavior from the perspective of individual end users' devices, such as laptops, desktops, or mobile devices.

- You want to troubleshoot issues specific to certain devices or locations, such as connectivity problems or application performance issues experienced by remote workers.

- You require insights into the end-user experience to optimize application performance and ensure a seamless user experience.

- You need to monitor network performance and application behavior outside of your organization's network, such as when users are accessing cloud-based applications or services from remote locations or home offices.

- You want to complement your network-wide monitoring with device-level visibility to identify and resolve issues affecting individual users or devices.

Chapter 3

1. What would be the purpose of running a synthetic test versus monitoring?

   Answer: Synthetic tests provide proactive monitoring by simulating user interactions, while monitoring captures real user data reactively.

2. What is the difference between an HTTP test versus a Page Load test?

   Answer: HTTP does not provide a waterfall view to see each element load.

3. What is the purpose of running a DNS Server test?

   Answer: You can monitor the availability and performance of DNS servers along with the records they contain.

Chapter 4

1. Can you create a custom alert that focuses on a specific metric?

   Answer: Yes, you can create custom alerts focusing on specific metrics.

2. Can alerts be integrated into other platforms?

   Answer: Yes, alerts can be integrated into other platforms using the ThousandEyes API or webhooks.

3. Can you change a rule to notify only if all agents met a certain condition?

   Answer: Yes, under the conditions of the Alert Rules, there is a setting to notify whether all agents meet a certain threshold.

Chapter 5

1. Can you create a widget that shows only alerts from Internet Insights?

   Answer: Yes, you can create a widget to display alerts specifically from Internet Insights.

2. Is there a way to extract the dashboard data to a web page?

   Answer: Yes, embed a widget and use an iframe.

3. When creating a widget, can you add more than one metric? If not, how can this be done?

Answer: Yes, you can use a Multi-Metric Table.

4. What would be the best widget to use when looking at end users' wireless signal strength?

Answer: Multi-Metric Table, Color Grid Table, or Number Table

Chapter 6

1. If an outage occurred at your company while you were on vacation, can you go back and view the data to see what transpired?

Answer:

- Yes, you can view data for up to the past 30 days for Cloud, Enterprise, and Endpoint Advantage (14 days for Endpoint Essentials).

- When an event needs to be saved for more than 30 days, a snapshot can be created. This will be available for 1 year (default retention value).

2. Can you see your network handoff to the ISP? Can you see the BGP routes?

Answer: Yes, the handoff can be seen by using Path Visualization. Yes, BGP Routing shows how BGP routes are distributed through the Internet.

3. Can you see latency or loss between two nodes that are not in your network?

Answer: Yes, as long as they appear in Path Visualization, ThousandEyes calculates forwarding loss and latency per hop, even across the Internet.

4. What is the difference between the MSS and the MTU?

Answer: MSS (Maximum Segment Size) refers to the amount of payload in a single TCP segment. MTU (Maximum Transmission Unit) refers to the size of the Layer 3 packet, including the IP and TCP headers.

Chapter 7

1. What is the use case for a Transaction test?

Answer: A Transaction test can be used to mimic the user interaction with a web page and measure metrics as the user clicks through a website.

2. How do you use a Transaction test to mimic a UX with a phone?

Answer: In the Advanced Settings tab of the Transaction test, set the Device Emulation option to **Phone**.

3. What are markers?

Answer: Markers are timestamps added to Transaction test results to correlate them with other data.

4. What other tests are associated with a Transaction test?

Answer: Tests associated with a Transaction test include HTTP Server (Web) and Agent to Server (Network). Additionally, BGP (Routing) monitoring of the public IP prefixes associated with the test target is available.

Chapter 8

1. What is the common theme with integrations?

Answer: Enhanced visibility and operational intelligence.

2. Are there any platforms that have bidirectional integration?

Answer: Yes, Cisco AppDynamics has bidirectional integration with ThousandEyes.

3. Can ThousandEyes monitor the underlay of Cisco SDWAN?

If so, how?

If not, why not?

Answer: Yes, ThousandEyes can monitor the underlay of Cisco SDWAN. Applying an agent to the transport VPN will allow the agent to see each hop. If the agent is applied to the service VPN, you may only see the overlay. NAT may be needed to view the underlay or other steering mechanisms in Cisco SDWAN to allow the agent traffic to gather data on the underlay.

4. What data does Webex ingest from ThousandEyes?

Answer: Webex correlates the data to see if its underlying infrastructure may hinder the UX of Webex, including Layer 3 and Layer 4 from the OSI model.

Chapter 9

1. Probing Modes apply to which type of network test, end-to-end or hop-by-hop?

Answer: Probing Modes apply to end-to-end network tests.

2. Path Trace Modes apply to which type of network test, end-to-end or hop-by-hop?

Answer: Path Trace Modes apply to hop-by-hop (Path Visualization) network tests.

3. When monitoring collaboration calls, Dynamic Tests are associated with which type of agent?

Answer: Dynamic Tests are associated with Endpoint Agents when monitoring collaboration calls.

Chapter 10

1. Can ThousandEyes Device Monitoring use SNMPv2 or v3?

   Answer: Yes, both

2. Do you need CDP/LLDP turned on?

   Answer: Yes, CDP/LLDP needs to be turned on to create a topology map in **Devices > Device Settings.**

3. How can you find throughput for an individual port?

   Answer: Navigate to the **Devices > Views** page and click the **Interface Table** tab.

Chapter 11

1. Is it possible to create a user that can make agent changes but not tests?

   Answer: Yes, by using RBAC, you can control what the user can do in the platform.

2. Can you segment two business units and allocate a certain number of test units per business unit?

   Answer: Yes, you can create account groups for the BUs and then set up a quota.

3. How can you determine how many units ten tests would consume?

   Answer: Navigate to the **Account Settings > Usage and Billing > Usage** tab, click **Calculate the Units You Need for This Account Group** to open the Unit Calculator, and click **Add Row**. Then, add the data needed to create a test and the calculator will supply the unit count for that test. The criteria will be Test Type, Interval, Agent Type, and how many agents to run the test.

Chapter 12

1. Is it possible to create a process to install an agent and then test?

   Answer: Yes, it's definitely possible to create a process to automate the installation of a ThousandEyes agent and run tests. This process typically involves scripting like Python or using a configuration management tool like Ansible to install. Once the agent is installed, you can use the ThousandEyes API to configure and trigger a test.

2. What is the benefit to using a GitHub webhook?

   Answer: GitHub webhooks are HTTP callbacks triggered by events that occur in a GitHub repo. They provide a way for external services to be notified when certain actions occur, such as pushing code changes or creating pull requests. Webhooks enable you to automate tasks or workflows in response to GitHub events. For example, you can trigger builds in a CI/CD system like Jenkins whenever code changes are pushed to a repo.

3. Can Endpoint Agent Labels be created to only show agents connected to specific BSSIDs?

Answer: Yes

4. Which is the preferred method of monitoring a data center using ThousandEyes?

Answer: You can both test to the applications hosted in the data center in order to see user experience and monitor the infrastructure connecting remote locations to the data center to keep a close eye on the network.

Troubleshooting

In this book, we have covered a substantial amount of Day 0 (initial setup or turn-up) procedures. However, there are times when things don't go as planned and troubleshooting becomes necessary. In this appendix, we explore some of the major topics and techniques used to troubleshoot issues in ThousandEyes.

Collect Logs

When gathering log data from a ThousandEyes agent, you can find the logs in the following directory. This applies to all types of agents except for the Virtual Appliance (a VM containing a prebuilt Enterprise Agent), for which logs can be found in the **Status** page.

```
/var/log/agent/te-agent.log
```

From the ThousandEyes Virtual Appliance proceed to the Status section upon login.

ICMP

Understanding the Internet Control Message Protocol (ICMP) types is crucial to understanding Path Visualization and even firewall rules for agents.

ICMP is a network protocol used to send error messages and operational information indicating issues in the communication between devices on an IP network. ICMP messages are typically encapsulated within IP packets.

One of the key features of ICMP is its ability to report errors and provide feedback about network conditions. ICMP achieves this through various message types, each serving a specific purpose:

- **Echo Request (Type 8) and Echo Reply (Type 0):**
  - **Echo Request:** This message is used by a sender (the ThousandEyes Agent) to request an Echo Reply from a receiver.

- **Echo Reply:** This message is sent by the receiver in response to an Echo Request, indicating that the packet has been received successfully.

- **Destination Unreachable (Type 3):** This type of message is sent by a router or a host to inform the sender that the destination network or host is unreachable.

- **Time Exceeded (Type 11):** This message is sent by a router when the Time-to-Live (TTL) value of a packet reaches zero, indicating that the packet has expired.

- **Redirect Message (Type 5):** This message is sent by a router to inform the sender that there is a better route for the destination network.

- **Parameter Problem (Type 12):** This message is sent by a router or a host to inform the sender about an error in the IP header of the packet.

- **Source Quench (Type 4):** This message is sent by a router to inform the sender to reduce the rate of packet transmission to avoid congestion.

- **Timestamp Request (Type 13) and Timestamp Reply (Type 14):** These messages are used to measure the round-trip time between two hosts.

Troubleshooting Path Visualization

Path visualization isn't always intuitive, so this section provides some pointers to help you define and troubleshoot issues if they arise.

Reasons for Loss Result Variation

The following conditions are the most common reasons for not being able to pinpoint an event further in the Path Visualization when Network Overview reports end-to-end packet loss:

- **Timing difference:** Although both network end-to-end measurement and path discovery processes occur within a specified interval, they may not start at exactly the same moment. If loss events are sporadic or clear rapidly, they may resolve before path discovery is performed.

  Additionally, tests are not guaranteed to be run at exactly the same moment from all agents assigned to the test.

- **Packet count difference:** Path discovery sends only 3 packets per TTL value, while end-to-end measurement sends a stream of 50 packets directly to the target. Therefore, an individual lost packet has a greater statistical percentage in Path Visualization (33% of packets sent) compared to the end-to-end loss, where a single packet represents only 2% of packets sent. This variation in statistical probability causes differences in the reported loss between the two views.

■ **Packet loss on the target:** There might be actual packet loss on the target while the path is clean. The traffic drop on the target might be caused by one of the following conditions:

  ■ The SYN backlog on the target is full. The target can't accept new TCP connections and is ignoring all new SYN packets. This only applies to SYN-based TCP measurements.

  ■ The target has reached the ICMP rate limit threshold and is therefore not generating new ICMP responses. This only applies to ICMP-based measurements.

  ■ The target has implemented a rate limiting algorithm and is currently dropping incoming traffic. This condition usually manifests itself as an initial test round showing zero packet loss, followed by one or more test rounds with high packet loss. This alteration between no loss and high loss is often periodic, producing a clearly visible pattern.

  ■ The recipient has an old TCP/IP stack with a "buggy" Selective Acknowledgments (SACK) implementation. This condition usually manifests itself as a constant low amount of packet loss in SACK-based TCP measurements.

  ■ The target's computing resources have been exhausted. The server can't cope with the network traffic. Although not very likely, this option should not be discarded.

■ **Agent count:** The forwarding loss might not be visible to all agents performing the test; for example, when the loss is occurring in a network segment that is traversed only by traffic from a single agent. If packets from a single agent are traversing the lossy network segment and one of the Path Visualization probe packets does not get responded to with the corresponding ICMP TTL exceeded message, then Path Visualization will not render the affected node with a forwarding loss (red circle). Instead, it will show the missing response as a parallel path with a blank node representing the missing response.

  Once the network segment is traversed by traffic from multiple agents, then the missing Path Visualization probe responses are marked as nodes that exhibit forwarding loss, regardless if such loss is detected by one agent or multiple agents.

Tips for Further Isolating Network Path Issues

Here are a few suggestions on how to adjust your testing strategy to pinpoint a network issue that is hard to spot in the Path Visualization:

■ **Inspect multiple test rounds of Path Visualization data:** If a small percentage of loss is consistently observed by the end-to-end measurement for a significant length of time, eventually even the path discovery process will hit the statistical "sweet spot" and show the forwarding loss. To spot it, you might need to check multiple rounds of Path Visualization results.

■ **Add more agents to the test:** Adding more agents to an individual test decreases the statistical influence of false positives or transient events caused by problems local to any individual agent. More agents in different locations will give a more real-world perspective on traffic conditions by using various providers and paths to reach the target.

Adding more agents is especially helpful when the packet loss is occurring closer to the target. Paths from source to target are often wildly different at the start, but then they converge more and more the closer they get to the test target. This causes more and more packets' TTL counters to expire on nodes closer to the target, resulting in a more sensitive forwarding loss detection.

■ **Run more parallel path traces:** Select **Cloud & Enterprise Agents > Test Settings > Test Type** and choose the **Advanced Settings** tab. The No. of Path Traces setting governs the number of parallel path discoveries that each agent will perform for this test. Its value defaults to 3 and can be increased up to 10. Increasing it up to 10 will cause each agent to perform 10 parallel path discoveries in each test round, increasing the probability of successful forwarding loss detection. In this case, the loss sensitivity of each agent is increased and, instead of the default 33% forwarding loss detection ability, even a 10% loss will be detected and pinpointed by a single agent.

■ **Isolate return path issues:** Packets often take a different return path on their way back from the test target to the agent. This can make pinpointing the exact location of forwarding loss more difficult in Agent to Server tests because it relies on response packets for accurate measurements. In such cases, an Agent to Agent test can help narrow down the results further. While Agent to Server tests require one agent to record all data, Agent to Agent tests have an agent on each side of the connection, enabling tests to measure unidirectional traffic.

■ **Change the test target:** If you are unable to deploy an Enterprise Agent in the same location as the test target (to act as a target for an Agent to Agent test), creating a new test specific to this diagnostic process may help narrow down the scope. To do so, perform the following:

  ■ In your original test's Path Visualization view, identify the furthest node that is functioning normally on the Path Visualization and will respond to pings.

  ■ Configure a new Agent to Server test targeting the node identified above. Use the ICMP protocol.

  ■ Once the initial test results are in, manually verify that the path displayed in the Path Visualization is identical to the original test.

If the results of the new test targeting the furthest functioning node from the original test are free of packet loss and if the discovered path matches the one observed in the original test, it confirms that the forward path up to that node is working as expected. This suggests that the issue causing loss in the original test likely occurs beyond that furthest node. Therefore, the troubleshooting focus can shift to investigating the path between that node and the test target, potentially leading to the identification and resolution of the network issue.

Troubleshooting Enterprise Agents on Cisco Devices

To understand how to troubleshoot an Enterprise Agent installed on a Cisco Device, you need to understand which commands are used for Cisco Application Framework. Table B-1 shows which commands are supported and the equivalent Docker commands.

Table B-1 *Docker Commands in Cisco IOS-XE*

Cisco IOS-XE CLI	Docker Commands
app-hosting connect appid MYAPP session	docker exec /bin/sh
app-hosting data appid MYAPP copy	docker cp
app-hosting activate appid MYAPP	docker create
app-hosting connect appid MYAPP session CMD	docker exec
app-hosting install appid MYAPP package <MYAPP.tar>	docker load
app-hosting move appid MYAPP log	docker logs
show app-hosting list	docker ps
app-hosting deactivate appid MYAPP	docker rm
app-hosting uninstall appid MYAPP	docker rmi
app-hosting start appid MYAPP	docker start
show app-hosting detail appid MYAPP	docker stats
app-hosting stop appid MYAPP	docker stop

Using **show app-hosting detail** enables you to see everything from the version to memory and runtime options, as shown in Example B-1.

Example B-1 *Example* **show app-hosting detail** *Command*

```
catalyst# show app-hosting detail appid thousandeyes_enterprise_agent
App id              : thousandeyes_enterprise_agent
Owner               : iox
State               : RUNNING
Application
  Type              : docker
  Name              : ThousandEyes Enterprise Agent
  Version           : 4.4.2
  Description       :
  Author            : ThousandEyes <support@thousandeyes.com>
  Path              : flash:thousandeyes-enterprise-agent-4.4.2.cisco.tar
  URL Path          :
```

```
Activated profile name : custom


Resource reservation
  Memory             : 500 MB
  Disk               : 1 MB
  CPU                : 1850 units
  VCPU               : 1
Attached devices
  Type              Name              Alias
-------------------------------------------
  serial/shell     iox_console_shell   serial0
  serial/aux       iox_console_aux     serial1
  serial/syslog    iox_syslog          serial2
  serial/trace     iox_trace           serial3


Network interfaces
  -------------------------------------
eth0:
  MAC address        : 52:54:dd:d:38:3d
  Network name       : mgmt-bridge-v21
Docker
------
Run-time information
  Command            :
  Entry-point        : /sbin/my_init
  Run options in use   : -e TEAGENT_ACCOUNT_TOKEN=TOKEN_NOT_SET
--hostname=$(SYSTEM_NAME) --cap-add=NET_ADMIN --mount
type=tmpfs,destination=/var/log/agent,tmpfs-size=140m --mount
type=tmpfs,destination=/var/lib/te-agent/data,tmpfs-size=200m -v
$(APP_DATA)/data:/var/lib/te-agent -e TEAGENT_PROXY_TYPE=DIRECT -e
TEAGENT_PROXY_LOCATION= -e TEAGENT_PROXY_USER= -e
TEAGENT_PROXY_AUTH_TYPE= -e TEAGENT_PROXY_PASS= -e
TEAGENT_PROXY_BYPASS_LIST= -e TEAGENT_KDC_USER= -e TEAGENT_KDC_PASS=
-e TEAGENT_KDC_REALM= -e TEAGENT_KDC_HOST= -e TEAGENT_KDC_PORT=88 -e
TEAGENT_KERBEROS_WHITELIST= -e TEAGENT_KERBEROS_RDNS=1 -e PROXY_APT=
-e APT_PROXY_USER= -e APT_PROXY_PASS= -e APT_PROXY_LOCATION= -e
TEAGENT_AUTO_UPDATES=1 -e
TEAGENT_ACCOUNT_TOKEN=nfhjzm8e8ikg07d4n31wcsws9bakcloh --hostname
Cisco-Docker

  Package run options  : -e TEAGENT_ACCOUNT_TOKEN=TOKEN_NOT_SET
--hostname=$(SYSTEM_NAME) --cap-add=NET_ADMIN --mount
type=tmpfs,destination=/var/log/agent,tmpfs-size=140m --mount
type=tmpfs,destination=/var/lib/te-agent/data,tmpfs-size=200m -v
```

```
$(APP_DATA)/data:/var/lib/te-agent -e TEAGENT_PROXY_TYPE=DIRECT -e
TEAGENT_PROXY_LOCATION= -e TEAGENT_PROXY_USER= -e
TEAGENT_PROXY_AUTH_TYPE= -e TEAGENT_PROXY_PASS= -e
TEAGENT_PROXY_BYPASS_LIST= -e TEAGENT_KDC_USER= -e TEAGENT_KDC_PASS=
-e TEAGENT_KDC_REALM= -e TEAGENT_KDC_HOST= -e TEAGENT_KDC_PORT=88 -e
TEAGENT_KERBEROS_WHITELIST= -e TEAGENT_KERBEROS_RDNS=1 -e PROXY_APT=
-e APT_PROXY_USER= -e APT_PROXY_PASS= -e APT_PROXY_LOCATION= -e
TEAGENT_AUTO_UPDATES=1

Application health information
  Status            : 0
  Last probe error  :
  Last probe output :
```

Depending on the situation, you might need to stop and start the container—for example, Enterprise Agent timeouts due to communication errors from a firewall rule or proxy.

If you find connection or DNS resolution errors in the log file, and the agent cannot connect to the ThousandEyes platform, ensure that the **app-vnic** command is configured properly on the Cisco device. From other devices, you may need to add DNS runtime options on a Docker host or an Open Virtualization Appliance (OVA). From a Linux distribution, you might need to update the etc/resolve.conf file.

The following is the code snippet for the **app-vnic** command:

```
9K(config-app-hosting)# app-vnic AppGigabitEthernet trunk
```

The AppGigabitEthernet port configuration needs to look like this:

```
interface AppGigabitEthernet1/0/1
  switchport trunk allowed vlan <vlan-id>
  switchport mode trunk
```

Linux-Based Agents

When deploying ThousandEyes Linux-based agents, there are a few critical considerations to ensure smooth and effective operation. Linux-based agents require specific configurations to communicate properly with the ThousandEyes platform and to maintain accurate time synchronization. Addressing these issues is crucial for maintaining the integrity and functionality of your monitoring setup.

The main issues commonly encountered with the Linux package include

- Ensuring that the built-in firewall is opened to allow the agent to communicate out to the ThousandEyes platform. (Check your Linux distro and see the default iptables.)

■ Ensuring that the Network Time Protocol (NTP) has been set up on the OS. This will avoid sync issues with the agent.

CLI Troubleshooting Utilities

ThousandEyes provides terminal-based network, DNS, and voice utilities, offering enhanced insight during troubleshooting. This section provides descriptions of these utilities and instructions for installing them on Linux distributions.

To install the utilities on a Linux distribution, use one of the following commands based on your distribution:

■ Debian/Ubuntu: **sudo apt-get install te-agent-utils**

■ Red Hat/CentOS: **sudo yum install te-agent-utils**

Adjust the commands according to your Linux flavor:

■ **te-ping:** A replacement for traditional ping, **te-ping** can be run in various application protocol modes, including SACK, SYN, ICMP, and VoIP. It provides metrics such as Loss, Latency, and Jitter and requires sudo permissions.

■ **te-pathtrace:** This utility runs a traceroute using methods similar to those used by ThousandEyes agents. It provides additional details such as quoted-ttl, response-ttl, and MPLS label values for each probe. To obtain consistent results with agent tests, use the option **-P 3** to run three sets of trace data. Sudo permissions are required.

■ **te-pathmtu:** Designed to quickly interrogate the path between endpoints, **te-pathmtu** finds the smallest allowed MTU on the path, which helps identify tunnel types or misconfigurations of MTU size on routers. By default, the MTU is set to 1500 bytes.

■ **te-bw:** A replacement for iPerf, **te-bw** measures bandwidth and estimated capacity between an endpoint and a target. It provides UPSTREAM and DOWNSTREAM bandwidth values, crucial for asymmetric links. Sudo permissions are required.

■ **te-dns-trace:** Similar to dig +trace, **te-dns-trace** follows CNAME records across zones to retrieve requested record types. It provides verbose feedback when trace attempts fail and does not require sudo permissions.

■ **te-rtp:** This utility initiates an instant voice call to a VoIP server with options to select Differentiated Services Code Point (DSCP) and codec values. It encapsulates voice packets with Real-Time Transport Protocol (RTP) headers and requires sudo permissions.

Virtual Appliance SSH

If the Virtual Appliance is experiencing issues, SSH access enables you to perform diagnostic tasks such as checking system logs, running network diagnostics (e.g., ping, traceroute), and examining system resources (e.g., CPU, memory usage). When SSH is used, this allows the administrator to access the underlying Linux OS.

To SSH into a ThousandEyes Virtual Appliance on Windows:

Step 1.   **Get an SSH client:** Download and install PuTTY, which includes PuTTY (SSH client) and PuTTYgen (SSH key generator).

Step 2.   **Create an SSH key pair:** Use PuTTYgen to generate an SSH key pair (public and private). Save both keys.

Step 3.   **Configure the Virtual Appliance:** Log into the ThousandEyes Virtual Appliance's web interface. Paste your public key in the SSH key field.

Step 4.   **Trim the key format:** Ensure the key format starts with **ssh-rsa**. Remove extra lines or comments if needed.

Step 5.   **Establish the SSH connection:** Open PuTTY, enter the Virtual Appliance's IP/hostname, set the username to **thousandeyes**, load the private key, and save the session.

Step 6.   **Connect:** Click **Open** to establish the SSH connection. Enter the passphrase if required.

Step 7.   **Confirmation:** Upon successful login, you'll see the prompt thousandeyes @appliance_hostname:~.

To SSH into a ThousandEyes Virtual Appliance on macOS:

Step 1.   **Obtain an SSH client:** macOS includes a built-in SSH client in the Terminal application, so no additional software installation is necessary.

Step 2.   **Create an SSH key pair:** Use the Terminal to generate an SSH key pair (public and private). You can use the **ssh-keygen** command to do this. Save both keys.

Step 3.   **Configure the Virtual Appliance:** Log into the ThousandEyes Virtual Appliance's web interface. Paste your public key in the SSH key field.

Step 4.   **Trim the key format:** Ensure the key format starts with **ssh-rsa**. Remove extra lines or comments if needed.

Step 5.   **Establish the SSH connection:** Open Terminal and use the **ssh** command to connect. Enter the command in the following format:

```css
Copy code
ssh username@hostname_or_IP
```

Step 6.   **Replace the username:** Replace the username with the SSH username and replace hostname_or_IP with the Virtual Appliance's IP or hostname.

Step 7.   **Connect:** Press Enter and enter your SSH password when prompted. If you've set up SSH key authentication without a passphrase, you won't need to enter a password.

Step 8.   **Confirmation:** Upon successful login, you'll see the prompt username@hostname:~ in the Terminal window.

Step 9.   **Install CA certificates on Enterprise Agents:**

Step 9a.   **Determine need:** Review scenarios where certificate errors occur during tests or administrative communications to identify if CA certificates need to be added:

- Issued by a private root CA certificate

- Decrypting proxy server

- Self-signed SSL server certificate

Step 9b.   **Convert to PEM format:** Ensure CA certificates are in PEM format. Use online converters or OpenSSL commands to convert if necessary.

Step 9c.   **Installation:** For Virtual Appliances, log into the web management console, navigate to the **Network** tab, and either paste the CA certificate or browse to the PEM-formatted certificate file in the CA Certificate section.

Make sure to include "-----BEGIN CERTIFICATE-----" and "-----END CERTIFICATE-----" markers if pasting.

Multiple CA certificates can be installed by concatenating them in the Add CA Certificate field.

Step 13.   Click **Save** to complete the operation.

Glossary

A

ACK (Acknowledgement) A TCP header flag. The ACK number specifies the next expected byte and is used in ThousandEyes tests to track the state of TCP connections.

agent A software component deployed in various locations to collect network and application performance data. ThousandEyes uses different types of agents, including Cloud Agents, Endpoint Agents, and Enterprise Agents.

alert A notification triggered by predefined conditions indicating potential network or application issues in ThousandEyes monitoring.

application programming interface (API) A set of rules and protocols that allows different software applications to communicate with each other. ThousandEyes offers APIs to integrate with other tools and automate workflows.

automation The process of automating manual tasks or processes using software tools or scripts. ThousandEyes supports automation for setting up tests and alerts.

autonomous system (AS) Used in routing protocols, a logical grouping of routers that share tables and updates. ThousandEyes uses AS information to analyze routing paths and detect issues.

B

Border Gateway Protocol (BGP) A routing protocol used to exchange routing information between autonomous systems on the Internet. ThousandEyes uses BGP data to monitor and troubleshoot routing issues.

C

Classless Internet Domain Routing (CIDR) A method for allocating IP addresses and IP routing. ThousandEyes uses CIDR to analyze network ranges and identify issues.

continuous integration/continuous deployment (CI/CD) A software development practice where code changes are continuously built, tested, and deployed to production environments. ThousandEyes can be integrated into CI/CD pipelines for continuous monitoring.

D

data center   A facility used to house computer systems and associated components, such as telecommunications and storage systems. ThousandEyes can monitor performance between data centers.

Differentiated Services Code Point (DSCP)   A field in the IP header used for packet classification and QoS (Quality of Service) prioritization. ThousandEyes uses DSCP values to analyze traffic prioritization.

Domain Name Service (DNS)   A protocol used for resolving domain names to IP addresses. ThousandEyes tests can monitor DNS performance and detect issues.

Dynamic Host Configuration Protocol (DHCP)   A protocol for automatically assigning IP addresses to devices on a network. ThousandEyes Enterprise and Endpoint Agents can use DHCP to obtain IP addresses.

F

File Transfer Protocol (FTP)   A protocol used for transferring files over a network. ThousandEyes can test and monitor FTP performance.

FIN (Finish)   A TCP header flag that signifies the completion of data transmission. Used in ThousandEyes tests to analyze TCP session termination.

H

Hypertext Transfer Protocol (HTTP)   A protocol for transferring web pages. ThousandEyes monitors HTTP performance to ensure web application availability.

Hypertext Transfer Protocol Secure (HTTPS)   A secure version of HTTP using SSL/TLS for encryption. ThousandEyes monitors HTTPS performance for secure web applications.

I

integration   The process of combining different systems or software components to work together seamlessly. ThousandEyes integrates with various tools for comprehensive monitoring.

Internet Control Message Protocol (ICMP)   A protocol used for network diagnostics and error reporting. ThousandEyes uses ICMP in ping tests to check network reachability and latency.

Internet service provider (ISP)   A company that provides Internet access. Examples include Time Warner, Comcast, AT&T, and Verizon. ThousandEyes monitors ISP performance to identify issues affecting end users.

J

Jenkins   An open source automation server used to automate building, testing, and deploying software. ThousandEyes can integrate with Jenkins for continuous monitoring in CI/CD pipelines.

L

line plot   In this graph, time is represented on the horizontal axis and the selected metric or quantity is shown on the vertical axis. This type of visualization is particularly useful for observing trends and patterns over a specified time period.

local-area network (LAN)   A network that connects devices within a limited area, such as a building or a campus. ThousandEyes can monitor LAN performance.

M

Maximum Segment Size (MSS) The largest amount of payload that can be sent in one TCP segment of data. ThousandEyes monitors and reports on the MSS used between Cloud and Enterprise Agents and their targets when tests are configured to use TCP.

Maximum Transmission Unit (MTU) The largest packet size that can be transmitted over a network. ThousandEyes uses MTU values to detect and troubleshoot potential fragmentation issues.

N

network address translation (NAT) A method used to remap IP addresses by modifying network address information in the IP header. ThousandEyes can monitor NAT performance and related issues.

network performance monitoring The process of monitoring and analyzing network traffic to assess the performance and health of a network. ThousandEyes provides tools for comprehensive network performance monitoring.

Network Time Protocol (NTP) A protocol used for synchronizing clocks across devices on a network. ThousandEyes uses NTP to ensure clock synchronization between agents.

O

OpenTelemetry An open source project that provides a standardized way to instrument, generate, collect, and export telemetry data for cloud-native applications. ThousandEyes integrates with OpenTelemetry for enhanced observability.

P

Path Maximum Transmission Unit Discovery (PMTUD) Also known as Path MTU Discovery. A technique to determine the maximum MTU size on the path between two IP hosts. This technique is used to avoid fragmentation. ThousandEyes uses PMTUD to determine MTU between agents and targets.

Ping An application that sends ICMP Echo Request messages to test network reachability and measure round-trip time. ThousandEyes uses ping tests to check network connectivity.

port address translation (PAT) A type of network address translation that enables multiple devices on a local network to be mapped to a single public IP address using different ports. ThousandEyes can monitor PAT configurations and performance.

Q

quality of service (QoS) The ability to provide different priority levels to different applications, users, or data flows. ThousandEyes uses QoS metrics to analyze traffic prioritization and performance.

S

scripting The process of writing scripts or code to automate tasks or processes. ThousandEyes supports scripting for custom test configurations and automation.

software-defined wide-area network (SD-WAN) A technology that uses software to control the management and operation of a WAN. ThousandEyes provides visibility into SD-WAN performance.

T

telemetry   The process of collecting and transmitting data from remote or inaccessible sources. ThousandEyes collects telemetry data to monitor network and application performance.

test   A measurement or evaluation of network or application performance conducted using ThousandEyes. Tests can be configured to monitor various protocols and services.

ThousandEyes IDE   An integrated development environment provided by ThousandEyes for creating and editing Transaction Tests using Selenium.

V

VXLAN (Virtual Extensible LAN)
A network virtualization technology used to encapsulate Layer 2 Ethernet frames within Layer 3 IP packets. ThousandEyes can monitor VXLAN performance.

W

webhooks   A method of augmenting or altering the behavior of a web page, application, or service through custom callbacks or HTTP requests. ThousandEyes uses webhooks for alerting and integration with other tools.

wide-area network (WAN)
A telecommunications network that extends over a large geographical area. ThousandEyes monitors WAN performance to ensure connectivity and performance across regions.

Index

Numerics

3-way handshake, TCP, 7, 207, 236

A

account administration
  account groups, 277–279
  Activity Log, 285–286
    add a filter, 287–288
    download logs, 288–289
    Quotas tab, 291–293
    time selector, 286–287
    usage, 289–291
  adding a new user, 275–276
  default roles, 276–277
  RBAC (role-based access control), 279–281
  SSO (single sign-on), 281
    identity provider setup, 282
    imported metadata configuration, 284–285
    ThousandEyes setup, 282–284
account groups, 277–279

Activity Log, 285–286
  add a filter, 287–288
  download logs, 288–289
  Quotas tab, 291–293
  time selector, 286–287
  usage, 289–291
Agent to Agent test, 53–56
Agent to Server test, 56–58
Agents
  Cisco Device, 44
  Cloud, 45–46
  Cluster, 39–40, 41–43, 274
  Docker container, 44
  Endpoint, 46–48
  Enterprise, 17–18, 159–160
    Docker container, 33–37
    installation, 18–24, 25–33
    Linux, 37–39
    placement, 44–45
    troubleshooting, 327–329
    utilization, 39–41
  Linux, 44
  VM (Virtual Machine), 44

packet loss, discards, 143–144

path visualization, reasons for loss result variation, 324–325

traditional, 125–127

transaction tests, 153–154

user experience, 239–240

TTL (Time-to-Live), 129

tunnel

explicit, 136

implicit, 136

opaque, 136–137

U

underlay network, 135, 138, 140–141

use cases

APM (application performance monitoring), 2

cloud and hybrid monitoring, 2

collaboration monitoring, 3

Internet and DNS monitoring, 3

network performance monitoring, 2

user account, creating, 275–276

user experience, 301

comparing, 304–305

troubleshooting, 239–240

utilization, Enterprise Agent, 39–41

V

value proposition, 310–312

views

device, 269–272

topology, 273

Transactions, 155–158

Views page, 123–124, 131–132

virtual appliance SSH, 330–332

VM (Virtual Machine) Agent, 44

voice layer, 76–77

RTP stream test, 80–82

SIP server test, 78–80

VXLAN, 307

W

web applications, 148

web layer, 66

FTP server test, 74–77

HTTP server test, 66–70

Page Load test, 70–73

Transaction test, 73–74

WebDriver, 148

Webex, monitoring

Cloud and Enterprise Agents, 218–219

Endpoint Agents, 218–221

webhooks, 105–107, 166–167

on GitHub, 296–297

options, 167–168

template, 167

testing, 167

widgets, 114–115

associated tests, 121

features, 120

iframe, 120

Wireshark, TCP SEQ tracking, 206–207

X-Y-Z

X.25, 5

Zoom, monitoring, 231

Cloud and Enterprise Agents, 232

Endpoint Agents, 232–234

Register your product at **ciscopress.com/register**
to unlock additional benefits:

- Save 35%* on your next purchase with an exclusive discount code
- Find companion files, errata, and product updates if available
- Sign up to receive special offers on new editions and related titles

Get more when you shop at **ciscopress.com**:

- Everyday discounts on books, eBooks, video courses, and more
- Free U.S. shipping on all orders
- Multi-format eBooks to read on your preferred device
- Print and eBook Best Value Packs

Cisco Press